# Trails of Western Idaho

Getting ready for a Hells Canyon hike

# Trails of Western Idaho

**Third edition, updated and expanded**

by Margaret Fuller

TRAIL GUIDE BOOKS

TRAIL GUIDE BOOKS

Published by
Trail Guide Books
P.O. Box 148
Weiser, Idaho 83672

Updated and expanded third edtion, second printing


Manufactured in the United States

Edited by Diana Hall
Maps by Jerry Painter
Cover and book design by Jerry Painter of Trail Guide Books

All photographs by the author unless otherwise noted

Cover photograph: Black Lake in the Hells Canyon area

*Library of Congress Catalog Card Number: GV199.42.12F83*
Fuller, Margaret, 1935–

ISBN 0-9664233-3-X

**For Ryan, Chris, Sierra, Ivy and Grace**

# Foreword

Margaret Fuller has done it again. Her latest guide book to Idaho's hiking trails is a "must" for outdoor enthusiasts who desire an accurate description of an area. It is also appropriate for people who need suggestions of where they might visit.

The trails described range from easy to expert and from remote to urban. Whether you have one day or one month, you will discover trails which were designed for you.

Idaho is dear to us and we hope our visitors will enjoy their time spent in the state. We are blessed with many areas where, by following Margaret's suggestions, one can be alone for as long as desired in an environment which will rejuvenate, while causing one to forget foreign travel. Beauty, solitude and the opportunity for enjoyment abound in Idaho. One only has to be properly prepared. By following Margaret's advice, you will experience a new world unfolding before your eyes with every step. All we ask is that you use the land, but don't abuse it. Our resources are finite and there are many generations to come.

**— Cecil D. Andrus**

# TABLE OF CONTENTS

## PAYETTE NATIONAL FOREST



## BOISE NATIONAL FOREST

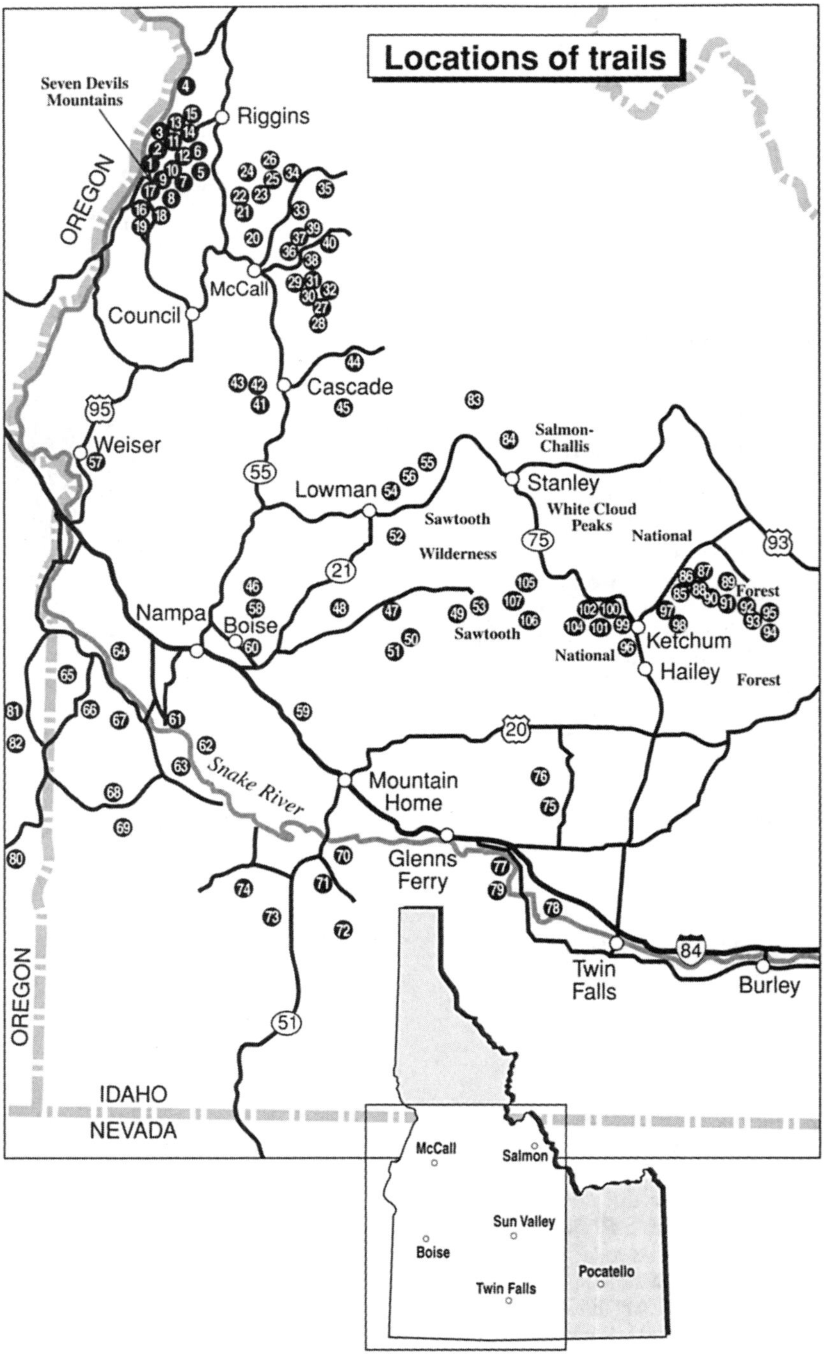

Locations of trails
Seven Devils Mountains
OREGON
Riggins
McCall
Council
Cascade
95
Weiser
55
Salmon-Challis
Lowman
Stanley
Sawtooth
Wilderness
White Cloud Peaks
National
75
93
21
Forest
Nampa
Boise
Sawtooth
National
Ketchum
Hailey
Forest
20
Snake River
Mountain Home
Glenns Ferry
84
Twin Falls
Burley
51
OREGON
IDAHO
NEVADA
McCall
Salmon
Sun Valley
Boise
Twin Falls
Pocatello

## BUREAU OF LAND MANAGEMENT

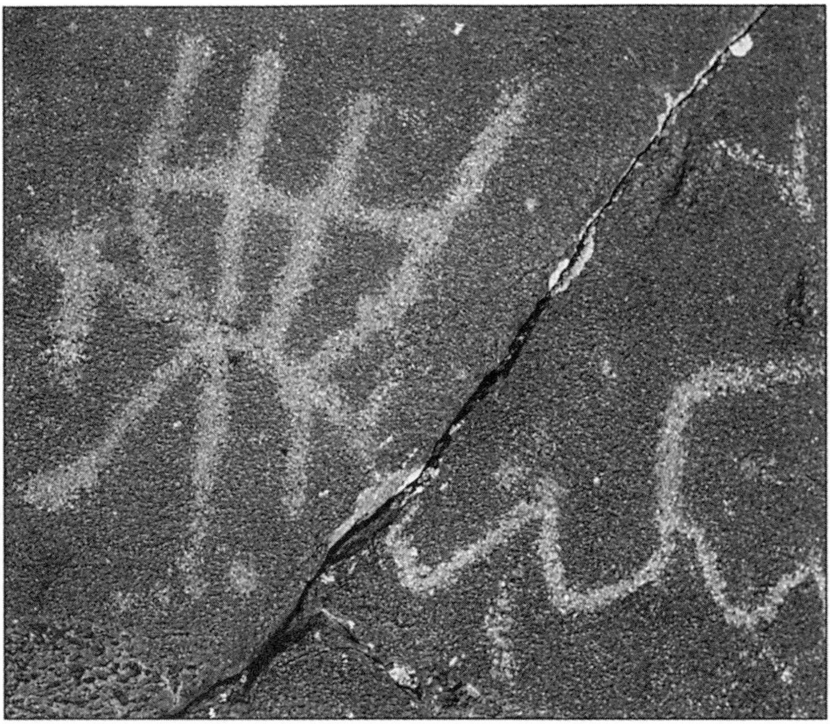

**Ancient Indian petrogylphs**

# Introduction

In southwestern Idaho, landscapes vary from sagebrush desert cleft with canyons to Douglas fir or lodgepole forests, mountain meadows and glacial cirques. In the mountains, aquamarine lakes contrast with gray and black peaks streaked with white, copper and rose.

In the Hells Canyon Wilderness, the Seven Devils Mountains of black rock run for 40 miles between the Little Salmon and the Snake Rivers. Along the western edge of these mountains, the Snake River flows through Hells Canyon. This canyon is 7,900 feet deep from the top of He Devil to the river. It is the deepest river-cut gorge in North America. As a result, snow covers the mountains above the canyon seven months of the year, although cactus grows along the river.

The Snake River begins near Yellowstone Park, flows south past the Tetons, then turns northwest into Idaho and curves in a great semicircle across the southern part of the state. Along the western boundary of Idaho, the river flows north through Hells Canyon on its way to join the Columbia. As the Snake turns north, it marks off a huge triangle of desert land in the southwestern corner of the state. The 8,000-foot Owyhee Mountains, covered with juniper trees and granite outcrops, occupy a northern corner of this triangle. This range hides remnants of old mining settlements like Silver City.

North of the Owyhees and the Snake River spreads the irrigated valley of the Boise River, usually called the Treasure Valley. Above this valley, forested hills rise to the north and east.

These ranges of the Boise National Forest hold sparkling lakes like the tiny Trinity and Red Mountain Lakes. North of Boise, the lakes, hanging valleys and glacier-scoured peaks of the Payette National Forest near McCall create a hikers' playground.

East of the Boise National Forest rise the green and beige hills of the Smoky Mountains in the Sawtooth National Forest. On the higher peaks, colorful stripes etch the cliffs. Located north and east of the Smokies, the Sawtooth, White Cloud and Boulder Mountains of the Sawtooth National Recreation Area are described in *Trails of the Sawtooth and White Cloud Mountains* by the author.

East of Sun Valley, the Pioneer Range features multicolored crags of metamorphic rock surrounding carpets of wildflowers. Since the Boise Valley touches the Oregon border, the guide includes three hikes at the edge of eastern Oregon. The Appendix of *Trails of Western Idaho* summarizes some hikes not covered in detail.

Visitors to western Idaho and Idaho residents will be surprised at the rich variety of hiking opportunities and the solitude of the backcountry described in this guide. With a few exceptions, these areas get much less use than the Sawtooths and White Clouds.

The purpose of this book is to give residents and visitors an idea of the many trails in southwestern Idaho. According to wilderness management specialists, information in a book on many possible trails helps distribute use. The desert hikes described extend the season for hiking from early spring to late fall. If many people become aware of the areas covered in this book, Idahoans may be able to keep some of these areas pristine.

## CHANGES IN THIS THIRD EDITION

Some hike descriptions have been removed in this edition, and others have been added, so that there are now five more hikes than there were before, for a total of 107. The five hikes at the edge of the Frank Church Wilderness are now included in *Trails of the Frank Church – River of No Return Wilderness* by the author, so they no longer appear in this book. Two other hikes have been removed from the book because the access is through private land and the owners have posted the land against trespassing. One hike has been removed because a landslide destroyed a section of the trail and the Forest Service doesn't plan to repair or maintain it any more. These hikes are listed in the appendix. For a few hikes, the access road or the trail differ because the trail has been rerouted. The author has added 13 new hikes including the Weiser River Trail and hikes near Jerome and Hagerman.

In the past few years, there have been dozens of fires in the areas covered by this book. Call ahead so you can plan to stay out of areas near current fires, and out of previously burned areas. Stormy or windy days cause washouts and falling snags in old burns.

For the convenience of readers the bits of history have been inserted in the hike descriptions nearest to the sites they mention instead of appearing in separate history sections as they did before.

While every effort has been made to make this edition as up-to-date as possible, there still may be changes of which the author is unaware. If you find any errors she would appreciate hearing about them. Her address is P.O. Box 148, Weiser ID 83672.

## HISTORY

The historical sections are intended to give backcountry users a respect for the historical remnants they will see. For those who want to read more about the history, a few books are listed under Suggested Reading. In this edition any historical material is located at the beginning of the hike descriptions, except where the trail leads past historical sites. In those cases the history is related at the point where a site is mentioned.

## HIKE DESCRIPTIONS

Information about each hike is listed at the top of its description. This includes the round trip or through mileage and the elevation gain or loss. Please note that if all of a hike is uphill with no downhill stretches which have to be reclimbed on the way back, there is no listing for elevation loss unless the hike is a loop hike. If you don't remember this you will keep looking through the book for non-existent elevation losses. Conversely, if a trail has no elevation gain, but only an elevation loss, the elevation gain will not be listed. Elevation gains and losses have been rounded off to the nearest 10 feet. Those with the additional note: "This section: x miles, y feet elevation gain" have miles given one-way rather than round trip. Please pay attention to the elevation gain because every 1,000 feet of climb will seem to add at least a mile in distance, although in reality it doesn't. If you don't remember this, you may think as one man's family did that the miles given here are "Fuller miles" and not accurate.

Also listed are the topographic maps needed, the round trip time to allow if on foot, and the length and quality of the access road. The time includes one hour at the destination for day hikes. Hike mileage usually starts at the farthest point on the access road that a two-wheel drive high-wheelbase vehicle can reach. However, a few roads such as the one to the Josephine Lake trailhead are recommended for four-wheel drive only. If obtaining water is a problem, the locations of water sources are described. Since trails are sometimes signed and sometimes not signed and this situation often changes from year to year, trail signs are usually not mentioned.

Unless the responsible agency has requested that the hike description state the kinds of use allowed on a trail (mountain bikes, motorcycles, jeeps, ATVs, horses, hikers), the kinds of uses are not mentioned. That's because they change frequently, too. You can find out what uses are permitted on a trail from the current travel plan map of the particular forest.

## ACCESS ROADS

Access roads for these hikes vary from paved to gravel, dirt and primitive. Because it is easy to get stuck or slide off, do not attempt to drive unpaved roads in wet or snowy weather or before they have dried in the spring. Also, traveling on these roads when they are wet damages them. It is wise to ask a ranger about the road and trail conditions before your trip. In some areas, such as Copper Basin, the roads can be muddy and treacherous until mid-July and after September 1, so it is essential to call the ranger district office in charge of the area before a trip during these times. Primitive roads are not suitable for passenger cars, but do not require four-wheel drive unless noted. On rocky roads, drive less than 20 miles an hour to prevent flat tires. Travel plan maps are available every year at each National Forest office. These maps show which roads and trails are closed to motorized vehicles. A few of the roads have deteriorated since the last edition of this book and the changes are noted. The road distances given here are only approximate. They were measured by the odometer of the author's car. Other odometers may show different distances.

## HIKE DIFFICULTY

These hikes are classified by difficulty. Easy hikes are less than 7 miles round trip, have less than 1,000 feet elevation gain, and require no cross-country travel. Moderate hikes are 7 to 10 miles round trip, have 1,000 to 2,000 feet elevation gain, and require no cross-country travel.

Strenuous hikes are longer than 10 miles round trip and have more than 2,000 feet elevation gain. If a trip requires several days, it is listed as strenuous. Some hikes are listed as expert because they have route-finding problems or treacherous footing. Some are listed as cross-country because there is no trail to the destination. A list of hikes by difficulty is found in the "Guide to Hikes" in the Appendix.

## MAPS

Topographic maps may be obtained from some engineering supply and backpacking stores, or online. The index map for Idaho will help you decide which maps to order. You can look at the index and maps to see which ones to buy or copy at university libraries. The topographic maps for each hike in this book are listed at the top of the description. Standard topographic maps are 7' minute size with 40-foot contour levels in a scale of 1 inch to 24,000 feet. A few have contour levels of 20 feet or 80 feet. The old 15-minute maps (with 80-foot contours) are obsolete. The newer maps are overprinted with Global Positioning System grids for those who wish to keep track of progress with a GPS unit.

Topographic maps omit apostrophes in place names, so this book does, also. Less detailed Forest Service and Bureau of Land Management maps, which can help you

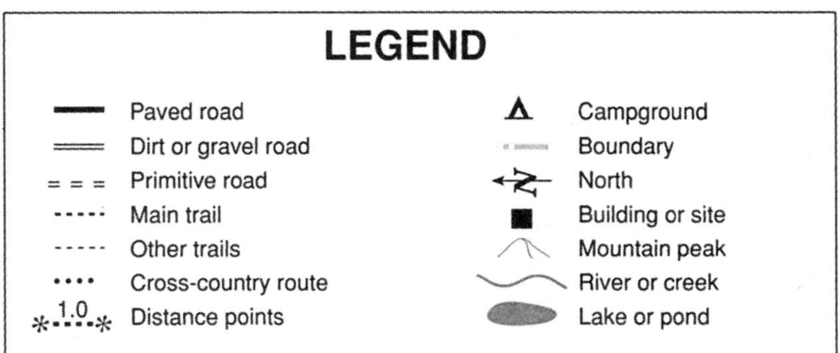

find and follow access roads, can be purchased at main offices for each national forest and BLM district. These addresses are listed in the Appendix.

## GLOSSARY

**Blaze:** small letter "i" cut in bark of tree to mark the official trail

**Cairn:** pile of rocks sometimes used as a trail marker

**GPS:** Global Positioning System: A system for determining your exact position on maps by way of a handheld device using the position of satellites

**Gully:** miniature canyon, ravine

**Rock bench:** large flat or rounded rock outcrop

**Saddle:** low point in a ridge

**Switchback:** a zigzag or to zigzag

**Talus:** loose rocks or boulders

## LOW IMPACT CAMPING AND HIKING

Now that so many people go hiking, backpacking, horseback riding and mountain biking everyone must learn how to use the backcountry without degrading it — to practice low impact camping. A vital part of this practice is to always carry out your garbage. Garbage along the trail or at campsites or trailheads offends most people. The Forest and Park Services and the BLM pick up trash, but they can't keep up with it. So please carry out all unburnable trash, including leftover food and disposable diapers. Never bury garbage because animals will dig it up, scatter it, and possibly eat it. Freeze-dried foil food envelopes will not burn and must be carried out. Take extra plastic bags for garbage.

Another important part is to select a campsite keeping low impact in mind. The low impact sites are often the most comfortable. Camp 200 feet or more away from trails, lakes or streams, and in a spot which has been used before, but not overused. The best sites are on needles or leaves with no vegetation underfoot. Don't dig trenches around your tent.

Avoid meadows because they are fragile and the short growing season in mountains means any damage will last many years. Meadows are also uncomfortable — damp, cold, lumpy and full of mosquitoes. When camping on an unused site, return it to its original appearance before leaving. Don't cut limbs or boughs from standing trees or pound nails into them. It is illegal to cut standing trees, dead or alive, in wilderness areas and without a permit in national forests.

To prevent fire scars and preserve wood supplies around campsites, use backpacking stoves for cooking. If you need a warming fire, either use an existing fire ring or plan to remove all traces of your fire. Build the fire on sand or earth from which all vegetable matter has been removed so it won't start a forest fire. To avoid leaving black marks on rocks, don't build fires on or against them.

To avoid polluting water, use special biodegradable soap or no soap. Wash dishes, clothes and yourself in containers away from the lake or stream and dump the water away from camp.

To dispose of human waste, dig a hole six to eight inches deep (no deeper) and fill it in after use. The bacteria in the top layer of soil will eventually dispose of the waste. Do not overturn a rock and then replace it on top of the waste! For groups, you can dig a shallow latrine at least 300 feet away from any water source. Carry out the used toilet paper in a plastic bag or burn it in your warming fire. Burn fish guts rather than throwing them in the lake or burying them. When fires are not allowed, carry out fish guts, toilet paper, all garbage including tampons and sanitary napkins in double plastic bags.

Another way to lessen your impact on the land is to select a little-used trail, or, if experienced with map and compass go cross-country, spreading out your party so it won't create a path if there isn't one. A list of little-used trails covered in this book is in the Appendix. Small groups have less impact, so try to travel with fewer than 10 people. Avoid taking shortcuts between sections of trail. Shortcuts cause erosion and walking them is a violation of Federal law. The more people who practice low impact hiking and backpacking, the fewer regulations will be required. Dull colors for tents, packs and clothing reduce your impact on other parties. So does being quiet.

## MOUNTAIN BIKES

When riding a mountain bike, taking precautions will help prevent hurting yourself or others and will prevent your annoying others or damaging the landscape. Always ride in control and sound your bell or horn or call out at corners. You should always stop and allow hikers and horseback riders to pass. Be sure horses, mules or llamas hear you coming and hear you talk so they know you are a person. Move your bike off trail on the downhill side if possible to let horses pass. Stay on designated roads and trails and out of wilderness areas — bicycles are illegal in designated wilderness. To keep from damaging trails, avoid riding on wet ground.

To avoid injury, a bicycle helmet with a hard outside shell and foam-padded interior is essential. You should also wear gloves, long pants and a long-sleeved shirt. Tuck pant legs into your socks or wear gaiters. Remember to look ahead for hazards. Practice riding on gentle smooth surfaces to develop the skill needed on steep, uneven slopes. Practice skidding on gentle, even slopes so you can control a skid on loose rocks or rough ground. Braking just before a curve, not within it, will help avoid skidding.

To be prepared for emergencies you should carry the same essentials you would if hiking. Carrying them in plastic bags inside the bicycle bags will keep your gear dry. Use rear-mounted bags; handlebar bags make it difficult to control the bicycle. In addition, carry bicycle tools, a pump and a tire patch kit.

## HORSES

To avoid trail damage, use as few horses or mules as possible. When meeting horses on the trail, stand still quietly on the downhill side while they pass, but greet their riders so the horses will know you are a person. If traveling by horse, use lightweight food and equipment so fewer horses will be needed. To prevent grazing damage to fragile meadows, carry in the feed, which by law must be certified to be weed free. Because you need to keep horses away from campsites and more than 100 feet from streams and lakes, take pans or buckets for their drinking water. To avoid killing trees, tie horses to them only while loading and unloading. You should protect the trees to which they are tied with burlap or pieces of garden hose.

Like you, horses need to get into condition for traveling and carrying packs in the mountains. They should be familiar with the feed and with the pickets or hobbles you plan to use. To avoid damage to the grass, picket only one horse and hobble the rest.

To make longer trips feasible for families with small children an outfitter can pack in gear to a base camp. To obtain a list of packers, call the Idaho Outfitters and Guides Association in Boise, which is listed in the appendix.

## LLAMAS

Information on llama packers is also available from the Outfitters and Guides Association. If you have your own llamas, and plan to use them for packing, they should already have been trained to halter, lead and walk on trails carrying packs and should have taken plenty of walks with you before the trip. They don't like going uphill, but will go readily if you insist. They are easier for the inexperienced to manage than mules or horses. It is important to remember horses are afraid of llamas. Therefore, have someone walk ahead of the llamas so if horses appear he or she can warn you to get the llamas out of sight off the trail.

## PACK GOATS

Some people have begun to use domestic goats as pack animals. They cost much less than llamas, and don't have to be led. However, the goats must be traveling with their owners for them to work well, because when they are very small they bond to their owner as though he or she were their mother. They tend to wander if their owner isn't with them.

## DOGS

If you wish to take a dog on the trail, be sure you can make it obey instantly, so it won't get into trouble. Never let a dog chase wildlife — the wildlife might turn out to be a porcupine. Bury the dog's waste as you do your own. Hold the dog if other trail users are approaching, especially if they also have dogs. Keep dogs out of the drinking water source and away from other parties. Lightweight cloth water bowls are available. It is a good idea to carry or filter the water for your dog because dogs can catch giardia from untreated water. Leashing your dog will help it avoid fighting with other dogs and help it avoid getting lost.

## ARCHEOLOGY

Please leave historical and archeological objects where they are so others can study and enjoy them. These things are protected by the Antiquities Act and the Archeological Sites Protection Act, which mandate large fines or prison terms. Some historical sites, especially old mines, are private property. If the property is posted no trespassing, stay out to avoid confrontation and possible arrest.

## ALLOWED USES

This book includes hikes in the Hells Canyon Wilderness and visitors need to know that all wilderness areas are closed to motorized and mechanical use, such as chain saws, bicycles, motorcycles, ATVs and game carts.

A few lakes and streams allow only catch and release fishing. Elsewhere you can keep at least some fish, but be sure to read the annual fishing guide put out the Idaho Department of Fish and Game and comply with its regulations. All bull trout (also known as Dolly Varden) must be released. Bull trout can be identified by the lack of spots on the dorsal (top) fin. Any sturgeon caught must also be released. In this area, they are found only in the Snake River. Wild salmon must be released as well.

Where registration boxes and cards or forms are found at trailheads, please register, since this helps managers plan trail maintenance.

# SAFETY

## ALWAYS LEAVE WORD

Always leave your itinerary with someone at home telling in detail where you will be each day and when you will return. THEN STICK TO IT. If far from home, leave word also at the nearest ranger station or other agency office. Then be sure to let this office know that you have returned.

## HYPOTHERMIA

Beware of hypothermia, which is a lowering of body temperature in cold or wet conditions that can cause death. It can occur even above freezing.

To prevent it, wear warm clothes, keep dry, and eat often. An uncovered head can lose up to 50 percent of the body's heat production at 40 degrees, so be sure to wear a woolly hat and your parka hood. Because wet clothing can draw heat from the body as much as 32 times faster than dry clothing, rain gear is essential. Plastic rain gear tears too easily. You need nylon waterproof pants and a nylon waterproof jacket or rain poncho. Waterproof breathable fabric like Goretex is more comfortable if you can afford it, but doesn't shed rain as well.

Your warm clothing should be wool or synthetic because those fabrics will keep you warm when wet. Down collapses if wet, and wet down and wet cotton draw heat from your body. Sweat dampens clothing, so when active remove extra clothes to avoid sweating, but put them back on when resting.

When you first feel cold, even with all your extra clothing on, make camp and build a fire. So you can do this on a day hike, be sure to carry an emergency shelter (such as a tarp or space blanket). Wind and rain add to the likelihood of hypothermia because wet clothing chills you and because wind chill dramatically lowers the temperature you feel. The higher the wind speed, the greater the heat loss. Therefore wear wind proof clothes or stay out of the wind.

Persistent shivering is the first danger signal of hypothermia. A shivering person needs to remove wet clothes and get into a warm sleeping bag. Then he or she should have a hot drink and a snack. If the victim seems confused, stumbles, or is semiconscious, the hypothermia has progressed to the second stage and hot drinks may make it worse. In that case put the victim into a sleeping bag, stripped, with another stripped person to warm by body heat, which is the fastest method of rewarming. At this stage, rough handling, keeping the victim walking, or too-rapid warming can be fatal. Send for medical help. Full recovery requires eight hours or more.

## FIRST AID

Someone in the party should have taken a first aid class, or at least have read and have in his or her pack the Red Cross first aid book. Red Cross instructions say that if someone is injured, first be sure the victim is breathing. If not, check for an open airway and then give mouth-to-mouth resuscitation. Next, control bleeding. Don't move the victim except to keep him or her from further injury. Cover the victim with a sleeping bag or jackets and treat for shock.

In case of serious injury, send for help. It is best to have a party of a least three, so that one can stay with the victim while the other goes for help. If the party is large enough, a person who is unable to walk can be carried out on a litter made of poles inserted in a sleeping bag, which has the stitching ripped out at the foot. A person with a suspected back or neck injury should only be moved by professional rescuers.

## CROSS-COUNTRY TRAVEL

To gain skill for cross-country travel, hikers should practice with a topographic map and compass or GPS unit while following trails. Off-trail hiking is an excellent way for experienced hikers to avoid crowds. Some off-trail areas may be closed to horse travel, so check with a ranger first. To avoid leaving a mark on the land, spread out your party so everyone takes a slightly different path.

## USING A COMPASS

You should have with you the U.S. Geological Survey topographic maps for the area. Check with a ranger in advance on trail conditions, since some trails (and roads) shown on the maps no longer exist or are no longer maintained. In addition, some current trails do not appear on the topographic maps.

Before starting out it is a good idea to find your trailhead and destination on the topographic map and then orient the topographic map with the land. That will help you keep track of where you are as you go along. To do this, place your compass on the map so the needle is parallel with the side of the map and the north end of the needle points to the top of the map. To allow for the angle of declination found in western Idaho turn the compass and map 19 degrees counter-clockwise. Now the compass needle will be pointing 19 degrees east of north, but the north mark on the dial will be pointing north. Look for landmarks such as cliffs or towers and then find them on the map by looking for close together contour lines.

As you travel the trail, constantly check where you are on the map. PANIC CAN KILL, SO IF LOST, STAY CALM, STAY PUT, BUILD A FIRE AND MAKE CAMP. With the map, calmly try to figure out your location. If unable to do this, wait for rescue.

## MINE SHAFTS

There are many old mine shafts and tunnels in Idaho's backcountry. Stay away from them and watch children closely near shafts and tunnels. Mine shafts may not always be evident on the surface as they may be hidden under piles of old boards.

**Mine tunnel above Black Lake**

## HIKING ALONE

Hiking alone always has an element of danger, but experienced hikers occasionally do go alone. Lack of water kills much sooner than lack of food. If you are injured or trapped by a rock, log, or mud you may not be able to get to water. In a little-traveled area, even on a day hike, solo hikers should carry a tent, stove, fuel, sleeping bag, signal flares, and survival kit at all times because if you can't get back to your pack for your sleeping bag you could die of hypothermia. Night time temperatures can be below freezing even in summer, and many of the areas described here don't have daily visitors. Avoid going cross-country alone. The most important thing when hiking alone is to leave a detailed itinerary with someone at home and then STICK TO IT! It is also a good idea to avoid taking trips of several days when hiking alone. If you suffer a serious injury and no one comes looking for you for a week or two, you may die before anyone finds you.

## TWELVE ESSENTIALS

Every hiker should always carry these 12 things even on day hikes because Idaho weather can change rapidly: a hot clear morning can produce an afternoon thunderstorm with two inches of hail or can be followed by a snowstorm.

1. Extra clothes (long pants, sweater, quilted parka, rain jacket or poncho and rain pants or chaps, wool hat, wool gloves)
2. Extra food (beyond the needs of the trip)
3. Pocket knife

4. Waterproof matches and their box or striker pad, or a butane lighter. (Keep any of these in a plastic bag for good measure.) Strike-anywhere kitchen matches often don't work well when struck on rocks even when kept dry.

5. Fire starter (purchased stick or jelly type, or homemade from paraffin and corrugated cardboard)

6. First aid kit including prescription pain medicine, which is vital in case of injury in preventing life-threatening shock

7. Flashlight or headlamp with extra bulb and batteries (some new headlamps will run 100 hours on one set of batteries)

8. Topographic map or maps

9. Compass and knowledge of how to use it

10. Sunglasses

11. Shelter — tent, tarp, bivy sack or space blanket

12. Water filter or kettle for boiling water

## CONDITIONING

A physical exam and several weeks of regular exercise should precede the first trip of the summer. The exercise should be aerobic, such as walking up hills, running or swimming. If possible, allow three days at the trailhead to get accustomed to the altitude. Full adaptation to a higher altitude takes several weeks. Those living at 2,500 feet and above will need less time to adjust than those living at sea level. Altitude sickness can cause headache, nausea, and even life-threatening pulmonary or cerebral edema.

Fatigue from being out of condition can lead to accidents. Lack of conditioning and trying to hike too far and too fast can cause altitude sickness and even a heart attack. For optimum safety on the trail, hikers should keep their pulses under their target rate (subtract your age from 200) and stop at least every half hour to rest for 5 or 10 minutes. If chest pains occur in the mountains, they aren't necessarily caused by heart problems, but should be investigated by a doctor. Other causes can be inflamed rib joints, sore chest muscles, spasms of the esophagus and digestive disturbances such as heartburn.

## CREEK CROSSING

CROSSING A CREEK OR RIVER IS OFTEN THE MOST DANGEROUS PART OF BACKCOUNTRY TRAVEL. Logs floating down a creek indicate water too high to cross without special equipment and training. If there is any doubt about a crossing, detour upstream to cross where the creek is smaller, or turn back, or change your destination. When detouring, do not attempt to pass cliffs at the edge of the creek. Large creeks are often not safe until after July 15 or later. Check beforehand with a ranger to be sure of conditions at stream crossings. River crossings are rarely safe and if they are it is only in late summer. If a creek is snow-fed, the water will be lowest in early morning, so that is the best time to cross.

Wading across on gravel in a wide part of the stream is the safest crossing. Rocks or logs can be very slippery. Keep boots and socks on when wading to prevent injury to your feet and to help your footing. If wearing a backpack, unfasten the hip belt. Face upstream and lean into the current. Use a trekking pole or find a sturdy stick in the forest to help with balance, planting it upstream from your feet. Then move your feet and the stick sideways as you cross the creek, keeping your feet still when you move the stick. Once across the stream, dry the insides of your boots with bandannas and change to dry socks to prevent blisters.

In the earlier editions of the book, footlogs were mentioned where they existed. Although some creeks have footlogs, these logs often wash away in spring runoff, so you can't depend on them. Because they are so likely to wash away this edition usually omits reference to them.

## WATER

The only way to be sure water is safe to drink is to boil it for five minutes at a FULL ROLLING BOIL, or to filter it with an water filter that includes iodine. Using drops of an iodine solution without also filtering kills bacteria and viruses but not the cysts of giardia lamblia and it takes 30 minutes to work. Boiling water for two minutes usually kills giardia, but killing other microbes requires at least five to 15 minutes of boiling. Therefore when car camping or day hiking, it is easiest to bring water from home if your planned campsite has no approved drinking water.

Diarrhea caused by giardia is becoming more common in Idaho because of increased backcountry use. Giardiasis, although not serious, is miserable. Up to 20 percent of the population may be carriers who have no symptoms. The incubation period is from six days to four weeks. This protozoa is also found in dogs, antelope, beaver and bighorn sheep.

In the desert, carry all water because desert water sources may be dry or contaminated with alkali, mud or minerals from old mines.

## BEARS

The black bear is the only bear living in the areas described here. However, the Fish and Game Department reports that grizzlies have occasionally been seen traveling through the Hells Canyon Wilderness. Black bears are considered only 25 percent as dangerous as grizzlies. Black bears may be any color from black to blonde, but have no shoulder hump like grizzlies and their claws are black. Few bears in remote areas will come near humans or campsites unless someone preceding you has allowed them to get into their food or garbage.

To prevent bear problems, keep food out of tents and pitch tents 100 yards from the cooking area. If a campsite is dirty, choose a different one or clean it up. If a campsite has bear scat in it, CAMP ELSEWHERE. Be sure to hang all food in a tree at night and in the daytime when you are going to be away from camp, and again, keep food away from sleeping areas. Hang the food in a heavy plastic bag inside a coated nylon sack at least 12 feet from the ground, five to 10 feet from the tree trunk and five feet below any branch. An alternative is to keep food in special bear proof containers, which you can buy at some outdoor stores.

Keep your campsite clean. Burn all scraps and fish guts or double bag them and hang with the food. Also hang any other garbage, including empty food packets. If fires are permitted, burn used toilet paper, tampons and sanitary napkins. Otherwise hang them with the garbage and carry them out in double plastic bags.

If you meet a bear, give it room, back away slowly, try to avoid eye contact and talk calmly to it. The bear will probably soon leave, although bear behavior is unpredictable. Mother black bears with cubs can be dangerous. It should be obvious that feeding bears is not only foolish, but can be deadly— if not for you, for the next person.

## SNAKES

The western rattlesnake (*Croatalus viridis*) is found in Idaho in deserts and foothills, usually only at elevations lower than 5,200 feet and rarely above 7,000 feet. This snake has a variety of background colors (pink, gray, green or brown) and diamond or hexagonal brown to black splotches. Therefore, when hiking in the desert, wear boots and long pants and look carefully where you are stepping or where you are placing your hands. Rattlesnakes will usually crawl away, but it may take a while. They strike only when frightened. Rattlesnakes often come out at night in the summer because they prefer temperatures between 80 degrees and 90 degrees. Night temperatures near freezing in spring and fall greatly reduce their activity.

Treat a bite only with a constricting band (not a tourniquet) and bed rest. Take the victim to a doctor, or send for medical help. Using antivenin in the field is dangerous because of possible allergic reactions, and using ice on a snake bite damages tissue. The "cut and suck" method damages tendons, blood vessels and nerves. In half the snake bites, little or no venom is injected anyway.

## INSECTS

Mosquitoes are the biggest insect problem. In early summer, even at high elevations, there can be clouds of mosquitoes so thick the sky looks charcoal gray. To keep them from biting you, wear long pants, a long sleeved shirt, a hat and, if needed, a headnet. Use plenty of insect repellant. The kind containing DEET seems to be the most effective. If backpacking, be sure you carry a bugproof tent. West Nile virus, a serious illness, is carried by mosquitoes. To prevent it, apply repellant containing 25 percent or more DEET or picaridin every four hours.

Scorpions are found under rocks in the Idaho desert and come out at night. The variety found here stings only a little more strongly than a bee, so a bite should be treated as a bee sting.

Ticks are found in the spring and early summer throughout Idaho. The common variety looks similar to a small watermelon seed. The ticks carrying Lyme disease are the size of a pinhead, but luckily only a few cases of the disease have occurred in Idaho. When outdoors in spring and early summer, you should examine yourself at least once a day for ticks. Long pants and long-sleeved shirts with tight cuffs will help keep off ticks. Ticks can carry Rocky Mountain Spotted Fever, tularemia, or Lyme disease, all of which can be cured by antibiotics.

Ticks usually crawl around for several hours before biting. When they do bite, they burrow painlessly into the skin. To make them back out, pull gently and steadily with tweezers, using care to prevent breaking off the head. If you find a patch of reddened skin a few days after a trip, consult a doctor. Such a patch is a symptom of Lyme disease.

In Idaho, bubonic plague is endemic in rodents, whose fleas carry the germs. Therefore, do not handle chipmunks or ground squirrels, and avoid pitching your tent close to their burrows.

Deer mice can carry hantavirus, so avoid camping next to or in old backcountry cabins or piles of lumber or branches. If you see mice droppings where you are camping or in a cabin, it is safest to assume they are from deer mice. To clean them up, don't sweep or vacuum because you risk breathing the virus. Instead put on plastic or rubber gloves and spray the droppings with antiseptic spray and then gather them up with damp paper towels.

## POISON IVY OR OAK

*Rhus radicans*, poison ivy, is the only species of poison ivy or oak in Idaho. Locally, people may call the plant either poison ivy or oak. In Idaho, poison ivy appears either as a shrub or a plant which grows mainly in desert canyons. The shrub can be identified by its shiny leaflets occurring in groups of three. Its leaves turn red in the fall and its white berries remain on the twigs all year. Another species, *Rhus diversiloba*, poison oak, appears only along the Pacific Coast and not in Idaho.

Both species have the same poison and will cause the same blisters and itching. Any part of the plant can produce the itchy ra sh. Scrub with strong soap and cold water immediately after exposure to avoid the effects. There are new over-the-counter lotions or creams that are more effective than soap in scrubbing off the itch-producing chemical from your skin and equipment. If blisters appear, cortisone ointment may help relieve the itching.

## AVOIDING GETTING STUCK ON ACCESS ROADS

Before attempting to drive backcountry roads, be sure your vehicle is in excellent condition. If planning to drive on dirt roads, get a Bureau of Land Management or Forest Service map of the area where you are going, topographic maps and a compass. Also take a shovel, pick, tow chain, 50 feet of tow rope, instant tire repair kit, tire pump, oil, duct tape, water, spare parts (such as a fan belt), tools and a small but sharp wood saw in case a tree falls across the road. Make sure you have all the parts for your jack and that you have a full size spare tire that fits the wheels of your car. Also take extra food and water, and sleeping bags, even on a day trip. Don't drive on dirt or primitive roads in rainy weather or until they dry in the spring. Rain makes these roads as slippery as grease. It can also create mud that builds up on tires so much they won't turn. In late summer and fall, some of the dirt roads turn into rivers of sandy dust that can require four-wheel drive. It is wise to explore bad roads in your vehicle only uphill, never downhill. Whenever in doubt, always walk down and look first, especially at washes and fords. In the desert it is a good idea to stay on the main roads

A high-wheelbase vehicle, such as a pickup or SUV, is recommended for primitive roads because such roads tend to damage passenger cars. A vehicle with four-wheel drive is a good idea; however, the wheelbase on small four-wheel drive vehicles is too low for these roads. If you get stuck, it is best to wait for rescue unless in a remote area.

## HEAT ILLNESSES

Sunstroke is life-threatening, and should be treated by immersion in cold water or covering with wet cloths. Symptoms are lack of sweating, hot dry skin, temperature over 105 degrees and possible unconsciousness. Get the person to a doctor as soon as possible. You can prevent sunstroke by drinking lots of water, resting in the shade in the hottest part of the day, and wearing a hat.

A victim of heat exhaustion has pale, moist, cool skin and a low temperature. He or she may also vomit or faint. Treatment consists of drinking lightly salted water or one of the drinks designed for sports and then lying down for awhile. Hikers may continue when they feel well again.

Remember that nights in Idaho are often cold, even in July and August when daytime temperatures are over 100 degrees in the desert and 75 degrees to 90 degrees in the mountains. Because of the daytime heat in summer, it is much safer to take desert trips in spring and fall.

## DEHYDRATION

Dehydration can have serious symptoms such as delirium, which may cause a person to become lost. Symptoms of dehydration are thirst, slow motion, lack of appetite, drowsiness and high temperature. Three quarts to a gallon of water a day per person are needed when hiking in warm weather. Extra salt is not needed—you get enough from food. In the desert, carry all your water, as water sources are uncertain. Don't rely on digging in dry stream beds or making solar stills for water. When they work, which is seldom, solar stills make only a pint of water in 24 hours.

Even in cold weather you can get dehydrated from sweating and from losing moisture in your breath. In the cold, dehydration reduces blood flow to hands and feet, increasing the danger of frostbite and hypothermia.

# GEOLOGY

A basic feature of the geology of Idaho's mountains is the Idaho batholith, which stretches from the Boise Ridge north to Kellogg and is one of the largest batholiths in the world. A batholith is a large mass of igneous rock which formed under the surface of the ground and was exposed by erosion. Idaho's 100-mile wide by 300-mile long batholith is composed mostly of granite and related rock. The rock was formed at a plate boundary when the heat generated by one plate sliding under another melted earlier rocks. The age of the rock in the batholith varies from 45 million to 180 million years old with the younger rocks on the eastern side. During the cooling of the hot magma, molten minerals flowed from the cooling liquid into nearby rocks to form many ore deposits. Before the batholith arose, Idaho was mainly seas and swamps.

Much of the rock in the Seven Devils mountains is part of the Wallowa Mountains — Seven Devils *terrane*, a geologic term for land carried to a continent by a moving plate. This group of islands was carried to North America beginning in the late Mesozoic about 130 million years ago.

During the Eocene epoch of the Cenozoic era, which began 70 million years ago, volcanoes began to erupt while lava flowed from cracks in the earth. On and around the Snake River plain the activity was due to the North American plate moving over an area of hot magma. Today this area sits under Yellowstone National Park. The Cenozoic era consisted of the Paleocene, Eocene, Oligocene, Miocene, Pliocene and Pleistocene. Later block faulting lifted the peaks and erosion and glaciation sculptured them. In the Eocene, redwood trees grew in southern Idaho, because no western mountains blocked the rain clouds when they came in from the Pacific. Therefore, the climate was much wetter than it is today. At this time, the mountain ranges which run north and south (the Lost River Range, Pioneers, and Sawtooth) were uplifted by block-faulting. Then in the Oligocene, the Challis volcanics covered most of these original ranges and uplift continued.

In the Miocene, rocks in the Seven Devils were eroded, folded and covered by the Columbia River basalts. When these basalts poured over the Snake River plain, they dammed rivers into huge lakes. One of these was geologic Payette Lake, which filled the Boise Valley and created the sand for the Bruneau Sand Dunes. Table Rock just above Boise is the remnant of a lake terrace of this lake. The vast sheets of lava covered an area 30 by 60 miles. Around the sheets of lava, elephants roamed among hardwood forests.

In the Pliocene epoch, the Snake River Valley sank 300 to 400 feet in a crescent shape along faults. The Blue Mountains, the Seven Devils and the mountains along the continental divide arose. Continuing lava flows created the final course of the Snake River. The most recent volcanic eruptions in Idaho occurred at Craters of the Moon about 2,000 years ago.

Tributaries flowing from the north into the Snake River became "lost" in the fissured lava and formed the Snake River aquifer, one of the largest underground reservoirs in the world. The rivers emerge into the Snake in the Thousand Springs area near Buhl in places like Malad Gorge and Box Canyon. Vegetation gradually became much more like the present, as the area became drier when the Cascades to the west arose.

In the Pleistocene, the climate became wetter and cooler, which caused glaciers to form during several ice ages. The Stanley Basin was full of ice, and even the Owyhees felt the nibble of small summit glaciers. Glaciers scooped out most of Idaho's mountain lakes. During this epoch, more minerals were deposited in rock fractures.

Humans probably came to Idaho 30,000 years ago by way of Canada and Alaska over a land or ice bridge. About 15,000 years ago, geologic Lake Bonneville in Utah overflowed and washed huge boulders from the canyon walls along the Snake River and rounded their corners. These boulders, today called melon gravel, traveled as far west as Homedale, Idaho. The flood also formed large river terraces where sediment collected behind temporary natural dams.

Idaho's nickname is the "Gem State" for its many precious and semi-precious stones such as jasper, opal, agate, petrified wood, garnet, sapphire, quartz crystal, amethyst and ruby. Many of them are found in the areas covered by this book, but some sites are on private land or within mining claims not open to the public.

# BOTANY

A wide variety of trees, shrubs, and plants grow in Idaho, due to its diverse terrain. The state flower is the syringa (*Philadelphus lewsii*), a 10-foot, spring-blooming shrub that has 1-inch fragrant white flowers with four long petals that form a cross. The state tree is the white pine (*Pinus monticola*), which is well-known for its knot-free white wood. Needles in groups of five and slender cones five to eight inches long identify this valuable timber tree, but it is absent from most of the areas covered in this book. The kinds of plants vary by location, and to try to make sense of their distribution botanists divide plant life into zones. Here is one of the systems used to describe plant zones in Idaho:

**Bear grass along Lick Creek Road**

**1. Sagebrush-grass:** big sagebrush, buckbrush, horsebrush, bluebunch wheatgrass, greasewood, hop sage, shadscale, winterfat and rabbitbrush.

**2. Wheatgrass-bluegrass:** Bluebunch wheatgrass, Idaho fescue, Sandberg's bluegrass and a few flowering plants. These grasses form a shortgrass prairie that is found in the Salmon, Clearwater and Snake River valleys.

**3. Fescue-wheatgrass:** In southern Idaho: little sunflower, arrowleaf balsamroot, paintbrush, sego lily, lupine, and geranium. In northern Idaho: wild rose, snowberry, chokecherry, cottonwood and hawthorn. This is also a prairie, so shrubs are small.

**4. Oak-mountain mahogany:** mountain mahogany, bitterbrush, serviceberry and buckbrush. There are no conifers and in Idaho there are no oaks in this zone in Idaho. It occurs mainly in southeast Idaho.

**5. Pinyon-juniper:** juniper, pinyon pine and limber pine. It lacks ponderosa pine and is usually found only south of the Snake River.

**6. Ponderosa (yellow) pine:** This zone lacks other conifers. It has grasses, plants and shrubs, such as ninebark, spirea, wild rose and serviceberry. North of the Snake River, it is the lowest forest zone.

**7. Douglas fir:** pine grass, elk sedge, serviceberry, bitter cherry, wild rose, buckbrush and mountain spray. Lodgepole and larch invade after a fire. This zone lacks grand fir, spruce or subalpine fir. It is the next higher forest zone above ponderosa.

**8. Arbor vitae (red cedar)-western hemlock:** This zone occurs only north of the Salmon River, so it isn't found in areas covered by this book. The other trees in it are grand fir, yew, western white pine and a little spruce and fir.

**9. Spruce-fir:** subalpine fir, fool's huckleberry, Engelmann spruce, grouse whortleberry, white-flowered rhododendron and woodrush. In southern Idaho, Douglas fir and lodgepole pine are common. It is the next highest forest zone above Douglas fir.

**10. Alpine:** This zone is found in isolated areas and has only a few cushion plants and lichens: Typical plants are mountain sorrel, mountain avens, alpine timothy, moss campion, dwarf willow and saxifrages. Just below this zone at timberline grow misshapen whitebark and limber pine. In the south timberline is at 10,000 feet and in the north 7,000 feet.

## WILDLIFE

Idaho wildlife is similar to the species found in areas adjoining it in the surrounding states. In addition, there are some unique subspecies. The state has many waterfowl, 24 species of game birds and animals, and 20 species of game fish. Idaho has some of the best deer and elk hunting in the country. Animals like elk, moose, mule and whitetail deer, badger, otter and others are found in several different types of habitats. In addition there are animals typical of certain plant zones.

Some of these are:

**Sagebrush deserts:** pocket mouse, sagebrush chipmunk, Townsend's ground squirrel and black-tailed jackrabbit

**Grassland:** pocket gopher, meadow mouse, antelope and white-tailed jackrabbit

**Ponderosa pine forest:** red squirrel and mule deer

**Spruce-fir forest:** flying squirrel, red-back mouse and snowshoe hare

**Subalpine forests and meadows:** pika and golden mantle ground squirrel

**Peaks and cliffs:** mountain goat and bighorn sheep

**Craters of the Moon:** chipmunk and pocket mouse (that is blackish to match the rocks)

One of the unique Idaho subspecies is the Idaho ground squirrel, which is found only on dry, rocky open ridges in Adams and Washington counties. This squirrel is dappled gray-brown on its upper parts and the buds of wild onions are its favorite food.

The Snake River Birds of Prey Area has the largest concentration of raptors in North America. Bald and golden eagles, peregrine falcons (an endangered species), prairie falcons and various hawks all live here. To take advantage of the opportunities to study these birds the World Center for the Birds of Prey is located just south of Boise.

The greater sandhill crane (a rare species) lives in remote marshes in the Boise, Challis and Sawtooth forest. It is gray-brown, long-necked and long-legged with a red crown and a rattling cry. If provoked, a sandhill crane can injure or blind a person with its heavy bill.

The endangered white sturgeon lives in Idaho in the Snake River. It is the largest freshwater fish in North America up to 13 feet. It looks like a shark but has no teeth. Instead it eats insect larvae, crayfish, clams and snails from the river bottom through a mouth which resembles the intake of a vacuum cleaner.

# HELLS CANYON NATIONAL RECREATION AND WILDERNESS AREAS

## 1.

## Hells Canyon Trail: Butler Bar to Bernard Creek (a National Recreation Trail)

**One-way distance:** 8 miles
**Elevation gain:** 1,100 feet
**Elevation loss:** 1,180 feet
**Highest point:** 2,000 feet
**Maps:** Squirrel Prairie, Hat Point, Old Timer Mountain
**Difficulty**: strenuous; time: 7 hours (part 1 of through trip);

**Access:** Before your trip, you need to arrange for a jet boat ride from Hells Canyon Dam to the trailhead at Butler Bar. To reach the dam from the south turn left (west) off U.S. Highway 95 at Cambridge onto paved Idaho Highway 71 and drive 63 miles to Hells Canyon Dam. Cross the dam to the Oregon side and go 1.2 miles more to the raft launching ramp. Then take the jet boat to Butler Bar. (You can also reach this trail section by driving from near Whitebird to Pittsburg Landing and hiking south for three days.)

Hells Canyon was labeled the Grand Canyon of the Snake on early maps. Some early boatmen referred to running Hells Canyon as a trip through hell, but the controversy in the 1950s over building a high dam is what gave it the name Hells Canyon. The first Europeans to see the lower end of the canyon were Lewis and Clark. Members of the Wilson Price Hunt party in 1811 saw part of the upper end of the canyon before cliffs turned them back.

In 1968, Idaho Power built three low dams on the Snake River in Hells Canyon. They are Brownlee, Oxbow, and Hells Canyon. As soon as their construction began, other companies began applying for licenses for dams farther down the canyon. When they did, conservationists formed the Hells Canyon Preservation Council to oppose the dams. In 1973, Idaho and Oregon senators introduced the Hells Canyon National Recreation Area bill, but it was two years before it passed

As you ride the jet boat to the trailhead, you may want to think about the 136-foot paddlewheel steamship, the Shoshone, built in 1866 to take people up and down the Snake as far as Olds Ferry near Weiser. After the railroad reached Winnemucca, Nevada, the next spring the ship was no longer needed and it was piloted down Hells Canyon to the Columbia. On the trip the ship lost eight feet of her bow going down Copper Creek Falls, the worst rapids on the river, which was at the site of today's Hells Canyon Dam.

Besides the Shoshone, other boats attempted to navigate Hells Canyon. The Imnaha began making runs from Lewiston in 1903, using ropes run through rings attached to the rock to get past the rapids, but it sank in 1904 at Mountain Sheep Rapids. Then the Norma, the steamship Albert Kleinschmidt built to carry ore mined

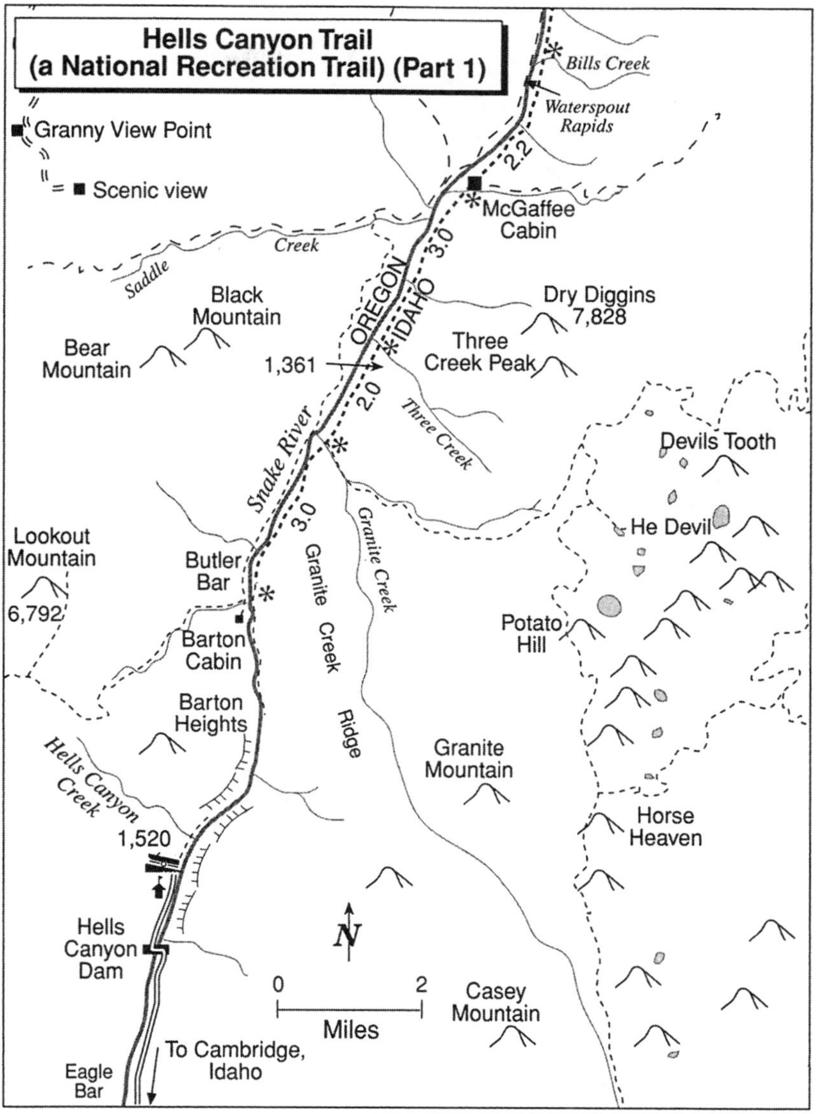


in the Seven Devils down the river, made only two runs before Kleinshmidt's company failed. In 1910 Ed McFarlane began a boat service on the Snake from Asotin, Washington, to Pittsburg Landing with a 36-foot gasoline powered boat, the Flyer.

By the 1920s people were attempting to take small boats and rafts down the river for fun. The first were John Mullen and Amos Burg in 1925 who went down in a canoe, although they let ("lined") the canoes down three rapids with ropes. In 1939, Buzz Holmstrom took the first woman down the canyon, Edith Clegg. Her boat ride was part of a transcontinental trip she was making by river. In 1954 Ms. Georgie White started a raft outfitting business and other outfitters soon followed

**Stone cabin at Bills Creek in Hells Canyon**

In Hells Canyon, rust and dark gray cliffs stair step thousands of feet up from the Snake River, which is cocoa brown, yellow-green or turquoise depending on the season and weather. A mantle of grass, green only in spring, covers the slopes between the cliffs. The river eddies along under the cliffs, breaking into rapids now and then. Occasionally a river terrace that is grassy and park-like with ponderosa pines, stands well above the river. In the bottom of the canyon, rolling heaps of gravel remain from the Bonneville flood 15,000 years ago. In addition, fan-shaped bars mark where side creeks have brought down sediment. Two of these, Granite and Bernard Creeks, drop 5,500 feet in less than 5 miles, tumbling down little canyons through tangles of netleaf hackberry, chokecherry and syringa.

The road continues a few yards past the ranch launching ramp to a visitor's center, where you can obtain information on the area and its natural and human history. From the center, a trail leads down the river about a mile before fading away. A trail also goes .2 miles along the Idaho side of the river to Deep Creek to provide fishing access. Because of cliffs, it does not connect with the through trail, so you must take a commercial jet boat and reservations are needed. Hells Canyon Adventures in Oxbow, Oregon, provides jet boat shuttle service.

In May, the trail is decorated by the 1 1/2 inch white flowers of the Bartonberry, a thornless raspberry that grows only in Hells Canyon. The bush is named after canyon settler Ace Barton's mother, who first told botanists about it. In early spring, flowers like pink grass widows and blue hyacinths embroider the grass, and underneath the grass there are flowers so small viewers have to lie down to see them.

Side canyons squeeze triangular hills from the canyon walls. Sagebrush grows in most desert areas in Idaho but there is little in Hells Canyon. Hikers may see mountain goats and bighorn sheep on ledges high above the trail, especially in early spring. Summer heat makes hiking Hells Canyon during July and August unpleasant. The fire danger is high then also — no open fires are allowed between July 1 and September 15.

The trail actually begins at Lamont Springs, but is hard to find and follow from there to Butler Bar as two parts of it are often underwater in spring. That is why it is best to start at Butler Bar. On the Oregon side, .5 mile before that point at Battle Creek, the old cabin where Ace Barton was raised stands on a fan-shaped bar. He came to live there with his family when he was three years old, and didn't move away from it until he was in his 50s. Later he helped Cort Conley write a book of history of the canyon called *Snake River of Hells Canyon.*

From Butler Bar, 5 miles from the launch site, the trail immediately climbs 300 feet up the side of the canyon. There is no water except from the river for the first 3 miles to Granite Creek during most of the year. About a mile beyond Butler Bar, the river breaks into Wild Sheep Rapids. Beyond the rapids, the trail descends to the river again.

Next, the trail gradually climbs 400 feet, passing under a rust-colored rock tower before dropping to Granite Creek at 3 miles. Here sandy flats among trees provide campsites. At the river's edge, boulders of greenstone have been so polished by the gigantic rock tumbler of the river they are slippery. The V-shaped canyon of Granite Creek rises from a grassy flat to pine-topped hills that are snow-covered in spring.

Beyond the bridge over Granite Creek is a junction with the Granite Creek Trail. A side trip up this trail .6 mile to the old Hibbs Ranch gives a fine view up Granite Creek. The trail from Granite Creek to Pittsburg Landing has been designated a National Recreation Trail.

There were many people who tried to make a living in the canyon. One of these was Ace Barton's grandfather, Martin Hibbs, who ranched on Granite Creek with his wife and six children beginning in 1902. Years later someone murdered Hibbs at his cabin and burned it.

Across the bridge, the trail cuts down to the water and runs under an overhanging cliff, a place called the "Tight Squeeze" at 3.5 miles. At high water, the trail is under water here. If it is, go back and go up the Granite Creek Trail .5 mile (600 feet up) and turn left (north) on an unsigned route that avoids the high water, but is difficult for beginning backpackers.

Some fine petroglyphs (designs carved into rock by prehistoric people) are 200 feet beyond the "Tight Squeeze," at 3.5 miles, where Granite Creek Rapids, one of the last remaining large rapids, churn the river and Cache Creek enters the river from the Oregon side. Ancestors of the Nez Perce Indians who lived in the canyon at the time of settlement came to the canyon as long as 30,000 years ago. They left petroglyphs, pictographs (rock paintings), and the remains of rock shelters and pit houses, which were houses that were dug into the ground and roofed with brush.

Beyond the Tight Squeeze, the main trail climbs 200 feet. It descends again, then climbs 150 feet, and drops to ford Three Creek at 5 miles, which is the last water until Bernard Creek. Beyond Three Creek, the trail continues high above the river with the narrow pine-studded flat called Two Bars across the way. At 6 miles, the trail goes along the high bar of Dry Gulch.

The green chasms of Saddle Creek and Hat Creek come down from the Oregon side at 7 miles. Between the two creeks a large bar of river stones forms an island in early spring.

From Dry Gulch the trail runs along the canyon wall to the grassy flat of Bernard Creek at 8 miles. Up that creek from a cabin and rusty machinery, you can see rock towers and pine and snow-covered hills. The cabin, known as the McGaffee Cabin, is on the national register of historic places and has interpretive signs and a visitor register. You can stay in the cabin, but it is so overrun with mice it is better to camp out. The best campsite is across the bridged creek on a high bar, just before two tiny beaches.

Bill Hiltsley, his wife and two children settled here in 1901, and constructed a log bunkhouse, board and batten cabin, and a wire enclosure to keep their children from falling in the creek. They raised fruit, cattle and chickens. The ranch is named the McGaffee Ranch after Fred and Billy McGaffee, who bought the ranch from Hiltsley in 1915, and raised cattle with the help of Fred's wife Gene. In 1935 Lenora Barton traded two other properties to acquire the ranch and in 1952 sold it to Bud Wilson.

# 2.

## Hells Canyon Trail: Bernard Creek to Sheep Creek

**One-way distance:** 6 miles
**Elevation gain:** 480 feet
**Elevation loss:** 560 feet
**Highest point:** 1,600 feet
**Map:** Old Timer Mountain
**Difficulty:** strenuous; time: 5 hours (second section of through trip)
**Access:** See Hike 1: Butler Bar to Bernard Creek. You can also reach this trail section by driving from US 95 near Whitebird to Pittsburg Landing and hiking south for two days to reach Bernard Creek, where this hike description begins.

Beyond Bernard Creek, the canyon widens so that the river bars, tufted with bunch grass, are up to 200 yards across and .2 mile long. Across the river from Sluice Creek, tiers of Columbia basalt with conifers rise between the layers rise to Hat Point Lookout. On the Idaho side, more than 6,000 feet above Bills Creek, Dry Diggins Lookout stands on a forested knoll. In this section, the side canyons carve gentle grooves instead of gulches and small prickly pear cactus peep from the grass.

From Bernard Creek the trail climbs 300 feet and goes along cliffs above No Name Rapids. At 1.5 miles, high water has sculptured a pothole four feet across and six feet deep next to the trail. From the pothole, the trail descends 50 feet, then climbs 200 feet to a grass shelf above Waterspout Rapids.

At 2.2 miles, the trail curves into the ravine of Bills Creek, near a roofless stone house built by Silas Bullock. Next, it goes .5 mile along the grass of Bills Creek Bar, where Dry Diggins Point can be seen upriver. At 3.4 miles, you can look up Sluice Creek to Hat Point and down to Sluice Creek Rapids seething below a landing strip.

At 4 miles, at Rush Creek, the trail wanders along Johnson Bar, which is 1.2 mile long and .2 mile wide. The ruins of the stone Bullock-Barton Cabin, built in 1914 by Ralph Barton (Lenora's husband) stand at the upper side. At the end of Johnson Bar, the trail descends to a sandy beach and campsite at 5.2 miles.

Now rock walls close in on the river and the trail climbs along them, then drops to a grassy bar split by Sheep Creek at 6 miles. The trail that used to go up the north side of Sheep Creek to Low Saddle has washed out. Near the mouth of Sheep Creek,

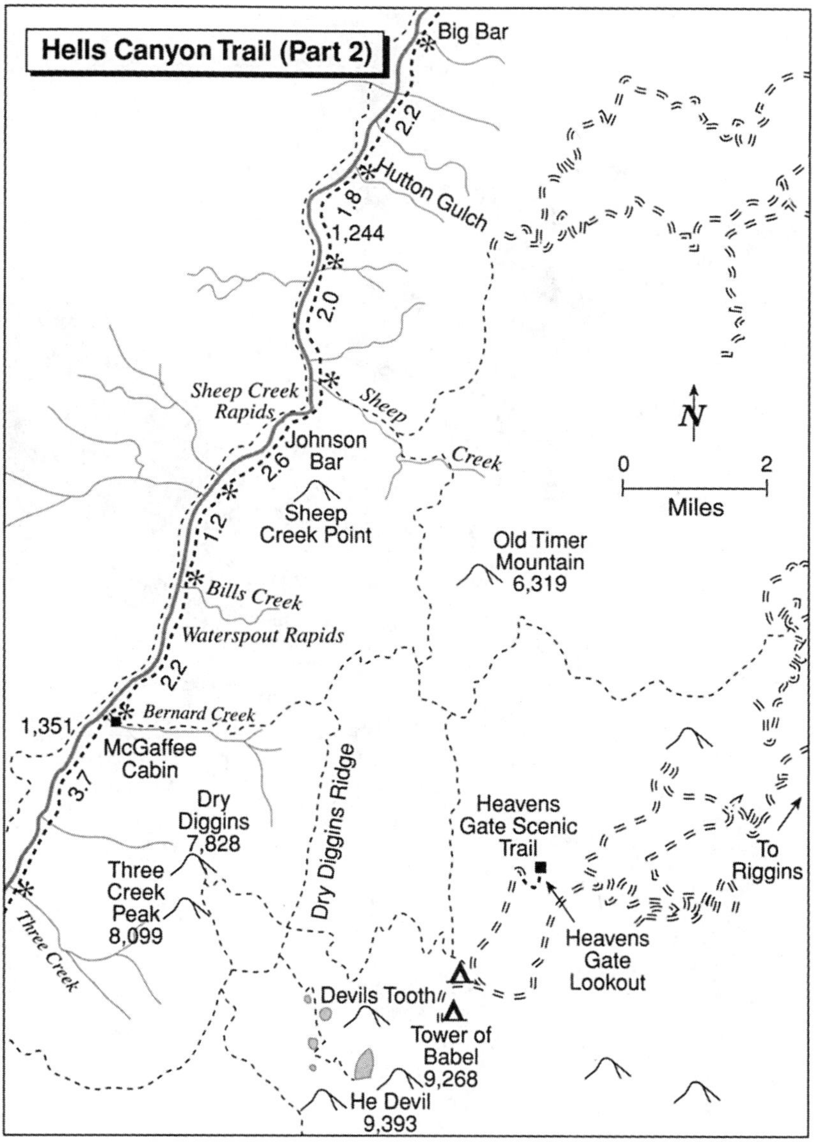


campsites are located on the two bars and in little flats, just across the wooden bridge. Cliffs and ledges flank Sheep Creek canyon through which Sheep Creek thunders down beside water birch trees and the house and barn of the Sheep Creek Ranch.

Bill McLeod, a Scotsman who homesteaded at Sheep Creek in 1884, built a rock dugout alongside the trail just below the present cabin. After he became ill in old age, the county sold his house to Fred and Billy McGaffee, who also owned a place at Bernard Creek. That is why on some maps there are two McGaffee cabins, one at

**Lookout at Heavens Gate**

Bernard Creek and one at Sheep Creek. Billy and his family lived at Sheep Creek, until they traded that ranch to Lenora Barton for a place she owned on the Imnaha River. From 1935 until 1952, she and her son Ace lived in the house the McGaffees had constructed, remodeled it, and built the outbuildings.

# 3.

## Hells Canyon Trail: Sheep Creek to Kirkwood Creek

**One-way distance:** 10 miles
**Elevation gain:** 1,100 feet
**Elevation loss:** 1,200 feet
**Maps:** Old Timer Mountain, Temperance Creek, Kirkwood Creek
**Difficulty:** strenuous; time: 7 hours (third section of four-day trip)
**Access:** See Hikes 1 and 2. You can also reach this trail section by driving from US 95 near Whitebird to Pittsburg Landing and hiking south for two days to Sheep Creek, where this hike description begins.

Below Sheep Creek, the hills become rounder, the cliffs fewer and the bars bigger. Now there is a lot of boating traffic, since the river below this point is considered navigable. (Only jet boats and non-motorized boats can travel the river from Sheep Creek to Hells Canyon Dam.) The big grove of ponderosa pines at Pine Bar seems like a bit of forest transplanted from a higher elevation. The trail in this section climbs the sides of two inner-canyon peaks. At the largest, Suicide Point, it traverses the side of a cliff 400 feet above the river. Between Sheep Creek and Kirkwood Creek there is water only at Meyer Creek. Len Jordan, his wife Grace, and their three children ranched at Kirkwood Creek during the Depression. Their old white clapboard house with a bathtub and sink which Jordan built himself out of cement is at Kirkwood Creek. Grace later wrote a book about their experiences called *Home Below Hells Canyon.* A staffed Forest Service interpretive center here is open year round.

From Sheep Creek, the trail skirts the base of cliffs and at .5 mile crosses Steep Creek, a small creek rising 600 feet from the river in .2 mile. At 1 mile, the trail traverses a hillside scattered with boulders and hackberries and then climbs 100 feet above the river along a cliff. Across the river at Sand Creek at 1.5 miles, a building on a high bar is used by Oregon Fish and Wildlife. The trail then drops to the tiny canyon of Willow Creek at 2 miles and passes the ruins of Indian pit houses. Today these are basins 12 to 16 feet in diameter and two to three feet deep. Once they were roofed with poles and brush. After this, the trail climbs 100 feet along a cliff where cement steps assist hikers.

Within about .3 mile of Willow Creek, it winds across Pine Bar where there is a campsite near the river. A grove of Ponderosa pines grows on this bar, far below their usual elevation in Idaho. From the pines orange gullies run up the mountain to orange outcrops. Then the trail rounds a few rocks to reach a rolling grass-covered hill called High Bar at 3 miles, where there is a last glimpse of Dry Diggins. About halfway

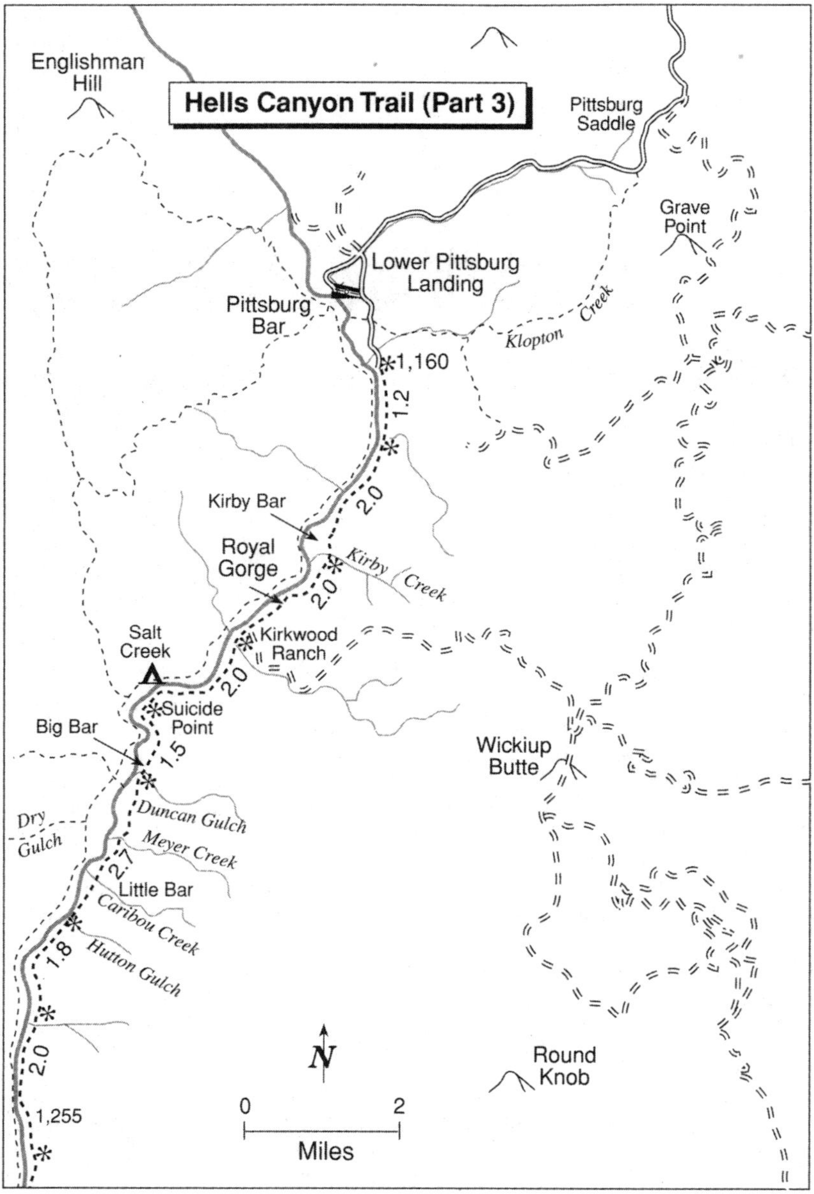


between Pine and High Bars, you can see pictographs beside the trail. Beyond the middle of High Bar, outcrops and cliffs dot high grassy hills. At Little Bar, Caribou Creek intersects the trail at 5 miles. Here a steep grassy hillside contains a mortared stone cellar.

The trail continues 200 feet above the river, curves into a dry gulch and runs back

**Hells Canyon**

into the deep canyon of Meyer Creek. Across the creek, an old pipe winds along the rocky point into Duncans Tunnel, which was built by blacksmith Ace Duncan by hand drilling the dynamite holes. Len Jordan hired him to build the tunnel to bring irrigation water from Meyer Creek to Big Bar. Although Duncan was 81 at the time, he accepted. The tunnel took him two years to complete. The trail climbs over a knoll 200 feet above the river, and then descends to Big Bar near a cabin at 6 miles.

At 8 miles across the river from a beach at Salt Creek, the trail hugs the face of Suicide Point and comes down onto a steep grassy slope where the beach of Half Moon Bar curves in at 9 miles. A lizard pictograph overhangs the trail 300 yards south of this. The trail reaches the large grassy bar split by Kirkwood Creek at 10 miles.

Across the creek from the Jordan house and the interpretive center is a white-washed fence and corral. A road up Kirkwood Creek leads 12 miles to Lucile. It serves as an alternate route in and out of the canyon. The bar beyond the corral has some campsites and restrooms. Pointed knolls of rock and grass guard both sides of Kirkwood Creek, across the river from the shadowy recess of Slaughter Gulch.

## 4.

## Hells Canyon Trail: Kirkwood Creek to Pittsburg Landing

**One-way distance:** 5.2 miles
**Elevation gain:** 800 feet

**Elevation loss:** 720 feet
**Highest point:** 1,600 feet
**Maps:** Kirkwood Creek, Grave Point
**Difficulty:** strenuous; time: 5 hours (fourth section of four-day through trip)
**Access:** See Butler Bar to Bernard Creek. You can also reach this trail section by driving 19.4 miles from U.S. 95 near Whitebird to Pittsburg Landing, a road that can be driven almost all year.

Down the river from Pittsburg Landing the Nez Perce under Chief Joseph crossed the river at Dug Bar during spring flood in 1877. Joseph was leading the tribe to the Lapwai Reservation as ordered by the federal government when they were met by troops after the battle of Whitebird that had been fought by another band of Nez Perce. The troops chased Joseph and his band 1,000 miles to just south of the Canadian border, where he, and the others still alive, surrendered.

The canyon closes in at Kirkwood Creek with fewer bars and more cliffs. The top of the canyon is now 2,000 feet lower than at Butler Bar, so the whole canyon wall is visible up to pine-clad summits. At the trail's end, travelers leave a gorge and enter the wide green valley of Pittsburg Landing. On the Idaho side, you see the first of the contact between the older rocks of the Seven Devils volcanics and the much younger black bands of Columbia basalts above. For directions to Kirkwood Creek, see Hikes 1, 2, and 3. The origin of the name Pittsburg for this place is unknown, but several families homesteaded there and across the river in Oregon as well, beginning in about 1885. Mike Thomason built a ferry here in 1891.

From Kirkwood Creek, the trail goes along the bar, then zigzags 400 feet in .5 mile up a hill of rock. It continues along the grassy side of the canyon 400 feet above the river, curving in and out of Royal Gorge at 1 mile. Then it descends a little, climbs 50 feet through a notch, cuts back into the canyon of Kirby Creek and crosses it at 2 miles. A campsite is on a sloping bar on Kirby Creek near the river.

Beyond here, the trail descends to the river at Cat Gulch, then climbs along cliffs 200 feet above the river. At 3.5 miles, it enters the shady recess of Line Gulch for 150 yards, then descends the gulch in poison ivy. Next, the trail slants across a rocky bar full of grass, cactus and hackberry down to the river bank at Corral Creek at 4 miles.

Beyond Corral Creek, the trail goes along cliffs edging the river. Finally it climbs off the cliffs down cement steps and goes along through grass and netleafed hackberry to the paved road at 5.2 miles.

To find the road to Pittsburg Landing from U.S. 95 as you are going north, turn left (west) at a sign for the Hammer Creek Recreation Area, which is south of the turnoff for the town of White Bird. This side road leads north to the recreation area. At 1.1 miles, turn left (southwest) on road 493 towards Pittsburg Landing. Mileage markers for the road begin at this point, but the author began the miles given here back at U.S. 95. The pavement ends at 2.2 miles and enters a ponderosa forest at 7 miles. Between 9 miles and the summit at 11.8 miles, the road can be very muddy in spring and fall and during rain. About .8 mile beyond the summit is a sign for Pittsburg Saddle and an overlook. From here the road drops in hairpin turns to Kurry Creek. At 17.7 miles is a junction with the road leading to the right 2.2 miles to the campground and marina. Take the road to the left (south) here signed Upper Landing. At 19 miles is a big parking area and at 19.4 miles the trail begins. There are picnic tables, a toilet, and parking for five or six cars here.

Driving from U.S. 95 to the trailhead takes 1 hour and driving from Cambridge to Hells Canyon Dam takes 1 1/2 hours. Driving U.S. 95 between the two turnoffs takes about 2 1/2 hours. Thus retrieving a car on a through trip is time-consuming.

# 5.

## West Fork of Rapid River (also known as the Rapid River Trail)

**Round trip:** 9 to 16 miles
**Elevation gain:** 1,800 feet
**Elevation loss:** 160 feet (return climb)
**Highest point:** 2,800 feet
**Map:** Heavens Gate
**Difficulty:** moderate to strenuous; time: 6 to 11 hours
**Access:** Going north on U.S. 95, turn west (left) onto a paved road 5 miles south of Riggins. Drive 2.9 miles to a curve in the road just before the picnic area at the Rapid River Fish Hatchery.

Idaho Power Company funds the fish hatchery at the trailhead because the three dams they completed in Hells Canyon in 1968 destroyed the Snake River salmon runs. The short stretch of the Rapid River below the hatchery is designated by treaty as Nez Perce salmon fishing grounds.

This trail punches through the jungle of chest-high grass, elderberry, wild rose, water birch, Douglas fir, Pacific yew, and other shrubs and trees which hide the canyon walls. Above 400-foot cliffs, grassy hills dotted with firs watch the canyon. In the spring, the river rushes with such force the water is completely white. When sitting on the rock knoll at the junction between the main river and the West Fork, you can hear the different pitches of the West Fork in one ear and the main river in the other. This hike is excellent for early spring and late fall because the access road is paved and the river crossings are bridged. In spite of the poison ivy, summer heat and rattlesnakes, many people hike the canyon, but because most of it is wooded, it still seems remote.

The trail begins as a two-wheel track where the road curves into the hatchery picnic area, which is for day use only. Don't be confused by a road a few yards farther that goes up the creek a short distance. You can't reach the trail from it. From the trail sign at the curve, the track goes through a gate 100 yards up and then turns to a trail. Idaho Power allows access through their land to reach the trail, which at about .2 mile enters the Nez Perce National Forest. The trail winds across an open hillside at the top of cliffs above the river for .5 mile. THE CLIFFS MAKE THIS HIKE DANGEROUS FOR SMALL CHILDREN. Across from a pale-orange cliff full of tiny caves, a trail for Cannon Ball Mountain turns off to the right (west).

At .7 mile, the trail passes a trickle of water in Thorn Gulch and then drops to edge the river. On a sturdy bridge at 1.4 miles, the trail crosses to the east side of the creek. Here the river is pinched between walls of rock. At 1.5 miles, where the wooded chasm of Blue Gulch rises across the river, the canyon widens and the trail goes

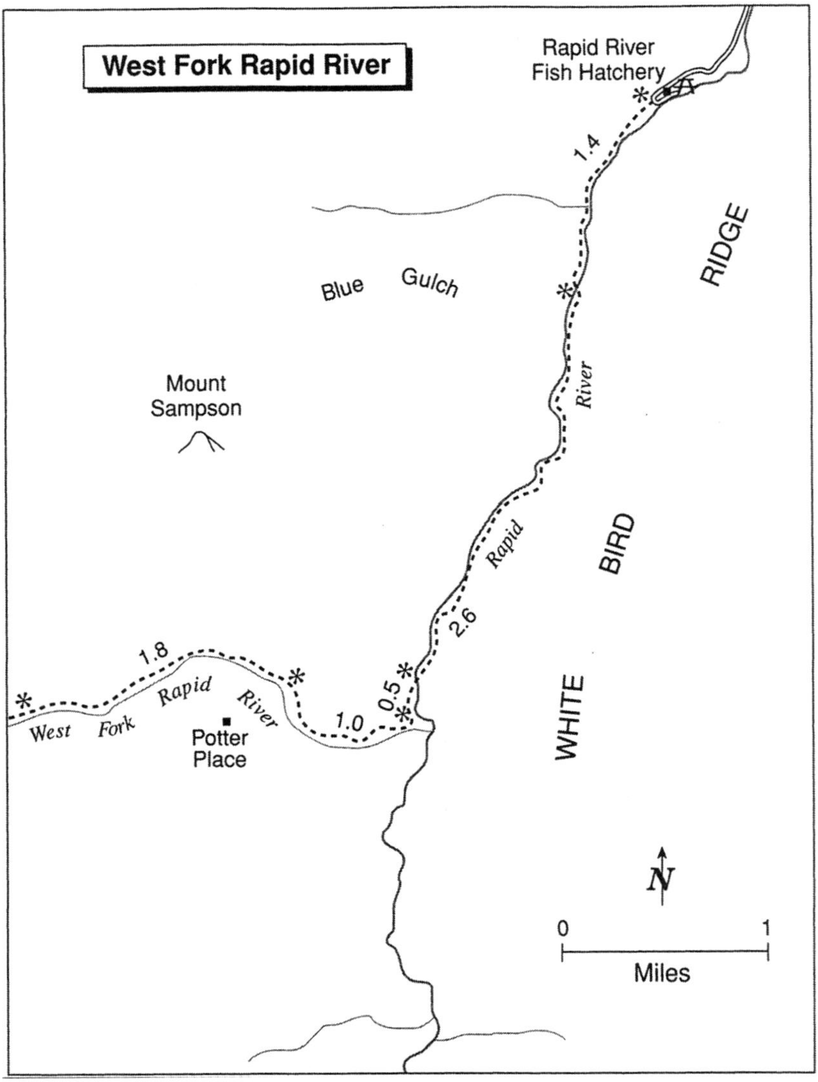


through chest-high grass. At 2.2 miles, it crosses a rocky area, and at 2.7 miles, leads 150 feet up a shrubby hillside. Then it returns to the creek at 3.2 miles where a few red-barked Pacific yew grow. Then the trail passes under mossy cliffs. At 4 miles, it crosses back to the west, and at 4.5 miles, treads a grassy hillside where the Main and West Fork trails join below a spur. The first possible campsite is here on a grassy flat next to the West Fork. From here on this hike description is of the trail to the right up the West Fork that connects with trails in the Seven Devils.

The trail up the West Fork climbs 400 feet in .5 mile on a hillside studded with short gray cliffs and in spring, wildflowers. From here there is a view of the cascading West Fork. As the trail enters forest again, a wooden gravestone honors a man killed in a mining accident. It continues beside the now placid creek through shrubs and trees in Potter Flat, which is named for George Potter, an early prospector and homesteader.

At 5.5 miles, a side trail goes across the creek and up 600 feet in .5 mile to the Potter Cabin, which is no longer open to public use. At the junction with the side trail to the cabin is a campsite suitable for a large party. From here, the main trail continues for 1.5 miles through the wooded creek bottom with cliffs and rocky points visible through a curtain of greenery. At 7.3 miles, it crosses Bridge Creek on a bridge, then climbs 400 feet along the base of an open hillside to the old McCrea Cabin at 8 miles. (This cabin is also no longer open to public use.)

Beyond the ranch, the trail continues up the wooded canyon of the West Fork, crossing Deep and Hanson creeks. At the Oxbow Bridge junction at 9.7 miles, one side trail climbs west 2.5 miles up Dog Ridge to the Boise Trail and another ascends Oxbow Creek to Bryan Mountain, 6 miles distant. From this junction, the West Fork Trail continues past Dog and Horse Heaven creeks into the Payette National Forest. The ruins of the old Rankin Mill are .2 mile north of Mill Creek, just before the trail meets the Jackley Mountain and Horse Heaven trails at 13 miles. The mill was also a nitric acid factory. Neither the mill nor the factory were a success.

# WINDY SADDLE AREA — NORTHERN SEVEN DEVILS LOOP

## 6.

## Boise Trail: Windy Saddle to Cannon Lake

**Round trip:** 8.6 miles (Windy Saddle to Seven Devils Guard Station .5 mile, Seven Devils Guard Station to Cannon Creek, 3 miles; Cannon Creek to Cannon Lake, .8 mile)

**Elevation gain:** 480 feet

**Elevation loss:** 680 feet (return climb)

**Highest point:** 7,200 feet

**Map:** He Devil

**Difficulty:** moderate; time: 4 hours (this section one-way)

**Access:** Going north on U.S. 95 turn left (west) one mile south of Riggins at a sign for the Seven Devils Road. At 1.7 miles, turn left on the Papoose Creek Road (517): From the highway it is 16.7 miles to the Windy Saddle trailhead.: 11 miles on gravel and 5.7 miles on a rough, primitive road.

A forest of fire-killed snags and young lodgepoles surrounds miniature green Cannon Lake. Black peaks splashed with lichen hang above like the underworld spirits for which they are named: The Goblin, The Ogre and She Devil.

Before driving up to Windy Saddle, stop at the Hells Canyon National Recreation

Area office in Riggins for information on road and trail conditions. The first 11.5 miles of the road has a gravel surface, but is steep. The last 5.2 miles is a dirt road with ruts, potholes and lots of football-sized rocks. A high wheelbase vehicle is necessary, and four-wheel drive is helpful, especially on the way down. Just beyond a high meadow where the road hairpins to the west at 16.5 miles, you can look east into the Salmon River Canyon. In a few yards, a side road with a locked gate leads downhill to the guard station. Continue straight ahead on the main road .2 mile farther to the Windy Saddle trailhead.

The trail that leads south from Windy Saddle is known as the Boise Trail because it follows the route of an old Nez Perce trail to the Boise River. Most of the forest along the Boise Trail burned over in the Rapid River Fire of 1994. The trail begins by descending a grassy hillside to the guard station road at a small barn and corral. Follow this road to the left (east) for 100 yards to reach the next section of trail. This section crosses a lower section of the same road before reaching the guard station at .5 mile.

From the guard station, the trail switchbacks down in the open and enters forest at .7 mile, then joins another trail at a gate. This unsigned trail along the fence downhill to the east is the trail to Saddle Camp and Cannon Ball Mountain. Go through the gate and follow the Boise Trail as it contours through forest at 1.3 miles. Note that the only water on this section of the Boise Trail is at Bridge Creek at 1.5 miles.

The junction with the Cannon Lake Trail is at 3.5 miles just before Cannon Creek. The side trail to the lake zigzags up through forest, then follows a little ridge in forest recovering from fire. Below the lake, the route crosses a creek and a marsh. Three campsites at the lake at 4.3 miles just beyond the marsh are overused. At the upper end of the lake, another site is beside the inlet, but camping at least 200 feet from the lake and creek will help preserve the shores.

# 7.

## Boise Trail: Cannon Lake Junction to Horse Heaven Lake

**Round trip:** 21.4 miles

**This section one-way:** Cannon Creek to Horse Heaven Lake Junction: 6.5 miles (980 feet gain, 400 feet loss). Side trail to Horse Heaven Lake: .7 mile (360 feet gain)

**Highest point:** 7,600 feet

**Map:** He Devil

**Difficulty:** strenuous; time: 5 1/2 hours this section one-way (second part of clockwise northern Seven Devils loop)

**Access:** See Cannon Lake (Hike 6) for directions to Cannon Creek 3.5 miles south of the Windy Saddle trailhead where this trail description begins.

Dark gray boulders and strips of bright green bunch grass surround the milky turquoise water of Horse Heaven Lake. On the west, low cliffs, one above the other, hold in two higher lakes (Slide Rock and an unnamed one). Behind these ledges rise the 400-foot cliffs of a black mountain, shaped like a chopped-off pyramid. A few feet south over a ridge is a tiny pond which dries up and becomes a meadow by late summer.

After leaving Cannon Creek, the grade is not noticeable, but the trail does climb. It circles into the canyon of Hanson Creek and crosses it at 2.5 miles. Here hikers can follow the creek 1.5 miles cross-country up to Lower Hanson Lake.

The main trail winds up a ridge and meets the West Fork of Rapid River—Dog Ridge Trail at 3.7 miles. Next it rounds the end of the ridge and heads up the canyon of Dog Creek in the open with a view of black peaks around Dog Lake. At Hanson Creek and Dog Creek are large, shady campsites, but both sites have burned snags that are hazardous when the wind blows because they could fall without warning. Hikers can reach Dog Lake by a 2-mile route that turns off 75 yards north of Dog Creek at the 4.5 mile point.

Beyond Dog Creek the main trail winds along in woods, crossing a side stream at 5.3 miles. At 5.6 miles it makes a big hairpin turn onto a grassy hillside. A junction with a route northwest to Horse Heaven Lake is at 6.5 miles just beyond a campsite and usually dry stream. The route to the lake gains 360 feet and passes through burned-over forest, over rock benches and across a meadowy hillside to the lake in .7 mile. From Horse Heaven Lake, hikers can climb cross-country west to an unnamed lake, then northwest to Slide Rock Lake at 1 mile, which lies below the Twin Imps.

# 8.

## Boise Trail: Horse Heaven Lake Junction to Horse Heaven — Seven Devils Trail Junction

**Round trip:** 24 miles
**This section one-way:** 2 miles (800 feet gain)
**Highest point:** 7,840 feet
**Map:** He Devil
**Difficulty:** strenuous; time: 2 hours this section one-way (third section of clockwise northern Seven Devils loop)
**Access:** See Cannon Lake and Horse Heaven Lake (Hikes 6 and 7) for directions to the Horse Heaven Lake junction 8.5 miles south of Windy Saddle.

Where the Boise Trail meets the Horse Heaven and Seven Devils Trails at the south end of the Seven Devils loop, there is a view of the grassy, tree-sprinkled hill of Horse Heaven. In summer it resembles a misplaced golf course. From the Horse Heaven Lake Junction, the trail climbs gradually through forest, then passes a rock slide just below Haas Lake at .8 mile. It then climbs east up the side of a wooded ridge. At .8 mile, it hairpins back to the west onto an open ridge. From here you can look south at black hills north of Black Lake that sweep up to sharp peaks, accented by the black spire of the Black Imp.

At 1.5 miles, the trail makes two switchbacks as it climbs a boulder field to the Horse Heaven — Seven Devils Trail Junction at 2 miles. (There is no obvious trace of the side trail shown on the map that leads from this junction down Two Creek to the Granite Creek Trail.)

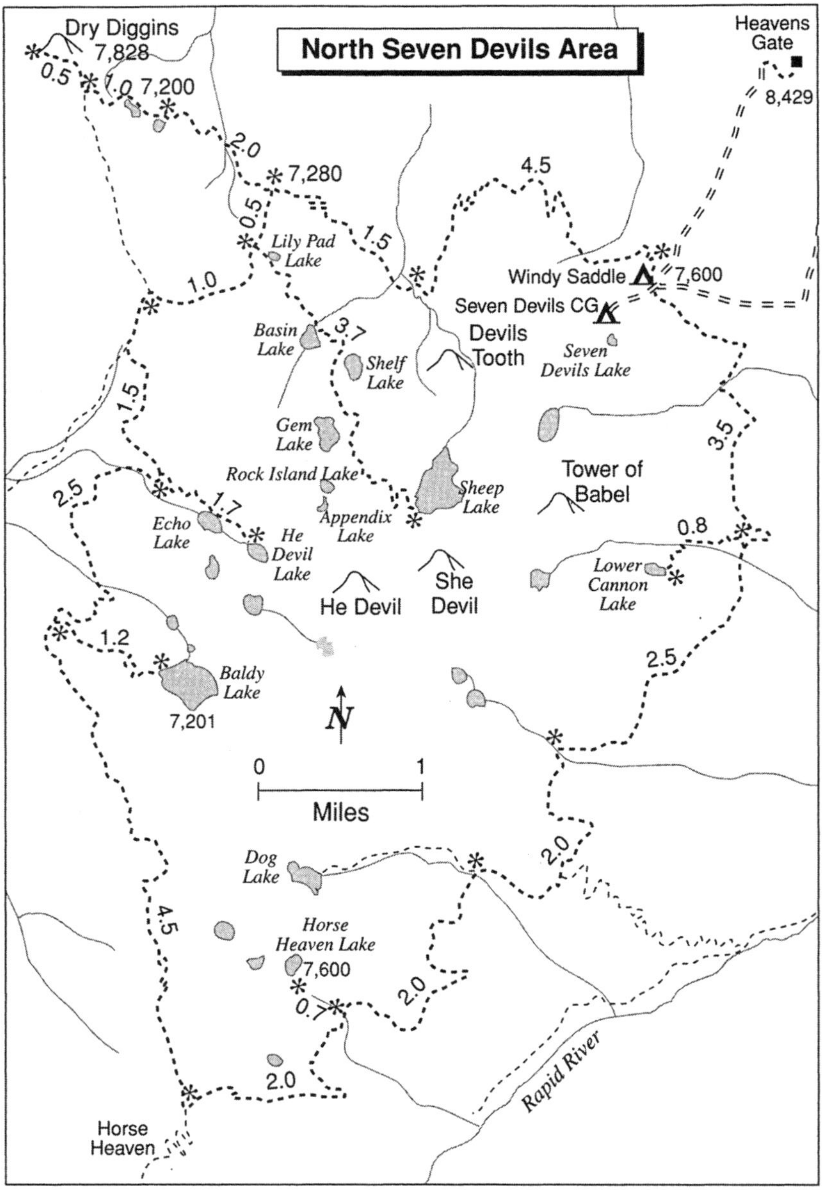

North Seven Devils Area
Dry Diggins
7,828
0.5
1.0
7,200
2.0
7,280
0.5
Lily Pad Lake
1.5
4.5
Heavens Gate
8,429
Windy Saddle
7,600
Seven Devils CG
1.0
Basin Lake
3.7
Shelf Lake
Devils Tooth
Seven Devils Lake
1.5
Gem Lake
3.5
Rock Island Lake
Tower of Babel
Sheep Lake
2.5
1.7
Echo Lake
Appendix Lake
He Devil Lake
0.8
Lower Cannon Lake
She Devil
He Devil
1.2
Baldy Lake
7,201
2.5
N
0
1
Miles
Dog Lake
2.0
4.5
Horse Heaven Lake
7,600
2.0
0.7
2.0
Rapid River
Horse Heaven

**The Seven Devils from Heavens Gate**

# 9.

## Seven Devils Trail: Horse Heaven — Seven Devils Trail Junction to Baldy Lake

**Round trip:** 35 miles via the Boise Trail and 25 miles via the trail to Dry Diggins

**This section one-way:** Horse Heaven — Seven Devils Trail Junction to Baldy Lake Junction: 4.5 miles (320 feet gain,1,200 feet loss)

**Side trail to Baldy Lake:**1.2 miles (300 feet gain)

**Highest point:** 7,920 feet

**Map:** He Devil

**Difficulty:** strenuous; time: 4 hours for this section one-way (fourth part of clockwise northern Seven Devils loop)

**Access:** See Horse Heaven Lake to the Horse Heaven — Seven Devils Trail Junction (Hike 8) to reach that junction where this description begins.

Half-mile long Baldy Lake fills a basin of hills of gray rock, backed by jumbled black peaks. One of them is He Devil, the highest mountain in the Seven Devils, and another is the Devils Throne, which sweeps up in tiers. Still another is a giant staircase of four jagged summits rising to a furrowed peak. Around the lake, young lodgepole pines rise above fallen snags that burned 60 years ago. Just below the lake, two tiny Little Baldy Lakes cluster along the outlet.

From the junction below Horse Heaven, the trail first runs along grassy Haas Flat with a 5,000-foot view into Hells Canyon. Later it passes the jumbled black boulders and pinnacles of the Devils Farm. In a flat above the trail, these boulders form mounds, as though they were the farmer's lumpy field.

Beyond its junction with the Boise Trail, the Seven Devils Trail first gently climbs meadows with Hells Canyon on the west. At .5 mile, bluebells and false hellbore 100 yards up a slope to the right (east) of the trail mark the location of Haas Flat Spring, the last water until the South Fork of Little Granite Creek at 5.5 miles, a mile past the Baldy Lake Junction. At .7 mile, the trail corkscrews down talus 400 feet in .5 mile. At 2 miles, it contours into the canyon of the Devils Farm, then skirts under Potato Hill, which is not visible, and heads east through trees to the Baldy Lake Junction at 4.5 miles.

The side trail to Baldy Lake contours along climbing 100 feet to cross a tiny side creek at .5 mile. Then it switchbacks 200 feet up to the lake 1.2 miles from the main trail.

# 10.

## Seven Devils Trail: Baldy Lake Junction to Echo and He Devil Lakes

**Round trip:** The shortest round trip, 21 miles, is via the Windy Saddle to Dry Diggins trail, rather than by the trail section described here. (On the Boise Trail the round trip is 44 miles.)

**This section one-way:** Baldy Lake Junction to Echo Lake Junction: 2.5 miles (320 feet gain, 800 feet loss); Echo Lake Trail to Echo Lake: 1 mile (400 feet gain); Echo Lake to He Devil Lake: .7 mile (200 feet gain).

**Highest point:** 7,920 feet

**Map:** He Devil

**Difficulty:** strenuous; time: 3 1/2 hours for this section, including lakes, one way; (fifth section of northern Seven Devils loop)

**Access:** See Cannon Lake (Hike 6) and the following hike descriptions to reach the Baldy Lake junction where this description begins.

From above, oval green Echo Lake seems to hang at the edge of Hells Canyon. From the east shore of He Devil Lake, talus rises to a 600-foot black cliff and on the southeast, the He Devil supervises his lake, which is accented by a round island sprouting trees from a bald, rock surface. To the right of He Devil, a humped black mountain defends a jagged low ridge.

Access for this section is either by 16 miles of the Boise and Seven Devils trails from Seven Devils Guard Station or by 10.5 miles of trail from Windy Saddle. From the Baldy Lake Junction, the Seven Devils Trail hairpins north 800 feet down through woods to the South Fork of Little Granite Creek at 1 mile. Once across, the trail climbs 150 feet up a boulder field, then contours along in trees. Finally, it turns east back into a wooded canyon to cross the Middle Fork of Granite Creek. At 2.5 miles

**She Devil from Sheep Lake**

**Hells Canyon from Dry Diggins**

in a clearing, it turns northwest just before the Echo Lake Junction.

The 1-mile side trail to Echo Lake begins by winding up a rocky hillside. Then it skirts the left side of the lake and corkscrews .7 mile up to He Devil Lake. From that lake, hikers can go south cross-country .2 mile to Triangle Lake and southeast .5 mile more to Purgatory Lake.

# 11.

## Echo Lake Junction to Sheep Lake Trail Junction

**Round trip:** 13 miles from Windy Saddle

**This section one-way:** Echo Lake Junction to Sheep Lake Junction: 2.5 miles (800 feet gain, 160 feet loss)

**Highest point:** 7,600 feet

**Map:** He Devil

**Difficulty:** strenuous; time: 2 1/2 hours for this section one-way; (sixth section of northern Seven Devils loop)

**Access:** See Cannon Lake (Hike 6) or Windy Saddle to Dry Diggins Trail (Hike 14). The shortest route (6.5 miles) to the Sheep Lake Trail is to go from Windy Saddle on the trail to the Dry Diggins Junction and then south for .5 mile.

From the Echo Lake Junction, the trail toward the Sheep Lake junction climbs a 800-foot grassy hill to meet the Little Granite Creek Trail near Hibbs Cow Camp. From the hill, there is a magnificent view of Hells Canyon to the west and ogre-like black peaks above Echo and He Devil Lakes to the east.

The first part of this section of the Seven Devils Trail climbs a hot, open slope until trees close in. At .7 mile, it crosses the North Fork of Little Granite Creek in a meadow. At 1.2 miles are two junctions 50 yards apart for a trail down Little Granite Creek 6.5 miles to the Snake River.

On the main trail, 200 yards beyond Little Granite Creek is another junction. Keep left here for 300 yards up a sandy hillside to a junction with the south trail to Dry Diggins Lookout at 1.5 miles. There is also a northern trail to the lookout, which is covered in Sheep Lake Trail Junction to Dry Diggins Trail Junction, Bernard Lakes and Dry Diggins Lookout (Hike 13). The main trail leads along an open ridge and then drops down a grassy hill and through trees to the Sheep Lake Junction, 2.5 miles from the Echo Lake Junction.

# 12.

## Basin, Shelf, Gem and Sheep lakes

**Round trip:** 20.4 miles

**This section one-way:** Sheep Lake Trail from the junction with the main loop trail to Sheep Lake: 3.7 miles (1,040 feet gain, 560 feet loss)

**Highest point:** 8,320 feet

**Map:** He Devil

**Difficulty:** strenuous; time: 4 hours this section one-way; (seventh part of clockwise northern Seven Devils loop)

**Access:** The shortest route to the Sheep Lake Junction where this description begins is via the Windy Saddle to Dry Diggins Trail Junction (Hike 14). It is 6.5 miles to the Sheep Lake Junction on this trail or 21 miles via the Boise Trail.

Black talus tumbles from a rock hill above the shallow bowl of green Basin Lake, the first lake on this trail. At Shelf Lake (the second lake) two black skyscraper-shaped mountains with a deep notch between them guard the inlet's inviting waterfall. On the east side of blue-green Gem Lake, the third lake, an enormous flat rock serves as a fishing platform, and above the south end rises a pale tooth-shaped crag.

The black face of the She Devil, splashed with yellow-green lichen, frowns over the south end of the tear-shaped fourth lake, Sheep Lake. Next to the She Devil, above a wildflower meadow, He Devil's ugly features are silhouetted against the skyline. Islands and peninsulas along the west shore face a crag across the lake that is named the Tower of Babel. It resembles the battlements of a castle nibbled by time.

Regulations require camping at least 200 feet from lake shores. Because all of these lakes get heavy use, it is a good idea to plan your trip to avoid camping at them.

The Sheep Lake Trail turns southeast from the main trail 1 mile east of the junc-

**Devils Tooth**

tion with the south trail to Dry Diggins Lookout and .5 mile south of the north trail to Dry Diggins. The Sheep Lake Trail comes to tiny Lily Pad Lake at .2 mile, then climbs over a little ridge to Basin Lake at 1 mile and on over a rocky ridge to Shelf Lake at 1.5 miles.

Beyond Shelf Lake, the trail climbs the inlet, threading rock benches and alpine gardens for .2 mile to a junction with a .2 mile trail to Gem Lake. The only places to camp near Gem Lake are between rock benches 100 feet above the east side of the lake.

From the Gem Lake Junction, the trail to Sheep Lake corkscrews up past rock outcrops and flowers, then skirts under the two skyscraper peaks. Beyond a snow pond, the trail winds up to a saddle at 3.2 miles, which is 800 feet above Shelf Lake. From the pond, hikers can go east 200 yards for a view of Rock Island and Appendix lakes below. Above the pond, you can see Dry Diggins Lookout. On the far side of the saddle, Sheep Lake spreads out under the menacing He Devil. From the saddle the trail drops 400 feet to the lake at 3.7 miles.

Sheep Lake can also be reached by a shortcut path from the campground at Seven Devils Lake, but it requires scrambling along cliffs and thus is recommended only as a climbers' route.

# 13.

## Sheep Lake Trail Junction to Dry Diggins Junction, Bernard Lakes and Dry Diggins Lookout

**Round trip:** 20 miles from Windy Saddle to the Sheep Lake Junction AND to Dry Diggins Lookout from the Dry Diggins Junction

**This section one way:** Sheep Lake Trail to Dry Diggins Trail Junction: .5 mile (80 feet loss); Dry Diggins Trail Junction to Bernard Lakes: 2 miles (320 feet gain, 320 feet loss); Bernard Lakes to Dry Diggins Lookout: 1.5 miles (640 feet gain)

**Highest point:** 7,828 feet

**Maps:** He Devil, Old Timer Mountain

**Difficulty:** strenuous; time: 3 1/2 hours for this section one-way (eighth part of northern Seven Devils loop)

**Access:** See Windy Saddle to Dry Diggins Trail Junction (Hike 14) and the preceding sections of the loop for directions for reaching the Sheep Lake Junction where this description begins.

Grass fringes the green water of Bernard Lakes below rounded black ridges. At the lower lake lodgepoles draped with the black strands of elk moss stand behind a large outcrop. At the upper lake the green pads and yellow flowers of water lilies set off a view of Dry Diggins Lookout. Camping is limited; be sure to camp 200 feet from the shores.

The abandoned Dry Diggins lookout perches 6,000 feet above the Snake River, separated from the chasm of Hells Canyon by black rocks and gnarled trees. Below these, cliffs and golden grass plunge to the dark blue river which is embroidered by white rapids. Haze often fills the whole canyon, bluing the opposite canyon walls. Ghostly outlines of the Wallowas loom to the southwest. Back to the east is an excellent view of the black figures of the Seven Devils.

This hike section contains three parts: a section of the Seven Devils Trail from the Sheep Lake Trail north to the Dry Diggins Trail Junction, the Dry Diggins Trail from there to Bernard Lakes, and the trail from the lakes to the lookout. The nearest access to the Sheep Lake Trail Junction is by 6.5 miles of trail from Windy Saddle, or by going around three-quarters of the loop for 21.5 miles from Windy Saddle.

To reach Bernard Lakes from the Sheep Lake Trail Junction, walk north .5 mile through grassy areas to the junction with the Dry Diggins Trail, which is sometimes called Iron Phone Junction, because it was once the site of a Forest Service telephone.

From this junction take the Dry Diggins Trail west. It switchbacks 400 feet into the canyon of Bernard Creek, passes a 100-foot cliff, and at the bottom, crosses Bernard Creek. Then it zigzags 320 feet up rock benches and past a lily pond to the first lake at 2 miles and the second at 2.1 miles.

Beyond the lakes the trail passes a lily pond and then ascends a dry, rocky hillside. At 3 miles, is a junction with a trail that runs south 2 miles to intersect the main loop trail .5 mile north of the Little Granite Creek Junction. If you go south on this trail to the first summit, which is called Three Creek Point, and walk 150 yards west off the trail, there's a wonderful view down Three Creek to the river.

Back on the Dry Diggins Trail, if you continue north to the lookout, the hillside levels and trees resume until the rocks of the lookout plateau begin at 3.5 miles. From the final switchback, the trail looks down to Bills Creek Bar on the Snake River.

# 14.

## Windy Saddle to Dry Diggins Trail Junction

**Round trip:** 12 miles
**Elevation gain:** 1,440 feet
**Elevation loss:** 1,780 feet
**Highest point:** 8,000 feet
**Map:** He Devil
**Difficulty:** strenuous; time: 7 hours this section one-way (ninth part of northern Seven Devils loop)
**Access:** Going north on U.S. 95 turn left (west) one mile south of Riggins at a sign for the Seven Devils Road. At 1.7 miles, turn left on the Papoose Creek Road (517). From the highway it is 16.7 miles to the Windy Saddle trailhead.: 11 miles on gravel and 5.7 miles on rough, primitive road.

Rugged views occur along the trail from Windy Saddle to the Dry Diggins Trail Junction since it goes down and up twice into and out of deep canyons. While descending into the canyon of Sheep Creek, you see a black spire called the Devils Tooth standing watch in front of He Devil, She Devil and the Tower of Babel. While passing the Tooth, you get a good view of Dry Diggins Lookout and Hells Canyon.

This description starts at Windy Saddle and goes west to the Dry Diggins Junction but it is the final section of the northern Seven Devils loop which, except for this section, is described in the opposite direction from that given here. The reason for this is to make the description easier to read for those planning to go only to Sheep Lake or Dry Diggins Lookout. Before starting your hike, it is well worth taking the time to drive down the road that leads .5 mile southwest to the Seven Devils Campground and around the loop, from which you can walk 150 yards down to the emerald tarn of Seven Devils Lake.

From Windy Saddle, the trail towards Dry Diggins drops 480 feet to the tiny East Fork of Sheep Creek. The trail edges a rock wall, then climbs 1,000 feet up the other side to where hikers can see Heavens Gate Lookout to the north.

At 2.5 miles, the trail rounds a spur, then contours to the end of the ridge and drops 1,300 feet to Sheep Creek. At 3 miles, it hairpins down under black towers, then cuts across a rockslide of gray, olive, russet, rose and white rocks, which is sprinkled in mid-summer with pungent purple horsemint.

At 4.5 miles, Sheep Creek splashes down in a waterfall, so following the creek is too steep a route to use in reaching Sheep Lake. The trail crosses two sections of Shelf Creek at 5 miles, then circles the head of the canyon and switchbacks 560 feet up a field of boulders to the junction with the Dry Diggins Trail at 6 miles. Because of the large elevation gains from Windy Saddle to this point, the loop trip is much easier if you begin by going south on the Boise Trail.

# 15.

## Heavens Gate

**Round trip:** 1 mile
**Elevation gain:** 300 feet
**Highest point:** 8,429 feet
**Difficulty:** easy except that trail is rocky; time: 1 hour 15 minutes
**Map:** Heavens Gate

**Access:** Going north on U.S. 95 turn left (west) one mile south of Riggins at a sign for the Seven Devils Road. At 1.7 miles, turn left on the Papoose Creek Road (517). From the highway it is 16.7 miles to the Windy Saddle trailhead: 11 miles on gravel and 5.7 miles on rough, primitive road. Turn right (north) on the bumpy road to Heavens Gate and drive 1.8 miles to a parking area.

Southwest of Heavens Gate Lookout, black and charcoal gray peaks of the Seven Devils jut from ridges at such varying angles they seem to dance. In early summer, snowbanks accent the peaks with white slashes. At that time mats of pink phlox soften and perfume the rocky slopes. From the lookout, which is usually no longer staffed, you can look west and north into the chasm of Hells Canyon and see the snowy Wallowas across it. To the north the lookout ridge continues in a series of grassy, bright green hills. Northeast are mountains in Montana, and east are the silhouettes of peaks like Sheepeater Mountain in the Frank Church Wilderness. The lookout has a stone basement, white wooden upstairs, and a flat metal roof with a radar antenna.

From the parking area the trail begins by winding south up grassy slopes, angling toward the top of the ridge beside whitebark pines. After about 10 minutes it begins to switchback, making two or three switchbacks before coming out on the crest of the ridge at .3 mile. Then it wanders along the ridge top through the rocks to the lookout at .5 mile. The trail may seem longer than .5 mile because it climbs so much for a short trail. The Boise Trail continues north from Heavens Gate, but doesn't begin at the lookout; instead it begins at the north end of the parking area below it.

# BLACK LAKE AREA

## 16.

### Six Lake Basin

**Round trip:** 10 miles
**Elevation gain:** 1,100 feet
**Elevation loss:** 920 feet (return climb)
**Highest point:** 8,080 feet
**Map:** Purgatory Saddle
**Difficulty:** moderate; time: 8 hours
**Access:** If going north on U.S. 95, in Council at a 90-degree turn at the City Square, turn left (west) on the Hornet Creek Road. (If going south on U.S. 95 you keep straight ahead at this corner.) Drive 30 miles to the village of Bear. Just before Bear the pavement ends at the junction with Road 002 to Cuprum. Continue straight ahead (Road 105) 4.3 miles past the Forest Service work center and the old schoolhouse to another junction. Take the left (north) fork and go .8 mile to another junction with a road to Cuprum. Here, turn right (northeast) and drive 13.1 miles to Black Lake on a rough primitive road (112). A high-wheelbase vehicle is required and four-wheel drive is preferred, for the road is listed as a four-wheel drive road in the Payette National Forest travel plan. The road usually opens only after July 15 because of snow on the section known as High Dive.

In midsummer, hills of light green grass and dark green firs roll across Six Lake Basin beside emerald green lakes, which reflect dark gray cliffs and boulders. Paintbrush, lupine, umbrella plant, purple horsemint and blue flax accent the hillsides. From the first saddle, the green hill of Horse Heaven shines to the north below high black peaks. Beyond Joes Gap, the pale shapes of the Wallowa Mountains drift in the distance.

Black Lake, where the hike begins, nestles in a circle of green ridges, rocky slopes and black cliffs. In early mining days, a tramway carried ore from a mine high above the lake to a mill below it. The mill was burned and its scrap iron collected to be melted down during World War II. A few yards off trail are the ruins of a wooden tram tower on the brink of cliffs. Above are a rusty cable, ore buckets, an immense wheel, a mine tunnel and the ruins of buildings.

The primitive, rough Black Lake Road climbs 2,400 feet in about 7 miles. At 40.2 miles from Council, a road turns off to the Smith Mountain lookout. Just before this there are two possible routes for the main road. The right hand one makes a large, rutted hairpin turn, while the left, which looks like a better surface, is a shortcut that goes straight uphill to intersect the other road after its switchback, but has huge pits in it at the top. A mile or so before the lookout road once stood a mill for the Placer Basin Mine. The mill was built in the 1930s and processed $3 million in gold.

From the junction with the lookout road, the main road continues 1 mile across

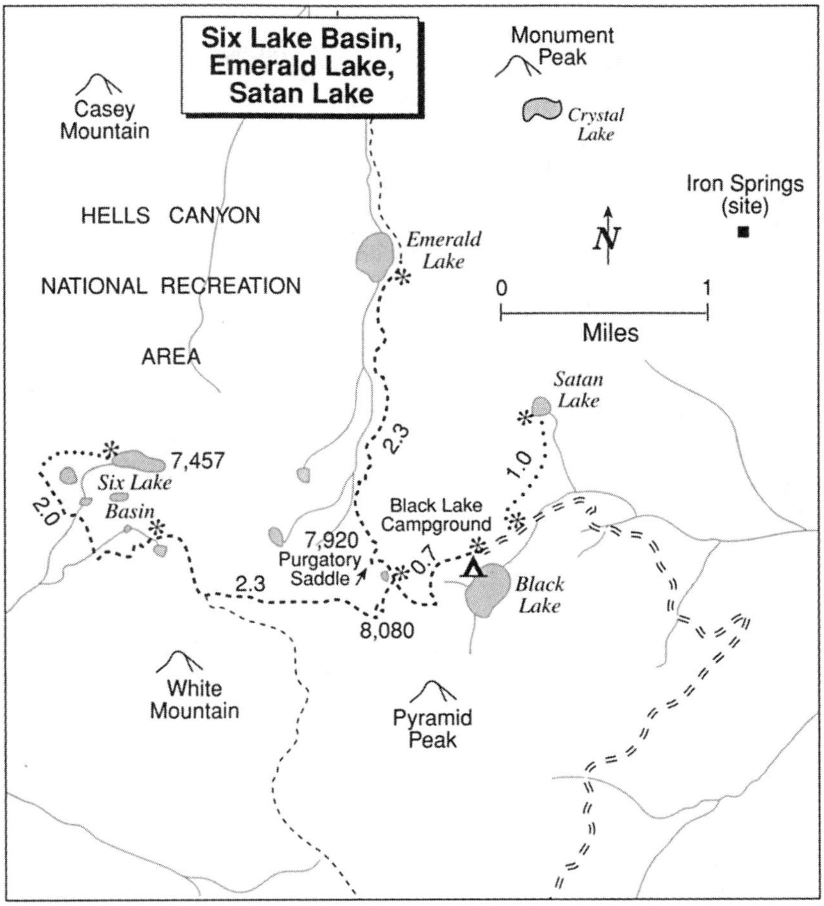


Lost Basin to a summit before plunging over the edge of "High Dive." Here the road appears to dive over a cliff but actually drives along the side of it. Then it traverses the canyon wall and turns up a second canyon to the lake at 13.1 miles.

The trail, a former mining road, begins 200 yards before the campground, which is on the north side of the lake. Do not be confused by spur roads just before the lake. An ATV trail turns right downhill to the ruins of the Rankin Mill at 46.7 miles (about .9 mile before the main trailhead.) If you plan to take an ATV on this trail to Rankin Mill you need to know that the area north of Paradise Creek beyond the mill is closed to ATV use. It is illegal to drive an ATV any farther than that — you could be arrested. On the Black Lake Road .3 mile beyond the track to Rankin Mill, a spur road to the right gives access to the cross-country route to Satan Lake, and in .1 more mile another track leads left to undeveloped campsites at Black Lake's outlet. The trailhead is about 100 yards beyond this turnoff.

On the main trail to Six Lakes Basin at .2 mile is a 30-foot boulder near rocks crusted with green malachite, a copper ore. At .5 mile, the trail switchbacks right, where a path to the left (southeast) detours to the old mining remnants.

Beyond the switchback, the main trail leads northwest up a grassy slope to a pond at .7 mile. In a gully below the pond is a junction with a trail to the left to Six Lake Basin. This trail zigzags up a hillside covered with three-foot curly dock to a saddle at 1 mile. (The right branch at the pond leads over Purgatory Saddle to Emerald Lake.)

Near the saddle on the Six Lake Basin Trail, the Seven Devils appear to the north. Beyond the saddle, a green horseshoe-shaped lake nestles under a dark peak at the upper end of Horse Pasture Basin.

The trail zigzags down the side of the saddle, dropping 320 feet, then climbing 160 feet through wildflowers to Joes Gap at 2.5 miles. Then it switchbacks down talus to the first blue-green lake at 3 miles.

Below this lake, the trail winds down through woods 200 feet, then crosses the outlet at 3.5 miles. At 4 miles, a second green lake is in the woods, with the third lake hidden to the east. The trail climbs around the end of an open ridge and heads north to the fourth lake, which is tea-colored. The trail to the fifth lake is an unofficial one. It goes up a grassy hill, turns east, and at 4.5 miles, intersects trails to Deep and Granite creeks. Beyond this junction is a campsite and horse area and at 5 miles the fifth lake. Peninsulas extend from the south shore into the .3 mile long lake and above the east end rise the dark cliffs of three rounded peaks. The sixth lake is a pond on the outlet of the first lake, .2 mile north of the trail.

# 17.

## Emerald Lake

**Round trip:** 6 miles
**Elevation gain:** 720 feet
**Elevation loss:** 1,120 feet (return climb)
**Highest point:** 7,920 feet
**Map:** Purgatory Saddle
**Difficulty:** moderate; time: 6 hours

**Access:** If going north on U.S. Highway 95, in Council at a 90-degree turn at the City Square, turn left (west) on the Hornet Creek Road. (If going south on U.S. 95 you keep straight ahead at this corner.) Drive 30 miles to the village of Bear. Just before Bear the pavement ends at the junction with Road 002 to Cuprum. Continue straight ahead on Road 105 for 4.3 miles past the Forest Service work center and the old schoolhouse to another junction. Take the left (north) fork and go .8 mile to another junction with a road to Cuprum. Here, turn right (northeast) and drive 13.1 miles to Black Lake on a rough, primitive road (112). A high-wheelbase vehicle is required and four-wheel-drive is preferred, for the road is listed as a four-wheel drive road in the Payette National Forest travel plan. The road usually opens only after July 15 because of snow on the section known as High Dive.

Emerald Lake gleams between black walls. On the west one, slices of dark lava are sandwiched between layers of green grass below a fluted face. To the left of the layers, a triangular rock head looks at the sky. On the east wall on a great dark cliff below Monument Peak, veins of lighter rock scribble pale lines. At Purgatory Saddle there is an excellent view of the canyon of Emerald Lake, the green dome of Horse Heaven, and a few of the northern Seven Devils.

The first .7 mile of this hike is along the Six Lakes Basin Trail; for directions, see Hike 16. At .7 mile, the Emerald Lake Trail climbs from the pond to Purgatory Saddle, which is a notch between dark gray cliffs. From just beyond the saddle you can look down on Emerald Lake. North of it at .1 mile, the trail zigzags a headwall, and then descends to grass and forest at 1.5 miles. It continues straight down the canyon, switchbacks twice, crossing a little stream twice. At 2 miles, it runs through dense woods along the main creek, and, at 3 miles, reaches the upper end of the lake. Recent reports indicate you are likely to see bears at Emerald Lake.

The trail goes around the east side of the lake to a big rock bench and a second inlet, then continues 5 more miles to Horse Heaven. Purgatory Saddle is 1,120 feet above the lake — remember you have to climb back up to it on your return.

# 18.

## Satan Lake

**Round trip:** 2 miles (cross-country)
**Elevation gain:** 320 feet
**Elevation loss:** 160 feet (return climb)
**Highest point:** 7,360 feet
**Map:** Purgatory Saddle
**Difficulty:** cross-country; time: 2 hours;
**Access:** If going north on U.S. Highway 95, in Council at a 90-degree turn at the City Square, turn left (west) on the Hornet Creek Road. (If going south on U.S. 95 you keep straight ahead at this corner.) Drive 30 miles to the village of Bear. Just before Bear the pavement ends at the junction with Road 002 to Cuprum. Continue straight ahead on Road 105 4.3 miles past the Forest Service work center and the old schoolhouse to another junction. Take the left (north) fork and go .8 mile to another junction with a road to Cuprum. Here, turn right (northeast) and drive 13.1 miles to Black Lake on a rough, primitive road (112). A high wheelbase vehicle is required and four-wheel drive is preferred, for the road is listed as a four-wheel drive road in the Payette National Forest travel plan. The road usually opens only after July 15 because of snow on the section known as High Dive. To find the correct turnoff for Satan Lake, notice an ATV trail that turns right downhill 46.7 miles from Council. This old road turns off about .9 mile before the main trailhead at Black Lake. Drive .3 mile beyond the ATV trail turnoff to a short spur road that turns off to the right (north) and park. This road is .4 mile before the campgound at Black Lake and just before another road leads left to campsites at the outlet.

Dark olive green Satan Lake nestles in a pocket below charcoal gray cliffs 1 mile from Black Lake. On the west, the black cliffs of a rounded peak spill part way to the

Satan Lake

shore.

To reach Satan Lake, walk along the spur road a few yards and then go to the right off it into a grassy area. Angle north downhill, keeping close to cliffs that are on your left. Beyond an area sprinkled with boulders, cross a belt of thick forest. Here keep going slightly uphill. At .5 mile, the route comes out of the trees onto steep talus slopes below cliffs. Cut across these slopes towards a whitish outcrop that is to the left of the apparent head of the deep canyon of Satan Creek. When you reach the outcrop at .7 mile, go up the left side of it. (About 20 feet of scrambling on solid rock is required here.) Climb the last few feet to the top of the outcrop, then climb to the top of the smaller earthen ridge holding in the lake and descend to the shore. The only place to camp is on the flattest part of this ridge, but there is no good site.

## CUPRUM AREA

## 19.

### Sheep Rock (a National Natural Landmark)

**Round trip:** .5 mile
**Elevation gain:** 80 feet
**Highest point:** 6,847 feet
**Maps:** Cuprum, White Monument
**Difficulty:** easy; time: 1/2 hour
**Access:** If going north on U.S. Highway 95, in Council at a 90-degree turn at the City Square, turn left (west) on the Hornet Creek Road. (If going south on U.S. 95 you keep straight ahead at this corner.) Drive 30 miles to the end of the pavement at the junction with the road to Cuprum (002). Turn left (west) here, passing the turnoff for the Kleinschmidt Grade into Hells Canyon at 36 miles, then turning right and passing through Cuprum at 37.5 miles. Drive about 1 mile farther, then go left on Road 106. Continue 11.5 more miles on a narrow dirt road to the Sheep Rock trailhead.

Cuprum, which you pass on the way in, was one of the most important towns serving the Seven Devils Mines. It had a smelter and still has an active copper mine. Levi Allen made the first discovery in 1862, when he found the Peacock Lode that under Albert Kleinschmidt later served the nearby town of Helena, Idaho. Beginning in 1885, he started mining there and at other area mines, and built a road to haul ore to the Snake River below. Helena was located beside Deep Creek just across Copper Creek from the Peacock Mine. The 1988 Eagle Bar Fire burned the remnants of Helena's buildings. The post office at Cuprum was established in 1897. At one time the town had three general stores, a hospital, six saloons, two hotels and a newspaper.

The Sheep Rock Trail is an easy way to get an excellent view of Hells Canyon. The trail is designed to be barrier free with 1/4 mile accessible for wheelchair use, so

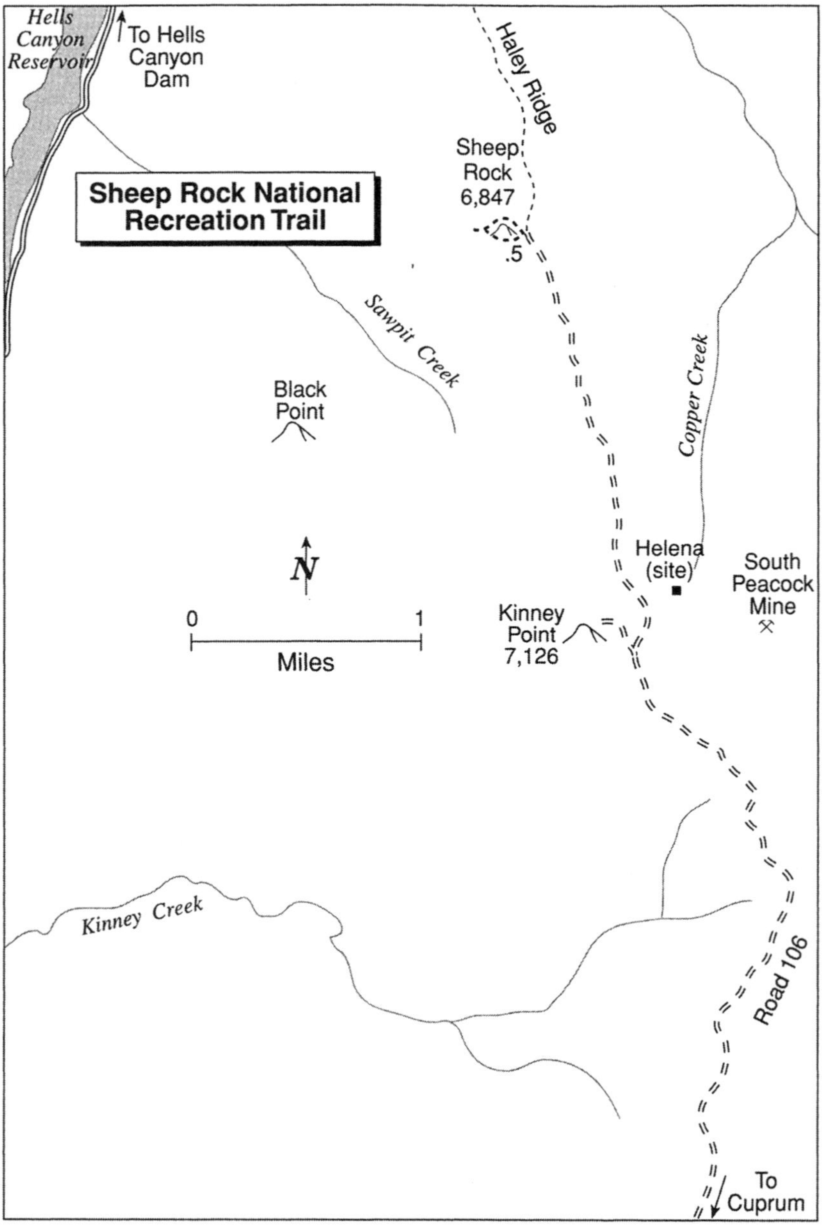


it has a gentle grade. However, the 50-foot side trail that leads from the loop trail to the overlook is not designed for wheelchairs. From the overlook you can look down into the canyon. The upper part of the canyon appears terraced because the earth between the layers of lava holds rows of trees. Cliffs lining the inner gorge block a view of the river. Across the canyon rise the Wallowa Mountains, which contain Oregon's Eagle Cap Wilderness. To see the river you can take the 1/4 mile primitive side road to Kinney Point 2 miles before Sheep Rock and walk 50 yards to an overlook. However, at this overlook you see Hells Canyon Reservoir instead of the wild Snake.

At the parking area for Sheep Rock, avoid a trail called the Copper Creek Trail which goes off to the right of the loop road leading to the parking area. Also avoid the Haley Ridge trail, which begins half way along the north side of the parking loop road. The nature trail begins at the parking area at the west end of the loop. Whichever end of the trail you take, it passes through a recently burned forest and circles around a group of 20- to 30-foot outcrops. On the canyon side of the loop about half way around, a side trail leads 50 feet or so over rocks to the overlook. The view is especially dramatic in mid-October or later when a couple of inches of snow on the trail often contrasts with the gold and black of the warmer canyon below. The lookout on a nearby hill to the south is Horse Mountain. Although the elevation is only 6,847 feet at Sheep Rock, a few whitebark pines grew here before the fire.

# PAYETTE NATIONAL FOREST
# NEW MEADOWS DISTRICT
# HAZARD LAKE AREA

## 20.

## Goose Creek Falls

**Round trip:** 2.6 miles
**Elevation gain:** 40 feet
**Elevation loss (return climb):** 680 feet
**Highest point:** 5,760 feet
**Map:** Brundage Mountain
**Difficulty:** easy, except that you may need expert ability to get the best view of the falls; time: 3 to 3 1/2 hours

**Access:** Turn right (north) 5 miles northwest of McCall from Idaho Highway 55 onto the paved Brundage Mountain Road and go 3.4 miles. Turn left and drive down to the huge snowmobile parking area at the trailhead. The trail is not on the topographic map.

On the way to the trailhead from McCall you pass the first McCall ski area, the Little Hill. It began in 1937, when local lumberman Carl Brown gave the town of McCall 80 acres to develop a ski area five miles from town. Club Hill, now more often called The Little Hill, was built on this land and is still running, with a t-bar, groomed slopes, day and night skiing, and groomed nordic trails.

Four miles from Idaho Highway 55, you also pass the turnoff for the much larger

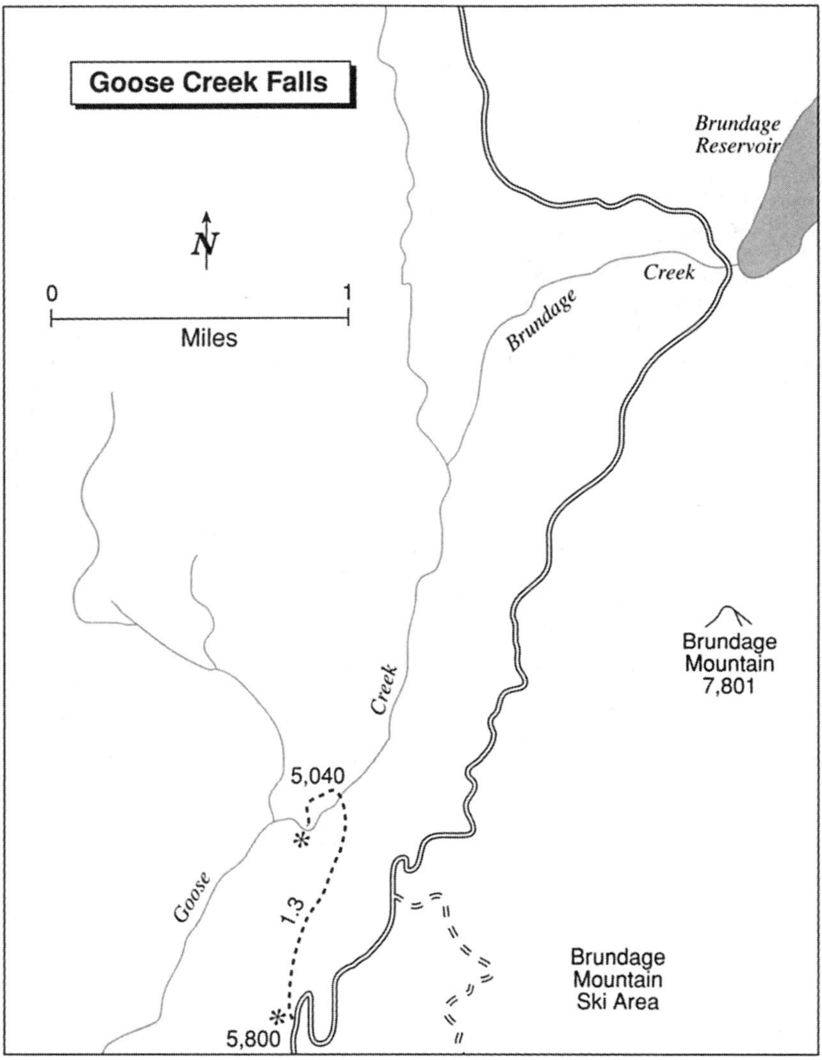


Brundage Mountain Ski Area. The first lifts (a double chair and rope tow) and lodge (an A-frame cabin) were constructed in 1961. Corey Engen, later the ski school director and head racing coach, was instrumental in starting the area. Best known for his ski jumping, he was captain of the 1948 U.S. Olympic team and competed in seven Olympic winter games. Two others who helped start the area were Jack Simplot, the potato magnate, and Carl Brown, a McCall lumberman. Brundage now has a large day lodge and 3 chairlifts, including a high-speed quad.

At Goose Creek Falls a vertical black boulder splits the creek into two plumes of white water. The water falls 60 feet into an olive green pool and then wanders down the canyon in cascades. Mist from the falls waters a hanging garden of ferns and

**Goose Creek Falls**

flowers on the far side of the creek. Reaching the best viewpoint of the falls requires scrambling down outcrops and steep gravelly slopes beside the falls. PLEASE BE VERY CAREFUL HERE, and stop as soon as the slope seems scary. IF YOU HAVE PRESCHOOL CHILDREN, the author recommends stopping at the trail bridge over Goose Creek, from which you can look down on a smaller unnamed falls.

The trail to Goose Creek Falls starts at the northwest corner of the parking lot. First it climbs for five minutes to the top of a little ridge at .2 mile. Then it angles north down into the canyon. The first 100 yards of this is the only steep place. The trail descends at first in a Douglas fir forest, then among alders, huckleberries and other shrubs. After about 20 minutes it levels off and goes up and down gently. A half hour along the trail, you cross a little side stream. Below this are large Douglas firs. At 1 mile there is a bridge over the creek. On the other side the trail goes both up and down the canyon. Up the canyon it reaches the Hazard Lake Road in a couple of miles. To see the falls, turn left (south) down the canyon on the level trail. In about .2 mile a signed side trail turns left .1 mile toward the falls. The main trail continues 2.5 miles down the canyon to Last Chance Campground. However, reaching the falls from that campground is not recommended because of a difficult ford of the creek.

Take the side trail toward the falls. It goes out over a rock outcrop and then down steeply to overlook the falls. A rock cairn marks where it is safest to stop.

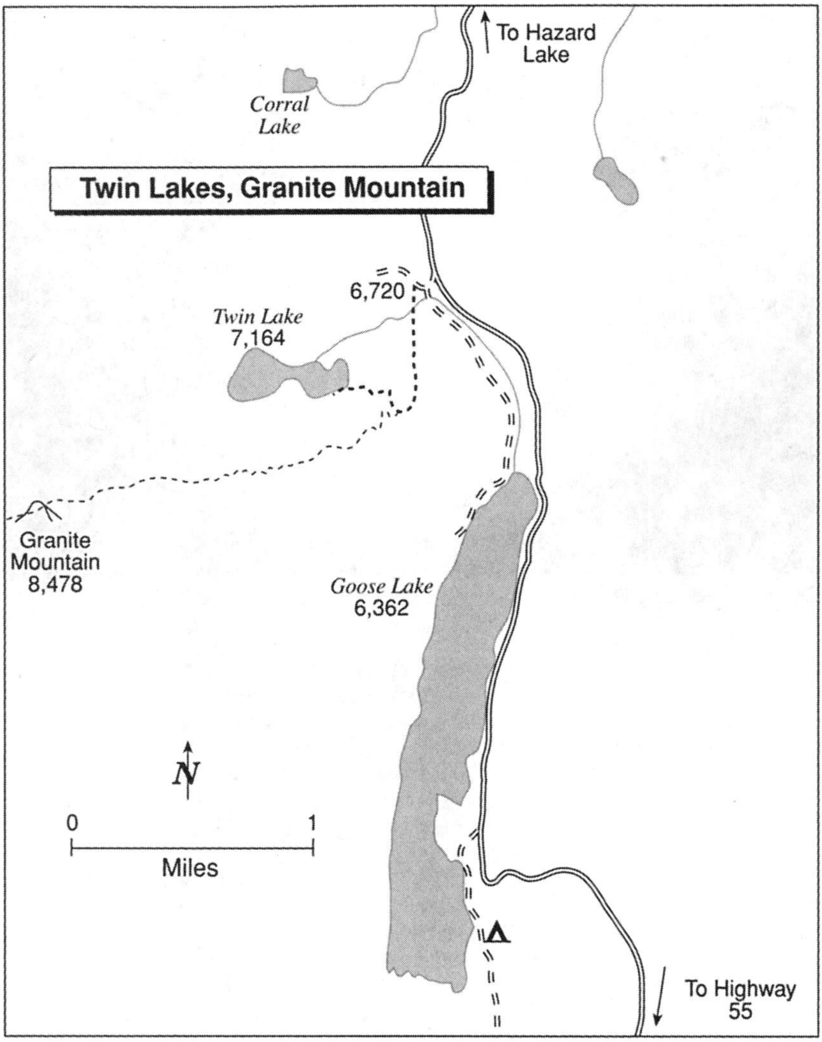


# 21.

## Twin Lakes (Granite Mountain Trail)

**Round trip:** 2 miles
**Elevation gain:** 450 feet
**Highest point:** 7,164 feet

**Map:** Brundage Mountain
**Difficulty:** easy; time: 2½ hours
**Access:** Turn right (north) 5 miles northwest of McCall from Idaho Highway 55 onto the paved Brundage Mountain-Goose Lake Road. Drive 4 miles on pavement and then on gravel, passing Goose Lake at 11.2 miles, to a sign for the Granite Mountain trailhead at 13.4 miles. Turn left (west) here and go .1 mile to the undeveloped trailhead. (Beyond the trailhead the road continues another .2 mile to a grazing association cabin. Please don't disturb the cabin or the cattle.)

The first permanent settlers in nearby Meadows Valley were Bill Jolley and Calvin White in 1877 and the Clay family in 1880. The Clays first lived in Packer John's cabin, which is now in a little state park. The cabin had been built by John Welch in 1862 for shelter on the pack trail from Pittsburgh Landing on the Snake River to the Boise Basin. Packer John was killed in 1864 in a robbery of his pack string. Idaho's first Territorial Democratic Convention was held there the year the cabin was built. There are two main groups of houses at New Meadows, one near Packer John's and the Goose Creek grade and one at the intersection of Idaho Highway 55 with U.S. Highway 95. There are two because the town began at the eastern site and then moved to the site at the highway junction when the P.I.N. Railroad reached its terminus there in 1911.

Glacier-sculptured Granite Mountain bulges over Twin Lakes, which are only one lake in spring, becoming two, later in the summer when the water drops, with dead logs littering their muddy shores.

Beyond Goose Lake, 13.4 miles from Idaho Highway 55, a dirt road turns left at a sign for the Granite Mountain Trail. Park beside a stream .1 mile from the main road. After 100 yards, the trail fords the stream into a forest which has recently burned. Follow blazes to the left (south) for 100 yards, then cross the outlet and find the trail again as an old road. At .5 mile, this track switchbacks northwest, then climbs gently with a view across the canyon of Slab Butte to the lower lake at 1 mile.

A trail to the summit of Granite Mountain leads off the Twin Lakes trail near the switchback and continues 2.5 miles to the top of the mountain, which has a view of the town of New Meadows and the Seven Devils.

# 22.

## Grass Mountain (Grassy Twin) and Coffee Cup Lakes

**Round trip:** 6 miles
**Elevation gain:** 840 feet
**Elevation loss:** 520 feet
**Highest point:** 7,800 feet
**Map:** Hazard Lake
**Difficulty:** easy; time: 6 hours;
**Access:** Turn right (north) 5 miles northwest of McCall from Idaho Highway 55 onto the paved Brundage Mountain-Goose Lake Road. Drive 4 miles on pavement

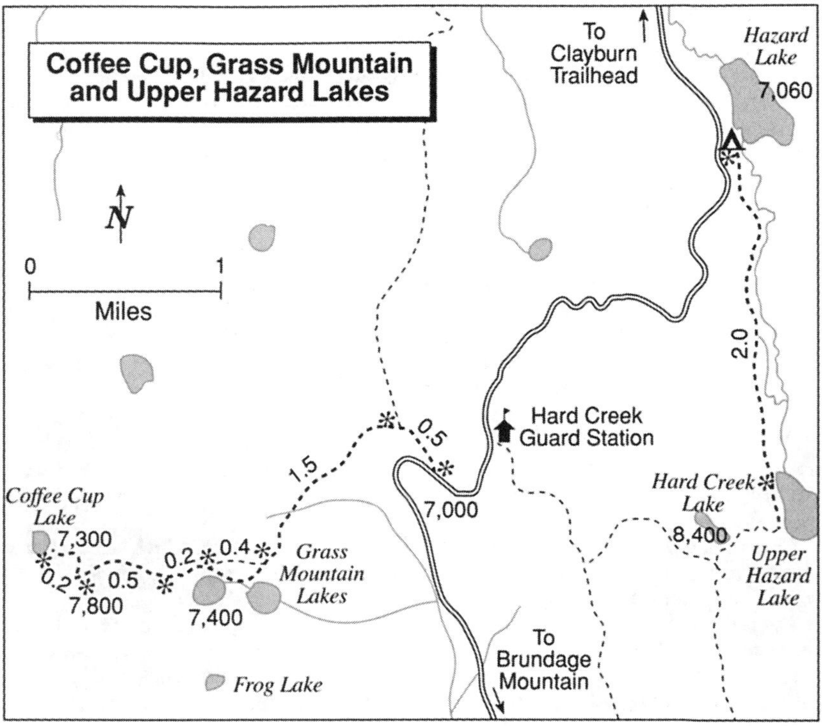


and then on gravel and dirt to the Grassy Mountain trailhead at 18.8 miles, which has a large parking area, and horse facilities. It is about .8 mile below the Hard Creek Guard Station.

From a grassy saddle above the brownish-green water of Coffee Cup Lake, the Seven Devils Mountains parade a row of goblins to the northwest and the Salmon River Canyon forms a gap to the north. Looking east across Hard Creek, you can see glacier-carved granite hills. Slabs, talus, and firs slide into the lakes from a pointed granite knoll 600 feet above. In July, golden carpets of buttercups and dogtooth violets surround the Grassy Twin Lakes. The trail leads through an area burned in the Corral Fire of 1994.

Across the road from the parking area, the trail leads southwest from the bend in the road. At first, it is a jeep track that crosses another track at 200 yards. It meets the Vance Creek Trail at .3 mile. Continue left (west) on the Grass Mountain Trail, which diagonally climbs an open slope spotted with clumps of subalpine firs and aspens. At .9 mile, the trail dips before climbing through forest. At 1.5 miles, a side trail leads .2 mile down a path through a meadow to the first lake.

The main trail to Coffee Cup Lake leads straight ahead here for 200 yards across the unmarked grass to blazed trees. Most people will want to take the fishing path which runs close to Grassy Twin Lakes instead. On this path, a rocky section beyond the lakes leads east to the main trail near a saddle at 2.2 miles, where a sign points ahead along the ridge to Coffee Cup Lake. The trail runs along the side of this open

**Grass Mountain Lakes**

ridge, then drops to a notch at 2.7 miles and descends .2 mile down a fir-filled gully to the shore at 3 miles.

# 23.

## Upper Hazard Lake

**Round trip:** 4 miles
**Elevation gain:** 360 feet
**Highest point:** 7,428 feet
**Map:** Hazard Lake
**Difficulty:** easy; time: 3 1/2 hours
**Access:** Turn right (north) 5 miles northwest of McCall from Idaho Highway 55 onto the Brundage Mountain—Goose Lake Road. Drive 4 miles on pavement and then on gravel to the Hazard Lake Campground at 22.4 miles and park in the day use parking beside the main road. At 22.2 miles, a sign for Upper Hazard Lake is for a future trailhead. (No trail as yet connects this point with the main trail.)

In July, meadows covered with yellow and white flowers creep into blue Upper Hazard Lake across from a fissured ridge of granite slabs. The ridge resembles a grizzly even to the hump on its shoulders, thus the name Bruin Mountain. Much of this area burned in the 1994 Corral Fire.

From the day use parking area hike along the campground road for .1 mile to the back of the loop where there is a sign for the trail. Follow the trail south along the edge of a big meadow, from which it leads through a fir forest to a second meadow at 1.2 miles. The trail goes through the meadow instead of above it as shown on the topographic map. When the trail levels in a clearing, the lake shines through trees ahead. A side path leads to the shore at 2 miles.

The trail continues along the west side of the lake past campsites, and at 2.5 miles, turns west and climbs and then descends 120 feet to tiny, narrow Hard Creek Lake in woods. By continuing for another 2.5 miles, hikers can make a through trip to the main road near the guard station.

# 24.

## Hard Butte, Twin and Rainbow Lakes

**Round trip:** 10 miles (7.4 miles for Hard Butte Lake; 2.6 miles more for Rainbow Lake)
**Elevation gain:** 540 feet
**Elevation loss:** 520 feet (return climb)
**Highest point:** 7,760 feet
**Map:** Patrick Butte
**Difficulty:** moderate; time: 7 hours
**Access:** Turn right (north) 5 miles northwest of McCall from Idaho Highway 55 onto the Brundage Mountain—Goose Lake Road. Drive 4 miles on pavement and then on gravel and dirt to the Clayburn trailhead at the end of the road at 27.4 miles. The trailhead is 3.6 mile past the turn for the Hazard Lake campground and 1 mile past a turnoff for Elk Meadows.

North of the trail to the lakes, lava cliffs and pillars lead towards the black face of a triangular partly wooded peak. Beyond it, blue hills drop toward the Salmon River Canyon. To the east, Hershey Point Lookout commands a tree-dotted hill, and south of it, a square blob of black lava marks Lava Ridge. A knife edge and spire of dark lava flank the 200-foot black hood of Hard Butte above Hard Butte Lake. Below it, a second tier of cliffs bristling with trees walls in the blue-green lake. In early summer, shooting stars cover the east edge of Rainbow Lake. Opposite them, above cliffs, a wall of pale granite runs north to Hard Butte. Two trails start at the Clayburn trailhead: The Clayburn Trail to Lava Ridge and the Elk Lake Trail.

Take the Elk Lake Trail north across flower-filled meadows. It goes gently downhill to cross a stream at 1 mile. At 2 miles, keep straight ahead where a track splits off to the left. At 2.5 miles, beyond the low point of Warm Springs Saddle, is a three-way junction, where you can take the left branch south 1 mile to Rainbow Lake, or the middle trail, which give access to both Elk and Hard Butte Lakes. The right trail, which is actually 50 yards beyond the junction, leads .7 mile to the Partridge Creek

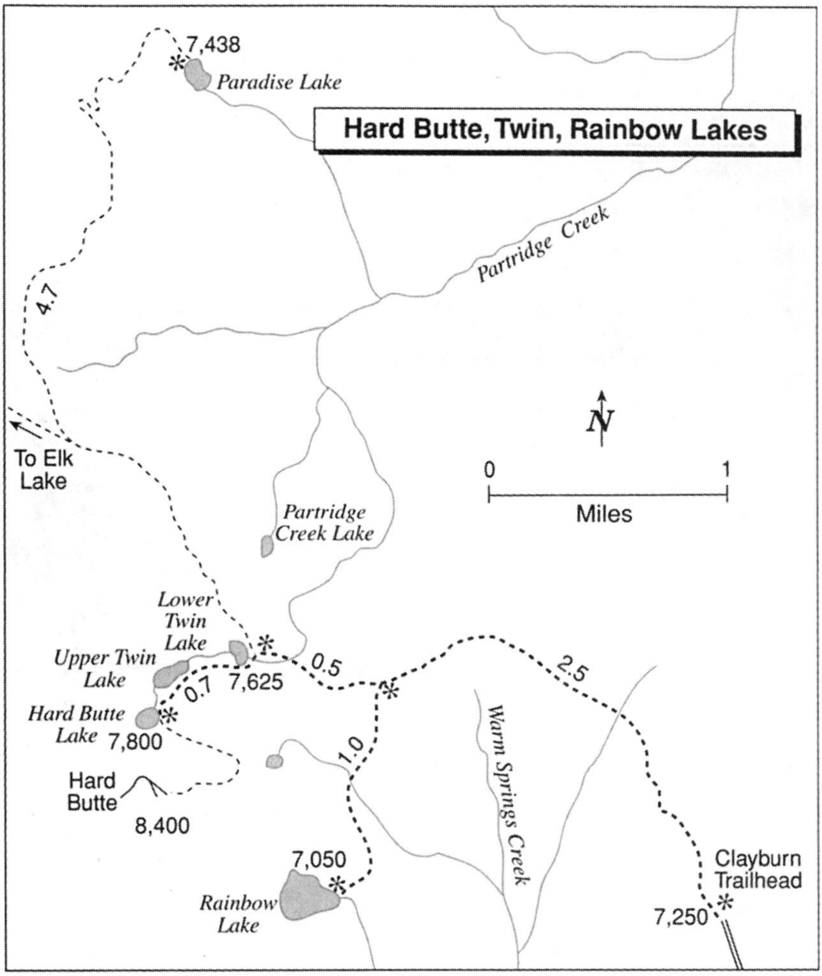


Lakes and eventually to the Salmon River.

Take the middle trail toward Elk Lake. It crosses the outlet of Twin Lakes .5 mile beyond the three-way junction. At a pond 200 yards beyond the outlet, turn left (west) and walk 100 yards to Lower Twin Lake at 3 miles.

To reach the upper lakes, go left (south), cross the outlet and take a path around the lake and up a ridge beside the inlet to Upper Twin Lake. The path continues along the south side of the lake and up its inlet to Hard Butte Lake at 3.7 miles.

Back at the Twin Lakes outlet at 2.3 miles, you can continue on the Elk Lake Trail another 4 miles and turn off it on a boggy side trail that descends to Paradise Lake, 7 miles from the trailhead. Below this lake, which is set in marsh grass, gray rock pavement is scrolled with veins of white quartz. There is a fine view from here toward the Salmon River canyon.

To reach Rainbow Lake, turn left (southeast) back at the three-way junction. The track drops across meadows and through bits of forest and past a grazing association cabin. One mile from the junction, a side trail runs .3 mile southwest to the lake, 240 feet below. Campsites are in the trees on the east shore. The side trip to Rainbow Lake will add 2.6 miles to your round trip. The main trail below the Rainbow Lake cutoff continues on to Hazard Creek and Black, Eden and Buck Lakes. On the return, .5 mile can be saved by taking a trail northeast from the cabin.

# 25.

## Scribner Lake

**Round trip:** 1 mile
**Elevation gain:** 150 feet
**Highest point:** 7,154 feet
**Map:** Hershey Point
**Difficulty:** easy; time: 1 hour
**Access:** Turn right (north) 5 miles northwest of McCall from Idaho Highway 55 onto the Brundage Mountain-Goose Lake Road. Drive 4 miles on pavement and then on gravel to a junction at 26 miles. Turn right (east) on the dirt Elk Meadows Road and drive 7.6 miles to a sign for Scribner Lake. This road is a two-wheel track but has some gravel on it.

A 400-foot granite face shaped like an earless elephant overlooks shallow, green Scribner Lake. Pale cliffs and brush line the west side of the lake below a grassy ridge.

From the Elk Meadows Road, the trail climbs through firs underlain by wildflowers. It then edges a jumble of enormous boulders and continues level through boulders and burned forest to the lake at .5 mile.

# 26.

## Lava Butte Lakes (a National Recreation Trail)

**Round trip:** 6 miles (includes 4-mile loop)
**Elevation gain:** 1,120 feet
**Elevation loss:** 400 feet
**Highest point:** 7,900 feet
**Maps:** Patrick Butte, Hershey Point

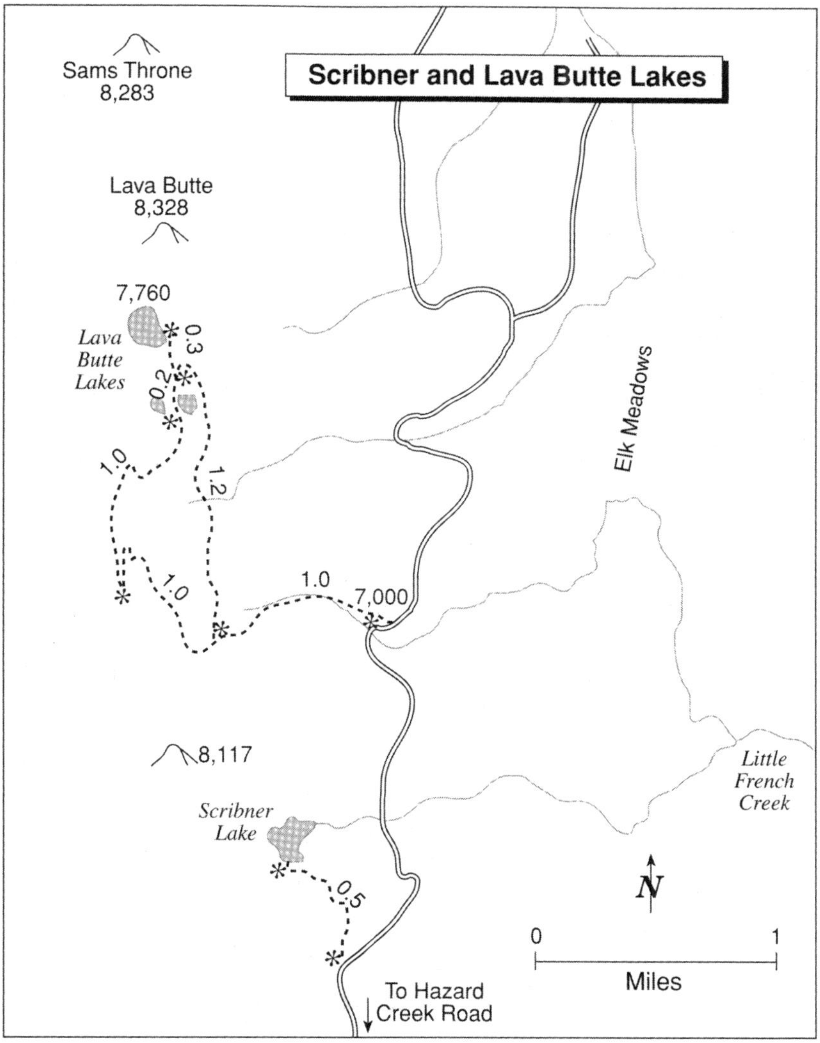


**Difficulty:** moderate; time: 5 hours

**Access:** Turn right (north) 5 miles northwest of McCall from Idaho Highway 55 onto the Brundage Mountain-Goose Lake Road. Drive 4 miles on pavement and then on gravel to a junction at 26.4 miles. Turn right (east) on the dirt Elk Meadows Road and go 8 miles to a parking area and a sign for the Clayburn Trail. (This is the east end of that trail.)

Above the three Lava Butte Lakes stand two peaks that resemble castles of black sand. In between them, an undulating ridge carries layers of grass and black cliffs from one peak to the other.

The trail begins as a jeep track that turns into a trail in 100 yards at a creek. It climbs through burned forest to a junction at 1 mile below lava bluffs at the edge of a long meadow. Here you can begin a loop that includes Lava Ridge and the lakes.

To go up Lava Ridge, take the blazed trail straight ahead to the west across the creek, then northwest up the ridge and along a grassy bench below lava cliffs. The trail switchbacks southwest to the top of the cliffs at 2 miles where it meets the Clayburn Creek Trail. Take this trail along the grassy ridge amid whitebark pines. At 2.5 miles, it turns off the ridge and begins descending toward the lakes. (The path continuing along the crest of the ridge is not the trail.)

Once below the cliffs, the trail descends a rocky hillside, skirts under the nose of the ridge and crosses crumbled lava. At 3 miles, a milky aqua lake is to the left (west) and a round green one is on the right. The highest, largest lake is north along a trail beyond these two, but has no good campsites. To reach it, take a path at 3.2 miles that angles north as the main trail turns northeast and go .3 mile. To complete the loop, after seeing that lake, turn left (east) where the path from the upper lake meets the trail. In a few yards, turn south (right) on a trail that circles back on the east side of the lower lakes. This trail climbs 40 feet over a ridge and down to the first of two meadows. Then it edges the long meadow where the loop began and returns to the junction at 5 miles, which is 1 mile from the trailhead.

# MCCALL DISTRICT
# PADDY FLAT AREA

## 27.

## North Fork Kennally Creek Trail (a National Recreation Trail)

**Round trip:** 5 miles (18 miles to lakes)
**Elevation gain:** 200 feet (1,600 feet to lakes)
**Elevation loss:** 120 feet (1,600 feet to lakes)
**Highest point:** 7,240 feet at lakes
**Maps:** Blackmare, Paddy Flat
**Difficulty:** easy as far as creek crossing; time: 4 hours (2 days for lakes)

**Access:** On Idaho Highway 55, drive 3.1 miles north of Donnelly and turn right (east) onto the paved Paddy Flat Road. In 1.5 miles the road crosses Farm to Market Road and the pavement ends. At 5.4 miles is the Paddy Flat summit. Just beyond it keep left on forest road 388, ignoring a confusing sign for Paddy Flat to the right. Although the forest map shows the Paddy Flat Road as an improved road, the northern (left) road has a better surface. Drive 10.5 miles to the junction of the Paddy Flat

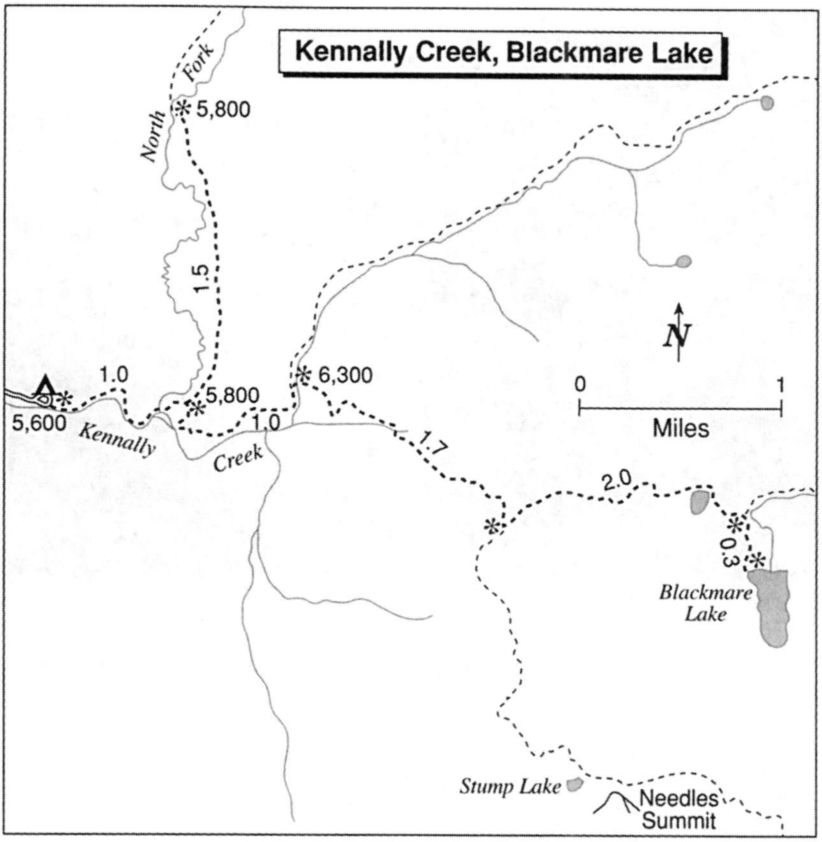


and Kennally Creek roads. Turn left (east) on the dirt Kennally Creek Road, drive 2 miles to a junction with the Sloans Point Lookout Road and turn left again and go east 1.6 miles to the Kennally Creek Campground.

If you go east of Donnelly on Roseberry Road, you reach the site of the original settlement of Roseberry when you cross Farm to Market Road. It was named after Lewis Roseberry, a trader who came to the area in 1882 and established a post office in his supply station in 1891. Most of the original settlers were Finns who had come there from mines in Wyoming about 1885. There is still a church, museum and a few other buildings at the site of Roseberry. In 1910 Roseberry had a post-office, flour mill, several stores, three churches, a bank and a hotel. In 1914 when the railroad was put in and it bypassed Roseberry, a new settlement, Donnelly, grew up next to the railroad siding.

At the trailhead at the Kennally Creek Campground, Kennally Creek foams over granite boulders beside dense lodgepoles, larches, and firs. Farther up on its north fork, transparent water flows over golden sand under banks of tall grass and flowers. Here in early July the foot-long white flower clusters of beargrass shine like lace lanterns when backlit by the sun. The first part of the trail to a creek crossing at 2.5

**Blackmare Lake**

miles makes a pleasant day hike, but the trail continues up the wooded canyon to Kennally Creek Lakes at 9 miles.

From the far end of the campground, begin by taking the East Fork of Kennally Creek Trail. After crossing the North Fork on a bridge at .7 mile, it reaches the North Fork Trail at 1 mile.

Turn left on the North Fork Trail and hike though forest and overgrown clearings. At 2 miles, the trail leaves the creek and climbs over a 100-foot hill and, at 2.5 miles, fords the creek. Here, light green brush and granite outcrops punctuate the wooded canyon walls. The route up the canyon to the lakes is much the same except the trail steepens for the last 2 miles.

# 28.

## Blackmare Lake

**Round trip:** 12 miles
**Elevation gain:** 2,280 feet
**Elevation loss:** 1,040 feet (return climb)
**Highest point:** 7,800 feet
**Map:** Blackmare
**Difficulty:** expert; time: 10 hours

**Access:** See North Fork Kennally Creek Trail for directions for reaching the trailhead. Hike up that trail for 1 mile to the junction of the North and East Forks of Kennally Creek trails where this hike description begins.

A huge floating platform of driftwood hugs the lower end of blue-green Blackmare Lake. At the upper end, a high rock knoll sits below a pointed mountain of crumbled granite cliffs. Trees diagonally stripe a long ridge of talus and slabs bordering the east side of the lake.

This hike is partly on an unofficial trail that drops 1,000 feet from a saddle on the East Fork of Kennally Creek Trail, so this must be climbed on the return. Another route on an official trail gains 2,800 feet in 11 miles from the South Fork of the Salmon. An unnamed lake 700 feet above Blackmare Lake on the route from Kennally Creek makes a fine destination itself.

From the point where the East and North Fork trails meet, take the East Fork Trail which zigzags 500 vertical feet up a wooded rocky slope. At 1.7 miles, this trail curves left (north) to a junction with the Needles Trail at 2 miles. The East Fork Trail continues from here 3.5 miles with a 1,400-foot climb to Blackmare Summit, where trails provide access to Cougar Ridge, Cougar Creek and Blackmare Creek.

At the junction, turn right (east) on the Needles Trail, which crosses the East Fork on a log, then angles through thick forest beside beargrass. It parallels but doesn't cross Kennally Creek at 2.5 miles. At 3.7 miles, a path leads uphill. There may be a sign here for "Blackmare Lake — no trail." It is 2.3 miles from this point to the lake. Take the path straight up the ridge and then over to the crest of a fold in the canyon wall at 4.2 miles from which Cascade Reservoir is visible to the west. Next, the path drops over the fold and heads east up a small side canyon. At a boulder field, it goes northeast to the top of a small wooded ridge at the head of the canyon at 4.7 miles, 600 feet above where the path left the official trail.

The path then drops to a tiny pond, skirts the pond on the north and reaches the small, unnamed lake at 5.5 miles. It continues around the north side of this lake, then plunges down the north side of its outlet to meet the trail from the South Fork at 5.7 miles. Turn right (south) on this trail, which crosses the outlet of Blackmare Lake, then climbs a brushy hillside to the lake at 6 miles.

# BOULDER CREEK AREA

## 29.

## Boulder and Rapid Lakes

**Round trip:** 9.2 miles
**Elevation gain:** 1,120 feet

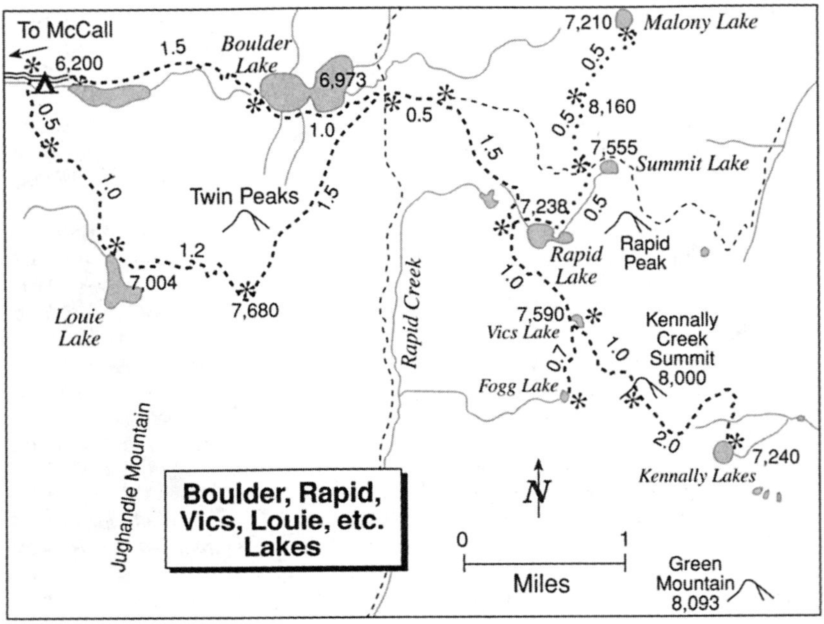


**Elevation loss:** 320 feet (return climb)
**Highest point:** 7,280 feet
**Map:** Paddy Flat
**Difficulty:** moderate; time: 6 1/2 hours

**Access:** From Lake Fork on Idaho Highway 55, go east 1.5 miles to the Farm to Market Road. Turn left (north) and go 3 miles to a bridge over the Lake Fork. (Or drive south from the traffic light at the McCall airport for 1.9 miles, turn left (east) on Elo Road and go 3 miles to the bridge.) At the bridge, turn east on a paved road; go 1 mile to the end of the pavement, and then drive a primitive road (403) to Boulder Meadows Reservoir at 5.1 miles, avoiding a road to the right at 4.3 miles and roads going left at 4.6 and 4.8 miles. From undeveloped campsites at 5 miles, take a road to the left, which ends at 5.1 miles in a tiny parking area just before the dam.

At the head of .2 mile-long Rapid Lake, small firs and brush climb gray and white 200-foot cliffs. Blue and red dragonflies flit above the shore, yellow pond lilies float next to marsh grass, and the white-flowered stalks of beargrass cluster on the peninsula that nearly cuts the lake in two.

Boulder Lake, .7 mile long, has an eight-foot rock dam, so muddy sand surrounds it in late summer. On the north, a pointed peak with charcoal gray cliffs rises above the lake, which is shaped like a "figure eight." From the beginning of the trail at the .5 mile long reservoir there is an excellent view of Jughandle Mountain, with its triangular face of cliffs.

The most difficult part of this trip is finding the trailhead. The Boulder Meadows Reservoir Road is muddy in early season, but can be driven in two-wheel drive most of the summer. You will probably want to park at a parking area on a side road to the right (southwest) of the undeveloped campground. since there is little space to turn around at the small one below the reservoir. The trailhead is most easily reached by walking up a rutted and rocky four-wheel drive road that turns left (northwest) at the beginning of the small parking area below the dam. This road switchbacks to the right and arrives at the north (left) side of the dam. The trail begins where the road starts across the top of the dam. (The road ends just across the dam.)

The trail to Boulder and Rapid lakes leads along the north side of the reservoir and up the canyon through thick forest. At 1 mile, it switchbacks, and at 1.2 miles passes a granite knoll with a view of the reservoir. At l.5 miles, the trail reaches Boulder Lake and goes along its south side.

Beyond the lake at 2.5 miles near a tiny pond is a junction with the Paddy Flat — Lake Fork Trail. A small sign 100 yards before this junction points southwest to the Jughandle Trail. Keep straight ahead toward Rapid Lake. The trail winds through wildflower meadows in season to a junction with the Buckhorn Trail to Summit Lake at 3 miles.

The Rapid Lake Trail continues southeast across the side of a grassy hill then descends through trees to a bog at 3.5 miles. The trail may be hard to find here. Next, it runs along the north side of the creek, crosses it at 3.7 miles and heads south uphill to a junction with a path to Rapid Lake at 4.5 miles. Walk 200 yards east on this path to the lake at 4.6 miles. Campsites are beyond the outlet and on and near the peninsula on the north side at 4.8 miles.

# 30.

## Louie Lake and the Jughandle Trail

**Loop trip:** 6.7 miles via Boulder Lake

**One-way:** 1.5 miles to Louie Lake; 2.7 more miles over saddle to Boulder Lake Trail

**Elevation gain:** 1,480 feet to the summit of the Jughandle Trail

**Elevation loss:** 1,480 feet

**Highest point:** 7,680 feet

**Map:** Paddy Flat

**Difficulty:** easy to Louie Lake; expert for the Jughandle trail; time: 6 hours for loop trip

**Access:** From Lake Fork on Idaho Highway 55, go east 1.5 miles to the Farm to Market Road. Turn left (north) and go 3 miles to a bridge over the Lake Fork. (Or drive 1.9 miles south of the traffic light at the McCall airport on Idaho Highway 55, turn left (east) on Elo Road and go 3 miles to the bridge.) At the bridge, turn east on a paved road; go 1 mile to the end of the pavement, and then drive a primitive road (403) to Boulder Meadows Reservoir at 5.1 miles, avoiding a road to the right at 4.3 miles and roads going left at 4.6 and 4.8 miles. From the undeveloped campsites at 5 miles just below Boulder Meadows Reservoir turn right (southwest) into a parking area at the trailhead. (This parking area is not the same as the very small one just below the reservoir's dam.)

The gray cliffs of Jughandle Mountain overlook dark blue Louie Lake, which is shaped like a witch's hat and contains two granite islands. The ruins of a log cabin sit near the eight-foot earth dam. From above on the Jughandle Trail, Payette and Little Payette Lakes spread robin's egg blue arms among green-black forest and Brundage and Granite Mountains frame one side of a view stretching to the Seven Devils. Jughandle is a dome that appears chopped in half, with the cliffs of the chopped edge facing the trail.

From Boulder Meadows Reservoir, the trail first crosses Boulder Creek on logs, then climbs 300 feet south to intersect the Louie Lake Jeep Trail at .5 mile. Walk east (left) up the jeep trail, which jogs north at .7 mile. It goes straight up through jack-o-lantern-sized boulders and forest to the .4 mile-long lake at 1.5 miles. The best campsites are opposite the jeep road and trail.

The Jughandle Trail turns southeast at Louie Lake's dam, follows the shore and then climbs a low ridge to the east. Where it crosses outcrops, the path is marked with rock cairns. The route then skirts the cliffs of Twin Peaks and reaches a saddle at 2.7 miles. The trail is difficult to follow beyond the saddle. It skirts the east side of Twin Peaks to another saddle at 3.2 miles, then follows the wooded crest of a ridge northeast. At 3.5 miles, it descends a grassy gully where a spring bubbles early in the summer. For most of the summer, the only water is at the lakes. Next, the trail descends a ridge to meet the Boulder Lake Trail at 4.2 miles, 100 yards west of the Paddy Flat — Lake Fork Trail Junction and 2.5 miles from Boulder Meadows Reservoir.

# 31.

## Summit Lake and Malony Lake

**Round trip:** 13.0 miles
**Elevation gain:** 1,890 feet
**Elevation loss (return climb):** 950 feet
**This section one-way:** 1.7 miles, 920 feet gain and 950 feet loss (return climb)
**Highest point:** 8,160 feet
**Map:** Paddy Flat
**Difficulty:** cross-country; time: 4 hours for this section, one-way;
**Access:** See Boulder and Rapid Lake for directions for reaching Rapid Lake where this description begins.

On Buckhorn Mountain, 800-foot gray cliffs hang above a talus-filled canyon leading to Malony Lake. Below forest and cliffs, silvered logs outline the shore of the milky blue-green lake. The other side of Buckhorn Mountain runs into the grass and lilies fringing 300-yard Summit Lake. From a saddle beside this mountain, there is a view north to the black peaks of the Seven Devils and south to pale blue Cascade Reservoir floating like a mirage..

Most hikers visit Summit Lake as a side trip from Rapid Lake because the Buckhorn Trail to the lake is poor. To reach Summit Lake, ascend a path from the peninsula at Rapid Lake up the left side of the inlet for .5 mile. Campsites at Summit Lake are lumpy grass. To get to the saddle beside Buckhorn Mountain, climb cross-country up a ridge to the west. Then go north as the ridge merges with the mountain and walk east to the saddle, 1 mile from Rapid Lake.

To reach Malony Lake from the saddle, walk northeast to the edge of a drop-off beside Buckhorn Mountain. Then turn left (north) for 100 yards along a ridge perpendicular to the saddle. Climb northeast down a green gap between sloping granite slabs to a tiny pond at 1.5 miles. Just above the pond, the way down is steep; BE CAREFUL. Beyond the pond, descend a gully toward a rock knoll overlooking the lake. Before the knoll, turn east down another gully into the canyon at the head of the lake. From here, it is an easy walk down to the lake, 1.2 miles from Summit Lake and 1.7 miles from Rapid Lake.

# 32.

## Vics, Fogg and Kennally Lakes

**Round trip:** 16 miles
**Elevation gain:** 2,040 feet
**Elevation loss:** 1,000 feet (return climb)
**This section one-way:** 4 miles, 640 feet gain, 1,080 feet loss (return climb); .7 mile extra, 240 feet additional gain for Fogg Lake
**Highest point:** 8,000 feet
**Difficulty:** strenuous; time: 3 1/2 hours for this section one-way;
**Map:** Paddy Flat
**Access:** See Boulder and Rapid Lakes (Hike 29) for directions for reaching Rapid Lake where this description begins.

Vics Lake is tiny and full of water lilies, but Fogg Lake, about the same size, is deeper with only a few lilies. Fogg Lake sits in a little pocket in the woods with a few granite outcrops that provide fishing platforms. East of these lakes on Kennally Creek Summit, a granite hogback bristles with pinnacles. The small and marshy Kennally Lakes sit in the woods surrounded by grass with a view of the hogback.

From the junction with the side path to Rapid Lake, the trail climbs over the crest of a ridge and drops 50 feet to Vics Lake at 1 mile, skirts the lake on the west and crosses the outlet. Beyond the outlet, a spur trail leads to the right (south) to Fogg Lake. This trail drops through trees .7 mile to the lake at a large campsite.

Back on the main trail, the section from the Fogg Lake Trail to Kennally Creek Summit at 2 miles gets little use. On the other side of the summit, the trail descends toward Kennally Lakes in the open under the hogback ridge, then goes into forest at 2.2 miles. At 2.7 miles, it crosses Kennally Creek to the north side, then at 3.5 miles returns to the south side. Here, turn off the trail and head southwest to reach the largest of the lakes at 4 miles.

# 33.

## Twentymile Lakes

**Round trip:** 13.4 miles to see all four lakes
**Elevation gain:** 2,360 feet
**Highest point:** 7,960 feet
**Maps:** Black Tip, Victor Peak, Box Lake
**Difficulty:** strenuous; cross-country for the upper lakes; time: 10 hours
**Access:** Drive 12.5 miles north of McCall on the paved Warren Wagon Road. The developed trailhead is on the east side of the road, 1.8 miles north of the turnoff for the Upper Payette Lake campground.

Behind blue East Twentymile Lake, pleated 400-foot gray cliffs rise to a pointed, buff-colored wall and to fractured cliffs forming a high cone. Red mountain heather and yellow buttercups grow on the shore. Above a waterfall, the cone-shaped peak dominates South Twentymile Lake. A band of trees separates North Twentymile Lake

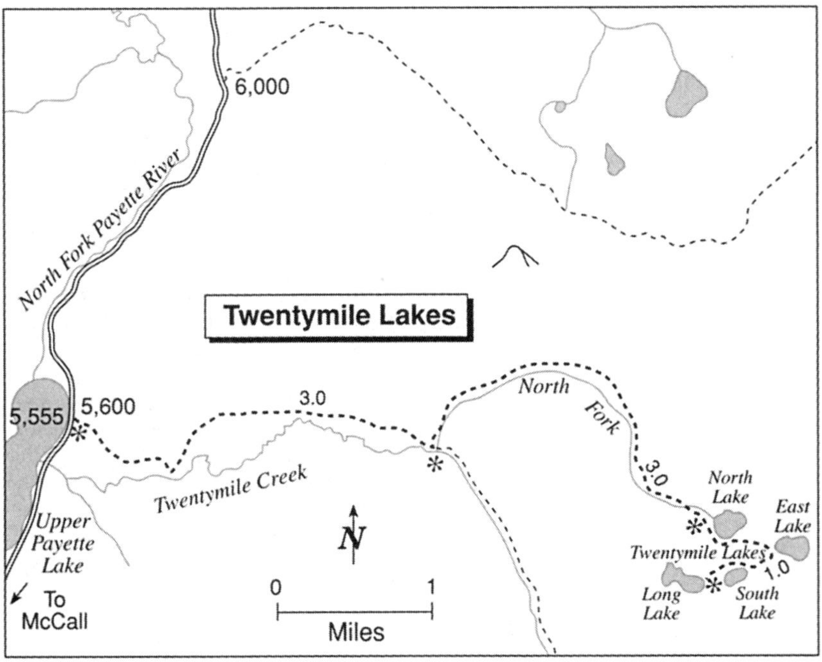

from the pleated cliffs. Deep blue Long Lake gleams among white boulders and outcrops. When planning your hike, note that the trail gains more than 1,800 feet between the junction with the Duck Lake Trail at 3 miles and North Twentymile Lake at 6 miles.

The trail climbs only 280 feet in the first 3 miles through a mostly burned forest carpeted with grouse whortleberry and beargrass. At 3 miles, the Twentymile Lakes Trail turns northwest off of the Twentymile Creek Trail which continues 10 miles south to the Lick Creek Road via Duck Lake.

The trail onto the lakes begins by climbing 200 feet in 200 yards along the North Fork of Twentymile Creek. At 3.5 miles, it crosses a side stream, and at 4.5 miles passes through open grassy areas. At 5 miles, it climbs 200 feet in 200 yards, and then flattens out, runs along the creek, and crosses it in a marsh just below North Twentymile Lake at 6 miles. The topographic map shows the trail crossing the creek and going to Long Lake, but it actually goes to North Twentymile Lake first.

To see the other lakes, go .2 mile south from the North Lake up a 100-foot ridge to the South Lake. Then go 200 yards down South's outlet to Long Lake. To reach the East Lake, go along the north shore of the South Lake, then climb 100 feet in .5 mile towards a talus-topped hill northeast of the pleated row of cliffs. To return to the North Lake, take a path down the southwest side of East's outlet until the route becomes too steep, then cut south and drop to the shore. Walking to the other three lakes adds 1.5 miles to the round trip.

# 34.

## Josephine Lake

**Round trip:** 1 mile
**Elevation gain:** 240 feet
**Highest point:** 7,400 feet
**Map:** Victor Peak
**Difficulty:** easy; time: 2 hours

**Access:** Drive north of McCall on the paved Warren Wagon Road past Upper Payette Lake at 15.5 miles and Secesh Summit at 22.3 miles to the Josephine Lake Road at 25 miles. Turn left (north) on the four-wheel drive road and drive 3.5 miles to its end if you have a four-wheel drive vehicle. Otherwise it is best to walk the road. Adding this distance round trip will transform the hike from easy to moderate.

A double waterfall splits the slanting cliffs on the south side of Josephine Lake. Above the falls, a 400-foot cliff and a nipple-shaped summit on the ridge called Squaw Point shadows a cirque above tiny ponds. On the west side of the blue-green lake, cliffs resemble a row of toppled dominoes.

One hundred yards before the end of the primitive, rocky Josephine Lake Road, follow a path leading southwest uphill, which angles left along the forest edge. At .2 mile is a pond in a meadow under cliffs. To see a waterfall on the outlet, take a path 25 yards before the pond. At .5 mile, the trail reaches the lake. Campsites are rocky

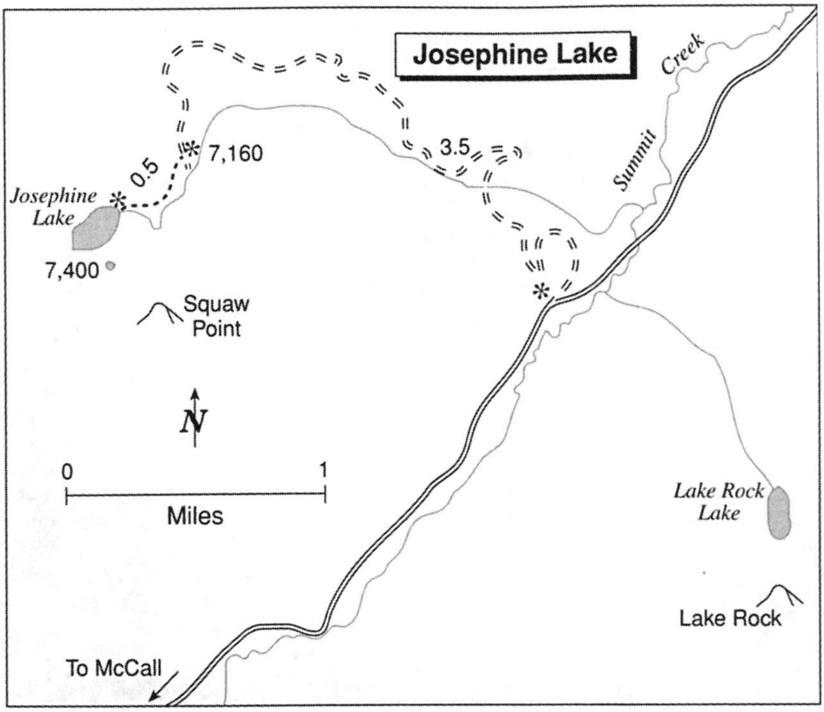


or slanting. A steep path FOR EXPERTS ONLY climbs the left side of the south inlet to the two tiny ponds. The area around Josephine Lake partly burned in the 1994 fires.

# 35.

## Loon Lake

**Round trip:** 10.8 miles
**Elevation gain:** 340 feet
**Elevation loss:** 180 feet (return climb)
**Highest point:** 5,840 feet
**Map:** Loon Lake
**Difficulty:** moderate; time: 7 hours

**Access:** Drive north of McCall on the Warren Wagon Road to the Burgdorf Junction at 28.3 miles where the pavement ends. Stay to the right (east) and drive the gravel road to a sign for the Chinook Campground at 36 miles. Turn right (south) on

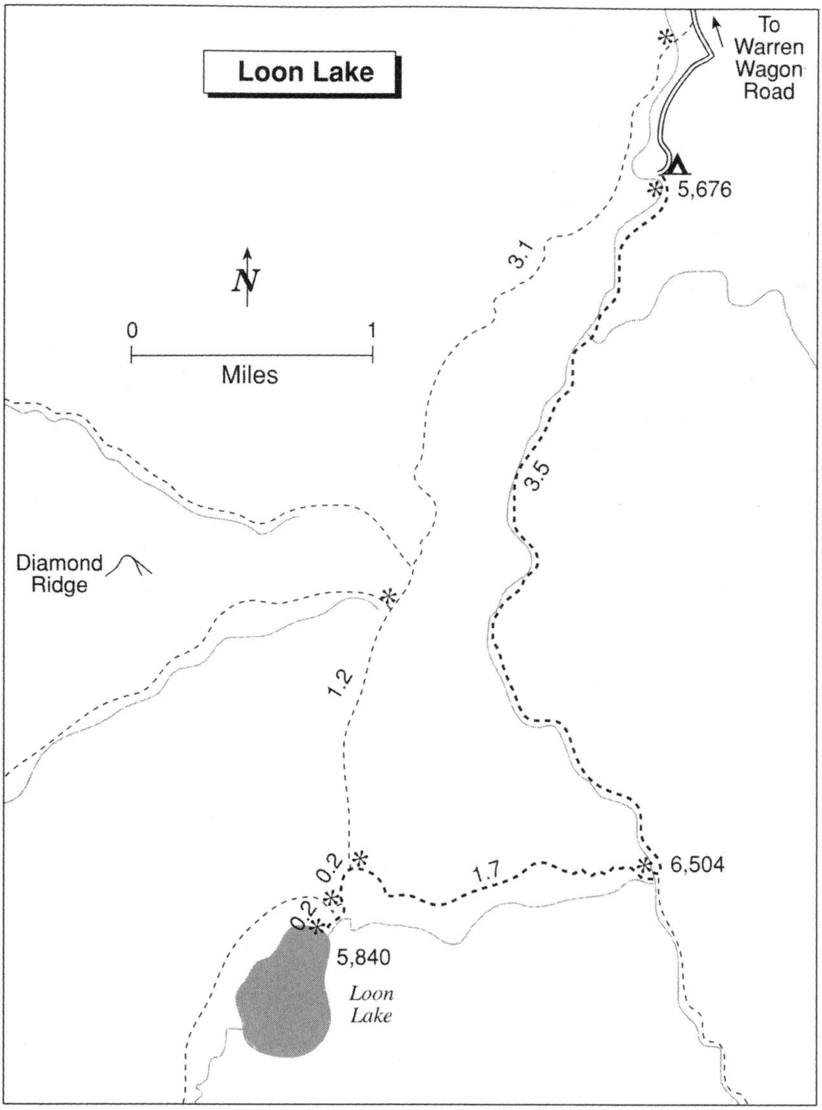


a primitive road and go 1.2 miles to the trailhead at the far end of the campground.

On the way to the trailhead you pass within a mile of the old resort of Burgdorf Hot Springs and come within 7 miles of the "ghost town" of Warren. You may wish to visit these sites on the way to or from the trailhead. At first called Warm Springs, the hot springs at Burgdorf were discovered in 1863 and became a stop on the main route from the Salmon River south to the Boise Basin. Fritz Burgdorf from Warrens homesteaded there and provided travelers with beef and hot baths and in 1870, built a hotel called Resort. He married a singer who stopped at Resort on her way to Warrens for a performance. After their marriage, she helped him run the resort. In 1914, she arranged for the post office to be renamed in honor of her husband. The pipes he carved from logs still bring the hot water to the swimming pool from the small pool where it upwells.

From Chinook Campground a trail leads down the Secesh River connecting with a branch trail to Loon Lake. A second trail to the lake goes across the river to the west side on a bridge at the north end of Chinook Campground and then follows ridges instead of the river. With the two trails you can make a loop trip to Loon Lake.

A wooded hill and granite ridge frame a triangular gray peak and pleated wall behind the big blue platter of Loon Lake. Wooded moraines and strips of meadow enclose the other three sides of the lake. The quiet outlet meanders in a hairpin bend before plunging to the Secesh River, which foams gold and green over orange-tinted granite.

In the trees on the south side of the lake is the wreckage of a B-23 bomber that attempted to land on the frozen lake on January 22, 1943. The plane was on a training mission when it met a heavy snowstorm. After waiting five days for rescue, three of the eight men hiked for 14 days down the Secesh River and then over Lick Creek Summit to the Lake Fork guard station. McCall pilot Penn Stohr landed on the lake ice twice to rescue the other men.

To reach the lake most easily, take the trail along the east (left) side of the Secesh, watching for mountain bikes as you go. The trail crosses Alex Creek at .7 mile. At 1.5 miles, it goes along a grassy slope and passes under an overhang at 2 miles. At 2.2 miles, Victor Creek comes in on the opposite shore and the canyon becomes more open and rocky at 3.2 miles.

The trail has descended 180 feet by the time it reaches a steel suspension bridge over the river at 3.5 miles. Cross the bridge and take the side trail to Loon Lake. This trail climbs the canyon of Loon Creek through lodgepoles growing in granite sand. At 4.5 miles, rounded granite peaks and a pleated mountain appear ahead.

The trail turns right (northwest) at 5 miles to skirt a meadow and reaches a junction with the alternate Loon Lake Trail at 5.2 miles. The alternate trail leads north along the ridges above the Secesh, connecting at 1.2 miles with the Victor Creek Trail that leads west to the Warren Wagon Road about 2 miles north of Upper Payette Lake. A few yards after that it connects with a trail leading northwest down Willow Basket Creek to Ruby Meadows. The trail reaches the new bridge over the Secesh at about 4.5 miles. The bridge is nearly a mile by road north of the beginning of the Secesh River Trail to Loon Lake. If you start at the beginning of the alternate trail and take it to Loon Lake the elevation gain is 670 feet and the elevation loss (return climb) 520 feet.

To continue to the lake from the junction with the alternate Loon Lake Trail in the meadow, go straight ahead across the meadow. On the far side of the meadow this trail splits. The left branch leads to a campsite at the bend in the outlet at 5.4 miles and then goes across the outlet and south along ridges to Split Creek and down it to the Lick Creek Road. The right branch leads 9 miles along the west side of the lake and south up its inlet to the Lick Creek Road.

To reach the plane wreck take the right branch for 1.7 miles and then go east across the inlet. Or you can bushwhack around the east side of the lake.

# LICK CREEK ROAD AREA

# 36.

## Blackwell and Crystal Lakes

**Round trip:** 11 miles (2 miles more for Crystal Lake)
**Elevation gain:** 1,950 feet plus 430 feet to Crystal Lake
**Elevation loss:** 720 feet (return climb) plus 520 feet for Crystal Lake
**Highest point:** 7,793 above Crystal Lake
**Maps:** McCall (20-foot contours), Fitsum Summit
**Difficulty:** strenuous; cross-country from Fall Creek Saddle to Crystal Lake; time:10 hours
**Access:** From Idaho Highway 55 in McCall, follow signs to Ponderosa State Park, turning east on Railroad, right on Hemlock, and left on Davis. Just beyond the McCall Golf Course at 2.2 miles, turn right on Lakeshore Drive. Go 2 miles to where the Eastside Road turns left (north). Turn your trip odometer back to zero here. Keep straight ahead (east) on the paved Lick Creek Road, passing Little Payette Lake at about 1 mile. The pavement ends at 4.1 miles. Continue on the rocky road to the undeveloped Fall Creek trailhead at 9.3 miles.

The route to the trailhead passes through the town of McCall. The town was named for Tom McCall who bought a cabin and 160 acres from the first settler, Sam Devers. McCall began a hotel in 1890, bought the sawmill on the shore of the lake in 1894, and in 1895 took the post office equipment to his hotel from Roseberry. The post office was then called Lardo because it had been started on Boulder Creek earlier with that name. Because McCall served liquor at his hotel he was cited for violating post office regulations and after that W.B. Boydstun became postmaster in his store across the Payette River. The area around his store became known as Lardo from the name of the post office. When McCall's mill burned he rebuilt it at Lardo. Later a second post office opened at Blackwell's store near McCall's hotel. McCall also had the townsite surveyed and donated land for a school and church and built an office for the Payette National Forest so it would move its headquarters to McCall. In 1914 a branch of the Oregon Short Line was completed from Boise to McCall.

That enabled the town to become a lumbering town. In 1910 Hans Hoff and his son bought McCall's mill, and after operating on a shoestring with a partner, Bert Bills, they got the contract for the ties for the new railroad. Their new partner was Carl Brown, and together they diversified the business, transporting freight by wagon in winter when snow stopped the trains, investing in ranches and building a box factory in Horseshoe Bend. In 1930 they split up, with Brown remaining at McCall and eventually selling to Boise Cascade. The mill burned after Boise Cascade sold it to developers.

A crescent-shaped island hugs the shore of Blackwell Lake near a gray log cabin. On the island, fused granite pebbles, resembling a pavement of petrified eggs, form outcrops. Water lilies circle the deepest water of the blue-green lake below a granite hill feathered with the skeletons of trees burned in the 1994 Blackwell fire. Because

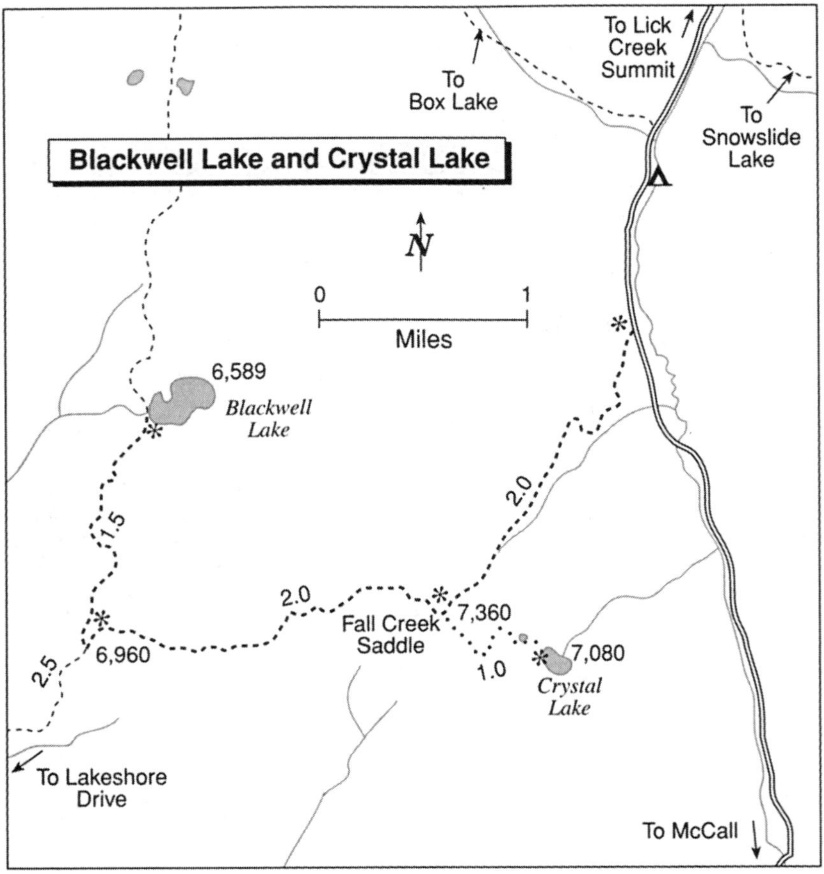


there is a small dam, stumps and mud ring the lake in late summer. In October, red huckleberry and orange mountain ash give a colorful accent.

White granite benches rim three sides of the blue-green oval of Crystal Lake. On the fourth side, the southwest, granite sheets fall into the water from a 600-foot peak. At the northwest end, granite slabs slant up to a tiny green pond.

The trail to Fall Creek Saddle provides a view of the canyon of the North Fork of Lake Fork clear to peaks near Lick Creek Summit. On a grassy ridge beyond Fall Creek Saddle, the hazy blue arms of Cascade Reservoir spread out in the distance. At the junction of the Fall Creek and Crestline trails, you can look down on the green peninsula of Ponderosa Park dividing two blue wedges of Payette Lake.

The recommended route to Blackwell Lake depends on your method of travel and your opinion of different kinds of trail users. The old jeep trail from Lakeshore Drive has been reopened for people to hike, mountain bike, ride horses, ride motorcycles and drive ATVs clear to Blackwell Lake and to Jumbo Basin on the Fall Creek Trail. To reach the old jeep trail, turn left (north) in McCall at the junction of Lakeshore Drive and the Lick Creek Road and drive 400 yards. Turn right (east) at a sign for the

Crestline Trail and drive 1.5 miles to a new developed trailhead. The trail leads about 2.5 miles up through a burned forest to join the Fall Creek Trail 4 miles from the Lick Creek Road. Because the author is a hiker, this description is of how to reach Blackwell Lake is via the other route, the Fall Creek Trail from the Lick Creek Road. That route is .7 mile longer and has an additional 100 feet elevation gain and 600 feet elevation loss (return climb).

From the 9.3-mile point on the Lick Creek Road, the trail climbs south through a forest of grand fir, Douglas fir, and Engelmann spruce, and crosses three small streams. After a 1,000-foot climb in 1 mile, the trail levels in grass and rocks, then enters the forest again along a stream. There are campsites at 1.5 miles, where cliffs border a flat meadow.

At the end of the meadow, find the trail by looking for blazes and cut-through logs. At 1.7 miles, the path reaches a rocky area and then zigzags 300 feet to Fall Creek Saddle at 2 miles.

Beyond the saddle, the trail turns right (north) up a ridge for 150 yards through boulders, and then goes northwest up the side of the ridge. On an open hillside at 2.2 miles, it heads west 200 yards to meet the old jeep trail. After meeting it, the track descends a spur of the ridge into the canyon of Tyee Creek. The track crosses this creek three times and at 4 miles, it meets the ATV trail from Lakeshore Drive, called the Crestline Trail, in a grassy saddle.

From here the Crestline Trail goes north to Blackwell Lake. First it cuts downhill to the left (northwest). At 4.5 miles, it crosses a creek, then contours west of a sagebrush hill, enters burned forest and turns downhill at 5 miles. At 5.2 miles, the track circles the east (right) side of a hill of granite slabs, climbs to its crest, and drops to the lake at 5.5 miles. Campsites are on either side of the outlet and on the island. The Crestline Trail continues north of the lake to Squaw Lake and to side trails or routes to Box, Brush, and Pearl lakes but it is not open to ATVs beyond Blackwell Lake. It is, however, open to motorcycles. The trail ends at an access road leading to the Warren Wagon Road.,

A cross-country route to Crystal Lake begins at Fall Creek Saddle. The Crystal Lake sign says "No Trail", but a path climbs southeast along the brink of the cliffs to a large grassy area near the summit of the ridge. The summit is 200 yards farther on, .5 mile from Fall Creek Saddle. There are views here of the lake below. The easiest route down to the lake is via a gully to the left (north) of a granite tongue. From there, go farther north to a tiny pond, then down the right (south) side of its outlet to the lake, 1 mile from the saddle. There are campsites near a small bay at the outlet.

# 37.

## Box Lake

**Round trip:** 6.4 miles
**Elevation gain:** 1,900 feet
**Elevation loss:** 340 feet (return climb)

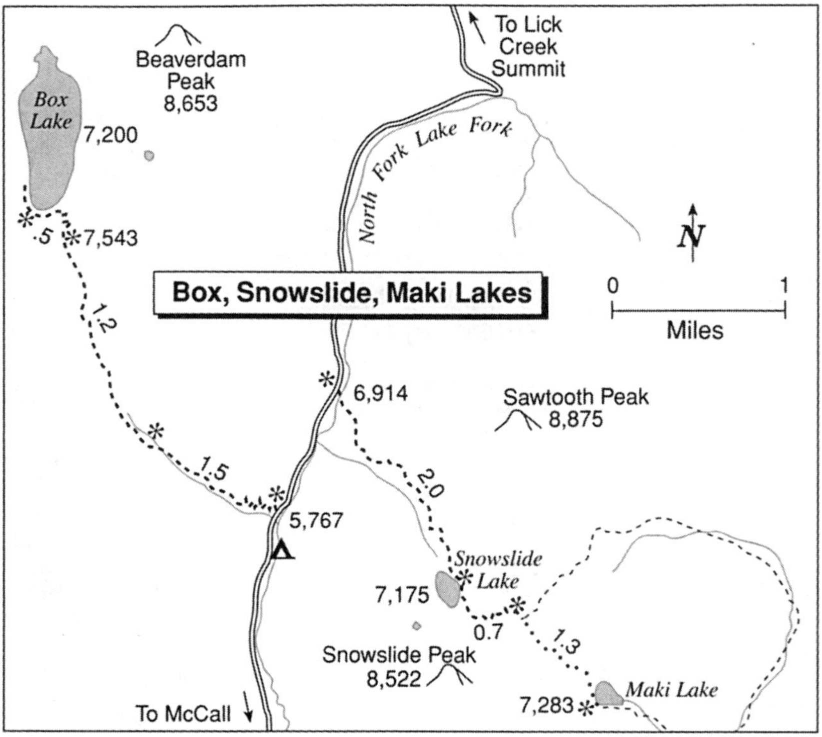


**Highest point:** 7,543 feet
**Maps:** Box Lake, Fitsum Summit
**Difficulty:** moderate; time: 6 1/2 hours
**Access:** From Idaho Highway 55 in McCall, follow signs to Ponderosa State Park, turning east on Railroad, right on Hemlock, and left on Davis. Just beyond the McCall Golf Course at 2.2 miles turn right on paved Lakeshore Drive. Go 2 miles to where the Eastside Road turns left (north). Turn your trip odometer back to zero here. Keep straight ahead (east) on the paved Lick Creek Road, passing Little Payette Lake at about 1 mile. The pavement ends at 4.1 miles. Continue on the rocky road to the undeveloped Box Lake trailhead at 11.1 miles. (There is a toilet and better parking .2 mile before the trailhead. at a primitive campground known as Black Lee.)

At the upper end of mile-long Box Lake, 600-foot cliffs shadow a swampy meadow and the wide white band of a 300-yard beach. Because of a dam at the lower end, stumps and silvered logs stud the water. Talus and brush cover the slopes of jagged Beaverdam Peak, which sprawls along the east side of the lake.

The trail to Box Lake is named the Black Lee Trail after the creek it ascends. From the Lick Creek Road, the trail switchbacks up 800 feet in the first mile through a lodgepole-fir forest. At 1.5 miles, it reaches a meadow and crosses the creek to another one. The trail runs through forest, crosses back over the creek at 1.7 miles, and comes out onto a brushy hillside. At 2 miles, it returns to the west side of the stream. Much of the area around Box Lake burned in the Blackwell Fire of 1994, and the trail has some loose rocks in it.

At 2.2 miles, the trail climbs a meadow of bunch grass, then passes granite pillars. There is a view of the canyon of the North Fork of Lake Fork and the black cliffs above Snowslide Lake.

At 2.5 miles is a .2 mile-long wet meadow. In a notch at 2.7 miles, you see Box Lake below. The trail hairpins down through brush to the lake at 3.2 miles. Two small campsites are east of the beach and several sites are at the lower end of the lake.

# 38.

## Snowslide and Maki Lakes

**Round trip:** 8 miles
**Elevation gain:** 1,980 feet
**Elevation loss:** 600 feet
**Highest point:** 7,890 feet
**Map:** Fitsum Summit
**Difficulty:** easy to Snowslide Lake except for ford of the North Fork of the Lake Fork at the beginning; cross-country to Maki Lake; time: 4 1/2 hours for Snowslide Lake, 7 hours for Maki Lake
**Access:** From Idaho Highway 55 in McCall, follow signs to Ponderosa State Park, turning east on Railroad, right on Hemlock, and left on Davis. Just beyond the McCall Golf Course at 2.2 miles, turn right on paved Lakeshore Drive. Go 2 miles to where the Eastside Road turns left (north). Turn your trip odometer back to zero here. Keep straight ahead (east) on the paved Lick Creek Road, passing Little Payette Lake at about 1 mile. The pavement ends at 4.1 miles. Continue on the rocky road past Slick Rock to the undeveloped Snowslide Lake trailhead at 11.9 miles.

Below an 800-foot black wall, a dark granite knoll overhangs Snowslide Lake. Across the lower end of the emerald lake, ripples of white granite cover a hill. On the trail side of the lake, dead logs point into the water like giant toothpicks. At blue-green Maki Lake, meadows studded with tiny lodgepoles and spruces hug beaches of white sand. The black hook of a peak lurks in the distance to the south.

The trail to Snowslide Lake first fords the North Fork of Lake Fork, then angles up through woods and grassy areas. (The ford will be difficult or impossible before mid-July.) At a gully filled with aspens and brush at .5 mile, the trail turns uphill to the southeast. Other brushy areas are at 1 and 1.5 miles. (Take special care not to lose the trail on the way back in the woods above the highest brushy area.) The path reaches the lake at 2 miles and passes three campsites. From the upper end of Snowslide Lake, the trail to Maki Lake is well-defined to the summit of the ridge, winding up the inlet through a wildflower meadow under black cliffs. At the top at 2.7 miles, a sign for a trail down the East Fork of Lake Fork points northeast, but that is not your route.

Instead, use your compass to go cross-country from the summit to Maki Lake by turning southeast and following the summit ridge toward its low point. Maki Lake is not in the canyon just below the summit, but rather over this ridge to the southeast. Someone has cut a line of blazes for the route. Keep well above the low point in the wooded ridges, almost at the edge of rock slabs. The blazes become more frequent at 3 miles and lead down the forested canyon with little trace of a path to Maki Lake at 4 miles. An alternate route to Maki Lake is to hike 5 miles up the East Fork of Lake Fork after fording it from the Lake Fork campground. Then take a side trail 1 mile to the lake in a 1,000-foot climb.

# KRASSEL DISTRICT
# LICK CREEK SUMMIT AREA

## 39.

## Duck Lake

**Round trip:** 2 miles
**Elevation gain:** 300 feet
**Highest point:** 6,840 feet
**Map:** Box Lake
**Difficulty:** easy; time: 2 hours

**Access:** From Idaho Highway 55 in McCall, follow signs to Ponderosa State Park, turning east on Railroad, right on Hemlock and left on Davis. Just beyond the McCall Golf Course at 2.2 miles, turn right on paved Lakeshore Drive. Go 2 miles to where the Eastside Road turns left (north). Turn your trip odometer back to zero here. Keep straight ahead (east) on the paved Lick Creek Road, passing Little Payette Lake at about 1 mile. The pavement ends at 4.1 miles. Continue on the rocky road to the large parking area at 16.4 miles, which is 1.1 miles beyond Lick Creek Summit.

Duck Lake has a green flower-dusted meadow at the upper end. On the east, a mountain covered with woods and talus barricades the lake from Hum Lake. In July so much beargrass is in bloom along the trail that the open areas seem like fields growing white lace. The drive up the North Fork of Lake Fork Canyon past the 800-foot glacier-polished dome of Slick Rock and over Lick Creek Summit is worthwhile by itself, especially in the fall when aspens and larches tint the canyon gold. Three new bridges along the trail make it much easier to travel than it was.

The trail crosses a small creek on a bridge at 200 yards, then leads through firs underlain by beargrass and grouse whortleberry. At .5 mile, it reaches the outlet, climbs along it, and then crosses it on a small bridge. Next, the trail leads gently along the stream and up through woods, crossing another side stream and passing a junction for the 3-mile trail that leads over the ridge to Hum Lake at .7 mile. The trail reaches Duck Lake at 1 mile near campsites. (The old trail from the lake to Hum

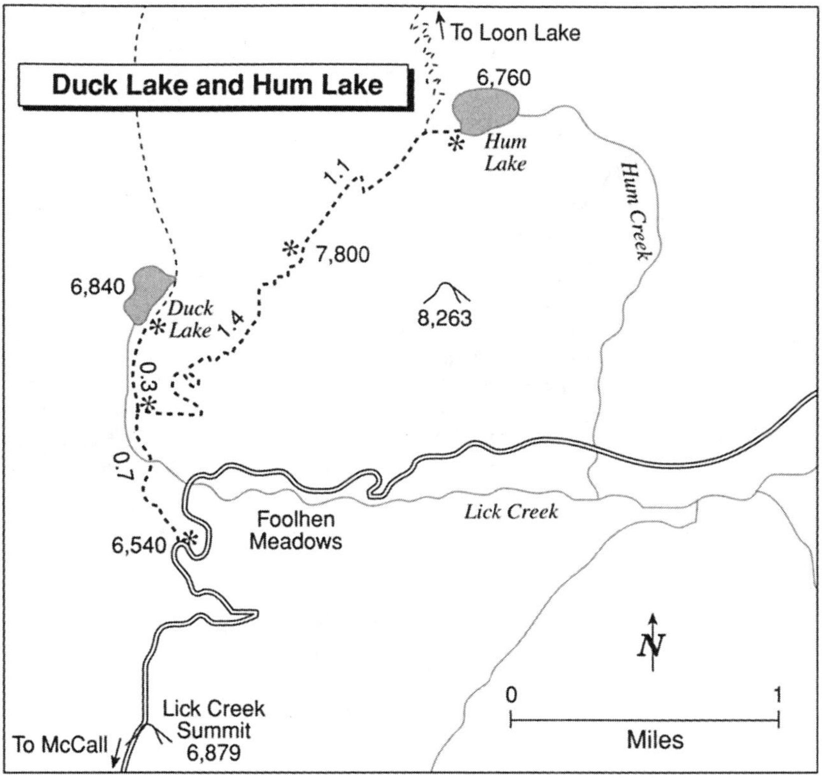


Lake has been abandoned.) The trail splits .7 mile north of Duck Lake. One branch climbs a pass to Loon Lake and the other goes along Twentymile Creek to the Warren Wagon Road at Upper Payette Lake.

# 40.

## Hum Lake

**Round trip:** 6.4 miles
**Elevation gain:** 1,260 feet
**Elevation loss:** 1,040 feet (return climb)
**This section one-way:** 2.5 miles
**Highest point:** 7,800 feet
**Map:** Box Lake

**Difficulty:** moderate; time: 6½ hours;

**Access:** Drive to the Duck Lake trailhead using access directions under Hike 39, and then hike .7 mile to a junction just below Duck Lake.

A circle of 1,500-foot rocky peaks cups Hum Lake. South of the lake, a roof-shaped peak with 400-foot cliffs hides behind a hill of granite slabs and trees. In the fall, the blue water reflects the glow of red-leaved bushes lining the shore. The trail described in the first edition of this book has been abandoned and replaced by a new trail over the ridge from Duck Lake.

This description begins at the junction of the new trail, .7 mile from the Duck Lake trailhead. The trail first goes east along the canyon of Lick Creek for .2 mile. Then it turns back to the left (west) and zigzags up the side of the canyon of Duck Creek among burned trees and granite outcrops. Soon, you can see a row of pleated cliffs on the wide triangle of Beaverdam Peak to the southwest. From the summit, 1.8 miles from the junction, you can look down over granite benches to Hum Lake.

The trail switchbacks down beside talus into alders and other brush. Near the lake, it edges a large meadow, then crosses two branches of the inlet in grass and reaches the shore at 3.2 miles (2.5 miles from the junction). There are campsites here.

# BOISE NATIONAL FOREST
# CASCADE DISTRICT
# WEST MOUNTAIN AREA

## 41.

## Blue Lake

**Round trip:** 2 miles
**Elevation gain:** none
**Elevation loss:** 480 feet (return climb)
**Highest point:** 7,680 feet
**Map:** Tripod Peak
**Difficulty:** easy; time: 2½ hours

**Access:** Turn left (west) off Idaho 55 at a four-way intersection 9.5 miles north of Cougar Mountain Lodge. Drive 2.1 miles to the end of the pavement, which is .8 mile beyond a bridge over the Middle Fork of the Payette River. Turn left (south) on the gravel Snowbank Mountain Road (No. 446) and go 8.7 more miles to Potters Pond. A new developed trailhead with parking, toilet, and horse facilities was constructed during the summer of 2003.

This little alpine lake near Cascade is only 2½ hours from downtown Boise. Two

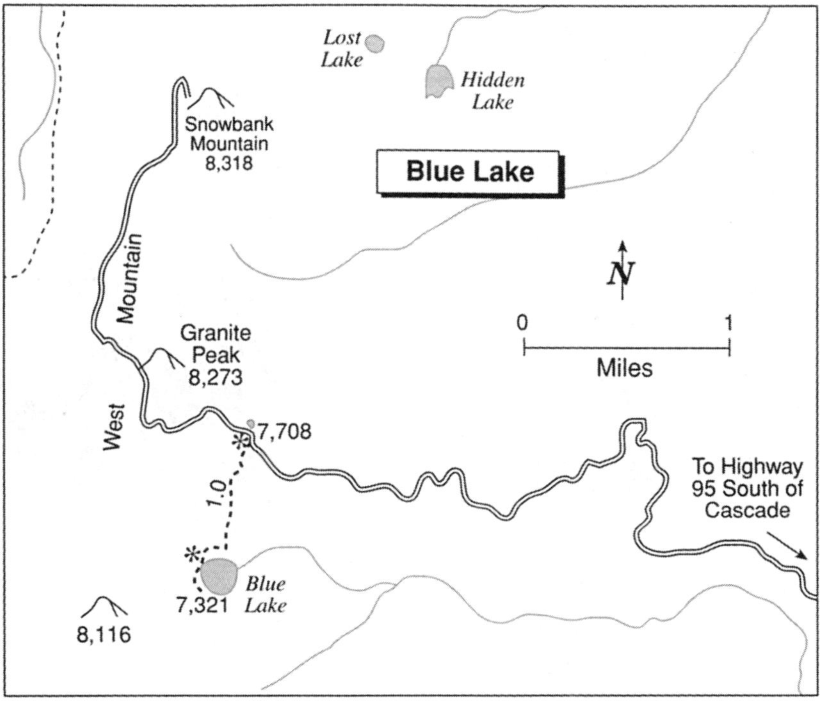


granite islands accent the blue water below gray granite knolls and cliffs which sweep up to an unnamed wedge-shaped peak. Woods and wildflower meadows surround the lake, and on the east side, the outlet cascades down a granite trough in a thin sheet of froth.

Beginning on the south side of the Snowbank Mountain Road across from Potters Pond, the trail leads south downhill over meadows and across two streams to the lake at 1 mile. In order to prevent overuse, make this a day hike.

# 42.

## Shirts Lake

**Round trip:** 3 miles
**Elevation gain:** 200 feet
**Elevation loss:** 1,120 feet (return climb)
**Highest point:** 8,200 feet
**Map:** Tripod Peak

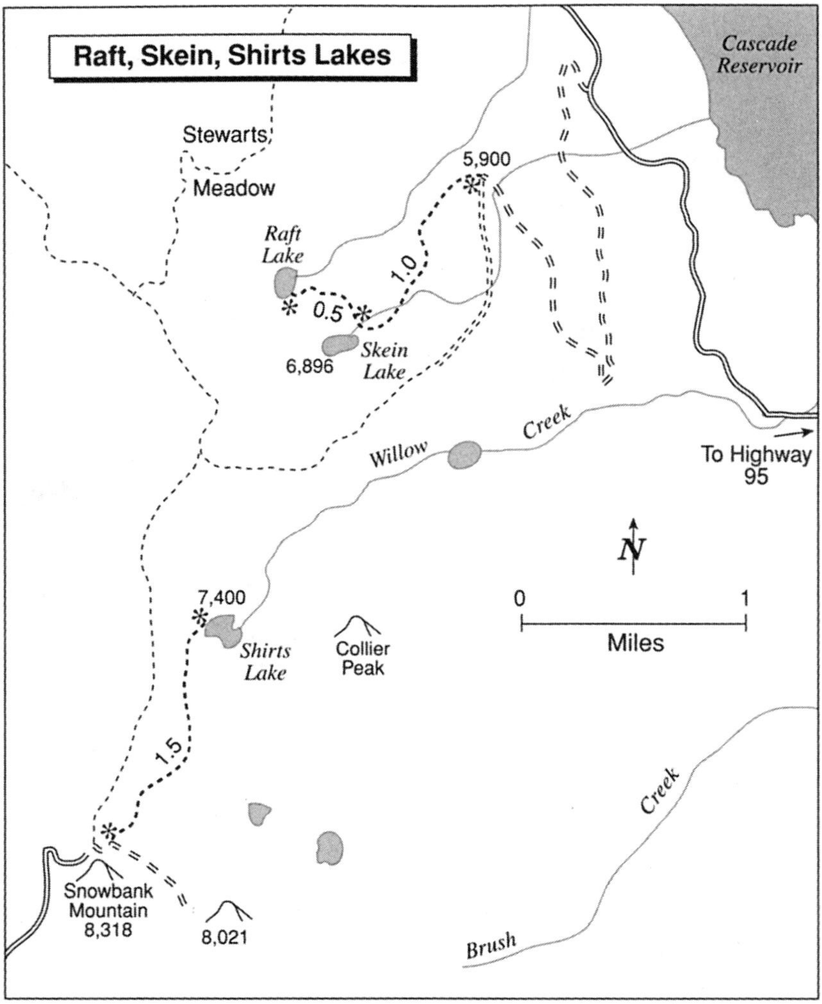


**Difficulty:** expert (not an official trail); time: 4 hours

**Access:** Turn left (west) off Idaho Highway 55 at a four-way intersection 9.5 miles north of Cougar Mountain Lodge. Drive 2.1 miles to the end of the pavement, which is .8 mile beyond a bridge over the Middle Fork of the Payette River. Turn left (south) on the gravel Snowbank Mountain Road (No. 446) and go 11.6 miles to the top of the mountain, where there is a radar installation. Continue east on road No. 446B for about .5 mile to the third switchback and a no motorized vehicles and trail sign at the beginning of an old jeep track.

The water of little Shirts Lake turns dark green as it reflects the dark granite banks. Above the upper end, a slope of grass and flowers runs up to cliffs. To the east, a sharp shoulder of Collier Peak guards the outlet. From the trail above the lake, Cas-

**Skein Lake**

cade Reservoir shines in the distance below, blue or silver with the changing light. In late June, yellow dogtooth violets (glacier lilies) bring sunshine to the trail.

From the third switchback below the top of Snowbank Mountain, walk north down the faint jeep track, which fades out in 100 yards in a grassy area. At the edge of the grass, take a poor trail down a tiny stream, which is usually dry. After descending 720 feet from the top of Snowbank Mountain, the trail levels at a swampy meadow. Just before it, look east to glimpse tiny Lost Lake. (From here you can take a cross-country side trip southeast down ledges to that lake and Hidden Lake beyond it.) Beyond the meadow, the trail climbs 200 feet north over a saddle, then descends a stream bed to Shirts Lake at 1.5 miles. There are no good campsites at the lake because of steep banks and willows.

# 43.

## Skein and Raft Lakes

**Round trip:** 3 miles
**Elevation gain:** 1,000 feet
**Highest point:** 7,000 feet
**Map:** Alpha

**Difficulty:** easy; time: 5 hours

**Access:** Turn left (west) off Idaho Highway 55 at a four-way intersection 9.5 miles north of Cougar Mountain Lodge. Drive 2.1 miles to the end of the pavement, which is .8 mile beyond a bridge over the Middle Fork of the Payette River. Turn right (north) on a gravel road that winds over grassy hills. At 14.1 miles it curves sharply to the left. At 14.3 miles, turn left (west) onto the West Side Road (422) which gradually curves north. Turn left again at about 16 miles, heading across meadows to the wooded west side of the lake, where the road is paved again. At about 18.5 miles, south of the Campbell Creek boat launch, there is a sign on the left (west) side of the road saying Willow Creek Trail. A road turns off here but is hard to see because it looks like a driveway. Drive up this primitive road, and at 1.2 miles keep straight ahead where a road turns off to the right uphill. At a second junction at 2 miles, turn uphill to the right. Continue driving, keeping to the best road and avoiding several side roads. The trailhead is where the road switchbacks to the left at 3.6 miles. A parking area here was constructed in the summer of 2003.

This trail has changed a great deal since the last edition of this book. By renovation of an old logging road, the trailhead has been moved 2 miles closer to Skein Lake and a trail from the lake to Raft Lake has been constructed.

Two rounded peaks guard dark green Skein Lake. The left one bristles with trees and the right one is accented by slanting rectangles of granite that resemble giant gray bricks. Near the lower end of the lake, a tin-roofed log cabin stands beside a huge boulder. Skein Lake is best for early season because mud rings it in late summer. Raft Lake overflows in early summer into a complex of little ponds. A rounded mountain and ridge above it are faced with cliffs.

The trail starts uphill steeply in a logged Douglas fir forest, where little lodgepoles are starting to grow. It soon follows the route of the old trail along the ridge between Campbell and Skein creeks. At .5 mile it turns downhill to the left into alders, then goes back up onto the side of a little ridge through a Douglas fir forest and then over open slopes. After .7 mile, the ground begins to level out and the trail goes through aspens. Keep right at an apparent junction just below the little cabin at .9 mile and go 100 yards farther to a better path before turning left toward Skein Lake. The upper path avoids a big puddle that may be a problem in early summer. There are no apparent campsites at the lake, but there are sites in a small flat area 100 yards before you reach the cabin.

To reach Raft Lake, go back to the junction above the cabin and turn north. The trail goes gently downhill and curves to the left. Then it climbs a few feet through huckleberries, subalpine fir and whitebark pine to the lake at 1.5 miles. There are a couple of small campsites as the trail approaches the lake. It takes about 20 minutes to get to Raft Lake from Skein Lake.

Back at the trailhead, if you were to drive up the road beyond it, you would reach the Willow Creek trail, which provides access to a trail along the crest of the main ridge of West Mountain, which is the ridge along the west side of Cascade Lake from No Business Mountain on the north to Snowbank Mountain on the south.

# WARM LAKE AREA

## 44.

## Vulcan Hot Springs

**Round trip:** 2 miles
**Elevation gain:** 130 feet
**Highest point:** 5,553 feet
**Map:** Rice Peak
**Difficulty:** easy; time: 2 hours
**Access:** Turn right (east) off Idaho Highway 55 one mile north of Cascade. Drive 25 miles on the paved Warm Lake Road and turn right (south) on the gravel road to Stolle Meadows. Although there are side roads, keep straight ahead and drive past Stolle Meadows at 5.8 miles to a developed trailhead at 6 miles.

Nearby Cascade sprang up as the result of the railroad being constructed in 1914 to bypass earlier towns in the area. Most of the houses of the earlier towns, Crawford, Thunder City and Van Wyck, were moved or taken apart and put back together next to the tracks. The new location was named Cascade after the nearby rapids in the North Fork of the Payette River known as The Falls. These rapids and the sites of the earlier towns were covered by Cascade Reservoir when it was completed in 1948.

The site of the early way station of Knox is a few yards down the South Fork of the Salmon River Road from the Warm Lake Road. The first to settle there was Charles Randall in 1898, who sold supplies and lodging to miners on their way to the Thunder Mountain mines. The settlement was named the Knox Ranch for John Knox who purchased several of the buildings when Randall left. The first hotel on the shores of Warm Lake was built by Bill and Molly Kessler, who also ran a fox farm there.

In a clearing amid a cloud of steam, Vulcan Hot Springs bubble from bowls of white rock streaked with orange algae. In June, yellow mimulus and blue camas cover the banks around the springs. The water is too hot to touch, but down the stream that begins at the springs, people have built pools with logs and plastic. The lowest pool is about 15 feet square and 2 1/2 feet deep with a sandy bottom. The water here is still so hot that a 10-minute dip brings on faintness. Because of the high temperature, heavy use, and unsanitary conditions, bathing is not recommended.

The walk to the springs makes a good conditioning walk because it is open by early June. That month Stolle Meadows is a sea of blue camas. Across the meadows rises the 2,000-foot ridge of Cougar Rock. The trailhead is near some interpretive signs about hot springs and their unique plants such as giant helleborine and panic grass and their unique animals such as hot springs snail and narrow-winged damselfly.

The trail begins by crossing the river on a log bridge. Beyond a small meadow, it goes over two more bridges. After the third bridge, the route joins the track of an old road, which leads gently up through a Douglas fir forest. (However, the trail is not

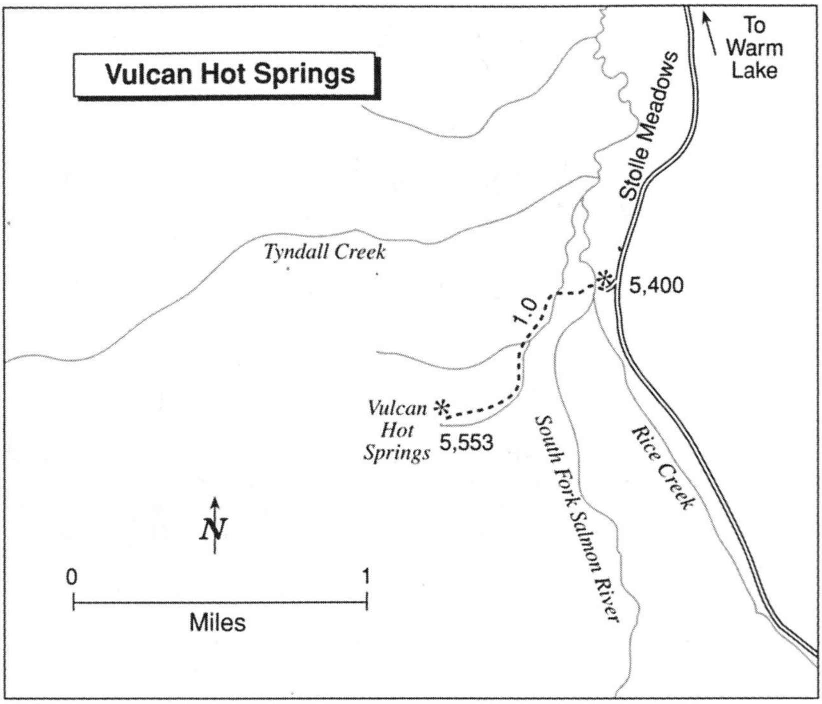


open to jeeps or ATVs. ) At .5 mile, the trail turns up the creek leading to the springs and at 1 mile, it reaches the lowest pool. To prevent overuse, make this a day trip.

# 45.

## Rice Lake, Rice Peak and Long Lake

**Round trip:** 1.4 miles to Rice Lake; 5 miles to Rice Peak; 10 miles to Long Lake
**Elevation gain:** 280 feet for Rice Lake, 1,400 feet for the lookout; additional 400 feet for Long Lake
**Elevation loss:** 760 feet (return climb) for Long Lake
**Highest point:** 8,693 feet
**Maps:** Rice Peak, Tyndall Meadows, Wild Buck Peak, Bernard Mountain
**Difficulty:** strenuous; cross-country from Rice Peak to viewpoint of Long Lake; time: 7 hours
**Access:** Turn right (east) off Idaho Highway 55 one mile north of Cascade. Drive 25 miles on the paved Warm Lake Road and then turn right (south) toward Stolle

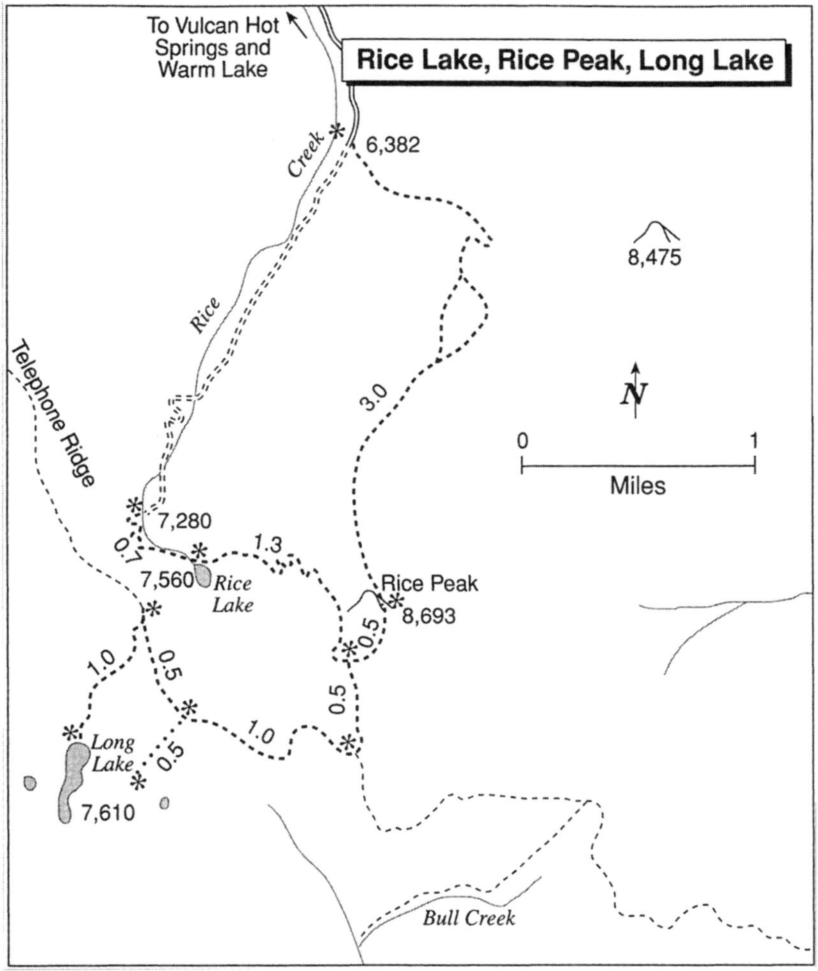


Meadows. Although there are side roads, keep straight ahead and drive past Stolle Meadows and the Vulcan Hot Springs trailhead to a junction with the road to Cupp Corral at 7 miles. Keep straight ahead on the now primitive road toward Rice Peak. Four-wheel drive is advised. At 10.9 miles, the Blue Point trail goes off to the left to Rice Peak Lookout. Beyond here the road has deteriorated to the point where it may be difficult even for four-wheel drive vehicles.

Grass and willows crowd the edges of the amber water of Rice Lake, which nestles under two gray granite knolls and the lookout on its hill of talus. The lookout oversees a circular rim of mountains. They include the blue points of the Sawtooths, the green and pink curves of the Salmon River Mountains, and the pale cream-colored peaks of the White Clouds. Warm Lake in a wooded basin to the northwest resembles melted blue wax. Cross-country hiking and an old trail lead to a view of blue-green Long Lake, which is squeezed into a narrow trough below the talus triangle of Rocky Peak.

The reason the road may be impassable even to four-wheel drive vehicles beyond the Blue Point trail is that a ditch has been dug in the road every 200 yards to drain it, resulting in a hump on the far side of each one. The ditches have deepened over the years so that the humps (often called water bars) are high enough to sandpaper the underside of your SUV or pickup. This section shouldn't be crossed until August 1 anyway most years because of mud, but the creek crossings are bridged. From the Blue Point trailhead, you can take that trail 3 miles to Rice Peak, or walk 2 miles farther along the road to the Rice Lake trailhead, then .7 mile to Rice Lake and 1.8 more miles to the lookout.

The topographic map shows a creek crossing the road 6 miles from the Cupp Corral junction. At this point, the Rice Peak Trail, built by the Youth Conservation Corps in 1975 begins. It angles left (east) through a fir forest and then climbs to the lake at .7 mile. The trail up to the peak crosses the outlet on logs and circles the east side of the lake past campsites. Then it ascends an open hillside and re-enters the forest after several switchbacks. At 1.4 miles, the trail crosses a cirque with a spring, and climbs talus to a saddle at 2 miles.

At a junction on the saddle, one trail leads up to the left (northeast) to the lookout, and an apparent trail drops south from the saddle. The trail to the lookout winds through whitebark pines to the summit at 2.5 miles. If you walked up the road from the Blue Point trailhead, at the lookout you have walked 4.5 miles. The Payette National Forest is preserving this lookout, so please treat it with respect.

To see Long Lake without a separate 12-mile round trip hike, take the apparent trail south from the saddle beside Rice Peak. It will disappear, but continue down 200 vertical feet until a much better trail angling uphill toward the west appears. Turn right and follow this trail west below the rock hill which adjoins the saddle and over a grassy spur onto the main ridge leading west.

The trail turns northwest with the ridge 1.5 miles from the saddle. Here a lower ridge with three rock hills on it joins from the southwest. For a view of Long Lake, turn off the trail and walk southwest along this low ridge. Keep to the top where deer have made a faint path. On top of the third hump, 2 miles from the saddle, the lake appears below.

To reach the shore of Long Lake safely, go back to the trail and follow it .5 mile northwest towards Telephone Ridge. Then turn left (south) on a trail that goes 1 mile to the lake, which is 5 miles from the Rice Lake trailhead. This route is about 1 mile shorter than reaching it by the Telephone Ridge Trail, which begins .2 mile west of the Cupp Corral Junction and goes 6.5 miles south to Long Lake in a 2,920-foot climb.

# BOISE NATIONAL FOREST
# MOUNTAIN HOME DISTRICT
# BOGUS BASIN AREA

# 46.

## Mores Mountain

**Round trip:** 2 miles
**Elevation gain:** 540 feet
**Highest point:** 7,237 feet
**Map:** Shafer Butte
**Difficulty:** easy; time: 2 hours
**Access:** From the intersection of Harrison Boulevard and Hill Road in Boise, drive 16 miles up the paved Bogus Basin Road to the ski area. Turn left (west) into the large parking area and drive through it to a road leading straight ahead to the nordic center. At 16.6 miles, just before the nordic center, the pavement ends. At 19.3 miles, turn right (east) onto the road to the Shafer Butte picnic area. At 20.6 miles, where a road to a gated group picnic area turns right, turn left to the trailhead at 20.7 miles. All vehicles parking here must pay a $4 day use fee. The main picnic area is beyond the trailhead.

Bogus Basin got its name because it once was the hideout of a gang of swindlers who made fake gold dust by adding other materials, such as gold-coated lead filings, to the gold dust. Eventually, Bogus Basin became a winter bonanza. Alf Engen snowshoed into the area in1937 to select a site for a ski area. Alf was one of the first professional ski jumpers in America and the U.S. alpine Olympic coach for the 1948 winter games. He came to the site of the future Bogus Basin while employed by the Forest Service to plan and develop winter sports areas. He also helped plan the Sun Valley and Alta ski areas.

The Civilian Conservation Corps (the Depression era project of the U.S. government to put young men to work) prepared the area for skiing and a rope tow was installed. The road was a one-lane dirt road, so drivers were allowed to go uphill only until 2:30 p.m. After 2:30, only downhill traffic was permitted. The old CCC building, which was heated only by a fireplace at one end, served as the day lodge until the Bogus Basin Recreation Association installed the Deer Point chairlift and built the first part of the Bogus Creek Lodge in 1962. Mores Mountain was named for J. Marion More, who led the party of prospectors that founded Bannack. It became the largest city in the Boise Basin and was later renamed Idaho City. More was also a legislator in the Washington territorial legislature, which included what is now Idaho.

Weather-beaten ponderosa pines and granite gnomes punctuate Mores Mountain. From it there are views of the Boise Ridge, the Treasure Valley and the Sawtooths. The many wildflowers which sprinkle the mountain in June seem planted by a master gardener. Along the trail, the pungent scent of chaparral refreshes the air. The trail, on which only foot traffic is allowed, was built by the Youth Conservation Corps in 1971, and reconstructed in 1988.

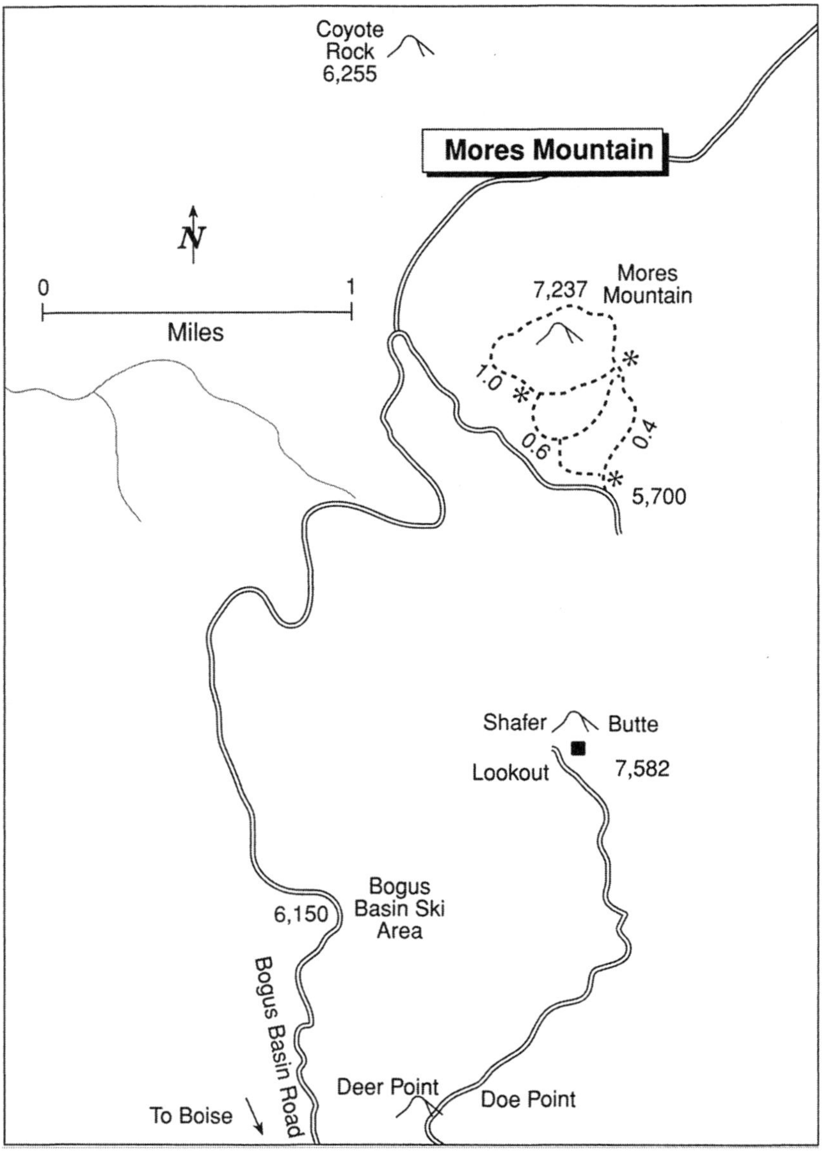


The Mores Mountain Trail has three interconnecting loops: a 1-mile interpretive trail, the 2-mile Valley View loop trail, and the 2-mile Mores Mountain trail. Neither the road to the picnic area nor the trail system are on the topographic map, but a sign at the trailhead has a sketch map of these routes. The trail crosses an open meadow for 50 yards and then runs northwest up into the woods, where another trail (the other end of the Valley View loop) goes off to the right.

To reach the top of the mountain, take the left trail, which winds gently up through trees and granite outcroppings. At the second outcropping, twisted pines frame a view of Shafer Butte and its ski runs. A signed junction with the beginning of the interpretive loop is at .6 mile. The interpretive trail goes off to the right (east) here. At about .8 mile, there is a sign for the Mores Mountain trail extension to the left. Take this trail, which leads around the north side of the mountain, circling just under the double summit at 1 mile. The eastern summit is covered with grass and chaparral with a few big trees. The western one is a rock outcrop with an excellent view. It is easy to leave the trail and go 100 yards up to either one.

The route descends east below the rocky summit through brush and across a little stream to meet the interpretive trail loop at its east end. For a shorter hike, you can return on it, or you can continue straight ahead down the Valley View loop which zigzags downhill through trees and follows the route of an old road back to join the other trail 50 yards above the trailhead.

# ARROWROCK RESERVOIR AREA

## 47.

## William H. Pogue (Sheep Creek) Trail (a National Recreation Trail)

**Round trip:** 10 miles (for section described here)
**Elevation gain:** 1,120 feet to Devils Creek
**Highest point:** 4,560 feet near Devils Creek
**Maps:** Twin Springs, Sheep Creek
**Difficulty:** moderate; time: 7 hours

**Access:** Turn right (north) off I-84 at the Gowan Road exit at the east end of Boise, Idaho. In 3.5 miles the road joins Idaho Highway 21. Continue to a side road for Lucky Peak and Arrowrock Reservoirs at 13 miles. Turn right (east) on a paved road. The pavement ends just before Arrowrock Dam, 5.7 miles from the turnoff. The road is improved but it is rough gravel and dirt and tends to develop a washboard surface. Drive along the winding arms of Arrowrock Reservoir and along the Boise River to the trailhead 30 miles from the Lucky Peak turnoff, passing the small resort of Twin Springs at 26.5 miles. The river runs through a cliff-lined gorge just before the road crosses a bridge to the undeveloped trailhead at 30 miles.

Since you drive along both Lucky Peak and Arrowrock Reservoirs on the way to this hike, you may want to know something about their history. By 1863, settlers were irrigating land on a small scale next to the Boise River, taking advantage of the

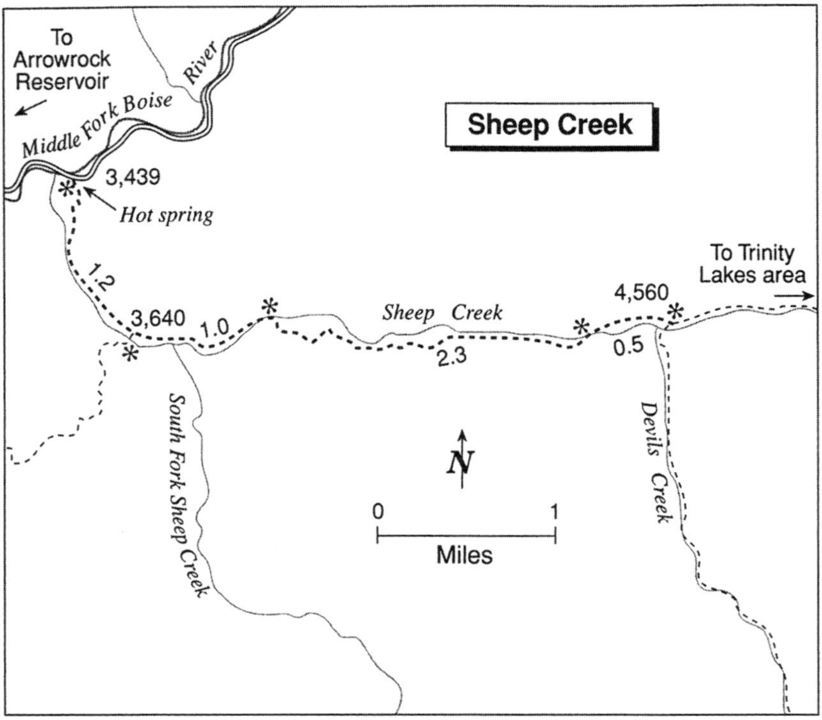


Homestead Act passed the year before. Soon canal companies sprang up. Irrigation expanded when the Desert Land Act, passed in 1877, gave 640 acres to anyone who bought and irrigated land in the next three years. This led to construction of the New York Canal in 1882, which ran from Diversion Dam east of Boise to Lake Lowell Reservoir near Caldwell. The Reclamation Act in 1902 enabled the federal government to build larger dams, such as Arrowrock in 1915. When it was constructed it was the highest dam in the world. Lucky Peak was constructed in 1952 at a cost of $20 million to control flooding.

In Sheep Creek Canyon, gray granite outcrops contrast with a green jungle of Douglas fir, ponderosa pine, alder, serviceberry and chokecherry. Yellow arrowleaf balsamroot flowers cover grassy hillsides in the spring. A 700-foot rock face just below Devils Creek resembles a dinosaur with a spiky back. This trail gives access to more than 50 miles of trails in unspoiled wilderness at Boise's back door. By using it, hikers can reach Trinity Lakes in 20 miles. It is also open to motorcycles. Some of it now passes through burned forest. The trail was renamed the William H. Pogue Trail to honor the Idaho Fish and Game officer shot in January 1981 by Claude Dallas. By then it had already been designated a National Recreation Trail.

The trail climbs steeply through trees and bushes and then up an open hillside. At .5 mile above a rocky knoll a side path goes downhill to the creek. Follow the main trail, which stays at least 100 feet above the creek. It climbs gently but lacks shade. The plants which at first glance seem to be poison ivy are really chokecherries. Rattlesnakes live here but are seen mostly in hot weather.

At 1.2 miles, the trail descends to a junction with the Corral Creek Trail. The main trail crosses Sheep Creek at 2.2 miles on a bridge beyond a campsite and enters burned forest. It then switchbacks away from the creek and, at 2.5 miles, runs along a steep hillside 200 feet above the creek. At 2.7 miles, as the trail climbs around a hill, a view of the canyon opens up. From here, a large rock face appears to block the canyon ahead. The Forest Service has been repairing sections of trail that were damaged by the flooding that followed the Foothills Fire.

At 3.7 miles, the trail descends and comes down to the creek across from the rock face at 4 miles. A campsite is at 4.5 miles in a meadow. Beyond here, the trail fords the creek. Across the creek, the trail meets the Devils Creek Trail at 5 miles on an open hillside.

The William H. Pogue Trail connects with several trails in the Trinity Lakes area to the east. One is the Roaring River Trail (045), which connects with the Roaring River Road (255) and the upper Roaring River trailhead near the Trinity Guard Station. The Pogue Trail also connects with the Snow Slide Trail (123) at the East Fork of Sheep Creek. This trail joins the Lava Mountain Trail (125), which passes Smith Creek Lake on the way to the Lava Mountain trailhead near Trinity Mountain.

# 48.

## Cottonwood Creek (Bald Mountain) Trail

**One-way distance:** 8 miles
**Elevation gain:** none
**Elevation loss:** 3,320 feet (no return climb with car shuttle, but shuttle is either on 10 miles of primitive road or requires driving along much of Arrowrock Reservoir)
**Highest point:** 7,040 feet
**Maps:** Arrowrock Reservoir Northeast, Twin Springs
**Difficulty:** moderate; time: 6 hours one-way
**Access:** Turn southeast off Idaho 21 one mile east of Idaho City onto the dirt Bannock Creek Road. Drive 10 miles to the top of the trail, which is 1 mile past a side road to Thorn Creek Butte Lookout. For the bottom of the trail, take the turnoff to Lucky Peak and Arrowrock reservoirs from Idaho 21 east of Boise and drive 14.5 miles on a rough gravel road to the Cottonwood Creek Road. Turn left (west) on the Cottonwood Creek Road and go 2.1 miles to the undeveloped trailhead.

Mining in the nearby Idaho City area began in 1862, when Moses Splawn and George Grimes led a party into the area looking for the Blue Bucket ore some people in a wagon train were said to have found. On their trip they found gold near what became the town of Centerville, but Indians killed Grimes. That fall hundreds of miners from Silver City went back with Splawn and started Idaho City and Pioneerville. In the next ten years the Boise Basin produced $100 million in gold, and by 1864 had 16,000 people living there. Placer mining in the basin was the most successful ever conducted in the United States. Parts of the town burned four times, but it remained the largest town in the territory for 20 years.

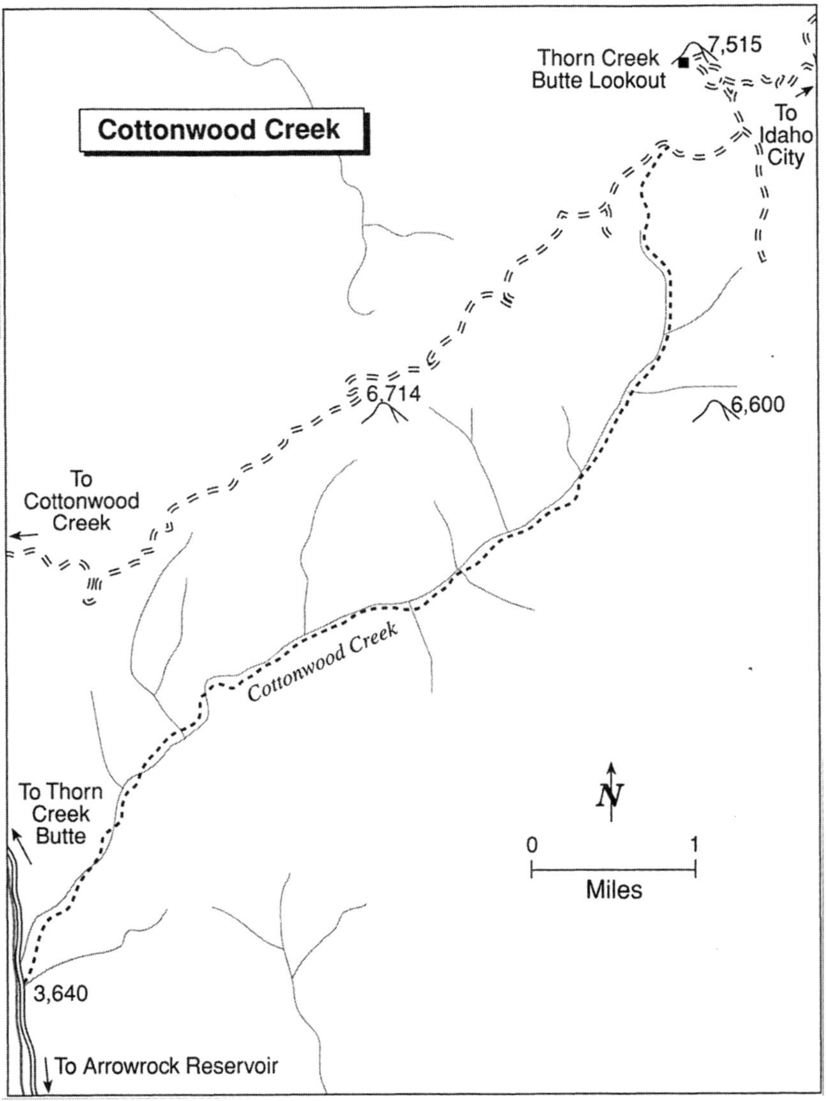


Note that this edition of the book reduces the hike mileage by 1.5 miles because it has you drive clear to the trailhead instead of starting at the lookout. If you feel like parking there or back at the campground, add 1.5 miles. The trail is limited to non-motorized travel. From the side of Thorn Creek Butte, Cottonwood Creek falls more than 3,000 feet to join its North Fork near the bottom of this trail. The creek tumbles through a green tangle of broadleaf trees and bushes. Aspen, dogwood, water birch and alder form thickets along the creek. Conifer trees along the route include Engelmann spruce and subalpine fir at the top and ponderosa pine at the bottom. Some of the ponderosas have trunks three feet across. If you take a side trip to the summit of Thorn Creek Butte, the view ranges from the snow-topped Sawtooths to the hazy Boise Valley and the blue Owyhees. In June, white blossoming shrubs and flowers like scarlet gilia, larkspur, mimulus and forget-me-not turn the trail side into a parade of colors. The lower part of this hike makes a pleasant walk in spring or fall. In early summer, it is fun to start at the top and walk the whole trail.

While driving up Thorn Creek Butte, avoid several confusing roads branching off the Bannock Creek Road (no map shows all of these roads). Keeping track of your progress on a Boise National Forest map and following the road with the best surface will get you to the top. At 10.9 miles there is a junction with two other roads. The one to the left goes to Bannock Creek. The one straight ahead continues to Bald Mountain Campground at 11.2 miles and then zigzags up to the turnoff for Thorn Creek Butte Lookout at 12 miles. In the campground a sign for the road up the mountain says "Road not maintained for public use." You can park here and walk, but you really need only a high wheelbase vehicle, not four-wheel drive, to continue. To reach the trailhead, drive straight ahead from the lookout turnoff for about .7 mile. The road descends about 200 feet before you reach the trail. In recent years, motorcycles and ATVs have made several confusing tracks so the trail is harder to find than it used to be, but a new trail sign will be installed in the summer of 2003. Beyond the trailhead the primitive road continues down the ridge west of Cottonwood Creek to join the Cottonwood Creek Road. Due to a landslide, you can no longer reach Idaho City from this road or the Cottonwood Creek Road.

The trail first crosses a tiny side stream at .2 mile and then fords a rushing side stream in aspens and alders at 1 mile. At 1.5 miles, at the East Fork of Cottonwood Creek, the trail crosses Cottonwood Creek to the west side.

The trail returns to the east side at 2.7 miles and then goes back over the creek after 300 yards. At 3.7 miles, it passes to the east side again for .2 mile before returning to the west. At 4.2 miles, the trail enters a meadow opposite Sawmill Creek, which once was the site of a water-powered sawmill. There is a beaver pond there now. The trail returns to the east side at 5.7 miles for .2 mile before crossing back. At 6 miles, it crosses Basket Springs Creek and at 6.3 miles goes to the east side once more and goes through a tunnel of alders.

After .3 mile, the trail returns to the west. Finally at 7 miles, it goes back to the east side for good. There are some burned areas along here and open hillsides that allow you views of Mt. Heinen across the North Fork of Cottonwood Creek. There are 10 crossings of Cottonwood Creek and only the three in the lowest 2.5 miles are bridged. In spring the others must be waded. The trail emerges into chaparral and grass at 7.5 miles, follows a fence, and drops to the lower trailhead at 8 miles.

Spanish Town

# ROCKY BAR AREA

## 49.

## Spanish Town

**Round trip:** 3.4 to 4 miles
**Elevation gain:** none on the James Creek route; 180 feet on the route from Sand Creek.
**Elevation loss:** 800 feet (return climb) on the James Creek route, and 480 feet on the route from Sand Creek.
**Highest point:** 6,320 feet
**Map:** Rocky Bar

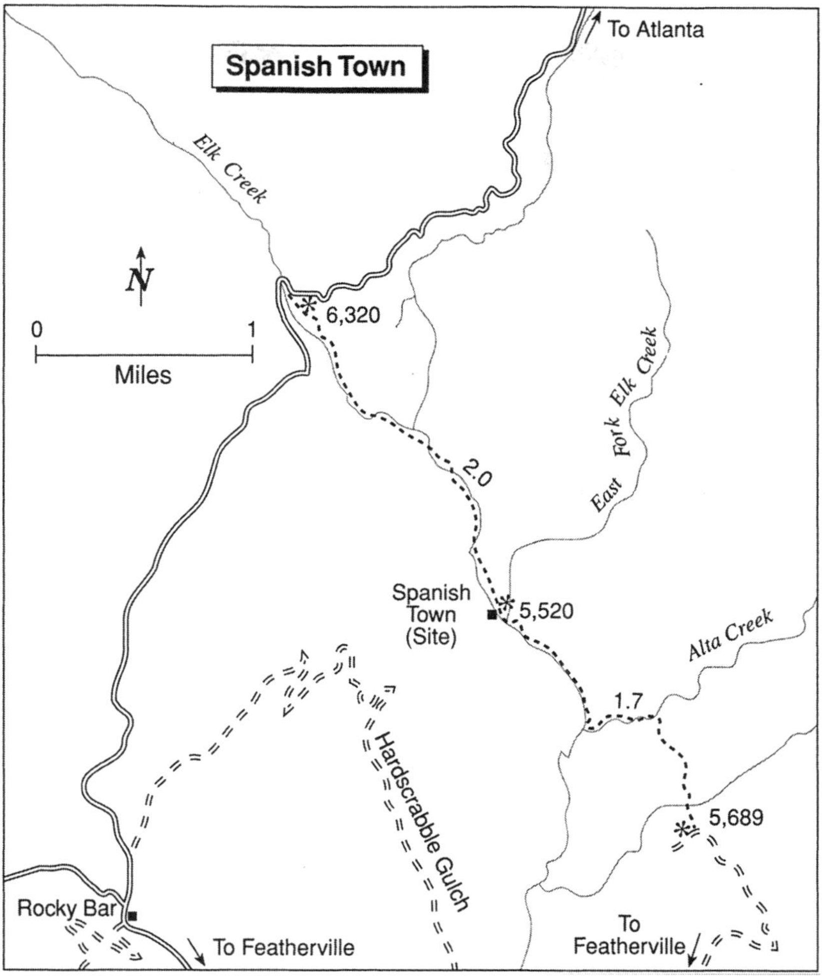


**Difficulty:** easy except for several creek crossings on the trail from James Creek; time: 4 hours

**Access No. 1:** Drive up the rocky, dirt James Creek Road either 3.5 miles from Rocky Bar or 9.5 miles from Atlanta to a switchback into a canyon at a waterfall. The James Creek Road runs from Rocky Bar to the Middle Fork of the Boise River Road 1.7 miles west of Atlanta. (See Grouse Lakes, Hike 49, for detailed directions to Atlanta.) To reach Rocky Bar, drive northeast of Mountain Home on U.S. Highway 20-26. Two miles east of Cat Creek Summit turn left (north) on a paved road to Pine and Featherville. Drive 25 miles to a junction with the road that goes east about 1 mile to Featherville. Just beyond Featherville, Road 168 turns north to Rocky Bar. The road up what is called the Boiler Grade over James Creek Summit is primitive and not recommended for passenger cars.

**Access No. 2:** From U.S. Highway 20-26 northeast of Mountain Home, drive 25.5

miles to a junction with the road east to Featherville. About 1 mile east of Featherville, turn north on the Cayuse Creek Road (135) and drive 3.9 miles to where an unsigned road (132) angles back off to the left. Take this primitive road, which may require four-wheel drive, and avoiding side roads including those signed 132 A, B, and C, go about 7.3 miles to an old Forest Service notice board and sign-in box. There is space for only one or two cars to park at this trailhead.

Miners flocked to nearby Rocky Bar in 1863 after lode gold was discovered on the Feather River and began working arrastras. A toll road was built to Featherville in 1864 and the neighboring town of Esmeralda was the first county seat of Alturas County, which no longer exists. By 1892, $6 million had been taken from the area's mines. The Alturas Hotel, ornamented with a gingerbread balcony, was the largest building in Rocky Bar. A fire destroyed most of the town in1892, leaving 150 homeless.

Robert Romig, the son of a homesteader who came to Spanish Town in 1931, says that early newspapers reported that miners first came to the area in 1863. When they arrived, they found a few stones from two primitive gold ore mills called arrastras and two cast iron Chilean mills. (Chileans were known to have participated in the California gold rush in 1849, so it is possible that the presence of the Chilean mills at Spanish Town meant Chileans reached Idaho or sold mills to those going there.) The miners in the 1860s had a mill at Spanish Town, and the ore came from over the ridge west of Elk Creek. Romig and his brothers built a small, corrugated-steel covered building in 1946 from the remnants of a large bunkhouse/cookhouse that had been crushed by snow. The Romigs also built other buildings and a flume, but there is little evidence of them. The family dug three mine tunnels east of Elk Creek and worked on three that were west of the creek, putting in 1,000 feet of tunnels.

At Spanish Town, a leaning log cabin, an old shack covered with galvanized steel, silvered boards, and the remains of piles of mine timbers stand silently. This is an easy shaded hike to an area containing 24 inventoried historical sites. All materials here are protected by the Antiquities Act, which provides heavy fines and jail time for anyone stealing or damaging any historical or archaeological objects.

**Trail from access No. 1:** From the James Creek Road, the trail down Elk Creek begins as a jeep track 200 yards up the Boiler Grade from a road bridge over Elk Creek below the waterfall. There is no trail sign and no parking except near the bridge. The track leads southeast downhill away from Elk Creek through aspens.

At .2 mile, the trail returns to the creek through Douglas fir among blue delphiniums. The track has been washed out into a narrow path 200 yards farther along. At .7 mile, it goes over the creek on logs to the southwest side. The trail crosses Elk Creek several times, and this may be a problem early in the summer.

At 1 mile there is another creek crossing, and at 1.2 miles, where the trail goes back to the southwest side of the creek, the canyon becomes rockier. At 1.7 miles, it crosses again to the northeast side. At a junction at 2 miles, take the Spanish Town trail northeast 100 yards to a building covered with galvanized steel and a log cabin beyond it. Additional ruins are a few hundred yards up the East Fork of Elk Creek and beyond where the trail crosses that creek.

**Trail from access No. 2:** From the trailhead at the end of Road 132 near Sand Creek, the trail crosses that creek at .2 mile, climbs through ponderosa pine and descends a gentle slope to little Alta Creek at .6 mile. It crosses the creek three times and a side stream once, as it follows that creek to Elk Creek at 1 mile. Then the trail goes along the right (east) bank of Elk Creek, and passes piles of timbers from the three mine tunnels. Then it crosses the East Fork of Elk Creek to Spanish Town at 1.7 miles.

# TRINITY LAKES AREA

## 52.

## Rainbow Basin Trail

**Round trip:** 9 miles; with 1.8 miles extra to see five lakes off the main trail
**Elevation gain:** 600 feet; 120 feet extra to see off-trail lakes
**Elevation loss:** 560 feet (return climb); 160 feet extra to see off-trail lakes
**Highest point:** 8,400 feet
**Map:** Trinity Mountain
**Difficulty:** moderate; time: 8 hours
**Access:** From Mountain Home drive 30 miles northeast on US 20-26 to paved FH61, the road to Pine and Featherville. Turn left (northwest) and go 29 miles. Just before Featherville, the road crosses the South Fork of the Boise. On the far side of the bridge, keep left away from town on Forest Road 172, the Trinity Creek Road. Go northwest up this road for 15 miles to FR129, avoiding FR183 where it turns south at about 7 miles. Turn left (south) on primitive road 129 and drive 3.2 miles to Big Trinity Lake. Turn left (east) and drive to the campground. Here, roads turn left and right to campsites. Turn left and drive .7 mile along the lake's north and east shores to the trailhead at the end of the road.

An 800-foot ridge of splintery, charcoal gray cliffs overlooks all three Rainbow Lakes. The middle lake has its own 400-foot set of cliffs below the higher ones. Thick forest and green water contrast with these dark cliffs. From a saddle on the trail nine lakes spread out below Trinity Mountain. The basin is unusual for Idaho because sagebrush is lacking. Near the trailhead, Big Trinity Lake, edged with grass and forest, sits below granite-covered knolls. There are campgrounds at Big Trinity and Big and Little Roaring River Lakes. This trail is one of the few trails in Idaho where only foot travel is permitted.

From the Little Trinity Lake campground on the east side of Big Trinity Lake, the trail first winds through meadows of lupine, paintbrush and sulphur flowers. At .2 mile, a path goes off to the lake shore and the trail joins the old trail, which has come .6 mile from Big Trinity Campground. Since the last edition of this book the trailhead has been moved from that campground to its present location, which has shortened the hike by .4 mile. From this junction the trail switchbacks 800 feet to the saddle with the view of the lakes at .6 mile.

From there the trail zigzags down grassy slopes to a stream at 1.1 miles (not on the map). Here a side path descends .2 mile to Green Island Lake. At 1.2 miles, a side path goes west to Fiddle Lake. At 1.4 miles, a path leads to Little Lookout Lake, which is only the eye of a marsh. At 1.6 miles on the main trail, a sign for Lookout Lakes points to a side path which goes southeast .2 mile up a stream to Big Lookout Lake, from which you can see Trinity Mountain Lookout above.

From the Big Lookout Lake junction, the main trail climbs past a spring in a

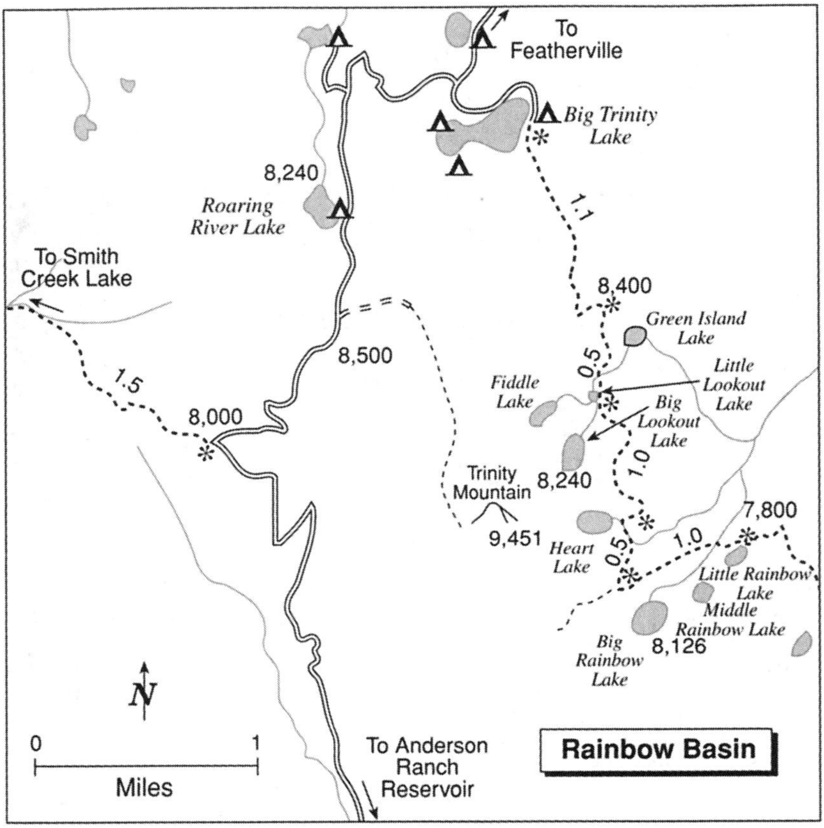


meadow and down to a 200-yard side path at 2.6 miles. This path goes .1 mile to deep blue Heart Lake, which glimmers below white granite and a gray cliff.

Beyond Heart Lake, the main trail contours over to a junction with the trail to Big Rainbow Lake at 3.1 miles. Here the main trail continues southeast and the trail to Big Rainbow turns off to the southwest to a pond at 3.5 miles and past it to the lake. Don't be confused by any paths leading west from the pond or near it because they do not go to the lake and are not Forest Service routes.

To reach the other Rainbow Lakes, return to the junction with the main trail that came from Big Trinity Lake and continues east. To reach the middle lake, walk .5 mile east on this trail, then turn right (southeast) on a side path and go .2 mile. To reach Little Rainbow Lake 3.6 miles from the trailhead, continue .5 mile farther down the main trail. Hideaway Lake can be reached by continuing .8 mile beyond Little Rainbow Lake. Any trace of a trail down the canyon of Parks Creek below Hideaway Lake is not on the Forest Service inventory so is not maintained.

If you want to reach the top of Trinity Mountain, the best route is to drive south from Big Roaring River Lake about 1 mile on the Fall Creek Road and then turn off on the lookout road and walk up it from the locked gate at .2 mile where it is closed to motor vehicles. The summit is about a 2 mile climb from the gate with a 1,450-foot elevation gain.

**Rainbow Basin**

# 51.

## Smith Creek and North Star Lakes

**Round trip:** 11 miles
**Elevation gain:** 1,830 feet
**Elevation loss:** 1,060 feet (return climb)
**Highest point:** 8,400 feet
**Maps:** Trinity Mountain, Prairie
**Difficulty:** strenuous; time: 8 hours

**Access:** Turn north off U.S. Highway 20-26 two miles east of Cat Creek Summit. Drive 17 miles on a paved road to Pine, and then 8.5 miles toward Featherville. Turn west on the dirt Trinity Creek Road and drive 11.6 miles to the Phifer Creek Road (129). Turn left (south) and drive 8.2 miles on a primitive road down six switchbacks on the Fall Creek Grade, past a small campground. Turn right (west) on a spur road that goes 200 yards to the Upper Lava Mountain trailhead, which is shown as a little loop road on the topographic map.

The trail to Smith Creek and North Star Lakes leads along grassy hills that resemble an island in the sky. Along the trail, waterfalls and streams thread meadows lacy with false hellbore, while lupine, paintbrush and scarlet gilia cover drier areas. These two lakes nestle under grassy ridges and rock benches like sapphires in green velvet. Near North Star Lake, the trail overlooks a quilt of green and gold fields on a flat shelf above the canyon of the South Fork of the Boise.

The trailhead for Smith Creek and North Star Lakes is now much farther down the

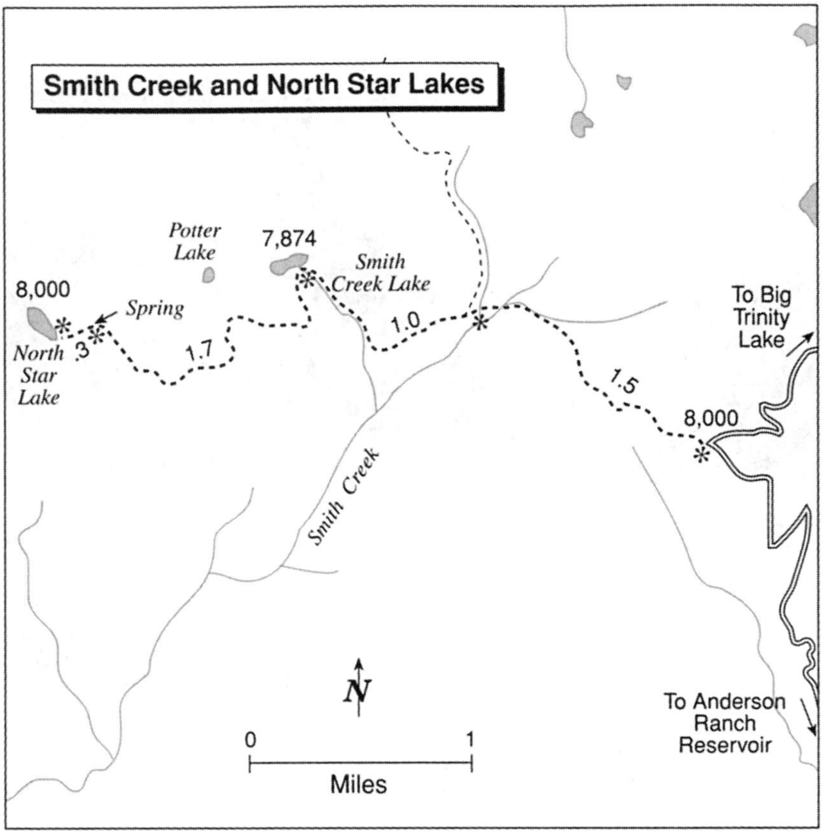


Fall Creek Road than it used to be, and starting farther down has added 2 miles round trip to the hike. The trail begins by climbing along the east side of the East Fork of Fall Creek. At 1.2 miles it curves 90 degrees to the left (west) and crosses a side stream below a small waterfall. At 1.5 miles at a saddle, it turns sharply north, then descends a ravine into the canyon of Smith Creek. At 2 miles, the trail crosses two small streams, enters tall grass where it is sometimes sketchy and at 2.5 miles crosses Smith Creek to the west side.

At a junction just beyond the ford, a poor trail turns north over a saddle into the drainage of Sheep Creek. The trail to the lakes climbs the side of Smith Creek Canyon and, at 3 miles, ascends the creek to Smith Creek Lake at 3.5 miles. The trail is shown on the topographic map as bypassing the lake, but the bypass shows less use than the trail to the lake.

From the lake, the route circles the shoulder of the next ridge, then curves into the canyon of Potter Creek. It ascends a wooded hillside to an open grassy slope at 5 miles where North Star Lake appears around a corner. The trail descends the hillside to a junction with a trail to Lava Mountain at 5.2 miles. The spur trail to the lake climbs 100 feet up a green hill to the shore at 5.5 miles. From the junction, the main Lava Mountain trail continues west 7.3 miles to road 222B about 9 miles from Prairie.

Jennie Lake

# IDAHO CITY DISTRICT
# MORES CREEK SUMMIT AREA

## 52.

## Jennie Lake

**Round trip:** 9.2 miles
**Elevation gain:** 1,940 feet
**Highest point:** 7,850 feet
**Maps:** Bear River, Jackson Peak
**Difficulty:** moderate; time: 8 hours

**Access:** Turn east on Forest Road 384 to Atlanta at Edna Creek Campground 18 miles north of Idaho City. Drive 7.3 miles on gravel and turn left (northeast) on the dirt Crooked River—Bear River Road (348.) Go 7.3 miles to Bear Creek. Here there is a parking area and horse loading to the right above the road, where another road turns 90 degrees to the left. The main road continues straight ahead but deteriorates immediately to a rocky, primitive road that is difficult to turn around on. Therefore, before the side road turns off to the left, look for the parking area and park in it. Then

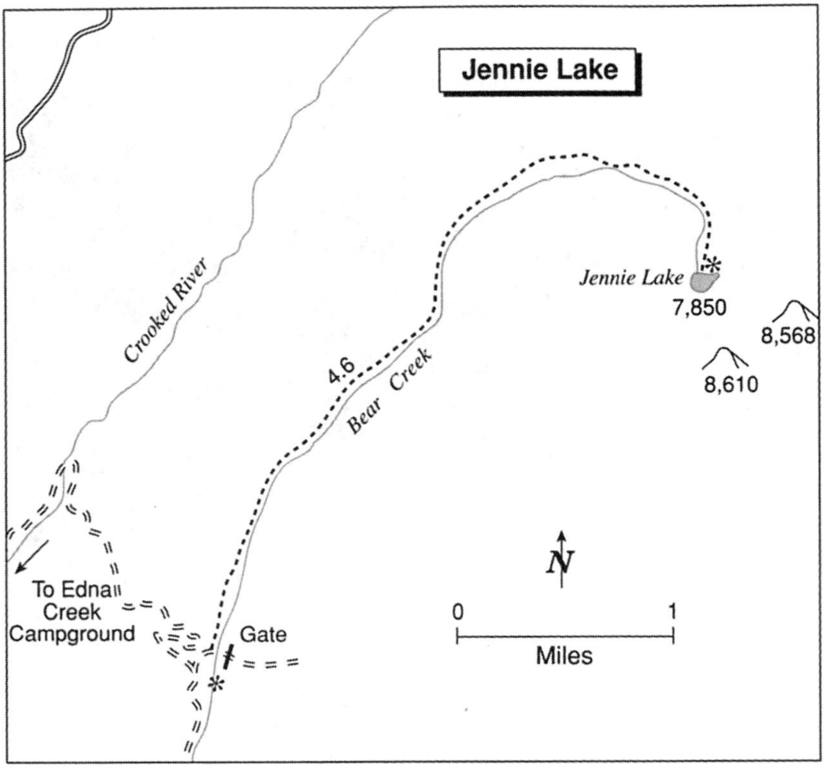


walk up the side road for 200 yards to where the trail begins at an interpretive sign. (Beyond the sign the side road crosses Bear Creek and then is gated shut.)

A 150-foot rounded knoll of gray granite, pitted by caves, guards the south side of dark green Jennie Lake. Behind the knoll, a high barren ridge holds 200-foot furrowed cliffs. To the east, light gray towers decorate more cliffs above shrubs which paint the canyon orange in autumn. The summit of Wolf Mountain, reported to be the home of mountain goats, rises behind the lake. The trail, which was rebuilt by the Youth Conservation Corps in 1980, is only two hours from Boise.

The trail climbs up the road bank onto a hillside. Then it goes along about 50 feet above and on the left (west) side of the creek through lodgepole, spruce and fir. It passes through shrubby clearings and open rocky areas. Ferns edge the creek, which flows over golden gravel. Some of the plants found are snowberry, delphinium, arrowleaf balsamroot and pearly everlasting. At 1.2 miles, an open area stretches up the side of the canyon; at 1.5 miles, the trail levels in small meadows. It passes two grassy hills on the east side of the creek at 2.5 miles, where it is cut into the creek bank. At 3.2 miles, it enters a series of larger sagebrush and grass meadows below a sagebrush ridge.

At 4.2 miles, the trail follows a tiny stream (not the outlet) east across the head of the canyon. After 200 yards, it turns left (south) up beside a pale green outcrop.

Finally it follows a small ridge up to the lake at 4.6 miles. The canyon circles as it climbs, so the trail which began by going north ends running south.

# ATLANTA AREA

## 53.

## Grouse Lakes

**Round trip:** 10.6 to 13 miles
**Elevation gain:** 2,375 feet; (to see upper lake, add .6 mile and 130 feet gain)
**Highest point:** 8,185 feet
**Maps:** Atlanta West, Atlanta East, Ross Peak
**Difficulty:** strenuous; time: 9 to 10 hours
**Access:** From Idaho Highway 21 at the Edna Creek Campground 18 miles north of Idaho City, turn off on Road 384 to Atlanta. Staying on 384, drive along Willow Creek and down Owl Creek to the North Fork of the Boise River Road (327). Turn left here and drive along the North Fork and then down Swanholm Creek to the Middle Fork of the Boise River Road (268). Turn left on this road, which goes east to the James Creek Road (126) at about 39 miles, 1.7 miles west of Atlanta. To find the Yuba River Road (289) turn right (south) on the James Creek Road, which angles off to the right of the main road. Then take an unsigned road that goes off to the left immediately. This is the Yuba River Road. Take this primitive road along that river for 2.5 miles through forest burned in 2000 to Decker Creek. Then turn left (east) on the narrow Decker Creek Road (207) and go 1.2 miles to the Grouse Creek trailhead.

The drive in to Atlanta is worth the effort even if you don't take this trail or the one from there up the Middle Fork of the Boise into the Sawtooth Wilderness. This mining town was founded in 1864, and named for a Civil War battle. In 1867 miners brought in a stamp mill by pack trail to process the ore, which was 75 percent silver. The basic unit in a stamp mill was a row of (usually five) steel posts about 3 inches in diameter mounted vertically in a framework and joined by a cam shaft. When the cam shaft was turned by steam power it made the posts rise and fall to crush the ore. Mining made little profit until the James Creek Road from Rocky Bar was built in 1878. An amalgamation plant installed in 1932 produced the most gold of any Idaho area from 1932-36.

A famous character in early Atlanta history was Pegleg Annie, who froze her feet when caught in a blizzard on the way to Rocky Bar for a dance in 1898. After her feet were amputated, she was still able to run a tavern and boardinghouse with the aid of peg legs.

Along the trail to Grouse Lakes, a mosaic of wildflowers in lavender, blue, red,

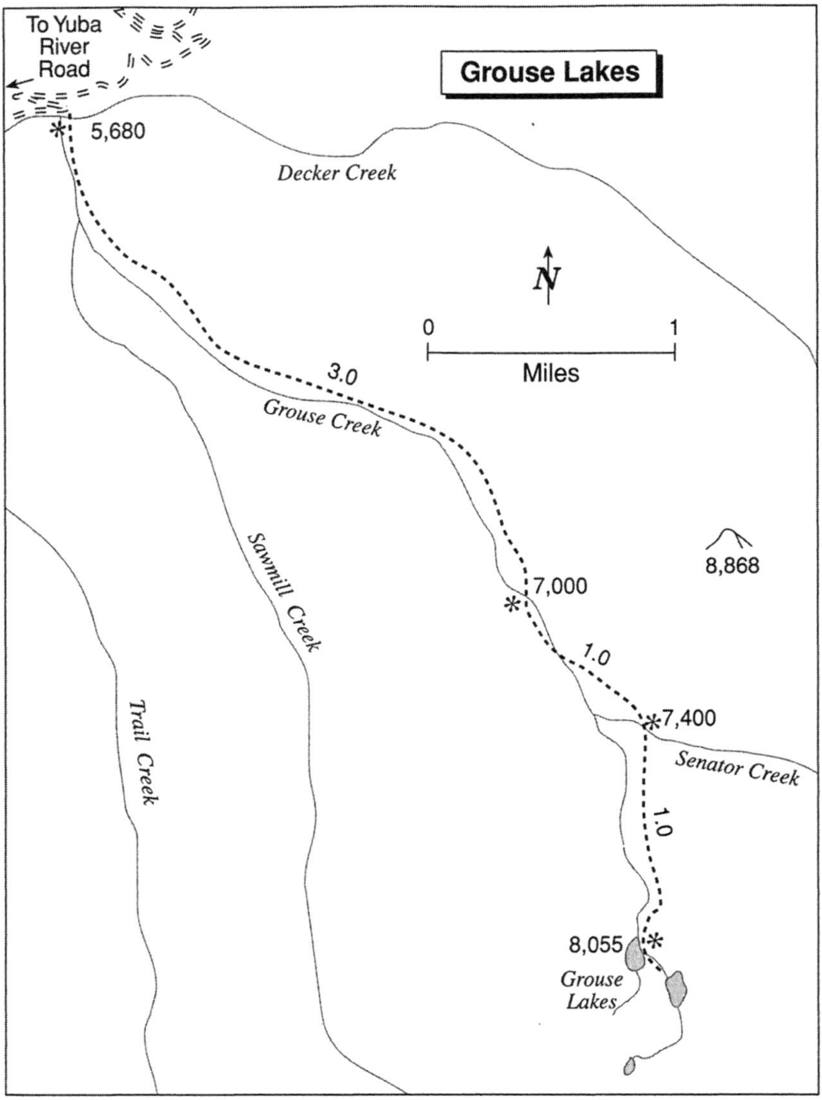


yellow and white covers a series of big meadows. By early August, they paint the grasses red-orange, light blue, and lavender. The lower lake lies in a soft cushion of marsh. A tangle of willows hides the green water of the upper lake, which is below 400-foot cliffs. Between the lakes, the stream splashes down in little waterfalls. The road and trail go through forest that mostly burned in 2000, giving an excellent opportunity to watch how a forest recovers from fire. You need to carry a wood saw in your car because burned trees will sometimes fall and block the road. For this reason, you should avoid the road and trail when it is windy or stormy.

Deep water bars (ditches followed by humps in the road) prevent passenger cars from driving the Yuba River Road. High wheelbase vehicles are necessary but probably not four-wheel drive.

The trail to Grouse Lakes begins at a switchback on the Decker Creek Road. The trail first crosses Decker Creek on a bridge, then goes southeast the left (northeast) bank through dead trees to the first of several meadows at .7 mile along of Grouse Creek. Watch out for nettles along the trail.

It used to be difficult to mark progress up the trail because forest hid the landmarks, but the fire has made it easier. Trail reconstruction in the summer of 2003 will eliminate the two creek crossings at 3 and 3.3 miles. Just before Senator Creek enters from the east, there is a junction marked with a cairn. That side trail isn't shown on the topographic map, but it is on the forest map. From here it goes up Senator Creek and over to Decker Creek and then down it to the Grouse Creek trailhead.

Stay on the main trail, which crosses Senator Creek in thick forest at 4 miles beside a large campsite. It traverses two clearings, then comes to a .5 mile-long meadowy hillside splashed with paintbrush, bluebells and yellow cinquefoil. There is one campsite where the trail reaches the lake at 5 miles and more small sites west of the outlet.

The upper lake is .3 mile beyond. To reach it, follow a path around the east side of the lower lake until it ends in a marsh. Skirt the marsh to the first inlet and follow it up a hillside of tiny firs to the lake. There are no campsites here because of the willows.

# LOWMAN DISTRICT
# LOWMAN AREA

## 54.

## Red Mountain Lookout and Lakes

**Loop trip:** 9.5 miles (1.4 miles extra to see highest lake)
**Elevation gain:** 2,560 feet
**Elevation loss:** 100 feet (return climb)
**Highest point:** 8,722 feet
**Maps:** Cache Creek, Miller Mountain East
**Difficulty:** strenuous; partly cross-country; time: 7 hours
**Access:** At Lowman, turn left (north) on the gravel Clear Creek Road (582) and go 12 miles to a junction. Turn right (northeast) on the Red Mountain Road (515) and drive 4.6 miles to a transfer camp with a large parking area.

Lowman, the closest settlement, was named for Nathaniel Lowman who built a home there in 1907, and in 1911 established a post office in his home. Several others

**One of the Red Mountain Lakes**

settled there much earlier, including Emma Edwards Green, designer of the Idaho state seal, the only woman to have designed a state seal. She entered the contest to design the seal in 1891 and won the competition.

Three of the Red Mountain Lakes nestle under 200-foot dark cliffs below Red Mountain. Bunch grass and flowers carpet the gentle side of Red Mountain between clumps of lodgepole pine and subalpine fir. From its summit, you see Trinity Mountain, Shafer Butte near Boise, Snowbank Mountain near Cascade, the Salmon River Mountains, most of the Sawtooths and some of the White Clouds. Pines, firs, red mountain heath, boulders and white granite benches enclose the tiny lakes. At the lowest of the three, a shoulder of Red Mountain rises behind water lilies. This is the only view of the peak where it looks red.

The trail begins at the far end of the parking area where the Clear Creek Road is closed to motor vehicles. First it runs along the old road on the left (north) side of Clear Creek in a deep, forested canyon, with a few open areas. At 1.4 miles, it crosses a side creek, Rough Creek, and the old road ends. Then it crosses a smaller creek at 1.6 miles. At 1.8 miles, it leaves Clear Creek to climb a ridge through chaparral and meadows. An open area and spring are at 2.9 miles. At 3 miles, the side trail to Red Mountain turns off. (The Clear Creek Trail continues east to a junction with the central section of the upper Kirkham Ridge Trail, which leads from Miller Mountain to Bull Trout Lake.) Turn north on the trail to Red Mountain. It climbs to the crest of a ridge and along it at the edge of trees. It angles northwest to a second ridge and switchbacks to the rocks holding the foundations of the old lookout at 4 miles.

From the summit, all three lakes can be seen. The easiest way to reach them is to descend cross-country. However, this route is rough walking. To reach the lake closest to Red Mountain, drop down a rocky gully southeast of the summit past a pond to the lake at .5 mile. Below this lake, a faint path leads .5 mile down the outlet to the lowest lake. (To make a side trip to the highest lake, walk .5 mile north along the lookout ridge to a wooded ravine and descend it .2 mile to the lake.)

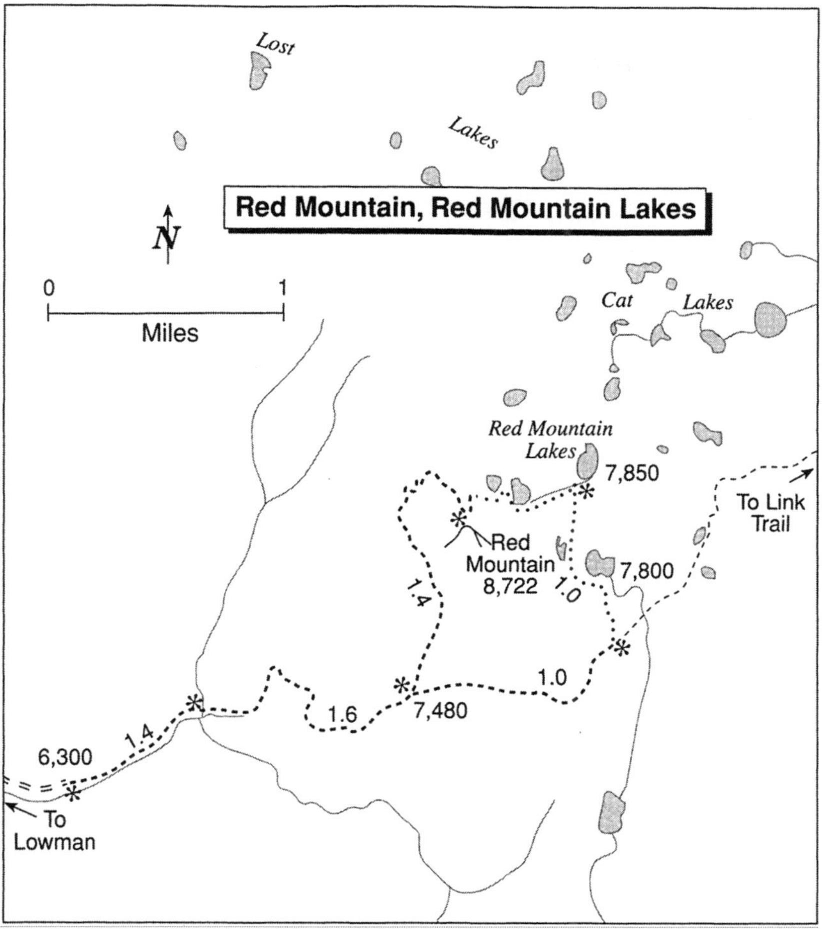


To return to the main trail from the lowest lake, turn south through a boulder-filled gap and pass a shallow pond in the rocks. Then turn east down to a pond, large enough to be called the fourth lake. These ponds are shown as marsh on the topographic map. From here, angle south across an open hillside to the upper Kirkham Ridge Trail, which is 1.5 miles from the summit of Red Mountain, and 1 mile east of the side trail to the summit. If you go north on this trail for .5 mile there are two more tiny lakes.

# 55.

## Upper Kirkham Ridge Trail: Bull Trout Lake to Cat Lakes and the Link Trail

**One-way distance:** 9.2 miles (add .2 mile for Cat Lakes spur trail)
**Elevation gain:** 1,360 feet
**Elevation loss:** 680 feet
**Highest point:** 7,670 feet
**Maps:** Bull Trout Point, Cache Creek
**Difficulty:** strenuous; time: 8 hours this section one-way
**Access:** Drive 1.5 miles north of Banner Creek Summit on Idaho Highway 21. Turn left (southwest) on the gravel road to Bull Trout Lake and drive .7 mile. Turn right (west) on a primitive road and go .5 mile to the road's end.

From the peninsula which juts into the lowest Cat Lake (sometimes called Catpaw Lake) from the east shore, the green water reflects dark firs and pale granite knolls. Behind the trees, two pointed peaks crowd an orange shoulder of Red Mountain. There are glimpses of the orange slabs and sand of Warm Spring Canyon along the trail, but most of the way you pass wooded hills. This trail should not be confused with the new, lower section of the Kirkham Ridge Trail, which is an ATV trail system that begins at Idaho Highway 21 near Kirkham Hot Springs. That trail system connects with the central section of the old Kirkham Ridge Trail, but the central and upper sections are not open to ATVs. Only the upper part of the old Kirkham Ridge Trail is covered here. The elevation gain is only 2,440 feet for a through trip from Bull Trout Lake compared to 4,630 feet when starting at the Warm Springs airstrip.

The trail starts at the edge of a flower meadow and crosses a swamp on flattened logs. Then it winds along Warm Spring Creek through lodgepoles to meet a trail to upper Gates Creek at .7 mile. At 1.5 miles, the main trail crosses three small branches of Warm Spring Creek in sandy hills. Then it winds through the woods and at 2.7 miles drops to a bridge over Gates Creek. From here, you can see orange talus and walls down Warm Spring Canyon. Next, it climbs 300 feet and at 3 miles follows Pass Creek. At 4.5 miles, the trail crosses to the south side of the creek (campsites here) and climbs 100 feet to a wooded pass at 5 miles.

On the other side, the trail switchbacks down an open area with a view up Cat Creek Canyon. At 5.7 miles at a large campsite, it crosses a side stream into meadows. At another campsite, at 6.5 miles, it crosses No Name Creek, then climbs around the end of a hill. The trail crosses the first of three branches of Cat Creek at 7.5 miles. At a fourth branch at 8.5 miles, an unsigned path leads up the right (north) bank and climbs 200 feet in .2 mile to the first lake at 8.7 miles. The other Cat Lakes can be reached cross-country from this one.

From the Cat Lake junction, the Upper Kirkham Ridge Trail climbs gently along

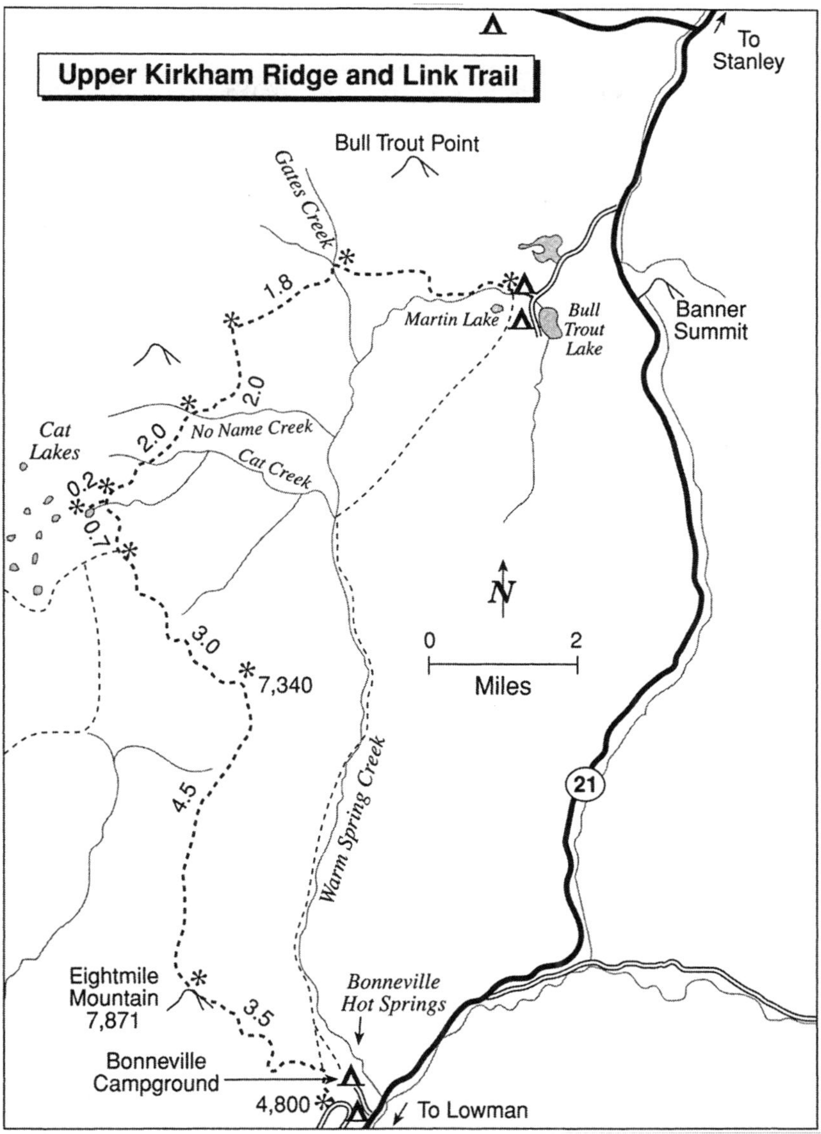


eroded gullies at the head of Cat Creek and drops to the Link Trail at .7 mile. This junction is at the point where the trail comes in here from the west from Red Mountain Lakes. From this junction, 9.2 miles from Bull Trout Lake, you can see the Sawtooths.

# 56.

## Link Trail: From Upper Kirkham Ridge Trail to Warm Springs

**One-way distance:** 11.0 miles
**Elevation gain:** 1,080 feet
**Elevation loss:** 3,950 feet
**Highest point:** 8,120 feet
**Maps:** Cache Creek, Bull Trout Point, Eightmile Mountain
**Difficulty:** strenuous; time: 2 days for this section one-way
**Access:** See the Upper Kirkham Ridge Trail: Bull Trout Lake to Cat Lakes and the Link Trail (Hike 55) for directions for reaching the junction of the Link Trail with the Upper Kirkham Ridge Trail where this description begins. To reach the lower end of the trail at the Warm Springs airstrip, turn left (west) off Idaho Highway 21, 18 miles east of Lowman. Drive 1 mile west to the site of the old guard station. Then turn right and drive 1.2 miles to the trailhead at the east end of the airstrip.

The view from the Link Trail includes more of the Sawtooths than you see from peaks in the range itself. For several miles, the trail hugs the top of a narrow ridge with a panorama of the Sawtooths resembling a giant mural. Near the upper end of the trail, Red Mountain presides over granite ridges, knolls and lakes.

The Link and Upper Kirkham Ridge trails join .7 mile south of the side trail to Cat Lakes, where the trail from Red Mountain Lakes comes in from the west. From here, the Link Trail contours southeast in and out of gullies with a view of Red Mountain. It crosses an open area at .7 mile and by 1 mile has climbed 600 feet above the junction. At 1.2 miles, it heads downhill, reaching a roof-edged saddle where the Sawtooths are visible at 1.5 miles.

From the saddle, the trail runs southeast along the side of the next hill on the ridge. In early July, this section at 8,000 feet, may have snow. At 2.5 miles, the trail continues southeast down a spur to Castro Creek and crosses it at 3 miles. A campsite below the crossing is the only good one as Castro Creek is the only water source except for one early season stream 50 feet below the trail at 6.5 miles.

From Castro Creek, the trail climbs the side of the canyon to a saddle at 4 miles where the Sawtooths appear again. It then climbs south up and down along the ridge top for several miles. In places, the canyon wall below the trail on the north has been eroded into a badlands of striped rock. USE CAUTION. At 6.5 miles, pine-needled flats provide campsites within reach of the early-season stream.

Then the trail climbs 160 feet, crosses an open area, and skirts the north side of Eightmile Mountain to a saddle at 7.5 miles. It switchbacks down the open side of the peak and the southeast ridge of Eightmile Mountain in firs and brush.

At 9.2 miles, the trail leaves the ridge and descends the canyon wall of the South Fork of the Payette next to Penrod Creek. It zigzags down a sagebrush and grass hillside to meet the Warm Spring Canyon Trail at 10.5 miles. Bull Trout Lake is 14 miles from here by the Warm Spring Canyon Trail, but that trail has a difficult ford and no view. Two-hundred yards below this junction, the trail crosses Penrod Creek. At 11 miles is a register box at the trailhead next to the airstrip, which is 2.1 miles from Idaho 21, 18 miles east of Lowman.

# FRIENDS OF THE WEISER RIVER TRAIL

## 57.

## Weiser River Trail

**One-way distance:** 84.4 miles
**Elevation gain:** 2,060 feet
**Highest point:** 4,160 feet
**Maps:** Weiser South, Weiser Cove, Mann Creek SE, Midvale Hill, Midvale, Cambridge, East of Cambridge, Goodrich, Council, Fruitvale, Tamarack, New Meadows
**Difficulty:** easy to strenuous, depending on length of section; time for whole trail: 2 or 3 days for mountain bikers and horseback riders; about a week for backpackers.
**Access:** There are several access points along the trail, so that hikers, mountain bikers and horseback riders may do a section of the trail at a time. From south to north access points include: Weiser, Unity Road, Galloway Dam site, Presley Bridge, Midvale, Shoepeg Road, Cambridge, Goodrich, Mesa Siding, Council, U.S. Highway 95 Bridge, Evergreen Campground, Pine Ridge store, Tamarack and Rubicon.

The non-motorized Weiser River Trail gives you an idea of the changing landscape of the west. The country along it includes completely wild sections, those being farmed and those used for recreation or retreat. You will see traditional farmhouses and barns, historical town buildings, old one-room schoolhouses, cabins, trophy homes and subdivisions with a few houses. Then there are the trestles constructed by the former P.I.N. railroad. Some are entirely of wood except for the new steel railings. They vary from ten feet long to over 200 feet. In April and May the bare hills along the lower part of the trail are such a bright green they resemble those in photographs of Ireland. In October, the sections above Cambridge display the golds of aspens and cottonwoods and the reds of serviceberry, chokecherry and huckleberry. Between Council and the end of the trail at the old siding called Rubicon the trail runs through hills covered with Ponderosa Pine and Douglas fir. Between Weiser and Council the hills along the trail are mostly treeless and covered with grasses, sagebrush, and in places bitterbrush. The miles are marked with new mile markers, with the numbers made of bent railroad spikes from the P.I.N. It is amazing how much work on this trail the private, non-profit Friends of the Weiser River Trail has accomplished in only ten years, especially since part of the railbed between Weiser and

**Weiser River Trail trestle bridge near the old siding called Concrete**

Midvale washed away in a 1997 flood. There is no charge for use of the trail, but memberships and donations are strongly encouraged and donations are deductible.

You can walk the trail most of the year. In winter, cross-country skis or snowshoes are often needed, especially for the upper half of the trail. At present, there is no grooming for skiing or snowshoeing.

From Weiser to Council the trestles have all been planked and had railings installed and the trail surface has no washouts. From now on it will be rolled at least once a year in the spring to smooth the surface and sink the railroad ballast rocks back into the dirt. In this section there are a few livestock control gates that can easily be opened if they are closed. The trail has been completed, except for the last few railings, which will be finished by Friends of the Weiser River Trail's tenth anniversary in June, 2007. Three sections in towns have been paved: in Cambridge, in Council, and from US 95 to paved parking and a restroom at E. 12th and Main in Weiser. Consult the Friends of the Weiser River Trail Web site at www.weiserrivertrail.org for more information.

Note that the mileages given in the descriptions below are consecutive, beginning with .5 mile at the beginning of the trail at U.S. 95 in Weiser. Union Pacific owns the first half mile of the old railroad, from the Weiser depot to U.S. 95. Because the elevation is low and the trail is next to water, remember to watch for rattlesnakes from April through October.

Friends of the Weiser River Trail owns the railway corridor under the Federal Railbanking Act. All the land outside of the old railway corridor along the trail belongs to someone else and most of it is private property. Please respect this and do not wander out of the trail corridor. The BLM maps of the area, Weiser for the southern part and McCall for the northern, show the land ownership.

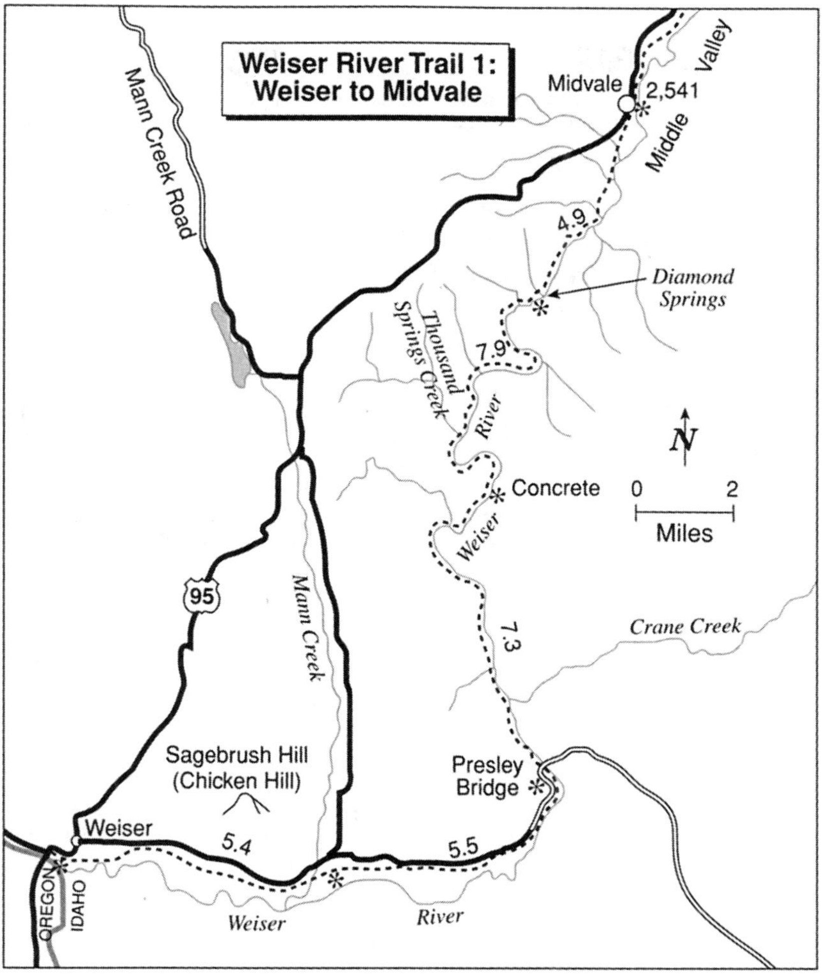


## Weiser to Unity Bridge: Mile .5 to 5.9

**Distance:** 5.4 miles
**Maps:** Weiser South, Weiser Cove
**Access:** The trail starts in Weiser just north of the bridge over the Weiser River on U.S. Highway 95.

From where the railroad crossed U.S. Highway 95, the trail goes along the southern edge of the City of Weiser. Note that the distances shown by the trail's mile markers are measured from the Weiser depot, .5 mile before the beginning of the trail. At .7 mile from U.S. 95, the trail runs through farm fields with views of the hills around Weiser, such as the high hill to the north called Chicken Hill by locals and Sagebrush Hill by the U.S.G.S. on the topographic map. This section has two trestles, a 15-foot one at 2.3 miles and one over Mann Creek, at 5.2 miles, which is about 40 feet long. At 5.9 miles the trail reaches Unity Road, an access point for the trail, where there is parking. On the railroad there was a siding here called Rebecca. Up on the nearby hills somewhere is an area designated the Rebecca Sand Hill Research Natural Area. It was established by the BLM to protect unusually large bitterbrush and a rare plant, Mulford's milk vetch, as well as the black-throated sparrow.

## Unity Bridge to the Galloway Dam Site and Presley Bridge: Mile 5.9 to 11.4

**Distance:** 5.5 miles
**Maps:** Weiser Cove, Mann Creek
**Access:** From U.S. Highway 95 in Weiser turn right (east) at the traffic light by Park School onto Park Street, which becomes the Weiser River Road. Just past the Mann Creek Road, turn right (south) at 5.3 miles on Unity Road. At 5.5 miles just before the road crosses the river it crosses the trail and there is a small place to park.

This section of the trail goes through farm fields, with views of the hills above, the river canyon and the scar of an old mercury mine on a hill ahead. The Weiser River is at a distance to the south until you get close to the Galloway Dam. From the Unity Road the trail goes along through fields and at about 7 miles crosses the Galloway irrigation canal to the right (east) side. From then on to the Galloway Dam the canal is between the trail and the river. At 7.3 miles the trail comes close to the Weiser River Road in a curve, and from 7.9 miles to the Galloway Dam at 10 miles goes right along the road. Just beyond the Galloway Dam is a parking area for fishing access that can be used for trail access.

Those with horses who are planning to ride up the canyon from the Presley Bridge will probably want to unload the horses and leave the trailers here. The road is paved to this point, then turns to gravel and climbs 100 feet above the river, descending to cross the Presley Bridge at 11.4 miles. The trail from the dam to Presley Bridge is enclosed in a canyon for the first time.

## Presley Bridge to Midvale: Mile 11.4 to 31.5

**Distance:** 20.1 miles
**Maps:** Mann Creek, Midvale Hill, Midvale
**Access:** From Weiser on U.S. Highway 95 turn right (east) at the stoplight by Park School onto Park Street, which becomes the Weiser River Road. Drive 10 miles to the Galloway Dam where the pavement ends. Continue to where the trail crosses the road just before the Presley Bridge at 11.4 miles. There is a new parking area between the Galloway Dam and Presley Bridge, about 11 miles from Weiser.

This is the truly wild part of the canyon, where for about 15 miles there are no houses and no farms. The hills gradually close in and become more than 1,000 feet high on both sides of the river. Lava cliffs and grotesque outcrops decorate their sides and tops. The canyon has only a few riparian shrubs and trees here, much less than you'll see higher up. Those traveling this section see a lot of wildlife: deer, elk, otter, beaver, great blue heron and golden and bald eagles. It is a long section for a day hike, but the Friends of the Weiser River Trail hasn't yet developed a campground in this section.

From the Presley Bridge the trail goes over a short trestle and passes a small farm and pasture. Along the river, some of the shrubs have clematis vines growing on them, which have large white to purplish flowers in spring and seed heads like grayish cotton balls in the fall. From 12.4 to 13 miles a bluff of cliffs rises above the trail on the left. Just past this, Crane Creek comes in on the other side of the river. At about 13.5 miles, you see on the other side of the river the last house for 15 miles.

Another steep bluff is above the trail on the left from 14.5 to 15 miles. At about 15.7 miles, a concrete hopper rises above the trail. It was used to store the rye raised nearby and to load it into railroad cars. From 15 to 16 miles, the trail curves gradually to the left on a big grassy flat, then goes along below cliffs where a couple of little canyons come in from the left. At 17 miles, the river and trail make a huge bend to the right (east) and you can see a long trestle ahead. At 18.2 miles, the trail crosses the trestle, which is above a little creek that has water all year.

Just beyond the trestle, the river makes a sharp-pointed turn to the left (north) and a more gentle one to the northeast. Now the hills begin to get taller on both sides of the river. From 18.7 to 19.5 miles the trail is double width. This was the old railroad siding called Concrete.

Next the river makes two huge hairpin bends, first left and then right. At the first bend a narrow flat bench is on the left and at the second bend a bigger, higher bench is on the right. Then a flat begins on the left side. It is cut by Thousand Springs Creek at 21.7 miles, which has a long, high trestle over it and flat patch of grass and some locust trees. A black lava mountain rises on the east just beyond here. At 23.5 Sheep Creek comes in on the left, and it too has a high trestle. Beyond here streaks of black lava talus run up through the grass and sagebrush of the canyon walls. The river uses 2 miles in making another hairpin turn from east to northwest. At this bend a little canyon comes in from the east.

At 26 miles, the river turns northeast, and the canyon narrows. From this bend you can see ahead a 40-foot black outcrop just above the trail. About 100 yards beyond it at 26.6 miles, a foot-wide creek rushes noisily down the canyon wall all year. Just beyond it, two-foot cement squares mark the location of a water tank for the trains. There are two more little springs before a small flat on the west side of the trail, then another spring and a creek. The area was called Diamond Springs by the railroaders and they had a section house, bunk house and tool house here. Bright green watercress grows in all the springs. North of the creek on the west side is a big, long flat. Three or four watercourses come down the hillside and above you can see rockwork holding up an old road that parallels the trail high above and then descends to the trail. Across the river at mile 29, Deep Creek comes in at an angle.

Now the trail comes out of the canyon onto farm fields and pastures south of Midvale. When the leaves are off the trees you may be able to see some heron nests in the cottonwoods on the right. The river comes close to the trail again in a bend at 30.5 miles, then moves away from it again. At 31.5 miles, it enters Midvale between a restaurant and an old tin-covered grain elevator.

## Midvale to Shoepeg Road and Cambridge: Mile 31.5 to 40.4

**Distance:** 8.9 miles
**Maps:** Midvale, Cambridge

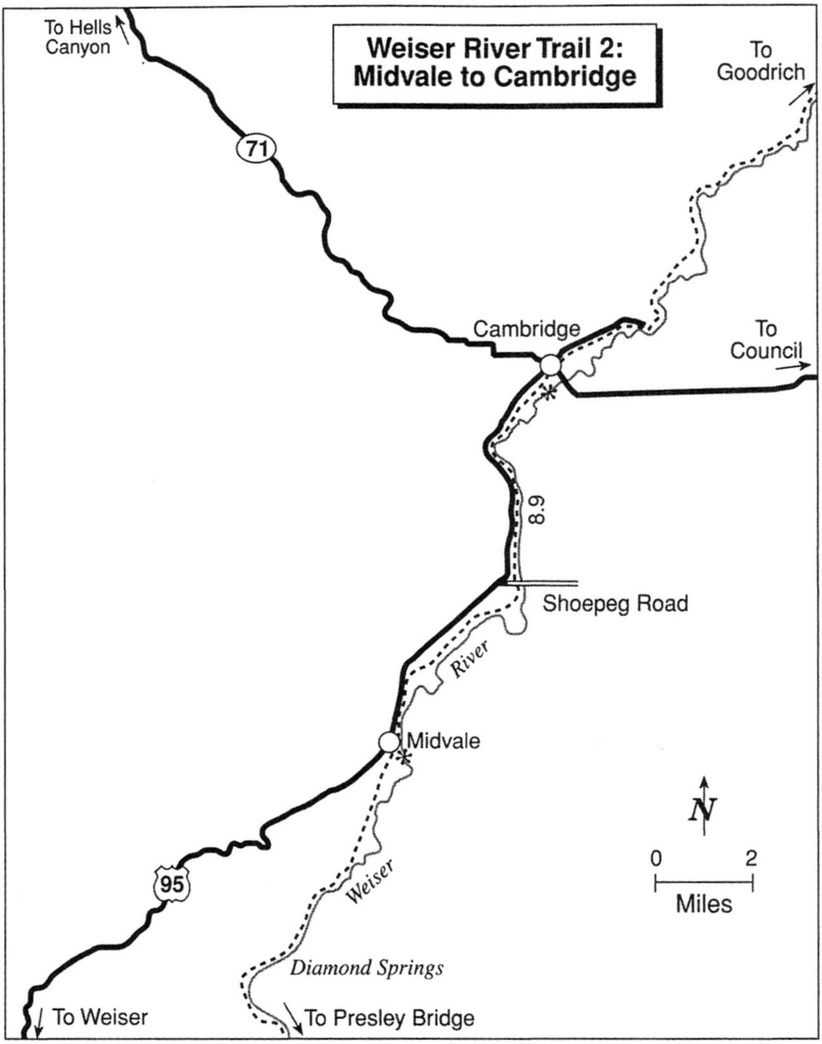


**Access:** On U.S. Highway 95 drive 20 miles from Weiser to Midvale. Park next to the trail at the Midvale City Park.

In the upper part of this section layers of dark lava stair step up some of the hills with grassy slopes between steps, resembling tiered cakes with runny icing.

From Midvale the trail goes through the town and farm fields along the east side of the highway for 1.2 miles. Much of this section was elevated above ground level in 1997 to prevent future flooding. At 32 miles, the trail is between the river and the highway, then the river loops away from the trail and returns near where Shoepeg

Road crosses the trail at 35.3 miles. At 35.8 miles, the trail enters a narrow canyon and runs along below U.S. 95 next to the west bank of the river. At 38.6 miles, the Little Weiser River enters the river from the east, just before a dirt road (the old highway) crosses the trail and ends at the river where a bridge washed out. There is parking by the trail here. Next, the trail crosses farm fields to Cambridge at 39.7 miles. It goes northeast through town a couple of blocks east of the highway and parallel to it. At 40.3 miles the trail goes through the Washington County Fairgrounds. In the center of town, U.S. Highway 95 makes a 90-degree turn to the right, so that the trail must cross it to continue north. Next to the trail, just before it crosses the highway at 40.4 miles, there is plenty of parking at the fairgrounds.

## Cambridge to Goodrich: Mile 40.4 to 49.8

**Distance:** 9.4 miles

**Maps:** Cambridge, East of Cambridge, Goodrich

**Access:** Drive to Cambridge on U.S. Highway 95 and find where the trail crosses the highway after the highway turns east. Park near the trail in the Washington County Fairgrounds south of the highway. You can also access the trail 2 miles farther north by keeping straight ahead in Cambridge where the highway turns east. In .2 mile when the road splits, turn right on Sawmill Road. Drive to where the trail crosses the road just before a road bridge over the river at 42.2 miles.

This section is semi-wild with lots of cottonwood and willow trees and riparian shrubs and the river winding back and forth in lazy curves below open hillsides. From Cambridge the trail goes through open fields, both before and after Sawmill Road, mostly at a distance from the river. At 44.5 miles, the trail and river enter a narrow canyon that within a half mile becomes thick with cottonwood trees and riparian shrubs, but there are still large flats beside the river. The canyon walls are steep grassy slopes with only the occasional outcrop. The vegetation is so dense black bears like it here and once there must have been grizzlies for Grizzly Creek is crossed on a trestle at 46 miles. At 49.7 miles, the trail goes over Goodrich Creek on a trestle and meets the Goodrich Creek Road.

## Goodrich to Mesa Siding and Council: Mile 49.8 to 60.3

**Distance:** 10.5 miles

**Maps:** Goodrich, Council

**Access:** From U.S. Highway 95 drive 16.9 miles north of the U.S. Highway 95 corner in Cambridge to a sign for the Goodrich Creek Road, just south of where the highway crosses the Middle Fork of the Weiser River. Turn left (west) and drive 4.5 miles on the gravel road to a junction with the Goodrich Creek Road. Here turn right (north) onto the Goodrich Creek Road, which goes up a hill and then descends to cross the Weiser River and the trail at 5.6 miles. Parking is limited. You can also reach this trail section by driving 3.4 miles south of the city square in Council to Mesa Siding, the point where the trail approaches the highway from the southwest and runs north along it.

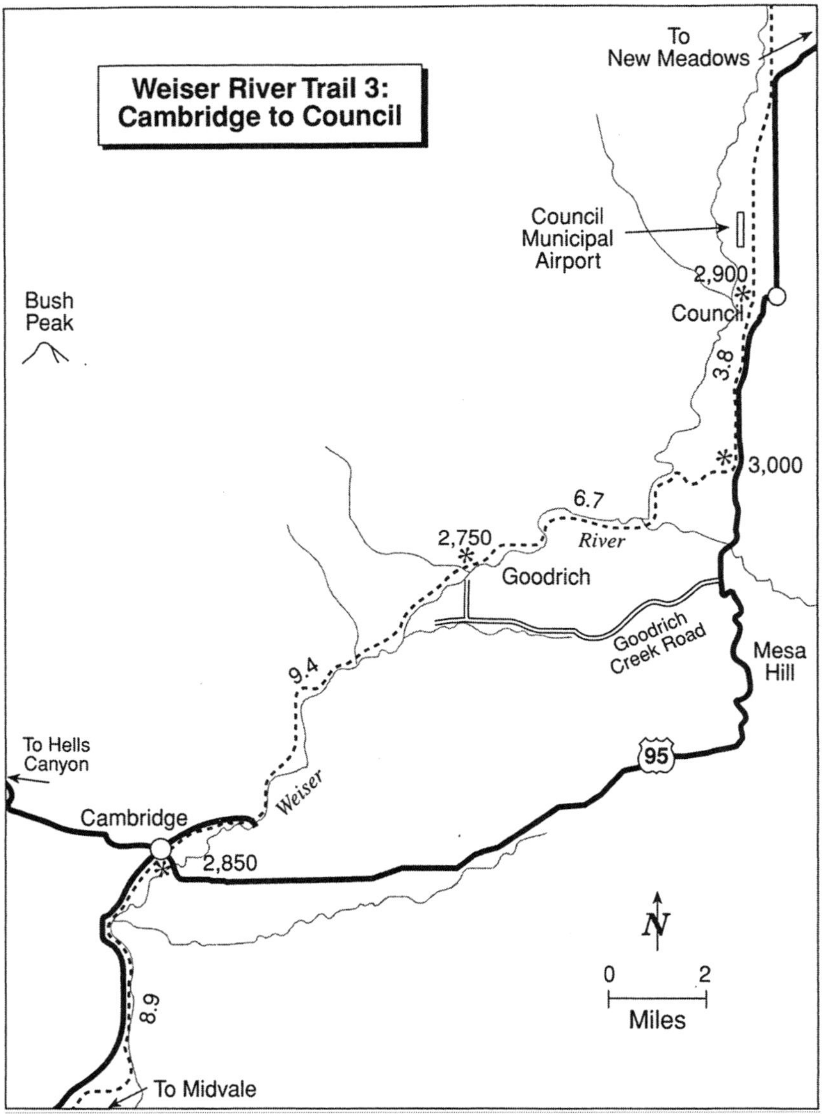


This section of trail is through another riparian jungle with many tall shrubs, big cottonwoods and large aspens. There are a couple of groves of ponderosa pines and Douglas firs above the trail. Highlights are the old school house at the village of Goodrich, and two steel bridges, one over the river and one over its middle fork. It is not as wild as the section from Cambridge to Goodrich because there are more houses and at the Mesa end the beginning of a subdivision.

As you begin walking, the old schoolhouse is behind the house with the blue roof on private land. The trail crosses a short trestle, then comes to an area of huge cottonwoods at Mile 50. The base of an occasional tree has been gnawed on by beaver. Dark clumps of bitterbrush are on the hills above. At Mile 51.5 the trail crosses the river to the right (southeast) side. The middle of the bridge is wider than at the ends and has only the steel walls as railings. At 52 miles, the trail goes along under the cliffs of a road cut, on a section of fill, with aspens on the uphill side. The river continues to wind across a broad, wooded plain. At 54 miles, the trail crosses the Middle Fork of the Weiser River on a curved steel bridge-trestle combination. Just before the bridge a road along the Middle Fork comes in from the highway and there are a couple of farms. Beyond here, the canyon is wild again and heavily wooded. At 55 miles, the river and the trail part company, with the river going north and the trail going east along the south side of an unnamed creek. Part way up is a house on the other side of the creek with a road leading from the highway to it. At Mesa Siding, which is next to U.S. Highway 95 at 56.5 miles, there is plenty of parking, so it is a good access point. The trail continues along the left side of the highway to Council, where it crosses the Hornet Creek Road at 60.3 miles.

## Council to U.S. Highway 95 Bridge: Mile 60.3 to 74

**Distance:** 13.7 miles
**Maps:** Council, Fruitvale
**Access:** In Council turn left (west) at the city square on the Hornet Creek Road that goes to Bear and drive about three blocks to the city park, where there is plenty of parking. This section has not yet been completed.

In this section the trail passes the Council airport at 61.3 miles, crosses fields north of Council and then enters a ponderosa pine forest, at first going along the left (west) side of the road between the road and the river. It goes along near the Fruitvale-Glendale Road past several cabins and houses, over a bridge at 67.6 miles and past the old Starkey hot springs at 69 miles (no longer open to the public). The bridge at 67.6 miles was washed out in the flood of 1997, removed, rebuilt and reinstalled by the Friends of the Weiser River Trail. After passing several cottages in the village of Glendale at 72 miles, the trail crosses back to the east side of U.S. Highway 95 by going UNDER the highway bridge that goes over the Weiser River between Council and Tamarack at 74.3 miles.

## U.S. Highway 95 Bridge to Evergreen Campground and Pine Ridge Store: Mile 74 to 81

**Distance:** 7 miles
**Maps:** Fruitvale, Tamarack
**Access:** Drive 9.9 miles north of Council on U.S. Highway 95 to where the highway goes over the Weiser River, just after it crosses the East Fork of the Weiser. Drive across the river on the highway bridge and turn left (west) onto the Fruitvale-Glendale Road, where there is parking. Walk across the highway to the east side, WATCHING CAREFULLY FOR TRAFFIC. Then look for a little dirt road that heads steeply downhill to the river where it connects with the trail at the north end of the highway bridge. The trestles on this section will all be planked and railed by the tenth anniver-

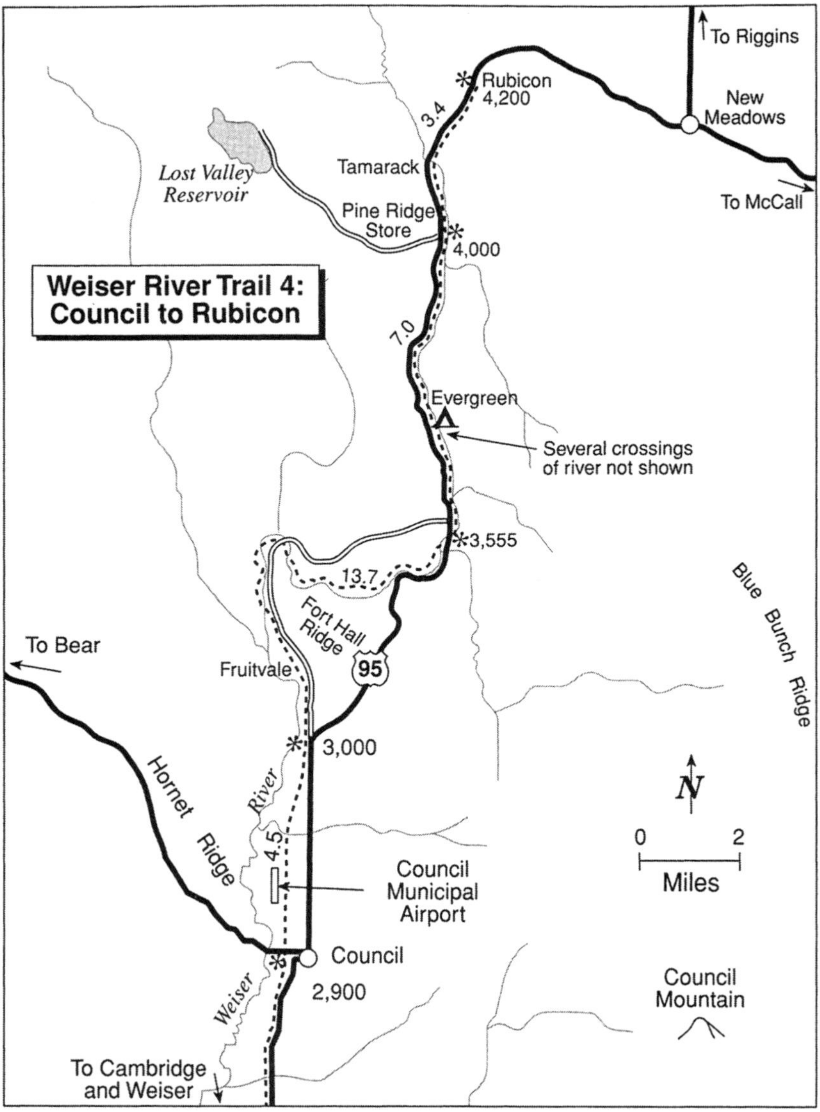


sary celebration in June 2007. A land exchange has opened land for a campground and trailhead at the Rubicon (north) end of the trail.

The hillsides along this section of the trail are heavily wooded and there are several houses, but because of the dense forest and thick riparian shrubs neither the houses nor the noise from the highway reduces the beauty of the green hills, the rushing river or the 15 old trestles.

Once you find the trail it is fun to look back and see it crossing the river under the

U.S. Highway 95 bridge. As you start north, the trail goes over the river twice more on trestles, so it is running along the left side of the river, between it and the highway. Just past a set of houses at 75.5 miles, the trail again crosses back and forth over the river. After passing another set of houses, the trail crosses to the right side on a long trestle into woods. At 76 miles, where the trail curves right, you see across the river the back of the old Evergreen store. At 77.8 miles, you are above the Evergreen Campground. A short, steep path leads down to it so you could reach the trail from the highway here. Beyond the campground is a hillside of bracken fern. At 78 miles, the trail returns to the left of the river, then at 78.6 goes back to the right. Within a short distance it crosses to the left again and comes out into an open valley with houses on the right and the highway next to the trail. Beyond the houses at 79.5 miles, the trail crosses back and forth twice more. At 79.8 miles, it comes to the impassable trestle. Here you must climb a few feet to the highway and walk along it. At 80.1 miles, the trail goes over Beaver Creek. After it does, you could cut down a steep brushy hillside from the highway to the trail or continue along the edge of the highway to the Pine Ridge store at 81 miles.

## Pine Ridge to Tamarack and Rubicon: Mile 81 to 84.4

**Distance:** 3.4 miles
**Maps:** Tamarack, New Meadows
**Access:** Take U.S. Highway 95 north of Council for 16.5 miles to the Pine Ridge store, which is at the turnoff to Lost Valley Reservoir. Park at the store and walk .2 mile north to where a road goes off to the right at an angle into a meadow and crosses the river on an old cement bridge. Walk over this bridge to the trail, which is on the east side of the river here.

This section runs along the opposite side of the river from the lumber mill at Tamarack and then goes through the pretty meadows of Price Valley. The official trail ends at Rubicon, which once had a 15-car siding, a section house, tool house and sawmill. The line reached New Meadows, but the railroad gave up that section years before the trail was begun. A large Y in the tracks at Rubicon allowed the trains to turn around, and there is plenty of parking there.

After the old road bridge crosses the river .2 mile north of the Pine Ridge store, go north along the trail. At 81.5 miles it crosses the river to the west side, but the trail leaves the railroad bed here to follow an old road along the east side of the river. This diversion allows the trail to bypass the lumber mill. The trail returns down a steep grade to the railroad bed at 82.3 miles, just past where the river turns west and runs under the highway. From there the trail goes right along the east side of the highway to its end at Rubicon at 84.4 miles. The rail bed continues to the Meadow Creek Road at 84.7 miles, but that small section is not part of the official trail.

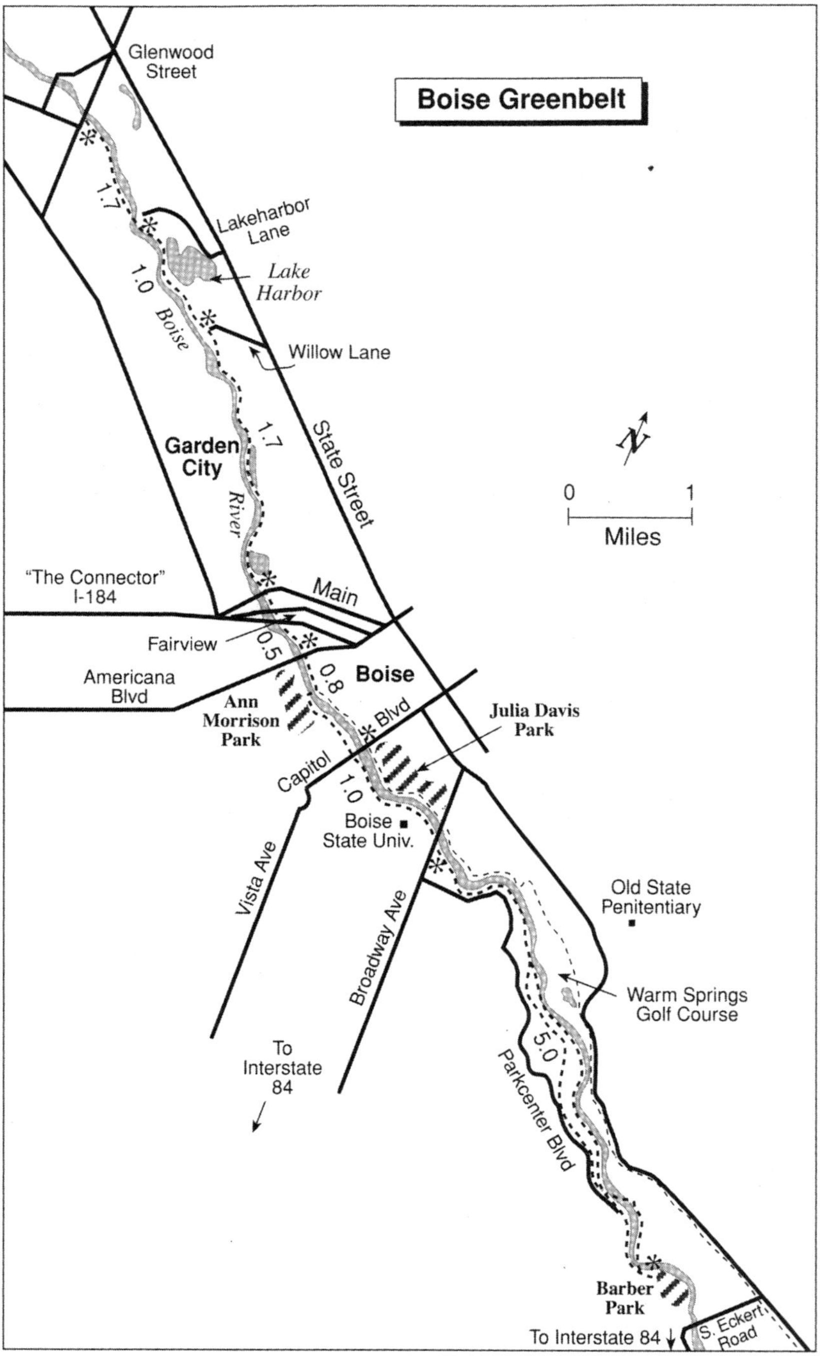
Boise Greenbelt
Glenwood Street
Lakeharbor Lane
Lake Harbor
Willow Lane
Boise River
Garden City
State Street
0 1 Miles
"The Connector" I-184
Main
Fairview
Americana Blvd
Boise
Ann Morrison Park
Julia Davis Park
Capitol Blvd
Boise State Univ.
Vista Ave
Broadway Ave
Old State Penitentiary
Warm Springs Golf Course
To Interstate 84
Parkcenter Blvd
Barber Park
To Interstate 84
S. Eckert Road
1.7
1.0
1.7
0.5
0.8
1.0
5.0

# CITY OF BOISE, DEPARTMENT OF PARKS AND RECREATION

# 58.

## Boise Greenbelt: Barber Park to Glenwood

**One-way distance:** 11.7 miles
**Elevation gain:** none
**Elevation loss:** 140 feet
**Highest point:** 2,780 feet
**Maps:** Boise South, Boise North, Eagle (20-foot contours); also, the Ridge to Rivers trail system brochure and the Boise Parks and Recreation Department brochure and website
**Difficulty:** easy to moderate, depending on length walked; time: 5½ hours for whole distance
**Access:** There are several access points along the river, especially Barber, Ann Morrison, Julia Davis and Veterans' parks.

The name Boise gradually came to be used for the present city's river. It was first called Wooded River by Robert Stuart in his journal of his 1812 trip from Astoria to St. Louis over a route that became the Oregon Trail. When Washington Irving wrote *The Adventures of Captain Bonneville* about Benjamin Bonneville's 1831 unsuccessful fur trapping expedition, he said Bonneville's French Canadian fur trappers exclaimed "Les Bois, Les Bois" when they first saw the trees lining the river. The anglicized version of this name stuck.

During three seasons, a curtain of leaves hides the buildings of Boise from those using the Greenbelt. Even though it is an urban park, sections of the Greenbelt seem remote from any city. The blue and silver river meanders through the town forming lagoons and islands which shelter ducks, herons and bald eagles. Along the banks, willows, wild roses, and currants tangle between elms and cottonwoods. At present, there are paved Greenbelt trails on both sides of the river much of the way from Barber Park to Glenwood Street. The route described here is the one that most conveniently provides a through route for walkers. CAUTION: For safety, women shouldn't walk the Greenbelt alone any more.

## Barber Park to Broadway

Most people walk, run or bicycle the Greenbelt a section at a time, but this book describes it beginning at Barber Park and proceeding west on the south side of the river to Ann Morrison Park and after that on the north side to Glenwood Street. Therefore, mileages given refer to the distance from Barber Park. However, mile markers on the Greenbelt pavement begin with zero at 8th Street (Capitol Boulevard) and run east and west, so they will not agree with the mileages given here. From the east end of Barber Park, a paved trail leads north to Idaho Highway 21 and then extends east out to Discovery Park just below Lucky Peak Reservoir. This section can also be accessed from Municipal Park via a trail running through the Warm Springs Golf Course. Going from Barber Park west almost to the Park Center area, the Greenbelt on the south side of the river includes a paved trail along Park Center Boulevard and a gravel trail which follows the river bank—both are wide enough for two to walk abreast. A portion of the trail is closed to bicycles as a wildlife corridor protecting nesting eagles and other birds of prey.

The gravel trail begins in Barber Park at a small parking area just north of the maintenance buildings. It travels through an undeveloped wooded area, the Barber Wildlife Refuge, and crosses a small ditch on a bridge at .8 mile. Beyond this, the trail is rocky for several yards until it enters the city of Boise. Then it passes near a subdivision, where the river area is being preserved in its natural state in return for the development of the subdivision.

The trail crosses a ditch on a culvert and comes to another habitat area, which is 50 yards from large homes. On the left is a creek and across the river is Warm Springs Mesa. The creek widens into a lagoon with cattails beside larger homes.

At the beginning of another subdivision, a paved trail joins from the south, but the Greenbelt continues as a gravel surface and goes under a high voltage transmission line. At 2 miles, the trail crosses a side creek at a sign prohibiting fishing because of trout rearing. Next is a section of the Greenbelt called Harper's Habitat, named for Hugh Harper who preserved the area.

The trail crosses a creek on a bridge into an area of the Greenbelt called Long Island, then goes along a tongue of land called Heron Lake Isthmus between the river and the creek. The 18-hole Warm Springs Municipal Golf Course is on the other side of the river, with the northern Greenbelt Trail going around it to connect with the trail along Idaho 21 to Lucky Peak.

On the south side of the river, the Greenbelt goes between the river and some condominiums. Beyond the condominiums at 3.5 miles from Barber Park, the trail is paved, and open to bicycle traffic. Soon the path goes between the river and a gravel pit pond, a private lake.

Next, the Greenbelt reaches the Park Center complex of office buildings. Here you can turn south on a side street to reach the Park Center Pond or the small, upscale Park Center shopping mall. The next section from Park Center to Broadway Avenue is across the river from Municipal Park. On the south side of the river between Park Center and Broadway, there are some observation decks overlooking the water..

On the north side of the river, between Municipal Park and the Idaho Fish and Game Department building is the Morrison-Knudsen Nature Center, a small park with a stream running from a hilltop to a pond. Underwater windows in the stream allow visitors to view the life cycle of trout.

On the south side of the river, the trail crosses a bridge over Loggers Creek. The creek is actually the remains of an old logging ditch. There are more office buildings and then the trail goes under the Broadway Avenue Bridge at 5 miles.

## Broadway to Capitol Boulevard (8th Street) Bridge, Boise State University and Julia Davis Park

On the south side of the river, the trail goes between a frontage road and the river at the north end of the BSU stadium. It continues along the river to a high arched footbridge (the Gibb Friendship Bridge) which leads over the river to Julia Davis Park and the northern section of the Greenbelt. The trail on the south side continues

**A view from the Boise Greenbelt**

past the classroom buildings and the Morrison Performing Arts Center. You may find it just as interesting to walk the Greenbelt path on the north side of the river through Julia Davis Park. The park contains Zoo Boise, the Boise Art Museum, the Julia Davis Rose Garden, the State Historical Museum, the Black History Museum and the Julia Davis Lagoon with paddle boat rentals. At 6 miles, the south side trail goes under the Capitol Boulevard Bridge.

## Capitol Boulevard (8th Street) Bridge to Americana: Ann Morrison, Kathryn Albertson and Shoreline Parks

Continuing on the south side of the river, the trail first goes under the old 9th Street Bridge, site of McClellan's Ferry which operated here from 1864 to 1868. Next it passes the health science building of Boise State University, a trucking agency and the offices of the Boise Park System and Recreation Department. When it enters Ann Morrison Park, there are picnic tables, shelters and restrooms.

Half way through the park, a footbridge crosses the river to Shoreline Park, giving access to Veterans Park and the section of the Greenbelt that continues to Glenwood Street. The bridge also leads to the Pioneer Walkway which goes north to River Street. Shoreline Park has observation decks and viewpoints and a skate and bicycle rental shop in season.

At 5.8 miles, the trail goes under the Americana Boulevard Bridge. If you decide not to cross the river until the Americana Bridge, you can take a side trip south along

Americana to Kathyrn Albertson Park, which emphasizes natural areas and a 3/4-mile walking loop. However, the Greenbelt does not continue along the south side of the river through this park.

## Americana to Main Street

To continue to Glenwood Street, the trail first goes along the north side of the river. This section passes under five bridges. The trail runs through Riverside Park, then crosses under the old metal railroad bridge and the Broadway-Chinden Connector Bridge. A side path (which is under construction) here leads across an old railroad bridge to Garden Street and Orchard Street.

Next, the Greenbelt trail goes under the Fairview Avenue Bridge. Beyond it, there is a gravel bar in the river large enough to host large shrubs. The trail then passes the grounds of an inn. At 7.3 miles, the Greenbelt runs under the Main Street Bridge.

## Main Street to the Willow Lane Park and Athletic Sports Complex

The paved trail continues along the north side of the river. Quinn's Pond, at 7.5 miles, provides a view of Shafer Butte and the rest of the Boise Front. The trail goes south over a slough of the river and veers to the left where a fence and gate are signed "no trespassing". This property will one day be a regional park for the City of Boise. West of the pond is a spur path to a parking lot on Pleasanton Avenue.

The Greenbelt trail crosses a small creek on a bridge and, at 8.2 miles, comes to Boise Cascade Lake, which has a fishing dock. This area is on the grounds of the old Idaho Soldiers Home, built in the 1890s. Beyond the lake, the trail meets a wooden footbridge that leads northeast into Veterans' Park. Continue straight ahead in a tunnel of trees. A slough is on your right and the river is on your left. At 8.8 miles, there is an automobile bridge over the river known as Veterans Parkway that provides access from Garden City to North Boise. The trail continues under the bridge of the parkway, then crosses the slough and jogs right and then left to the sewage disposal plant. It travels through landscaped grounds to a Greenbelt parking area and restrooms at 9 miles.

## Willow Lane Park and Athletic Sports Complex to Lake Harbor

This 1-mile section of the Greenbelt has been completed since the last edition of this book. From the parking area at the sewage disposal plant the trail goes along the east side of the tournament soccer field and across the river end of it. Next it passes a large parking area, then goes along the south side of the fenced playing fields. There is a "Swedish jogging trail" with exercise stations here. After passing some houses, it reaches Willow Lane at 9.5 miles.

From Willow Lane, the Greenbelt trail curves toward the river and enters an area that is heavily wooded with lots of big cottonwoods and maples. There are signs for wildlife habitat. The path crosses three small bridges and one longer one over wet areas and sloughs. Then it goes along the edge of a subdivision where you see the river on the left and a sign asks you not to disturb the bald eagles that live here. Soon you see the lake of Lake Harbor on your right and a road runs between it and the Greenbelt. Beyond the lake is another subdivision and Lakeharbor Lane at 10 miles.

## Lake Harbor to Glenwood

From Lake Harbor Lane, the paved trail curves toward another lake, called Silver Lake, and meets a side trail. The Greenbelt trail continues west to the bank of the river and along it on the south side of Plantation Golf Course. Then on footbridges, the path crosses a channel of the river, then an island, and a second channel to the south side of the river at about 11 miles. Beyond the second channel, a paved trail comes in from the east that extends a short distance along the south side of the river. Turn right (west) on the final section of the Greenbelt Trail, which sneaks between the chain link fence enclosing the stables and trailer area for the Fairgrounds and reaches the Glenwood Street Bridge over the river, 11.7 miles from Barber Park. West of Glenwood there is 1 to 2 miles of Greenbelt trail on the south side of the river only.

# BUREAU OF LAND MANAGEMENT
# LOWER SNAKE RIVER DISTRICT
# BOISE AREA

## 59.

## Oregon Trail at Bonneville Point

**Through trip:** 4.7 miles
**Elevation gain:** 20 feet
**Elevation loss:** 810 feet (return climb)
**Highest point:** 3,860 feet
**Maps:** Indian Creek Reservoir (20-foot contours), Lucky Peak
**Difficulty:** easy; time: 3 1/2 hours one-way, plus shuttle driving time
**Access:** Turn off I-84 at the Blacks Creek exit 10 miles southeast of Boise's Gowen Field exit and turn left (north) off the exit road. Drive 2.7 miles east on the paved Blacks Creek Road to a junction. Turn left (northeast) onto a gravel road and drive 1.3 miles to the interpretive site (or for an additional hike go straight ahead for 1.3 miles to where the marked Oregon Trail intersects the road).

After hundreds of miles of barren desert, the Oregon Trail, now a National Historic Trail, tops Bonneville Point with a view of the oasis of the Boise Valley. Bonneville Point is named for Captain Benjamin Bonneville, whose fur trappers supposedly first saw the Boise Valley from here in May 1833. He was following the route pioneered by the Astorians in 1812, described in writing by an expedition member,

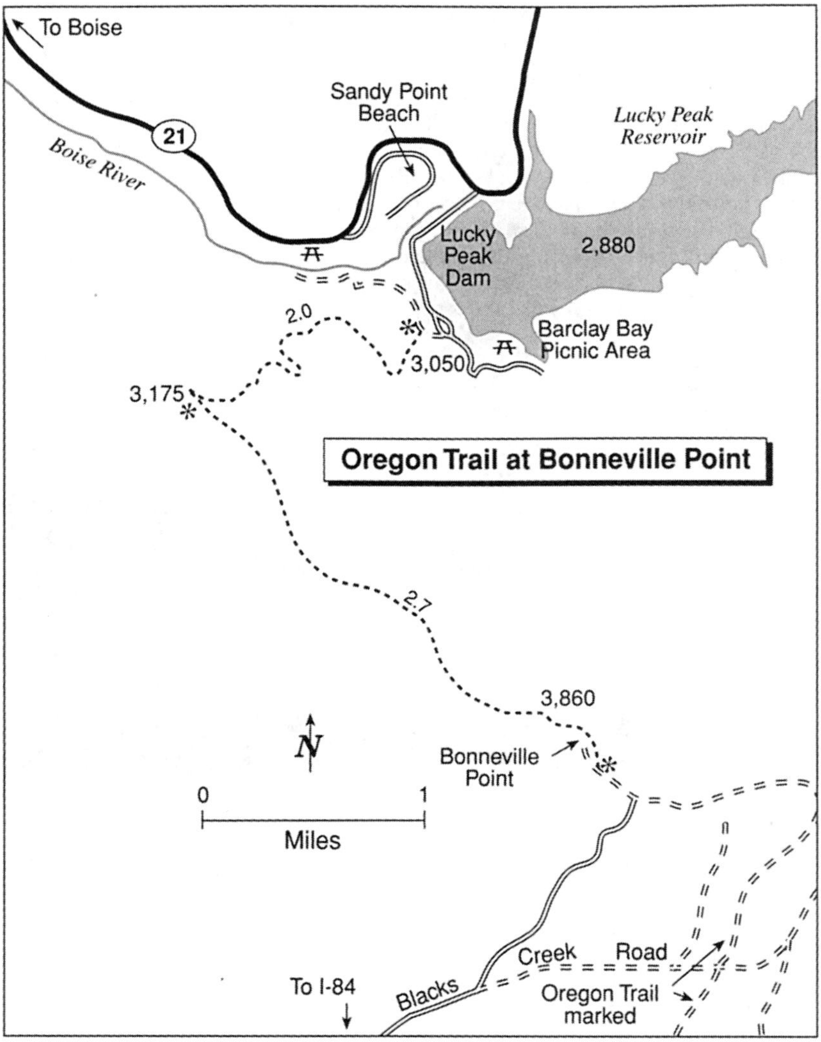


Robert Stuart, and later used as the Oregon Trail.

The archeological site of the Foote House is near Lucky Peak Dam, but it hasn't been marked for the public. Mary Hallock Foote lived in Idaho while her husband, Arthur, worked as the engineer for the initial unsuccessful effort to build the New York Canal. While living there, she wrote and illustrated novels and short stories of life in the West. Her narratives of life in this house were used by Wallace Stegner as the basis for part of his novel *Angle of Repose*.

Hiking along the Oregon Trail near Bonneville Point gives you an idea of what it was like to travel the Oregon Trail. Part of the original track still shows among the sagebrush as a great groove in the land. The Bureau of Land Management has marked the route near here with four-foot cement posts. Near the end of the hike, Lucky Peak Reservoir spreads out below wrinkled velvet hills. To feel the drama of pioneers seeing the Boise Valley for the first time, continue straight ahead on the Blacks Creek Road when the side road to Bonneville Point turns off and go 1.3 miles to where the Oregon Trail crosses the road. Then walk to Bonneville Point along the 2.5 miles of marked Oregon Trail. At the Bonneville Point interpretive site are trees, a stone memorial and an interpretive display. Do this hike in May, if possible, when wildflowers like yellow arrowleaf balsamroot are in full bloom.

To hike towards the Boise Valley from the interpretive site, follow the cement markers downhill from the northwest end of the site along a section of the original trail and across a fence to a dirt road at 150 yards. At .4 mile, this road splits. Take the left branch to follow the markers, which soon leave the road for a section of the original route. At 1 mile, the cement posts rejoin the road and the two roads merge. The road passes a jeep track on the left at 1.5 miles, and at 2 miles, descends beside a gully. At 2.2 miles, the markers leave the road to climb along a hillside on the right. From here, the Oregon Trail drops back to the road at 2.7 miles near a junction with a primitive road leading northeast to Lucky Peak Dam.

Hikers can continue northwest along the road to the edge of Boise, but it is more interesting to follow the primitive road to Lucky Peak Dam. At 3.7 miles, it runs above dark lava cliffs which brood over the Boise River and frame a slice of green valley. (Farther west, a section of the Oregon Trail descends this lava rim to the river.) At 4 miles, there is a gate. Beyond it at 4.2 miles, the road turns left. It passes a track on the right at 4.5 miles. The dam and boat launch are at 4.7 miles.

# 60.

## Hulls Gulch

**One-way distance:** 3.5 miles
**Elevation gain or loss:** 1,120 feet one-way
**Highest point:** 5,000 feet
**Maps:** Boise North, Robie Creek
**Difficulty:** easy; time: 2 to 3 hours one-way

**Access:** Drive north on Boise's 8th Street to a sign for Hulls Gulch that gives mileages to the different trailheads. At present the pavement ends .2 mile beyond this sign. At .6 mile is the first parking lot for the lower trailhead for the Lower Hulls Gulch Trail, and the second at .8 mile. The road beyond here has a dirt surface. At 3 miles, you pass the gate where the road is closed in the winter. At 3.2 miles and 3.5 miles are two more trailheads. Beyond here the road is rutted and rough. Continue to the upper trailhead at 6.2 miles. This hike description starts there and covers the Upper Hulls Gulch Trail, which runs from there to two trailheads that are at 3.2 and 3.5 miles on the road. At those trailheads the upper trail changes its name to the Lower Hulls Gulch Trail. The Hulls Gulch Trail is not on the topographic map, so it is difficult to measure your progress; however, a Ridge to River System map, avail-

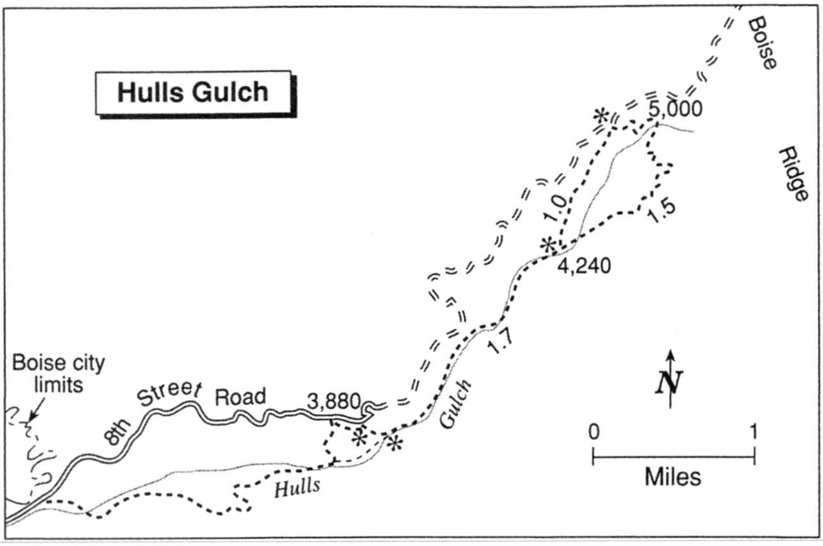


able from outdoor stores, may help you do this.

The boom in the Boise Basin gold camps led to the beginning of Boise City. Farmers began to farm nearby land to supply the miners with food and a military post was established to protect travelers to the mines. In 1863, Frank Davis built the first cabin in the Treasure Valley. Later that year, Major Pinckney Lugenbeel was dispatched to build a fort to protect the area from Indians. On July 4, Lugenbeel found a site for the fort along the road from Boise Basin to the Owyhees. On July 7, farmers met in the Davis-Ritchey cabin to form a town. Henry Riggs laid out the town and named it Boise for the river. To obtain materials for the fort, Lugenbeel constructed a mule-driven sawmill up Cottonwood Creek and dug a quarry, the signs of which still exist near the Old Penitentiary.

Built by the Bureau of Land Management and volunteer groups, this trail winds along a rushing stream beside wildflowers, willows and other shrubs only 15 minutes from Boise. In June the upper slopes are blanketed with blue flax in bloom, and the lower slopes may be hopping with Mormon crickets. Above, dark pines blanket Boise Ridge and below spreads the entire Treasure Valley. Since the last edition of this book, Hulls Gulch burned in the Foothills Fire of 1997, and a flood then knocked over the burned trees along the creek and washed out the bridges, which have now been reconstructed. Another change is that the lower trail now connects with the upper, so you can hike the whole trail if you wish.

To walk the upper trail easily, it is a good idea to use two vehicles and hike from the sign for the upper trail down to one of the two middle trailheads. By way of a cut-off trail, you can also make a 2.5 mile loop hike from the upper trailhead. The trail is closed to motorcycles and mountain bikes. Even in spring it is often hot, so be sure to carry enough water. The road to the trailhead is open from early spring to late fall, but it may be too hot in midsummer except for morning and evening. There are restrooms at the trailheads but none along the trail.

From the upper sign, the trail slants across a sagebrush hillside towards two branches of the creek in Hulls Gulch. Fifty vertical feet below the sign at .2 mile, the cutoff trail that allows a loop trip from the upper trailhead turns off to the right downhill. The main trail curves back in and out of gullies, and crosses two little streams in ravines; the second of these has a small waterfall below it. The trail crosses the southern branch of the creek.

Wildflowers such as arrowleaf balsamroot, larkspur and pink phlox decorate the trail in spring. Sagebrush, bitterbrush and grasses grow on the open hillsides. Due to fire, overuse and motor vehicle damage, most of the Boise Front, the hillside region above Boise, no longer has enough deep-rooted perennial grasses to prevent erosion on these hillsides.

After you have climbed down the steeper part of the trail, it crosses back to the northwest side of the creek below the junction of the two branches. At 1.5 miles is the junction with the 1- mile cutoff trail that climbs back to the upper trailhead, forming a 2.5-mile loop. To continue to the upper of the two middle trailheads, keep straight ahead here for 2.3 more miles. Beyond the junction, the main trail follows the creek with granite outcrops of the Idaho batholith just above, staying farther above the creek than it did before the fire and flood. The creek, larger now, gurgles along over rocks and beside syringa, bitterbrush, red osier dogwood, golden currant and elderberry. In the fall, the canyon glows with red and gold leaves of these shrubs and the golden flowers of rabbit brush. The trail crosses the creek back to the east side at 2 miles, but soon returns to the west and then the east again. At 3.2 miles, is a junction with a trail called the Crane Gulch Connector, which continues down the creek to the Lower Hulls Gulch Trail. (On this trail and the Lower Hulls Gulch Trail you can hike down 3 miles over open slopes to the second of the lower parking lots .6 mile up the 8th Street Road.) To reach the middle parking lots and the end of the Upper Hulls Gulch Trail instead, turn right (north) at this junction and follow a trail up a sagebrush hillside to the upper one of the middle trailheads. At the top of the hill you climb on the way up to this trailhead from the gulch, a level .2 mile trail connects the parking areas for the two middle trailheads.

# SNAKE RIVER BIRDS OF PREY NATIONAL CONSERVATION AREA

## 61.

## Halverson Lakes

**Loop trip:** 3 miles
**Elevation gain:** 100 feet
**Highest point:** 2,360 feet
**Maps:** Walters Butte, Initial Point

**Halverson Lake**

**Difficulty:** easy; time: 3 hours

**Access:** From the Nampa Boulevard-Marsing exit on I-84 go south, crossing 2nd and 3rd streets and continuing on Yale, which curves left and becomes 7th. Go 7 blocks to 12th Avenue. Turn right and follow 12th Avenue as it curves left and goes south past the high school and Mercy Medical Center. Continue south on this road, which becomes Idaho 45. At 15.2 miles, turn left (east) off this highway toward Melba. At 18.2 miles, turn right (south) on Can-Ada Road. At Baseline Road, turn left for half a block then right on a continuation of Can-Ada Road. At 22.3 miles, turn right (west) on Victory Road at a sign for Celebration Park. The road makes three sharp turns and then winds downhill toward the river and the end of the pavement at 24.7 miles. When it branches at 25.4 miles take the left branch that turns away from the Celebration Park Headquarters and goes south along the river. It goes through a campground at 26 miles and continues to a parking area at 26.5 miles. The road goes .2 mile more before it is gated to motor vehicles, but that section is very rough and there is no parking at the gate.

There is a system of trails around Halverson Lakes, two lakes set among big black boulders of "melon gravel", which is the name geologists have given to boulders torn from the canyon walls and rounded by the Bonneville flood. This flood occurred about 15,000 years ago when prehistoric Lake Bonneville overflowed at Red Rock Pass into the Snake River drainage. The overflow caused erosion of the pass and a flood 150 times as large as the highest water since then on the Snake. It lowered the lake 300 feet to its present level — Lake Bonnevillé is now known as the Great Salt

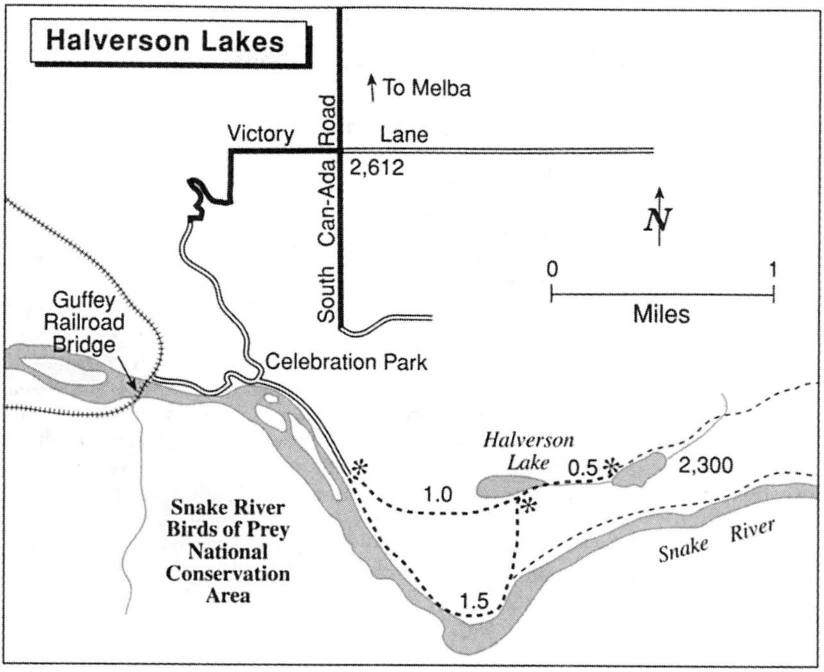


Lake.

The first Halverson lake, which is long and narrow, resembles lakes in the eastern United States because it is surrounded by shrubs and broad-leafed trees, such as cottonwood. Huge black boulders form peninsulas and islands in the lake's usually blue water. Outside the ring of trees is desert. The other lake is a desert lake surrounded by sagebrush, melon gravel boulders and distant lava cliffs. There are only a few shrubs, all at the upper end. Beyond it rises a little butte that looks like stacks of buttons. A strip of sloping white sand divides the lakes from the basaltic columns of the canyon wall. The first lake is named for Albert and Roy Halverson, who once owned property to the north of it. The other is unnamed, but is referred to as Little Halverson Lake. In pre-settlement times the lakes held water only in the spring. They were deepened by homesteaders and when irrigation arrived filled up from irrigation runoff. Now they dry up in the winter only occasionally. The trail system was created when the area around the lakes was closed to motorized vehicles in 1996.

From the trailhead for Halverson Lakes, the trail at first goes along the river. In 100 yards at a sign and map, it splits into three trails. This junction is just east of Sign Island. To reach the lakes, take the middle trail, which climbs a few feet onto a sloping plain covered with thousands of black melon gravel boulders. It winds through the boulders and approaches the side of the first lake at 1 mile. Continue on the trail along the side of the lake, past a junction with a trail that goes south to the river, and cross the little creek between the lakes to the east side. As the trail starts downhill to the second lake, remnants of an old stone house are off to the left. The second lake is at 1.5 miles.

To make a loop along the river trail return .5 mile to the junction with the trail to the river and follow it. It rounds a headland at 2 miles and then goes along a narrow strip of land between riparian shrubs and a 40-foot high earthen bank to the trailhead at 3 miles. In the fall, the river trail is so sandy it is difficult to walk on it. You can return instead along a trail under the canyon wall that stays away from the river and then parallels the road high above it. This trail joins the road near where the river road turns off the road to Celebration Park. On this route the round trip distance is about 4 miles if you park at the road junction.

You can make a longer loop by going around the north side of the second lake and continuing east along the base of the canyon wall to where the wall comes close to the river at 3.5 miles and then returning on a trail along the river. This loop is about 7 miles from the trailhead and goes completely around the button-like butte.

After seeing the lakes you will probably want to tour Celebration Park, which is a Canyon County park. It has a visitors center, usually open only in summer, a large parking area and a picnic area. Paths lead to petroglyphs and the Guffey Bridge. In 1899, a this bridge was built from Guffey, a former village on the north side of the river, across the river to extend a railroad to Murphy, then called Striker Springs, and to the mines at Silver City. However, the tracks never reached Silver City because of recessions in the early 1900s. The bridge still stands and is being preserved as a historical landmark. Murphy, named for an assistant engineer on the railroad project, served as a freight center for Silver City and the surrounding towns, but the railroad tracks have long since been removed. You can walk across the bridge and hike up the river on old roads and paths all the way to Swan Falls.

# 62.

## Birds of Prey Area at Swan Falls

**Round trip:** 5 miles
**Elevation gain:** 80 feet
**Highest point:** 2,340 feet
**Maps:** Sinker Butte (20-foot contours), Wild Horse Butte
**Difficulty:** easy; time: 3 hours

**Access:** Take the Meridian exit from Interstate 84 and drive south and west to Kuna. At 7 miles, the road curves west into Kuna, then at 9.1 miles curves north. At this curve, turn left (south) on a paved road signed Swan Falls. Beginning at 22 miles the road makes a few right angle turns. At 24.7 miles is Dedication Point with a nature trail and a scenic overlook. At 27.7 miles the road starts down into the canyon in a 12% grade with one hairpin turn. Parking and a restroom are at 29.2 miles. Continue driving east along the river through the picnic area to the pavement end and past a boat launch at 29.9 miles. The road continues to the top of an inner canyon hill but is not maintained for public use, so it is best to park near the boat launch.

In the 1840s, parties who wanted to avoid crossing the Snake River twice used the south alternate of the Oregon Trail, which runs through today's Snake River Birds of Prey National Conservation Area on the south side of the Snake River. Military

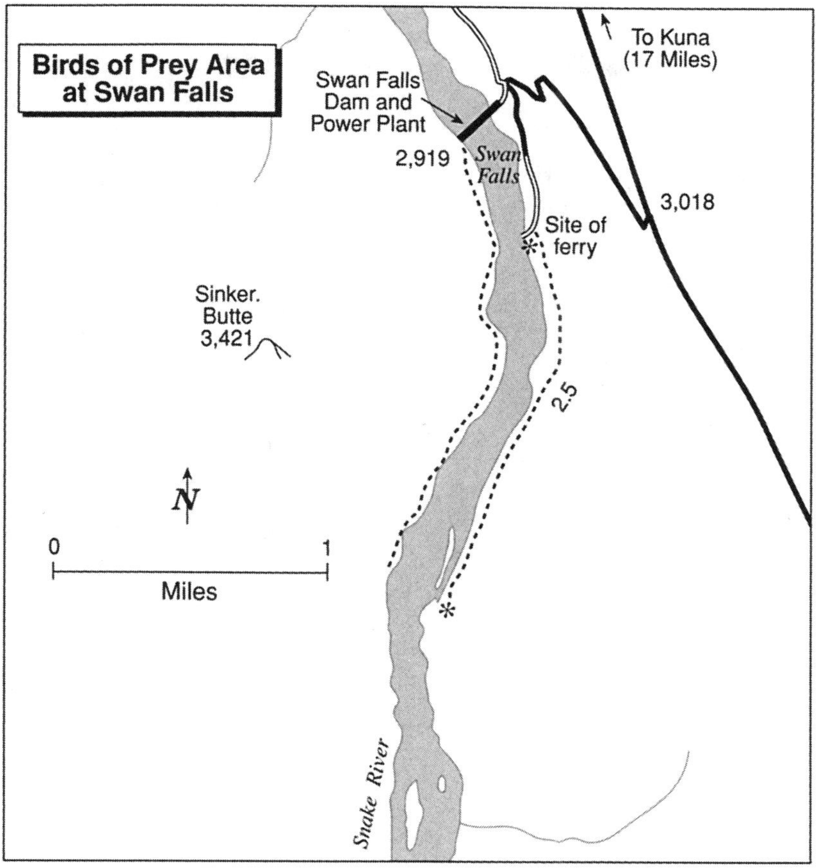


escorts were supposed to meet wagon trains on the south alternate, but they couldn't always prevent Indian trouble. In1901 Swan Falls dam was built to supply nearby Silver City with electricity.

Because the canyon is a major world habitat for raptors, the Snake River Birds of Prey Area was first established here in 1971. It is now officially called the Snake River Birds of Prey National Conservation Area. In addition, the World Center for the Birds of Prey was independently constructed south of Boise by the Peregrine Fund in the late 1980s. The Peregrine Fund, a non-profit organization started to conduct captive breeding of peregrine falcons, moved its headquarters to Boise from Colorado. They did this to be near the Snake River and its raptors and because Boise State University had one of the few programs in the nation studying raptor biology. The raptors here include eagles, falcons, hawks and owls. Golden eagles and prairie falcons are the most abundant species.

The food supply is unique because it is above the canyon nests, which enables birds nesting there to save energy by coasting back down to their nests with their prey. They hunt from two to 10 miles from the canyon, looking for Paiute ground

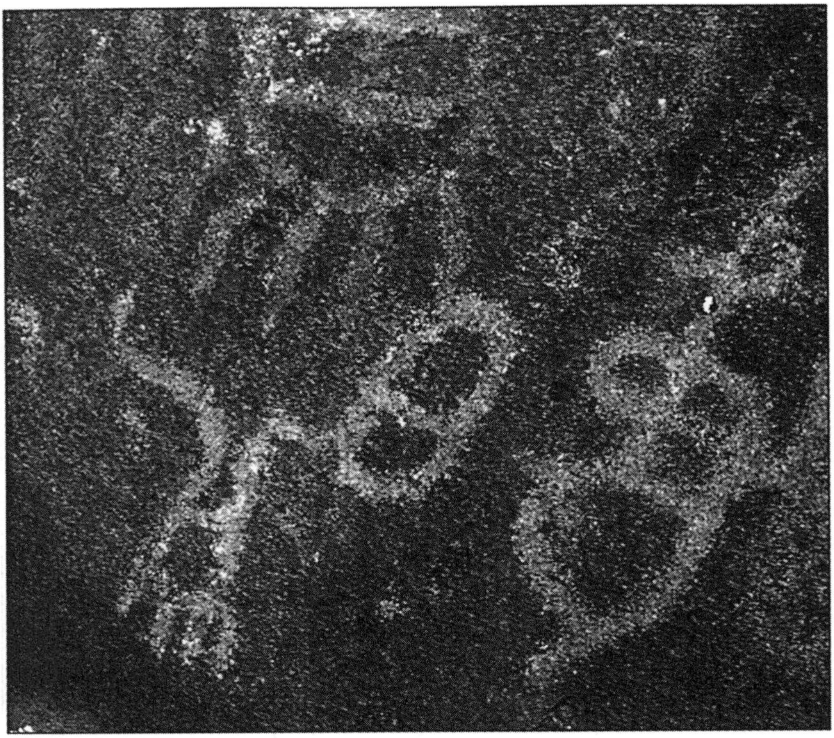

**Ancient petroglyphs**

squirrels (*Spermophilus townsendii*). The birds search mostly north of the canyon because the soils on that side are much finer-grained, allowing easier burrowing for the ground squirrels.

In addition to the birds and their nests, the area contains hundreds of unique Indian petroglyphs. Descriptions of where these petroglyphs are located have never been included in this book because many had already been vandalized when the author first saw them.

In the Snake River Birds of Prey Area, eagles and falcons soar above the cliffs where they nest. In spring, desert wildflowers and shrubs bloom in the bottom of the canyon. On both sides of the river, a wide caramel-colored band of rock stripes the black lava cliffs. It is usually 10 degrees warmer in the canyon than on the plain above, so this is a good hike for cool weather.

This description begins at the boat landing. First, walk along the road beside lava outcrops, keeping to the remnants of the lowest road. A new two-wheel track goes up a steep hill to the edge of the canyon wall. The road along the river becomes a trail at about 1.5 miles that winds beside lava boulders and squeezes past 300-foot black cliffs. At about 2.5 miles on an outcrop, it disappears. From here the lava ship of Sinker Creek Butte looms ahead on the other side of the river. From the outcrop, you may return the same way or continue cross-country along the river for any distance. Birds of Prey brochures are available from the Bureau of Land Management Office at 1387 Vinnell Way in Boise.

At Swan Falls, visitors are welcome at the historic dam and power plant, which provide access to a trail on the other side of the river. This trail leads from the dam upriver for about 2 miles before it dwindles to a deer path. To reach it, walk across the river on a walkway that is joined to the power house and dam. From the first part of this trail you get an excellent view of the dam and powerhouse.

# 63.

## Oregon Trail South Alternate Near Sinker Creek

**Loop trip:** 5.2 miles
**Elevation gain:** 600 feet
**Elevation loss (return climb):** 600 feet
**Highest point:** 3,000 feet
**Map:** Sinker Butte (25-foot contours)
**Difficulty:** moderate, but no sign for trailhead; time: 4 hours

**Access:** Turn left (east) off Idaho 78 onto the paved Murphy Flats Road 3.2 miles south of Murphy. The road turns 90 degrees to the right at 4.1 miles. The road comes to a T-intersection at 4.6 miles. Turn left here on the paved road. At 5.1 miles, the road turns to the right. Where the Murphy Flats and Sinker Butte roads intersect at 8.1 miles, keep straight ahead on the Murphy Flats road. At a Y in the road, where the pavement ends at 8.6 miles, keep straight ahead. The two-wheel track to the left is the other end of the loop hike, so you may want to park or leave a car here. If you drive, the road drops into the canyon of Sinker Creek and enters private property. The road ends 2.2 miles from the Y (10.8 miles from the highway.)

In late summer, much of Sinker Creek dries up. Some say that is the reason for its name. Others say the name is from travelers on the Oregon Trail South Alternate, who used nuggets found there for fishing sinkers. At one time, people believed the 1860 Indian attack on the Utter party occurred at Sinker Creek, but research has shown the attack occurred near Castle Creek, a few miles to the east. Another party may have been attacked at Sinker Creek, since wagon parts and skulls were found there by early settlers. However, travelers' accounts describe doubling their teams to get wagons up the grade at Sinker Creek, so the wagon parts and skulls may simply show the danger of that grade.

Murphy, the nearest town to Sinker Creek, was founded as the terminal for the Boise, Nampa and Owyhee Railroad to serve the Silver City mines. The line reached the town of Guffey on the north bank of the Snake in 1898. The only reason Murphy still exists is because it became the county seat in 1935 after workers in a nearby Civilian Conservation Corps camp voted for it over Homedale

This hike along a section of the old stage road to Silver City and the South Alternate of the Oregon Trail has changed little since pioneer days. This route ascends the hill travelers considered to be the worst on the South Alternate. Sinker Creek is

**Old stagecoach road near Sinker Creek**

guarded by 300-foot cliffs striped in rust, brick and gold. Outcrops are scattered along the canyon like lava boats on a rocky sea. As you descend into the canyon you get an excellent view of the old stage road, which follows the route of the South Alternate. From the end of the road at the bottom of the canyon, fenced and posted private land blocks access down the canyon to the river.

You can either walk or drive the first 2 miles of this loop hike down a ranch road that follows a side canyon down into Sinker Creek. If you see anyone from the nearby ranch, please ask their permission to be there on the road. Across the side canyon at 1.5 miles is the steep grade of the old stage road and Oregon trail. The elaborate rock work was built to support the stage road. At 1.7 miles, the road passes under gold cliffs banded with stripes.

To begin the next part of the hike, squeeze through the pole fence onto BLM land before the ranch gates at the bottom of the canyon. Please respect the private property north and east of Sinker Creek by staying off it, by packing out your trash and by acting in a quiet, polite manner.

From the fence, walk over to the bottom of the stage road and climb it. At 2.5 miles, it switchbacks north and, at 2.7 miles, joins a gully that is the Oregon Trail. The track runs over sandstone at 3 miles with well-defined wheel ruts, then it climbs northwest around Sinker Creek Butte and drops to a two-wheel track leading southwest beside a dry wash at 4 miles. Take this road to the left (southwest) and follow it back to the Y at 5.2 miles.

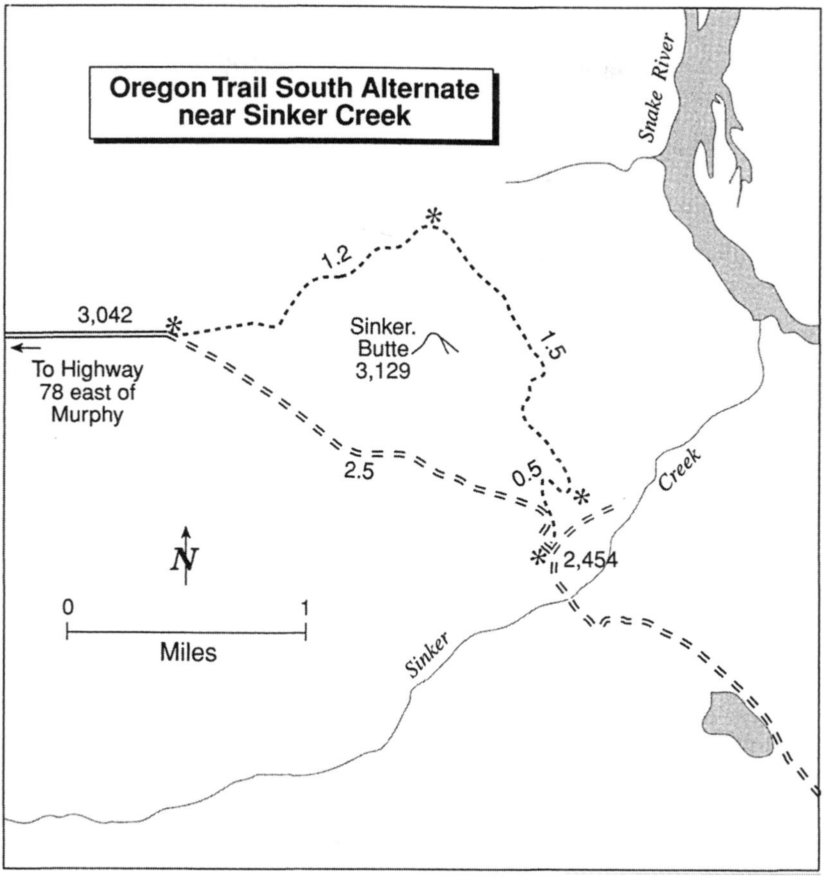
Oregon Trail South Alternate
near Sinker Creek
Snake River
1.2
3,042
Sinker.
Butte
3,129
1.5
To Highway
78 east of
Murphy
2.5
0.5
Creek
2,454
N
0
1
Miles
Sinker

# 64.

## Lizard Butte

**Round trip:** 1 mile
**Elevation gain:** 400 feet
**Highest point:** 2,634 feet
**Map:** Marsing (20-foot contours)
**Difficulty:** easy; time:1 hour
**Access:** Take the Karcher Center exit from Interstate 84 just west of Nampa. Drive west on Karcher Avenue (Idaho 55) across Nampa-Caldwell Blvd. Continue for 9.5 miles to a point where the road curves left (south) at Sunnyslope. Three miles beyond this curve, turn left (east) onto Symms Road. Drive .2 mile to a gate on the south side of the road and park. The landowner requests that only hikers use the track up Lizard Butte. Because the butte is private property, please respect it by not littering and by conducting yourself in a respectful manner.

In May near Lizard Butte, new grass tints the bases of the snow-capped Owyhees and the pastures on the nearby farms a delicate green. The white and pink blossoms of orchards cover the hills between the butte and the blue ribbon of the Snake River. Dark alcoves mark Jump and Squaw Creek canyons in the foothills to the south. (To see the black top of the butte as a giant lizard with upraised head, splayed feet and long tail, drive west of Marsing on Idaho 78 for 3 or 4 miles.)

From the gate walk up a dirt road .2 mile to the cement stage used in Easter services. From the stage, paths lead 200 yards to the 10-foot cross on the summit. Lizard Butte makes a rewarding "mountain" for small children to climb, although they MUST be watched carefully at the top because of the cliffs.

# 65.

## Jump Creek

**Round trips:** Falls: 1 mile, Overlook Trail .2 mile, and Rimrock Trail and extension: 3 miles
**Elevation gain:** Falls: 50 feet, Overlook Trail: 25 feet, Rimrock Trail and extension: 740 feet
**Highest point:** 3,342 feet on the extension of the Rimrock Trail

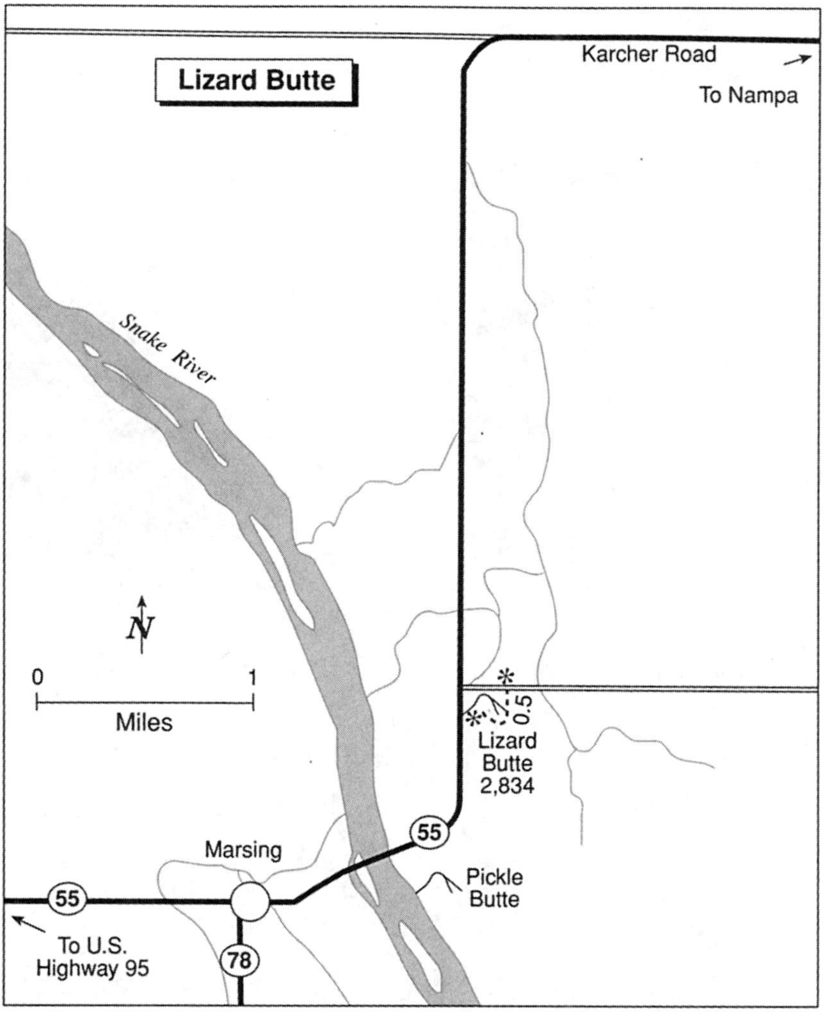


**Map:** Jump Creek Canyon

**Difficulty:** easy, moderate for Rimrock Trail and extension; time: Falls: 1 hour, Overlook: 20 minutes, Rimrock Trail and extension: 2 hours

**Access:** Drive 2.5 miles south of junction of U.S. Highway 30 and U.S. Highway 95 west of Marsing and turn west (right) on Poison Creek Road. At 4.7 miles from the US 30-95 junction, there is a sharp turn to the left and at 5.3 miles there is one to the right. At 5.8 miles, at a four-way intersection, turn left onto a gravel road and at 6.3 miles turn right over a cattle guard. A road goes off uphill at an angle to the right near where you pass the gate of a ranch at 6.5 miles. Keep straight ahead. At 7.3 miles two halves of a loop road join. Keep right and go to the end of the loop at a big parking area at the edge of the canyon at 7.6 miles. Leave passenger cars here. With a pickup or four-wheel drive vehicle, you can descend a short, steep road to the park-

Jump Creek Falls

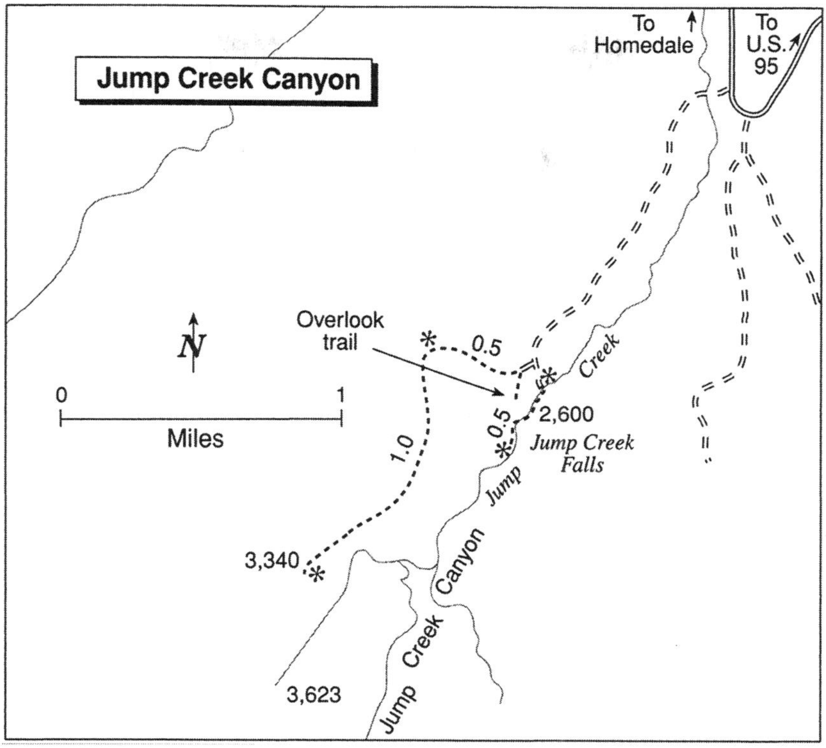


ing area for the Falls Trail at 7.8 miles. Since the last edition of the book, the road to the large parking area has been graveled, but it still isn't recommended for use in wet weather.

At Jump Creek, a white stream of water plunges 75 feet into a shallow pool shadowed by brown cliffs. In the spring, the falls are fluffy, like a bride's veil. During the rest of the year, they shrink to a white ribbon. Above the falls, the upper canyon is lined with rock towers and battlements. The trail to the falls winds under and around boulders and beside poison ivy and caves. Never attempt to climb the cliffs above the falls. THERE HAVE BEEN SEVERAL FATALITIES. If you want to see the upper canyon, an extension of the new Rimrock Trail provides much safer access.

From the lowest parking area, the Falls Trail leads southwest along the right side of the stream. At 200 yards, two 20-foot high caves are across the creek. At .3 mile, the trail descends to the creek, crosses it on rocks to the left (east) side, and climbs above it. Soon you can look into another big cave across the creek. The trail drops back beside the stream as it reaches the pool below the falls at .5 mile.

From the upper parking lot, the Overlook Trail leads .1 mile to the left to an excellent view of the falls and lower canyon. A path continues beyond this point but it is VERY DANGEROUS and the BLM requests that you stay off it for your safety and the protection of water quality and the plants that grow on the rocks. To see the upper canyon, an extension of the new Rimrock Trail is much safer and gives you a much better view. From the upper parking lot, the new Rimrock Trail leads to the right (west) for about .5 mile before ending at a fence. To see the upper canyon, turn left (south) here and climb up a steep path to the left of a ravine. In about 200 yards, the path becomes much less steep and is pleasant walking. Continue up this path, keeping to the right of a depression that drops off into the canyon, to a relatively flat ridge top that parallels the canyon at a distance from it. Walk along the ridge top, which has a fine view of the upper canyon.

Two routes BLM personnel use to climb down into the canyon can be reached from this ridge. They are hard to find, and if you get off route, you will be descending cliffs, so the author strongly recommends that you talk to someone from the Boise District of the BLM before attempting either of them. Both require some scrambling and once there you will find the canyon choked with head-high poison ivy. To find these routes a 7´ minute topographic map and experience in route-finding are essential. The first route begins on the far side of the depression that is to the left of the trail to the ridge. This route begins at the number 3,000 on the topographic map that is at the beginning of the ridge and leads down a ravine into the canyon. The second begins at the south end of the first flat part of the ridge where it widens and steepens ahead, and descends into the main canyon just after it has bent 90 degrees to the west. That route goes down a little wrinkle from the 3,200 to the J in Jump Creek on the topographic map.

For views of the higher part of the upper canyon and to find other routes into the canyon, continue along the ridge top to the spur of a four-wheel-drive road that comes toward the canyon from the northwest, at about 1.5 miles. The spur, which is not shown on the topographic map, ends on a little hill at 3,347 feet and is just above a side canyon that joins Jump Creek from the west. From the hill you can also see into the canyon of a creek that joins Jump Creek from the east. Where the spur road joins the four-wheel drive road on a little saddle a few yards south of the hilltop, a path angles down into the canyon of the western side creek. Following this canyon down to the bottom of the main canyon looks possible from above and on the map, but the author didn't try it and therefore can't recommend it. The path may require some scrambling and be difficult in spring when the side creek runs high. Also, that path may have been made by cows and the author has found that cow paths show no logic in their routes. Another possible way into the canyon would be from a saddle on another spur of the four-wheel drive road about .1 mile southwest of a hill labeled 3,623 feet. This spur road is shown on the map. DON'T try to climb down into the canyon except at the four places mentioned above because the walls are too steep and dangerous.

# 66.

## Squaw Creek

**Round trip:** 3.4 to 4 miles
**Elevation gain:** 240 feet
**Highest point:** 2,800 feet

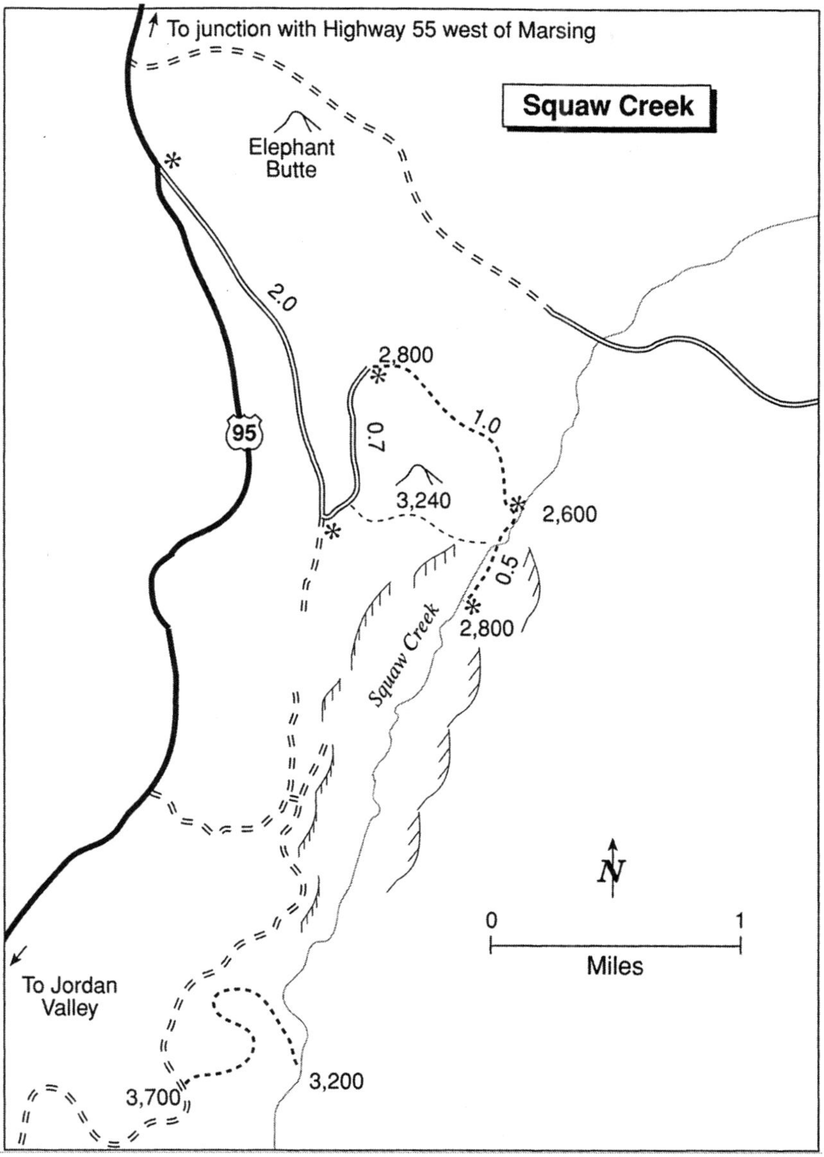


**Map:** Opalene Gulch

**Difficulty:** easy to moderate; time: 2 hours

**Access:** From the intersection of U.S. Highway 95 with U.S. Highway 30 west of Marsing, go 6.1 miles towards Jordan Valley on U.S. Highway 95 and turn (left) southeast on the two-wheel track that follows the old route of U.S. Highway 95 before it was rerouted a few years ago. (The topographic map and the current BLM map show only the old route.) Drive along the track, opening and shutting a gate at about .6 mile. At about 2 miles the road hairpins back on itself to the north as it heads up a hill. (Here a jeep road goes off to the right — don't take it.) Continue another .7 mile and park where an old jeep road heads east down into the canyon. It is best NOT to attempt to drive down this section because the bottom of this track is on private land, and you need to walk around it. Be sure to take a litter bag and pick up any litter you find.

South of Marsing, Squaw Creek Canyon cleaves 800-foot dark cliffs, pocked with caves, where cliff swallows sometimes build their mud nests. The sagebrush in the creek bottom is 10 feet tall, but little poison ivy grows here. In the spring, red paintbrush and pink and white phlox accent the sagebrush slopes. In the fall, the canyon glows with the yellow leaves of cottonwoods and the brilliant red of poison ivy.

This edition of the book describes a different route into the canyon than the earlier editions. The original access to the canyon was from the Sommercamp Road through private property and the landowners have requested that people stay off their property. However, all but the beginning of the canyon is BLM land and there is another route for entering the canyon that doesn't require going through private property. It is more difficult to find the right access road for this route as it is unsigned, but it is a good road.

From the main access road described above, turn right (east) at the 2.7 mile point, and walk down the two-wheel track toward the bottom of the canyon. When you get near the bottom you can see the ruins of a rock and pole shelter built by the Boy Scouts years ago on the other side of the creek. At about .7 mile you reach the private property, which is not fenced. To avoid it turn right, (south) up the hillside cross-country. Within 200 yards you will intersect a track that has come up from the road. From the top of it, you can cut below a large prow-shaped butte down a grassy slope to the creek at 1 mile. The old route went up the right (west) side of the creek here. Turn right (south) and follow this trail about 200 yards until a fence parallel to the creek gets in the way. Here cross the creek to the left (east) side and follow a path up that side of the creek to the point where the canyon closes in at 1.5 miles.

To go farther up the canyon, you must walk in the creek. In the spring, this will result in a thorough soaking, and even in the fall, the water is knee deep. To make a more challenging loop hike, go back down the canyon to the end of the fence and walk up the right (west) side of it until it ends at some cliffs. Below these cliffs, a gully goes west part way back to the access road. Hike up the gully cross-country until you intersect a jeep track that will take you back to the access road just above where it doubles back on itself.

In the author's search for a way into Squaw Creek that doesn't go through private land, she found a second point of access higher up the old highway. This route is all on BLM land. To find it go back to U.S.Highway 95, and drive south toward Jordan Valley. About 300 yards beyond where you emerge from the deep road cut and can look down into Squaw Creek Canyon, a paved side road (the old highway) leads off to the left (southeast) toward a ranch. Take this paved road, which passes a ranch gate and turns to a gravel two-wheel track at 1.5 miles. At 2.3 miles, park in a small pull-out beside (to the left of) a little hill that has a jeep track up it. Walk up the rutted track to the right (east) until it splits on the north side of the hill. Turn left (north) and follow this track down to the bottom of the canyon. It goes down very steeply at first, curves northwest, and makes a hairpin turn southwest. It continues to the bottom of the canyon and ends beside the creek just north of the base of a brown tooth-shaped tower. Except for the tooth, this is not the spectacular part of the canyon, but you may be able to walk cross-country down the creek and through the water to the path at the

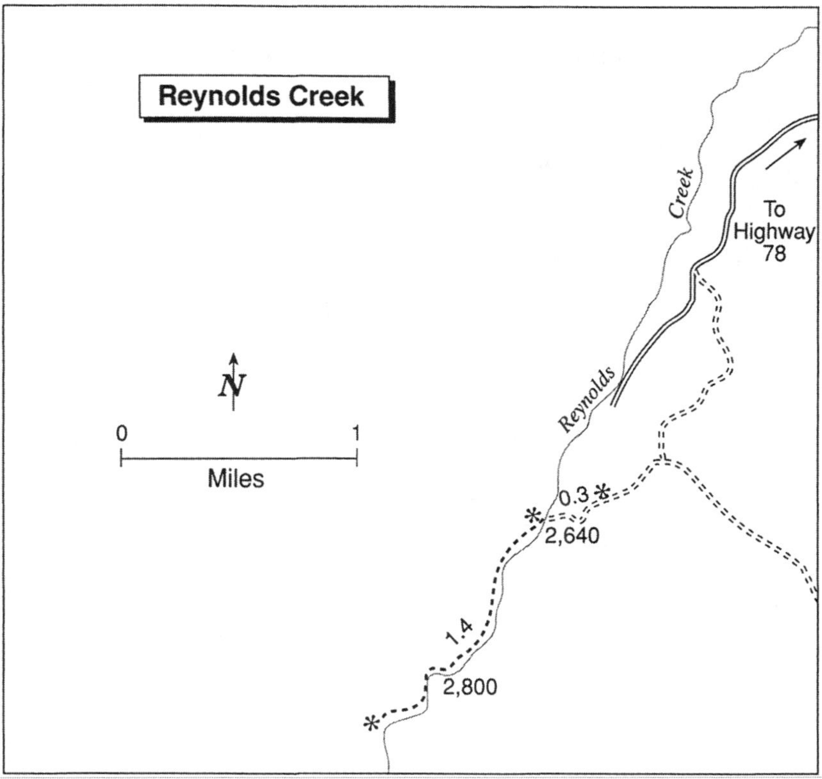


other end. The descent from the old highway to the creek is about 600 feet, so you need to plan for that steep climb back in planning a round trip hike.

# 67.

## Reynolds Creek

**Round trip:** 2.8 to 3.4 miles
**Elevation gain:** 180 feet
**Elevation loss:** 60 feet
**Highest point:** 2,640 feet
**Map:** Wilson Peak
**Difficulty:** easy, but no signs; time: 4 hours

## Reynolds Creek Trail

**Access:** To reach Reynolds Creek, drive 17 miles south of Marsing on Idaho Highway 78 towards Murphy. Turn right (west) 5.5 miles beyond Givens Hot Springs onto Wilson Cemetery Road. This turn is .7 mile past the Wilson Creek Road. (Or you can take Idaho Highway 45 south of Nampa, cross the river at Walters Ferry and turn right towards Marsing on Idaho Highway 78 for 2.6 miles.) On the gravel Reynolds Creek Road at .3 mile keep left, although a road goes off to the right to the cemetery. At 1.3 miles, near some trailers turn right (south) at a T-intersection. At 1.6 miles, at a sign for a private lane straight ahead, turn left (east) toward the "Canyon." From here on the road is primitive with bumps and beds of sharp lava rocks. A high wheelbase or four-wheel drive vehicle is a good idea. The road goes along the right side of a little hill. It passes the stone foundations of an old house at 2.2 miles. Next, the road curves right and left and then goes along the left (east) side of a fence. At a corner of this fence at a four-way intersection at 2.4 miles, turn right (west) again and follow the road across a flat. At another four-way intersection at about 2.8 miles, keep right again. Continue toward the canyon and down a ravine to Reynolds Creek at 3.2 miles. The road down the ravine is rough, so it is wise to leave passenger cars on the flat before it begins if you haven't already parked. Doing so adds .6 mile to the round trip

Resembling logs stacked vertically, 500-foot cliffs of rust-colored rock columns line the canyon of Reynolds Creek. The walls become more than twice as high farther up, but they are not as close to the creek. The 300-yard width of the gorge leaves plenty of room for hiking. An elaborate old irrigation canal system of stones, built by the Chinese in the early mining and farming days of Owyhee County, provide good trails for 1 mile in the canyon, which stretches 9 miles from its mouth toward the village of Reynolds.

From the bottom of the ravine walk along a ditch at the side of the creek for 100 yards to a tiny dam. Here cross the creek on rocks and follow a path along the east side for 300 yards. Look up on the hill above to find a stone canal leading up the canyon. Climb 100 feet to the dry, overgrown canal, turn left (south) and walk up the west side of the canyon on the canal banks. On the east side of the creek is another shorter canal. At .9 mile, the canal ends at a sharp bend in the creek.

Now, follow an overgrown path along the creek and under an overhang at 1.2 miles. At 1.4 miles, a side canyon comes in from the northeast. A path runs up this canyon that connects in .7 mile with a jeep road branching off the Wilson Creek Road.

# SILVER CITY AREA

## 68.

## Avondale Basin

**Round trip:** 5 miles
**Elevation gain:** 1,100 feet
**Highest point:** 6,800 feet
**Maps:** Silver City, DeLamar
**Difficulty:** moderate but no signs; time: 5 hours

**Access:** Take the Karcher Road exit from I-84 at Nampa. Go east to 12th Avenue and follow that road south. It becomes Idaho Highway 45 and at 19 miles crosses the Snake River at Walters Ferry. At 19.4 miles, turn left (east) on Idaho Highway 78 toward Murphy, which is at 29.5 miles. Turn right (southwest) for Silver City 3.5 miles south of the Murphy courthouse. The Silver City Road is paved for 7.4 miles. Continue on a gravel surface that gradually turns to dirt as it goes over New York Summit at 18 miles, after a climb of 3,400 feet. At a small white sign for Silver City at 19.2 miles, turn right (northwest) on the road to Jordan Valley. This road is much worse than the Silver City Road and requires a high wheelbase vehicle. At 20.6 miles, park beyond a bridge over Jordan Creek at the second parking area below the road and either drive or walk down a steep side road to a flat area beside Jordan Creek. The trail, which is an old road, begins across the creek, on its north side and leads north.

The Owyhee Mountains were named for three Hawaiians who disappeared in 1819 while trapping on the Owyhee River. Michael Jordan and W.T. Carson from the Boise Basin discovered gold on Jordan Creek in the Owyhees while looking for the legendary Blue Bucket Mine. The next spring, Michael Jordan and W.T. Carson led

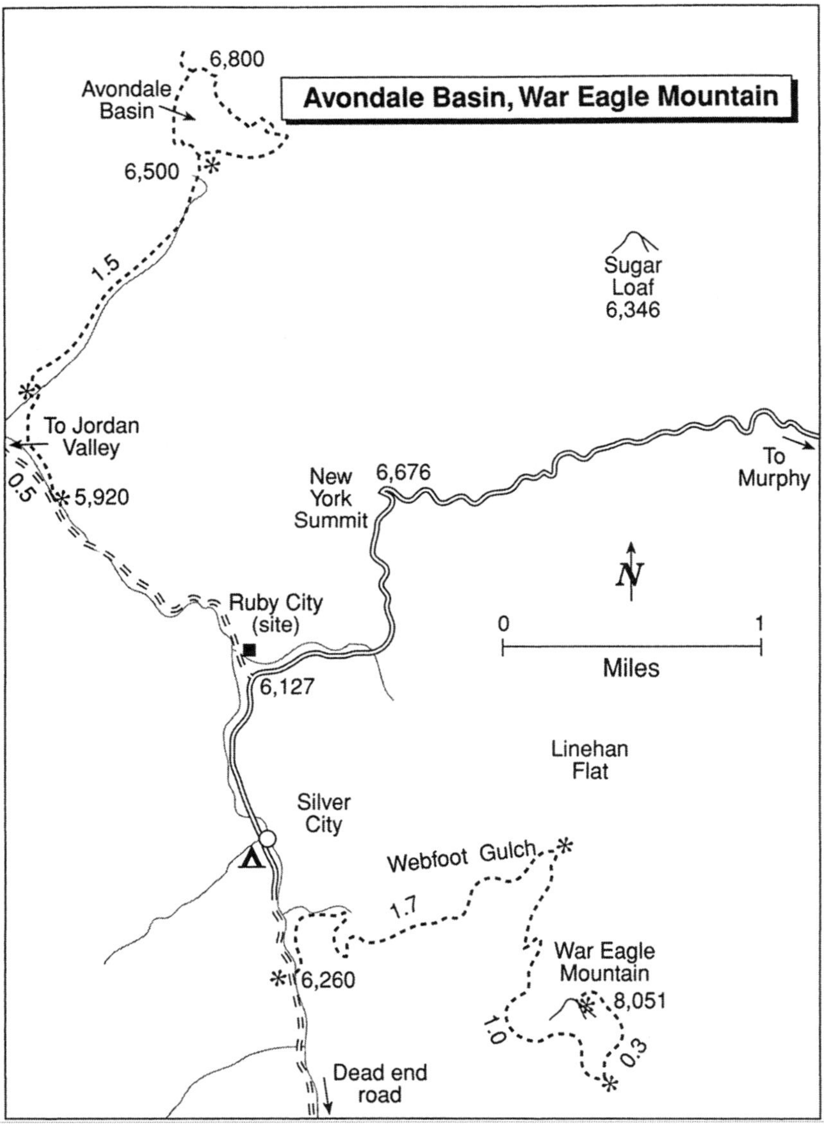


29 men from Placerville in the Boise Basin to the Owyhees to search for the Blue Bucket. Soon prospectors found silver there also.

The first settlement in the area was named Ruby City after the ore ruby silver, which is silver and antimony sulphide occurring in red metallic crystals. Timber was so scarce that within six months the nearby hills were barren and miners had to build stone and dugout houses. The discovery in 1864 of the Orofino and War Eagle lodes resulted in a new town, Silver City, to serve the new mines. After Michael Jordan's partner, Colonel Dewey, built a toll road between the two towns, the better buildings were moved 1 mile to Silver City. When Michael Jordan flipped a coin with Colonel Dewey to see who fought the Indians and who stayed home, Jordan lost, went off to fight and was killed. In 1865, the first newspaper in Idaho, The Owyhee Avalanche, was started in Ruby City. The next year, Silas Skinner built a toll road from Silver City down Reynolds Creek that crossed the Snake River by ferry and continued to Boise.

Silver City was the nation's second largest silver producing area at the time when the Comstock Lode in Nevada was the first. Mining in the Owyhees has continued sporadically. Many of the old buildings in Silver City have been restored as summer homes.

Above Avondale Basin, weathered granite spindles and turrets cap hills clothed in dark green juniper and gray-green mountain mahogany. At the low point of the sloping basin, a tiny spring-fed meadow holds a collapsing log corral. Several old roads that have been taken over by ATVs wind through the area. From one of these tracks you can look out across the Boise Valley, and get close to some of the granite towers. Because Avondale Basin hasn't been mined, it shows what the area was like before the miners came.

To reach the trail to Avondale Basin, ford the creek from the parking area and immediately turn left (west) on a track that goes close to the creek. (At high water, park before the road bridge and walk along the north side of Jordan Creek for 1 mile to this point.) Within 200 yards the track turns uphill along a side creek, Presby Creek. (You can also access this track by parking at Presby Creek, fording Jordan Creek and walking up the west side of the creek to join the track.)

The track crosses the creek at .5 mile, becoming rockier as it climbs past junipers, sagebrush and grassy spots. Use of the track by ATVs has eroded away the dirt that used to cover the rocks. A steep drop off at .8 mile almost goes into the creek. At the head of the creek at 1.5 miles, the track climbs northwest over a knoll and turns left (west) into a meadow in which are the ruins of a corral. This area is Avondale Basin.

For a closer view of the rock towers, follow one of the several roads up the ridge to the north. One can be reached by crossing the meadow to the east. This road has come north from New York Summit. Turn north along this road, which climbs to the ridge top, and continue along it to see as many of the rock towers as you wish. Walking along this road and going out on a spur track to the north for views of the rock towers and Treasure Valley, then dropping back into the basin cross-country is about a 2-mile trek from Avondale Basin. Because of ATV use the topographic map no longer shows all the tracks. The author no longer recommends making a loop by going west to Cunningham Creek and down it to the Jordan Valley Road, because that route goes through private property.

# 69.

## War Eagle Mountain

**Round trip:** 6 miles
**Elevation gain:** 1,850 feet

**Highest point:** 8,051 feet
**Maps:** Silver City, Cinnabar Mountain
**Difficulty:** expert; time: 6 to 7 hours;
**Access:** Take the Karcher Road exit from I-84 at Nampa. Go east to 12th Avenue and follow that road south. It becomes Idaho Highway 45 and at 19 miles crosses the Snake River at Walters Ferry. At 19.4 miles, turn left (east) toward Murphy, which is at 29.5 miles. Turn right (southwest) for Silver City 3.5 miles south of the Murphy courthouse. The Silver City Road is paved for 7.4 miles. Continue on a gravel road that gradually turns to dirt as it goes over New York Summit at 18 miles, after a climb of 3,400 feet. At a small white sign for Silver City at 19.2 miles, turn left (south) and drive through town to the campground .8 mile from that junction. Walk along the main road for about .4 mile to the second of two small roads that go down to the creek. Two well- defined tracks lead up the other (east) side of the canyon from the creek. The hike begins on the left one leading at a gentle angle over to Webfoot Gulch.

You'll find it difficult to find the right place if you drive clear to the beginning of the trail, and there is no place to park anyway except at the campground. If you come to a house you have gone too far. Note that the author has changed the recommended route for this hike from a loop to going up and back the same way. The reason is that the old route up Jordan Creek to the ridge top goes through a large section of private property. There are patches of private property up on the mountain also, but because of the number of old roads and tracks it is pretty well accepted for recreational users to follow them up the mountain.

There are several anecdotes about the mining on War Eagle Mountain. One is that in 1875, the 1,500 members of the miners union of Fairview, a settlement on the northeast side of the mountain, held their mine superintendent captive for three weeks. He was released only when company officials in San Francisco assured them they would be paid the wages they were lacking.

On War Eagle Mountain, mining shacks cling to rocky hillsides surrounded by mine diggings and shafts. From the radio tower on the peak, hikers overlook the wooded basin of Silver City and can see the Treasure Valley stretching to pale blue Shafer Butte. In the distance, C.J. Strike Reservoir glimmers in wrinkled hills. Subalpine and Douglas firs grow on the cool north side of the mountain and its neighbors, and mountain mahogany, juniper, sagebrush, and grass cover the south sides. This hike follows some of the old wagon and mining roads.

The track begins by climbing north at a gentle angle to Webfoot Gulch and then climbing up it for a short distance before switching back to the right at .5 mile. At .7 mile, it switches back to the left, then climbs the side of the canyon above the gulch, passing shacks and mine shafts. BE CAREFUL! At 1.7 miles it crosses the creek to the north side and intersects the Slaughterhouse Gulch Road, a four-wheel drive road coming from a flat at the bottom of New York Summit.

From here there are two possible routes, one a half-mile shorter than the other. The longer one has more named mines along it and thus more potential for property owners to care about your presence. The route the author recommends is to climb southwest from the junction of the Webfoot Gulch track with the Slaughterhouse Gulch road on an old jeep trail. This goes up to the west ridge of the mountain and across the southwest face of it to a saddle at 2.7 miles. There are several old mine shafts and diggings close to the trail so again BE CAREFUL! At the saddle, the road that went around the east side of the mountain past the site of Fairview joins. From here, a road goes north up the mountain. Take that road to the radio tower and summit at 3 miles. You can return the same way or try going back around the east side of the mountain.

Sand lilies at Bruneau Sand Dunes

# BRUNEAU AREA

## 70.

## Bruneau Sand Dunes

**Loop trip:** 5 miles
**Elevation gain:** 490 feet
**Elevation loss:** 490 feet
**Highest point:** 2,930 feet
**Map:** Sand Dunes (25-foot contours)
**Difficulty:** easy; time: 4 hours
**Access:** Turn left (east) 15.6 miles south of Mountain Home off Idaho Highway

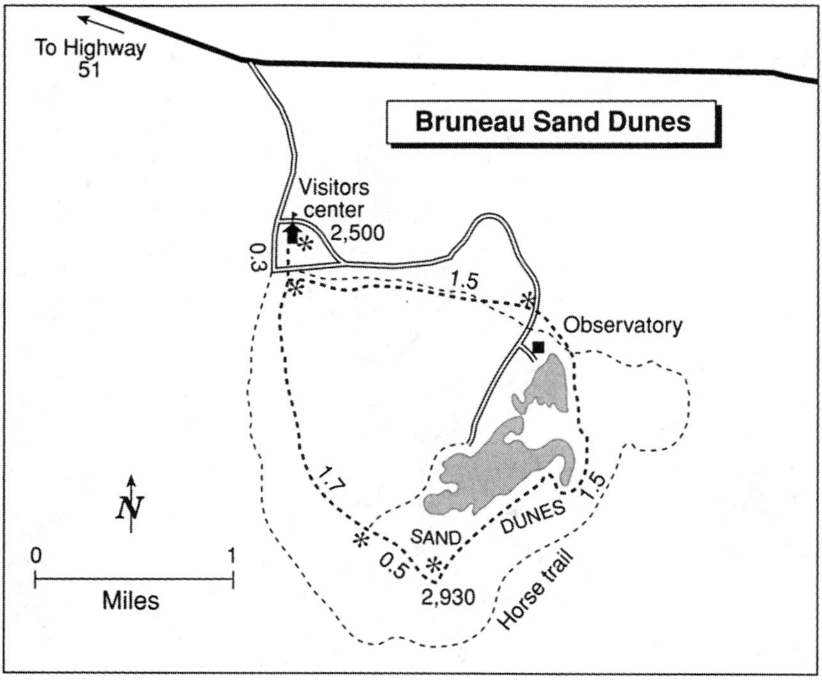


51 onto Idaho Highway 78. At 1.8 miles, turn right (south) onto the paved Bruneau Dunes Road. Go 1 mile to the Visitors' Center.

The Bruneau Sand Dunes resemble an ocean beach in high sagebrush tablelands. Shallow blue lakes are nestled beneath gray mountains of sand. The tallest dune is 462 feet high and is the largest single sand dune in North America. Green bullrushes and gray-green Russian olives rim the shores of the lakes. Fishing is good for bluegill, sunfish and large-mouth bass. On a windy day, the sand spins out from the crest of the dunes like ocean spray. Sometimes this sand fog is so thick that the top of the big dune is invisible.

The dunes are a state park, created in 1968, featuring a five-mile loop hike which climbs to the summit of the largest dune. The Visitors' Center has displays and literature on the dunes' natural history. These tell that the construction of Strike Dam on the Snake River in 1952 raised the water table enough to create the lakes. Organized groups can arrange for programs about the dunes. Facilities include a picnic area, boat launch, and landscaped campground with hot showers and a new astronomical observatory. Driving off-road here is not permitted.

The five-mile trail crosses sagebrush flats from the visitors center to the lakes and edges them. Then it climbs the largest dune and wanders back to the center across the sagebrush and sand flats. Posts mark the trail, although wind on the sand keeps any paths erased. Outside of the loop trail for hikers is another longer trail for horses.

From the visitors center the hiking trail heads south, and at the first post splits into the loop. You can go either direction. If you continue south the next two posts guide

**Indian Bathtub**

you around the marsh, then the third post points you to the top of the highest dune, which has an excellent view of the dunes, lake and ponds. From here you go east down the crest of the big dune, and passing posts 4 and 5 cross a small dune and circle the picnic area. Then the route veers northwest and at post 6 intersects the road from the campground to the boat launch. Continue northwest across tiny dunes and sandy flats back to post 1 near the visitors center.

For a shorter hike, find this trail at the picnic area and follow it along the east edge of the lake. Work your way around the end of the lake and follow a path on the west side of the lake which leads to a road that returns to the picnic area.

Sledding is possible on the big dunes. A flat-bottom sled without runners works best. Skiers can even ski with an old pair of skis if they have the energy to climb up the sand. It is hot here in summer, so when hiking the five-mile trail check with the ranger before and after the hike and USE CAUTION during it. Carry lots of water and wear a sun hat. Spring and fall are the most pleasant months to visit, but the park is open year round. Swimmers need to beware of the flatworm larva in the lakes. They burrow into the skin and cause a painful inflammation called "swimmers' itch," which can be prevented by toweling or showering immediately after swimming.

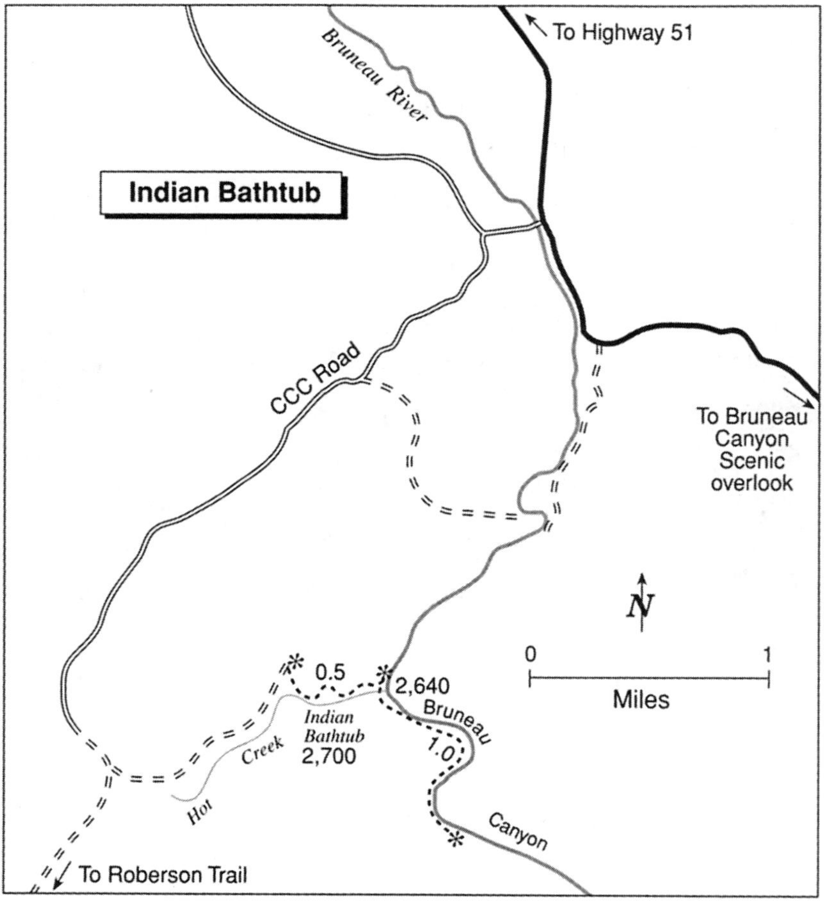


# 71.

## Indian Bathtub

**Round trip:** 3 miles
**Elevation gain:** 25 feet
**Elevation loss:** 85 feet (return climb)
**Highest point:** 2,700 feet
**Maps:** Sugar Valley, Hot Spring (both 25-foot contours)

**Difficulty:** easy, but no signs; time: 2 hours

**Access:** Turn (left) southeast off Idaho Highway 51 on the paved Bruneau Canyon Road, 20.3 miles south of Mountain Home. Drive 7.6 miles and turn right (southeast) on a gravel road. Cross a bridge and at 1.4 miles, turn left (south) on a dirt road signed for the Bruneau River. This road is also marked with a green post with a white CCC on it, because it is known as the CCC Road. Soon a signed road for the Bruneau River turns left. Keep straight ahead. At 3.1 miles, an unsigned dirt track goes off to the left downhill to the Indian Bathtub. Turn left (east) on it and go 1.5 miles to the end of the road.

Hot water from a spring at the base of 50-foot cliffs fills occasionally dry Indian Bathtub. The bathtub may have been first created by Paiutes or Shoshoni who dammed Hot Creek to make a swimming pool. Years ago, a unique species of wild orchid grew beside the pool. Desert tablelands covered with sagebrush and grasses rise above Hot Creek Canyon. The bases of some of the cliffs on these tablelands are red where hot lava baked clay into natural brick.

In the nearby Bruneau River Canyon, 100-foot gray and pink striped cliffs overlook the twisting river, which flows clear in the fall but rushes cocoa brown in the spring. Willows and cottonwoods grow on islands and netleaved hackberry trees cluster in tiny side canyons. In winter, the greenish-white berries of poison ivy bead leafless stalks, like sinister grapes.

To climb safely down to the tub from the end of the road, take a path that descends southeast to Hot Creek and then climbs 50 yards south to the pool. USE CAUTION in bathing, as the water can be murky and contains biting bugs.

From the tub, a path leads down Hot Creek on the north side .5 mile to the Bruneau River. A private property owner allows access here, so be respectful, be quiet and carry out your trash. From the edge of the river, a path goes up the river and appears and disappears for miles, but large amounts of poison ivy cover it within 1 mile of Hot Creek. The canyon here is only 150 feet deep, contrasting with the 800-foot depth at the scenic overlook 8 miles south on the other side of the river.

# 72.

## Bruneau Canyon — Roberson Trail

**Round trip:** 2 miles
**Elevation gain:** none
**Elevation loss:** 640 feet (return climb)
**Highest point:** 3,680 feet
**Maps:** Hot Spring, Sugar Valley, Broken Wagon Flat, Crowbar Gulch
**Difficulty:** expert; time: 2 hours;

**Access:** Turn left (southeast) off Idaho Highway 51 onto the paved Bruneau Canyon Road, 20.3 miles south of Mountain Home. Drive 7.6 miles and turn right (southeast) on a gravel road. Cross a bridge and at 1.4 miles, turn left (south) on a dirt road signed for the Bruneau River and marked by a green post with a white CCC on

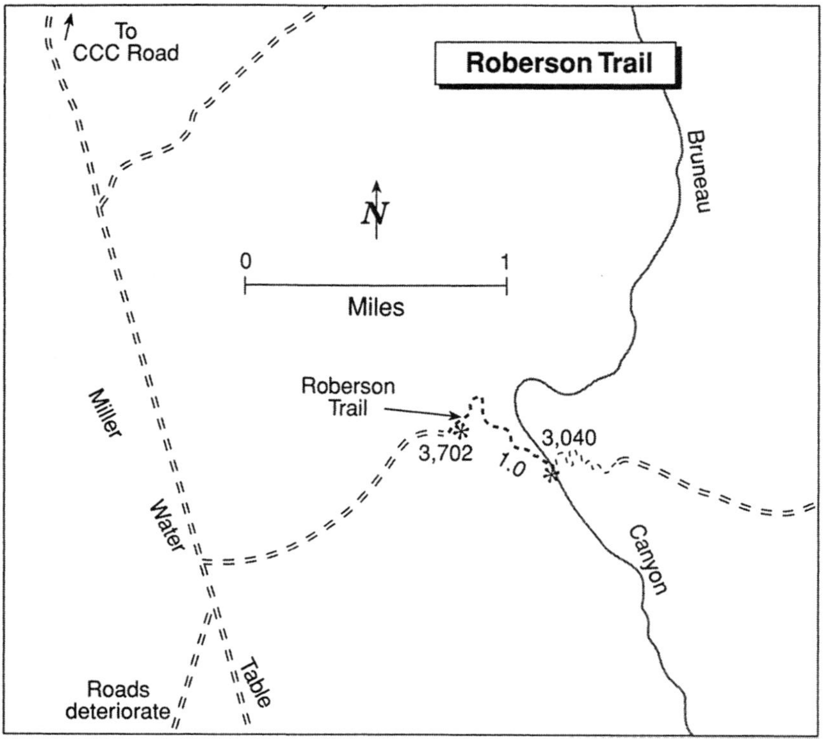


it. Soon a signed road for the Bruneau River turns left. Keep straight ahead. At 3.1 miles, an unsigned dirt track goes left downhill to the Indian Bathtub. Continue straight ahead. At 5.5 miles, turn left uphill on an unsigned dirt road. This road is labeled Blackstone-Grasmere on the topographic map. In the fall, the sandy dust on this part of the road may be deep enough to require four-wheel drive on a couple of hills.

At a Y in the road at 11.3 miles the right hand road goes through a fence at a cattle guard. (The left hand road is a worse road than the right.) About 1 mile before the Y, the road passes a corral and small water tanks. About halfway between the corral and the Y, a little road goes off to the left beside one of the water tanks, but it is not plain until you are past the tank. Follow it toward Bruneau Canyon, which soon can be seen ahead. At 1 mile, park at the highest point before the road goes downhill to its end at the brink of the canyon. (From this high point you can see another road across the canyon coming to its edge and a trail down into the canyon leading from it.) To find the trail on your side from the high point, walk BACK along the road 250 yards to a grassy area 200 yards wide. Walk east-northeast in the lowest part of this on a faint jeep track to a ravine and continue down it. Just as you see the canyon falling away ahead you will find an overgrown trail running just above the bottom of the ravine on its right (southeast) side. Because the trail is difficult to find, all four of

**Bruneau Canyon from the Roberson Trail**

the topographic maps that show the approach to it are listed above, but Crowbar Gulch is the one that shows the trail.

The Bruneau River was probably named for a Canadian trapper, Jean Baptiste Bruneau, who may have discovered it in1815. For 80 miles the canyon is from 600 to 1,200 feet deep and is as narrow as .2 mile. Abraham and Martha Roberson and their five sons began farming at Bruneau in April 1869 and started living there in the spring of 1870. During the Bannock War of 1878, 26 people took refuge in "Settlers Cave" which the Robersons' sons had dug in a sandstone and clay bluff. The cave had a long hall, four small rooms, and a ventilation hole. A friendly Indian, Bruneau John, who warned the settlers so they could hide in the cave in time, received a medal from President Garfield for his warning.

In the dark chasm of Bruneau Canyon, black columns of basalt, broken occasionally by horizontal bands of light red rock, form the canyon walls. Hot lava baked clay into brick to create these bands. From the bottom of the canyon, a 600-foot tower of dark basalt gives an idea of the depth of the canyon at the overlook downstream across the river. The deep and narrow gorge is mostly in shadow all day. Green junipers edge the river amid a jungle of wild roses, currants and poison ivy. The spikes of scouring rush and marsh grasses flank white sand beaches. Above on the plateau in early spring, the grasses under the sagebrush are sprinkled with tiny pastel flowers like the pink ones of longleaf phlox. The river has been proposed as a National Wild and Scenic River and the canyon is a BLM wilderness study area.

Once you find the trail, follow it as it goes out across the hillside for 50 yards and then returns to the ravine. The trail soon leaves the ravine by turning southeast between two tiers of cliffs and contouring a grassy hillside toward other cliffs. It switchbacks below these cliffs through rocks and sagebrush to the river at 1 mile. From here, faint paths run up and down the river, but there are no campsites.

The trail fords the river in a possibly DANGEROUS ford and climbs the east wall of the canyon to a primitive access road which can be reached by heading south from the Bruneau overlook and taking the correct road at each of several turns. This route is rougher and more difficult to find than the roads described here. The Roberson Trail is abandoned, so the switchbacks through the rock and brush are hard to find. It is NOT RECOMMENDED for children because of the drop-offs.

# 73.

## Big Jacks Creek — Parker Trail

**Round trip:** 3.2 miles
**Elevation gain:** none
**Elevation loss:** 640 feet (return climb)
**Highest point:** 4,680 feet
**Map:** Wickahoney Crossing
**Difficulty:** easy, but poor trail; time: 3 hours
**Access:** From Idaho Highway 78, 2 miles west of Bruneau, turn south onto Idaho Highway 51, which goes through Grasmere to Nevada. (Or drive south from Mountain Home on Idaho Highway 51 to this point.) At 22.5 miles from the junction with Idaho Highway 78, turn west on the gravel Wickahoney Road and go 4.6 miles. Turn north on a dirt road and drive about 2.5 miles. Park before the road starts downhill towards the canyon.

In the canyon within a canyon of Big Jacks Creek, 100-foot gray cliffs rim the upper gorge above 200 feet of slanting talus. In the inner canyon, the blue-green creek hairpins back and forth from rock wall to rock wall across a wide band of grass. Obelisks of rock serrate the top of the winding inner canyon walls, which form alternating intersecting lines resembling feather-stitching. Along the route, Simpson's barrel cactus grows under sagebrush or in holes in the rock together with a species of prickly pear. Please be careful not to harm the cactus. Big Jacks Creek is a BLM wilderness study area.

From where the road starts downhill, park and start walking. At .4 mile, it crosses a dry wash. From there it continues level for .3 mile and then turns to a trail at a stile (a walkover ladder) that climbs over a fence at the edge of the canyon. From it, the trail descends into the canyon. At .8 mile, it goes down a gully until the gully drops

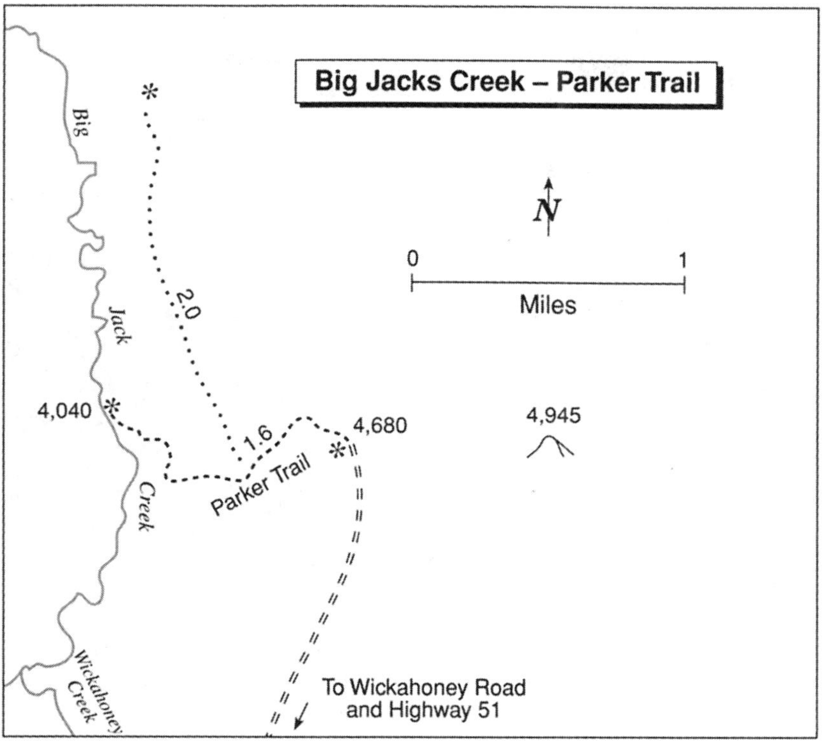


off in cliffs at 1.2 miles. Here the trail leads uphill 200 yards to the north along the side of the gully to the brink of the inner canyon. From there it descends through grass and sagebrush to the creek at 1.6 miles.

A faint path goes along the grass in the canyon bottom. However, in the spring it is necessary to wade the creek several times to follow it. Back at the beginning of the hike you can get a wider view from the top of the canyon wall. To do this, walk north cross-country along the canyon rim for 2  miles to the west side of a point that is between the main canyon and the side canyon formed by the dry wash. From here you can see the creek repeating the pattern of a winding canyon within a canyon for several miles.

# 74.

## Little Jacks Creek

**Round trip:** 2.8 miles (1.4 miles cross-country travel)
**Elevation gain:** 360 feet

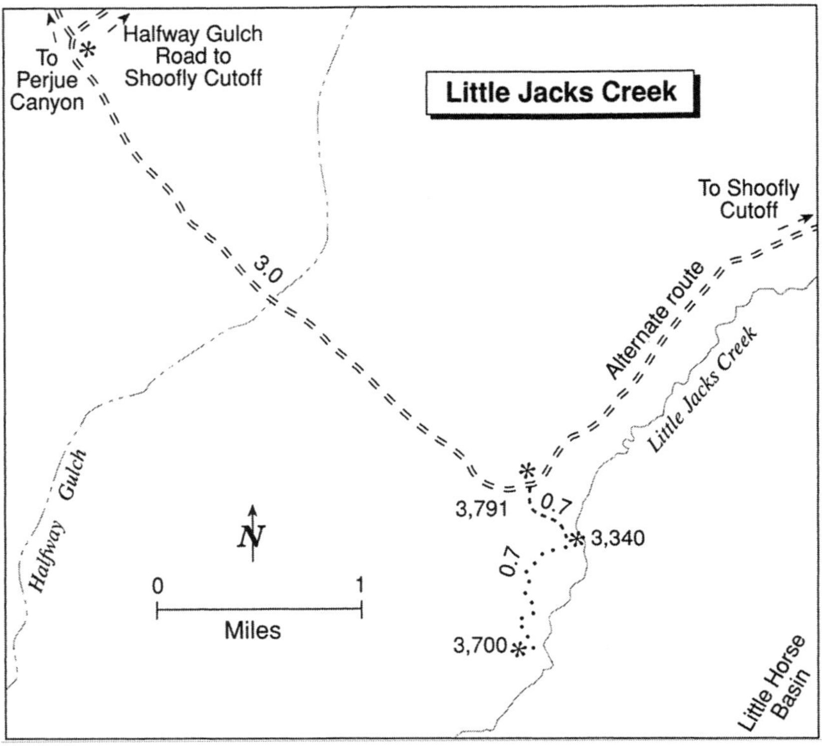


**Elevation loss:** 420 feet (return climb)
**Highest point:** 3,760 feet
**Maps:** Perjue Canyon, Chalk Hills, Ox Lake, Big Horse Basin Gap (20-foot contours),
**Difficulty:** expert; time: 3 hours
**Access:** Go south of Mountain Home on Idaho Highway 51 for 22.3 miles to the junction of Idaho Highway 51 and 78. From this junction, there are two relatively good ways to go to the beginning of the spectacular part of Little Jacks Creek canyon and more than one difficult way. To take the one the author is familiar with turn right (west) at this junction onto Idaho Highway 78 and go 15.1 miles to the paved Mud Flat Road (also called the Owyhee Uplands Scenic Byway). Here, 2 miles before (east of) Grandview, turn south on this road. At 7.6 miles, turn left (southeast) on the gravel Shoofly Cutoff Road and go 2.6 miles. Turn right (southeast) on an unsigned, primitive but not rocky road, which is known as the Halfway Gulch Road and is maintained by a local rancher. (There is a cattle guard near the beginning of it.) The road runs along Halfway Gulch for the first few miles, which means there can be muddy places on it in the spring. At 2 miles along this road, a road goes off to the left (east) where the road you are on curves west. At 2.5 miles, a road goes off to the north. Keep straight ahead. Continue as the road curves south and crosses the occasional wash.

At about 5 miles, the roads begin a confusing maze. Continue straight ahead where each of three roads turn off or cross your road in the next mile. At 7.6 miles there is a four-way intersection where one of the roads goes toward the mountains ahead for quite a distance. Turn left (southeast) here toward Little Jacks Creek. You can begin to see its canyon in the distance. At 8.2 miles, another road turns off to the right toward the mountains. Keep straight ahead. At 10.8 miles, the road curves 90 degrees to the left (north) near the edge of Little Jacks Creek canyon and a jeep trail curves to the right toward the canyon. Park at the beginning of this track.

The road that comes south to this 90-degree curve is another route to this point, which is probably drier in the spring. To use that road as a route to the canyon, go south from the intersection of Idaho Highway 51 and 78 on Idaho Highway 51 toward Grasmere for about 8 miles and turn right (west) on the Shoofly Cutoff Road. At about 1.4 miles, turn left (southwest) toward Little Jacks Creek. When you get close to the creek the road splits. Don't take the left branch along the creek. Instead, take the right (northwest) branch which soon curves south and follows the Chalk Hills above Little Jacks Creek to the 90-degree curve in the road mentioned above. This is about 15 miles from the highway by that route. DO NOT try the route that begins at Shoofly Creek (Perjue Canyon) off the Mud Flat Road even though it looks shorter. It is very steep and rocky, crosses several rocky washes, and the first steep section has a DANGEROUS sidehill slant.

Grassy slopes slant between layers of cliffs on the hills which form the canyon wall of Little Jacks Creek. These stair-stepping layers make the hills resemble wedding cakes before they are frosted. Willows overhanging the creek provide shelter for an endemic fish, the red-banded trout. Carpets of poison ivy creep between the willows. This canyon, the deepest in the Owyhees (1,350) and a BLM wilderness study area, gets little use because it is challenging hiking as well as difficult to reach. You need the Triangle and Glenns Ferry BLM maps, as well as the topographic maps mentioned above, plus a good sense of direction and maybe even your compass or GPS unit. The topographic map doesn't show all of the Halfway Gulch Road. You need to take the topographic and BLM maps with a grain of salt because neither show all the roads that exist and they also show some roads that don't exist.

From the 90-degree curve in the road near the edge of the canyon, walk along the jeep trail down grassy slopes. When the track ends at .6 mile, find a path to the right and take it to the canyon bottom at .7 mile. Across a ford, a path climbs to meet a jeep trail on the other side. Don't take it. Instead, turn right before the ford and go cross-country up the right (west) side of the canyon to a viewpoint of the upper canyon. You used to be able to hike along the canyon bottom from the ford for a mile or so, but since the BLM fenced the creek to protect it from cattle, the shrubs and plants have overgrown too much to do this any more. Just climb along the west side of the canyon on the grassy slopes following faint cow paths where they are helpful. Between one set of cliffs and the next, ascend a steep grassy slope to the top of a knoll at 1.2 miles. Continue to a second knoll at 1.4 miles for a view of the upper canyon. For a glimpse of the inner gorge, descend from either knoll to the edge of the cliffs. Adventurous, well-prepared hikers can continue cross-country for many miles up the canyon or along the plateau above it.

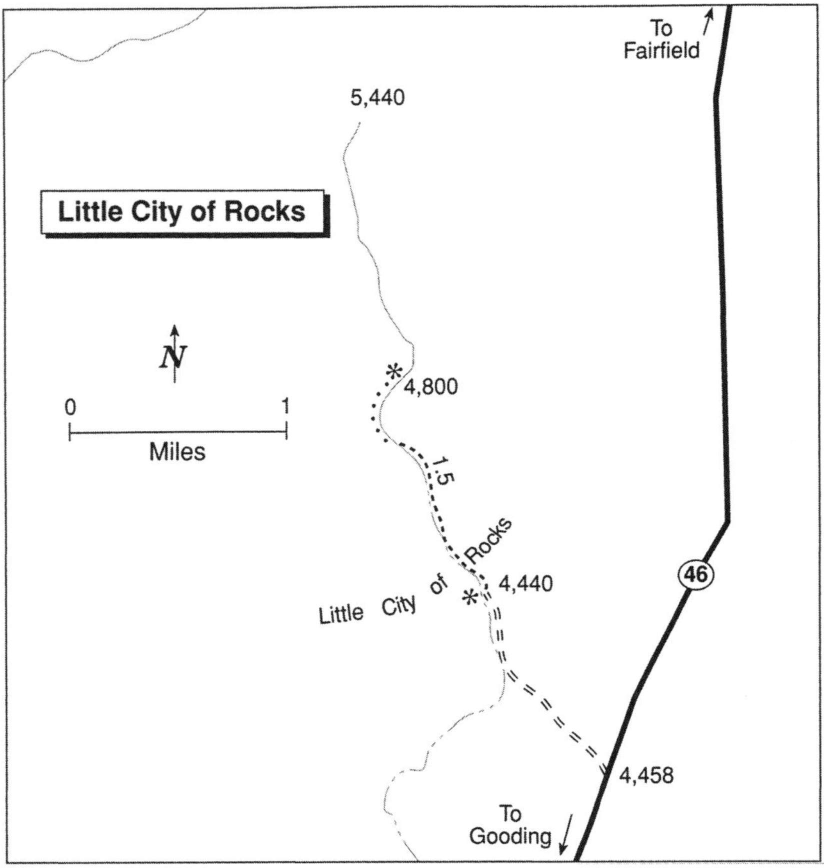


# SHOSHONE DISTRICT
# BENNETT HILLS AREA

## 75.

## Little City of Rocks

**Round trip:** 3 miles
**Elevation gain:** 480 feet

**Highest point:** 5,000 feet
**Maps:** Thorn Creek SW, McHan Reservoir
**Difficulty:** easy for first mile, expert for next .5 mile; time: 3 hours
**Access:** From U.S. Highway 20, drive 4 miles east of Fairfield and turn south on Idaho Highway 46. Go 18.3 miles toward Gooding to a signed turnoff. Or turn left (east) off I-84 at Bliss and drive 11 miles to Gooding and then go north 12.7 miles on Idaho Highway 46 to the turnoff. Turn west on a dirt road and drive 1.1 miles to a parking area just before an old stone dam.

Goblins of rock seem to dance in and on the walls of the canyon called the Little City of Rocks. These formations are called hoodoos and they peer, they lean, they gyrate. Their ripple marks and twists are due to variations in the hardness of the rock. The rock is covered with black lichen and dark desert varnish, but underneath it is brown and beige welded tuff, a rock made of volcanic ash that fused together over time. Frost split this rock into columns and water eroded away the softer sections, leaving the towers.

From the parking area, walk northwest up the old road that goes around the east end of the dam and up the canyon. The canyon is no longer open to motorized travel because it is a BLM wilderness study area. As you walk you see that earth covers the back side of the dam. The vegetation is sagebrush, bitterbrush and grass with a few riparian shrubs along the seasonal creek that winds through the canyon. By mid-summer the creek dries up and the grasses turn golden. The track winds up the right side of the creek, and as it does so, the hoodoos back off from the valley floor. Just before the old road ends at .8 mile it crosses to the left side of the creek and then back again. Where the road ends a small, steep side canyon comes in from the right.

The old road becomes an unofficial foot trail here where the canyon curves left. The trail crosses to the left side of the creek and begins to climb. It crosses back and forth over the creek twice more and curves to the right before a small side canyon comes in from the left at 1.2 miles. On the north, a group of high towers divides the side and main canyons. The trail continues up the left side of the main canyon, now and then climbing over big rocks with gravel on them. The canyon narrows and the creek to your right falls over two-foot steps of black lava. When the creek is dry you can see the shine on the steps from the water polishing them. It is best to turn back at the point where the trail climbs an immense gravel-covered boulder and there is a steep drop off below at 1.5 miles. The path continues beyond here, but it is DANGEROUS.

# 76.

## Gooding City of Rocks: Upper Coyote Creek

**Round trip:** 4 miles (or more)
**Elevation loss (return climb):** 360 feet
**Highest point:** 5,200 feet
**Map:** Fir Grove

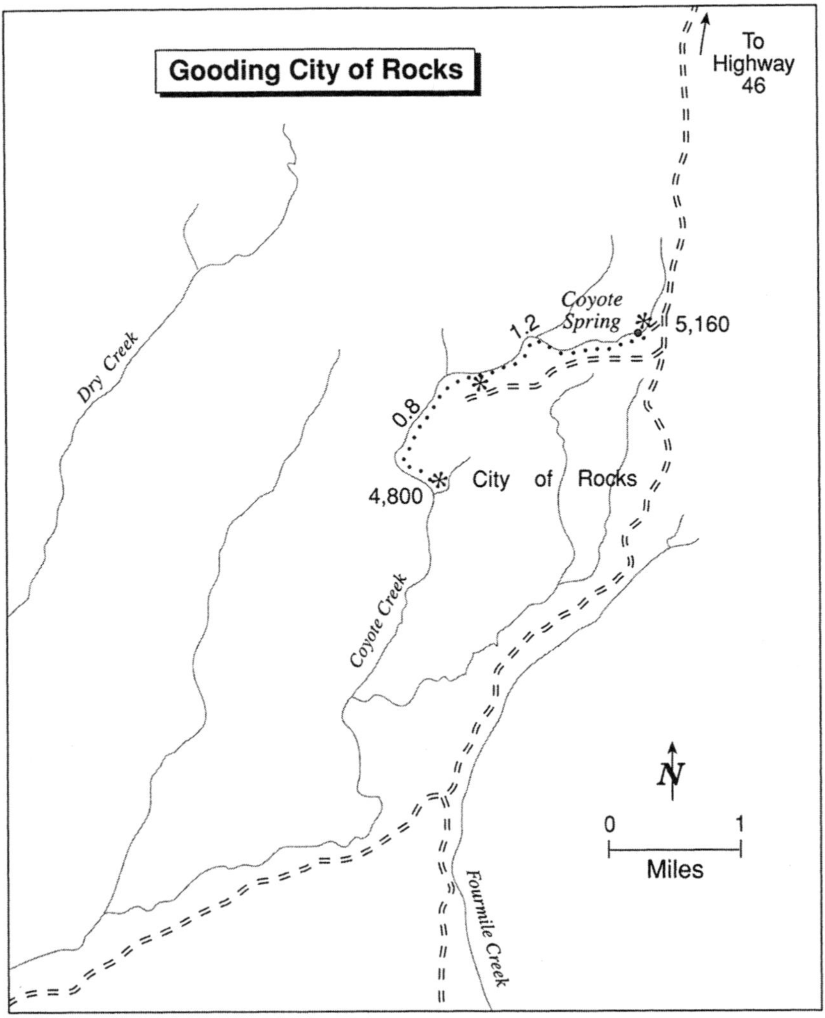


**Difficulty:** cross-country; time: 3 to 4 hours

**Access:** From U.S. Highway 20, drive 4 miles east of Fairfield and turn south on Idaho Highway 46. Go 13.8 miles south toward Gooding to a signed turnoff. Or turn left (east) off I-84 at Bliss and drive 11 miles to Gooding and then go north 17.2 miles on Idaho Highway 46 to the turnoff. (The turnoff for this hike is 4.5 miles north of the one for the Little City of Rocks.) Turn west on the gravel Gooding City of Rocks Road, and drive to a junction with the road to Fir Grove. Turn left (south) on a dirt road and go .9 mile to a junction with the road to Davis Mountain. Turn left again here and continue to the short towers labeled Gooding City of Rocks, which are 8.7 miles from the highway. The road ahead is labeled "dead end — no turnaround." Walk or drive back toward the highway .3 mile to where a dirt track goes off to the

**Coyote Creek at Gooding City of Rocks**

west.

This hike is along the upper canyon of Coyote Creek on a series of faint paths. At first it is a smaller canyon with shorter rock towers than the one at the Little City of Rocks. Walking along the little creek and squeezing past the rocks gives you a feeling of being in a cowboy and Indians movie. Later the towers grow taller and blacker than the ones at the Little City and stand back from the creek. Some of them resemble hooded figures.

From the main road, walk west along the little track, which drops down a small hill and ends in a loop at .1 mile. From here, follow a path down to a long stock tank filled with water from Coyote Springs by a bubbling pipe. Ahead, the path leads over tiny grassy flats past 20-foot hoodoo towers. A thick tangle of shrubs such as willow, chokecherry and golden currant grows next to the creek. Soon you pass a thin, vertical cave. The canyon narrows so you are pushing your way through the shrubs at times and must squeeze under an overhanging outcrop in one place. Then at about .4 mile, you have to climb uphill to the left of the creek through brush with not much of a path for about 50 feet. This detour is necessary to get past a place where big boulders have fallen across the creek and blocked the canyon.

Past this spot the canyon opens up and you can see very tall towers ahead. At .6 mile, a side canyon comes in from the right as the main canyon curves to the left. Another from the same side comes in at 1.2 miles. As the canyon opens out and widens at about 1.6 miles, the riparian shrubs disappear. At 2 miles, a side canyon comes in from the left. You can continue down the canyon quite some distance, although the map shows a couple of narrow places that will require climbing around. By mid-summer the creek usually dries up along much of the upper section.

# IDAHO STATE PARKS
# HAGERMAN AREA

## 77.

## Malad Gorge State Park: Devils Washbowl Loop

**Round trip:** 2.2 miles
**Elevation loss (return climb):** 40 feet
**Highest point:** 3,281 feet
**Map:** Tuttle
**Difficulty:** easy; time: 1 to 1½ hours
**Access:** On I-84 from the eastern (141) of two exits at Bliss, continue east for 6.3 miles. Turn off the interstate at Exit 147, which is signed for Malad Gorge State Park. Turn right (west) here at the end of the exit ramp. Then turn right (north) .6 mile from the exit ramp. At a road closed sign at 1 mile turn left into the park where there are picnic tables and a sign for Devils Washbowl on the right. Turn right and go .3 mile to a parking area.

The whole Malad River is only 12 miles long from the point where it emerges from the Snake River aquifer to where it joins the river. It got its name when some of fur trapper Alexander Ross's men became ill from eating tainted beaver meat they trapped here. Malade means sick in French.

This trail gives you views of the 250-foot gorge that retreating waterfalls carved in the basalt flows of Gooding Butte, 9 miles away. First, you overlook the Devils Washbowl, a dark pool in a lava basin, fed all year by a 60-foot waterfall. Farther along, you look down into another pool, this one emerald green. In the fall, the pool is clotted with black algae at the edges and lime green algae on the surface. White streaks in the lava above its head show where water feeds it in the spring. The walls surrounding the emerald pool are vertical and so are the walls of the main gorge. The trail goes out on a narrow tongue of land between the main gorge and the gorge with the pool in it. From the end of the tongue, you can see a gray-white concrete flume carrying water over the black lava into the canyon of the Snake River to the south.

This state park opened to the public in 1979. Sections of the Oregon Trail's north alternate and the Kelton stage line went through the north part of the park. You can

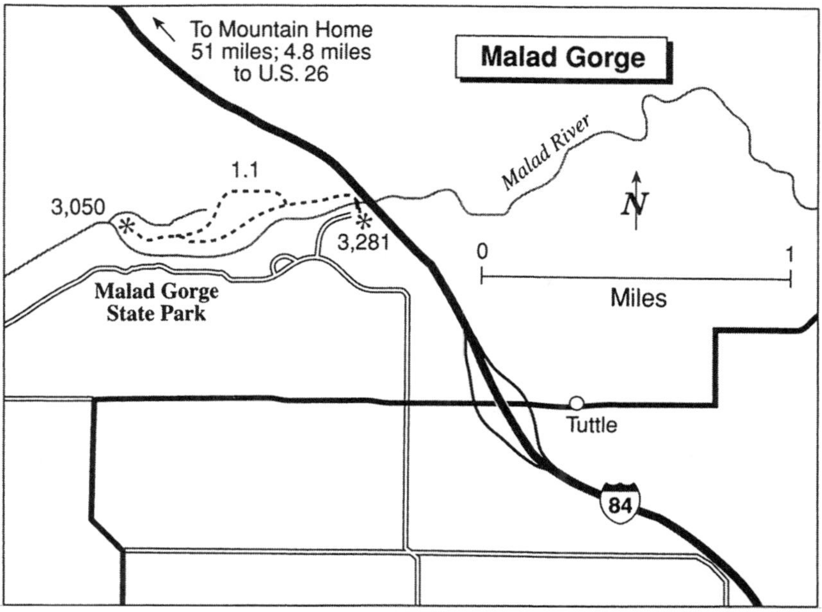


hike north on the other side of the freeway on a tour guided by park staff to see the remnants of one of the stage stations and to see wagon wheel ruts in lava. Tours must be arranged in advance.

From the parking area, walk 100 feet northwest on a paved trail to the information kiosk, where there are displays about the park. Then walk 50 feet more to a steel bridge over the gorge. Cross the bridge, using caution if it is wet or snowy, to the west side of the gorge. The trail goes south from there along the rim of the gorge for about .2 mile to more information panels and an overlook of the gorge and Devils Washbowl.

The trail continues as a dirt path 200 yards to a 10-foot deep side canyon and descends into it. There is a junction with the loop trail here. If you take the left branch, you'll continue along the rim of the gorge, walking over occasional beds of lava in the trail that resemble tiled floors. These are the tops of jointed columns formed by the basalt as it cooled. After .8 mile, the tongue of land you are on narrows to only a few feet. Here you can step over to the edge of the other gorge for a view of the green pool. At first, there is only one trail out along the tongue of land, but then it divides again. When it divides, take the branch along the rim of Malad Gorge to the end of the tongue of land at 1 mile. Return on the branch that runs along the gorge of the emerald pool. At the head of this gorge, the trail goes about halfway along the head wall, providing a good view of how the lava splits off to form the gorge. From a junction, a path continues along the head wall. Turn right (north) here on the main trail which curves across a flat grassy area back to the trail junction in the little side canyon at 2 miles. From here it is .2 mile back to the parking area on the paved path.

# 78.

## Box Canyon

**Round trip:** 1.4 miles to view of pools, 2.4 miles to the bottom of the canyon (not recommended)

**Elevation loss (return climb) to the bottom of the canyon:** 160 feet

**Highest point:** 3,200 feet

**Map:** Thousand Springs

**Difficulty:** easy for views; expert for bottom of the canyon; time: 1 to 2 hours

**Access:** On I-84, from the eastern of the two exits at Bliss, drive 14.5 miles to the first Wendell exit. Turn right (west) on the Wendell-Hagerman Road at the end of the exit ramp. Go 3.2 miles to a road signed 1500 East with an arrow sign for Buhl. Turn left (south) here and drive 4.5 miles, passing the West Point Store, to a sign "Earl M. Hardy Box Canyon Preserve" and parking area on the right (west). Another alternative is to take the second Bliss exit and drive south on U.S. Highway 30 to Hagerman. As you drive through Hagerman, notice the Hagerman Fossil Beds office on your left. Continue south for 2.4 miles from this office and turn left (east) at a sign for Wendell onto the Wendell-Hagerman Road. Go 5.3 miles to 1500 East, turn right, and go south 4.5 miles to the parking area for the preserve.

At the head of this vertical-walled side canyon of the Snake River are two aqua-green pools where water bubbles up through the basalt at their edges, creating shifting streaks of white sand at their centers. A cascade laced with curls of white water connects the two pools. From the lower pool the creek continues in cascades toward the Snake in an S-curve, dropping in a twenty-foot waterfall .2 mile below the pools. Around the pools and along the creek, riparian shrubs create a cloud of greenery, except in the fall and winter when the colors are rusts and grays. At the S-curve a few junipers add dark green to the palette. Along the edges of the canyon, immense chunks of lava have partially split off from the main mass of lava that underlies the plain, showing how the canyon formed.

From the parking area walk west along the old road, passing a house, a barn and a cultivated field. At .5 mile, the track goes through a fence, curves left (south), descends a few feet and passes through a grove of the introduced tree, Russian olive, decorated with magpie nests. Just beyond are some portapotties where the canyon rim is only a few yards to the right. Turn off the old road here and walk to the edge of the canyon at .7 mile for an excellent view of the two aquamarine pools. When you have taken enough pictures, return to the old road and walk south along it. After about .1 mile another old road angles off to the right through tumbleweeds toward the canyon. Turn off on that road and continue to a grassy area where another old road comes in from the east. At the edge of the canyon 1 mile from the parking area, a sign "Caution, unimproved trail. Use at own risk." marks a sketchy path to the canyon bottom. THIS IS A DANGEROUS ROUTE. At the top, this path makes a hairpin turn just under the canyon rim. At this turn, a fragile-looking cable has been strung to help hikers descend the cliff. Note that the cable is rusty and has sharp protrusions. Below the cable, the ground becomes slightly less steep and the path winds through boulders

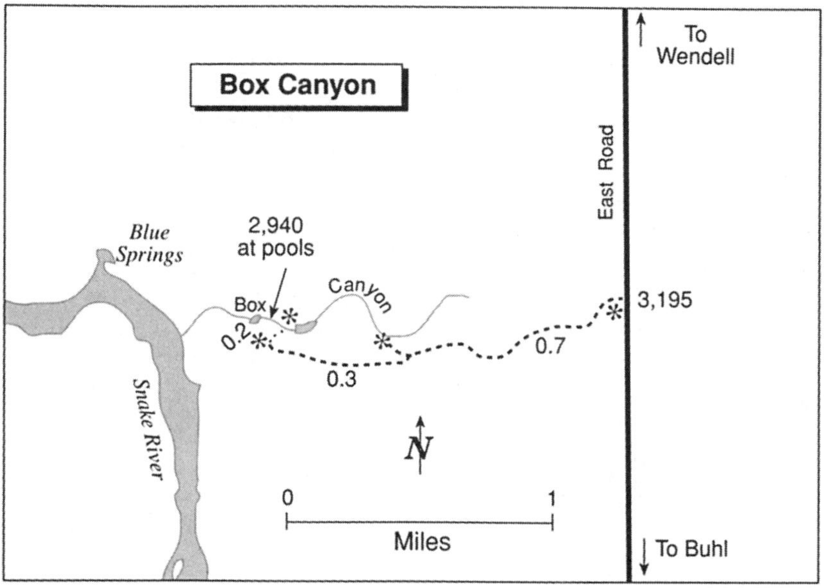


and shrubs to the edge of the creek at 1.2 miles. The two pools are a few yards to the north, but walking along the creek to them is very difficult because of a jungle of shrubs and hidden rocks. It is easier to walk down the canyon, where in .2 mile there is a 20-foot waterfall. Be aware that there is lots of poison ivy in the bottom of the canyon, as well as rattlesnakes. The route of the trail to the canyon and the location of the pools vary from what is shown on the topographic map.

# NATIONAL PARK SERVICE

## 79.

## Hagerman Fossil Beds: Emigrant Trail and Oregon Trail Overlook

**Round trip:** .5 mile for the Oregon Trail overlook; one way trip of 3 miles for the Emigrant Trail

**Elevation gain:** 575 feet for the Emigrant Trail

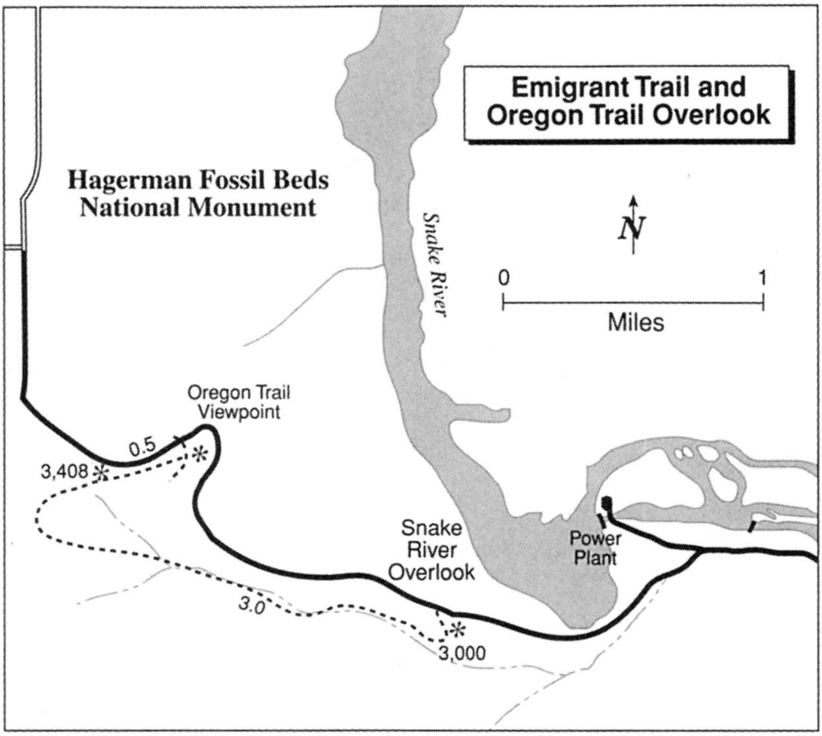


**Elevation loss (return climb):** 25 feet for the Oregon Trail overlook,

**Highest point:** 3,475 feet

**Map:** Hagerman

**Difficulty:** easy; time: 1/2 hour for overlook; 2 hours for Emigrant Trail with a car shuttle

**Access:** On I-84, at the eastern of the two Bliss exits (141), turn south toward Hagerman on U.S. Highway 30 and drive through Hagerman. From the Hagerman Fossil Beds office continue south and cross the bridge over the Snake River. On the other side of the bridge, at 4.8 miles, turn right (west) on a paved road along the south side of the river. Begin hiking the Emigrant Trail across the road from the Snake River Scenic Overlook at 7.5 miles or continue to the top of the grade to a large parking area for the upper end of the trail and the Oregon Trail Overlook trail at 10.2 miles.

The Oregon Trail overlook gives an excellent view of blue or silver curves of the Snake River winding in two directions. Near the beginning, you can see the big groove cut in the land by the Oregon Trail as it climbs the steep escarpment from the low land along the river below. To preserve the remnants of the Oregon Trail here, the National Park Service has constructed another trail parallel to it. This trail, the Emigrant Trail, gives you an excellent idea of the hilly, sagebrush-covered landscape the Oregon Trail traveled much of its way through Idaho. The little valley and hillside the

Emigrant Trail follow have no water and are dominated by typical great basin shrubs, including rabbit brush. Unfortunately, the introduced plants, tumbleweed and rush skeleton weed, now grow here in abundance as well. It is too bad the Oregon Trail travelers weren't able to see the area in spring, when the hillsides turn bright green and are decorated with wildflower jewels.

The Overlook Trail begins at the northeast corner of the parking lot and goes about .2 mile to a hilltop overlooking the paved road and the river. Near the parking lot, it passes the head of a steep gully that has Oregon Trail ruts and signs requesting you not to walk on them. Past the gully, one branch of this trail goes left a few yards for a better look at the river and another branch goes right a few yards for a look at the Oregon Trail.

The Emigrant Trail runs from the upper trailhead to the Scenic Overlook of the Snake River back about three miles toward Hagerman. You can walk or ride a horse along the trail from either end. Bicycles and motorcycles are not allowed. To get an idea of the difficulty the pioneers had climbing the escarpment to the plain above you need to start at the bottom trailhead.

The trail begins across the highway from the Snake River Overlook. First, it angles east down into the little valley that runs below the road here, then it turns straight downhill and goes through a gate. From here you can see shrubs and trees in the next valley to the southeast. Next, it turns right and goes west up the center of the little valley, crossing to the left of a small watercourse after about 200 yards. As a dusty or muddy track, the trail continues west along the little valley through the sagebrush and tumbleweeds. At 1.4 miles, the canyon splits and the trail goes up the right (north) branch. Above, power lines remind you that this is not the 1850s. At about 2 miles, the trail begins to angle up the left wall of the canyon, running parallel to the bottom of it. When the trail nears the top of the steep walls at the upper end at 2.6 miles, it turns 90 degrees to the right (north) and climbs along the side of the ridge that forms the headwall of the canyon. Underfoot in this section are scattered pieces of whitish limestone or caliche. This sedimentary rock overlies additional sedimentary deposits of the Glenns Ferry formation, in which has been found the largest concentration of fossil horses in North America. The trail comes to the top of the ridge, goes along it to a gate and goes through it to the parking lot at 3 miles.

# BUREAU OF LAND MANAGEMENT: VALE DISTRICT (OREGON)

## 80.

### Coffeepot Crater

**Round trip:** 1 mile
**Elevation gain:** 90 feet

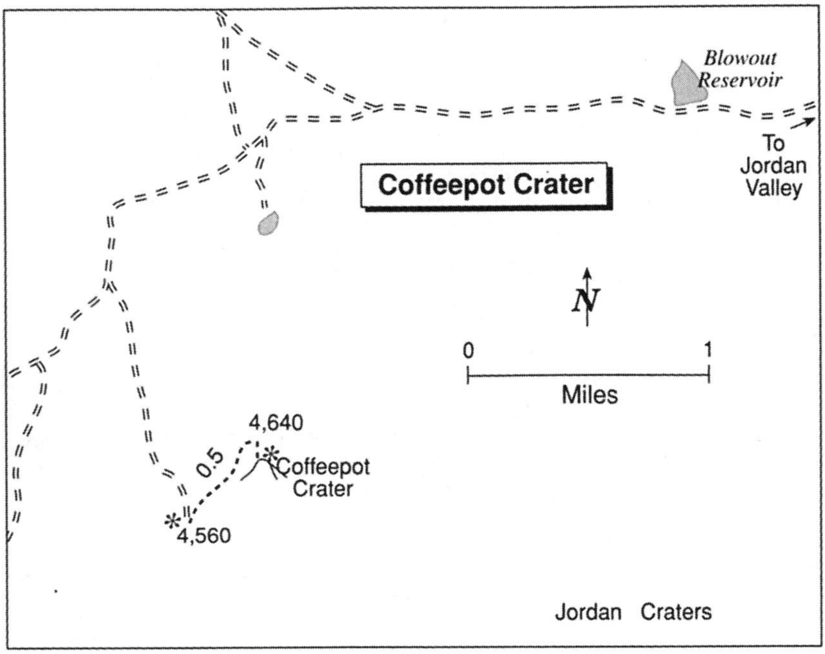


**Elevation loss:** 100 feet (return climb)
**Highest point:** 4,640 feet
**Maps:** Jordan Craters North (Oregon), Vale District BLM map
**Difficulty:** easy, except for finding the crater by road; time: 1 hour

**Access:** From the junction of Idaho 55 and U.S. 95 west of Marsing, drive 36.4 miles south on U.S. Highway 95. Turn right (west) on a dirt road signed Jordan Craters and drive 9 miles. Then veer right (north) and go 8 miles, avoiding roads to the left to Cow Lakes. Take the left (west) branch of the road and go 7 miles to a junction just before a short track turns south to seasonally dry Coffeepot Reservoir. At the junction, turn left (west) and drive 1 mile. Avoiding a road to the right, turn left (south) and drive 1 mile to the end of the road beside a large crater. (There are few or no signs for these turns, but once you see the big crater it is not hard to find the way to the base of it.)

Jordan Valley was first settled in 1864 when John Baxter built a stone house at Jordan Creek on Skinner's toll road to Silver City. He operated a store, post office and a hotel from the house. Later, the settlement became a supply station for the Silver City mines. At first ranchers raised cattle, but a bad winter in 1888 killed most of the cattle, so they brought in sheep and Basques from Spain to herd them. Some of the herders started buying and raising sheep themselves and their descendants still live and ranch in the area.

Near the Idaho border northwest of Jordan Valley, Oregon, Jordan Craters rise from a six-mile square of rough black lava. From the end of the road beside Coffeepot Crater, an unmaintained path climbs the crater wall and descends into the center where bright green and orange lichens blotch the pink-striped inner walls. The path angles up the south side of the crater, goes around its rim to the left and drops into the crater from the north, reaching the bottom at .5 mile. BE CAUTIOUS, only the surefooted should attempt to descend into the crater. Children will especially enjoy the several small craters which cluster around the big one like coffee cups.

After exploring the crater, you may want to walk cross-country out on the lava fields. BE CAREFUL because the lava has many sinkholes and drop offs. It is best not to take small children or dogs. The area is similar to Craters of the Moon National Monument near Arco, Idaho, but doesn't have as many craters or caves.

# 81.

## Three Fingers Rock

**Round trip:** 2 miles
**Elevation gain:** 700 feet
**Highest point:** 4,828 feet
**Maps:** Three Fingers Rock, Pole Creek Top (both Oregon)
**Difficulty:** cross-country; time: 3 hours
**Access:** 5.1 miles west of Homedale, Idaho, on Oregon Highway 201, turn left (south) on the Succor Creek Road. Drive 18.5 miles, passing picnic areas and campgrounds and climbing 1,000 feet out of the canyon. Then turn northwest on an unmarked dirt road 1 mile beyond a 400-foot red-brown rock (known as Negro Rock) and go 3.5 miles. The road is not passable before May 1 or in rainy weather. Avoid driving it when thunderstorms threaten. For the 3.5-mile side road you now need four-wheel drive. You can also reach this road from the McBride Creek Road from U.S. Highway 95. On this route, after driving 10.4 miles from the highway to the Leslie Gulch turnoff, it is about another 5 miles to the side road at Negro Rock. The last 6.5 miles to the turnoff is rocky and can have a washboard surface, so it is slow going.

As you drive the Succor Creek Road on the way to Three Fingers Rock, you are following a road that was the main highway to Jordan Valley until U.S. Highway 95 was constructed about 1920. Before that there was Skinner's toll road, which went up Poison Creek to Rockville and then up Jordan Creek to Silver City. The old stage station at Poison Creek is still standing. Another stage station was at Rockville (named for two big rocks used by freighters for storing hay and grain). The site of Rockville is 1.7 miles south of the junction with the side road to Leslie Gulch on the Succor Creek Road.

From the top of Three Fingers Rock, buttes, rocks and tablelands stretch toward the Treasure Valley and to the Owyhee Mountains. Grass-lined notches split the 200-foot rock into three sections 40 feet below the top. Because the top of the rock is the highest point for miles, it is a landmark in the Treasure Valley. It is easy to scramble up the east section of the rock. Spring is the best season for this trip as phlox, balsamroot, Indian paintbrush and penstemon peek out from beneath the sagebrush.

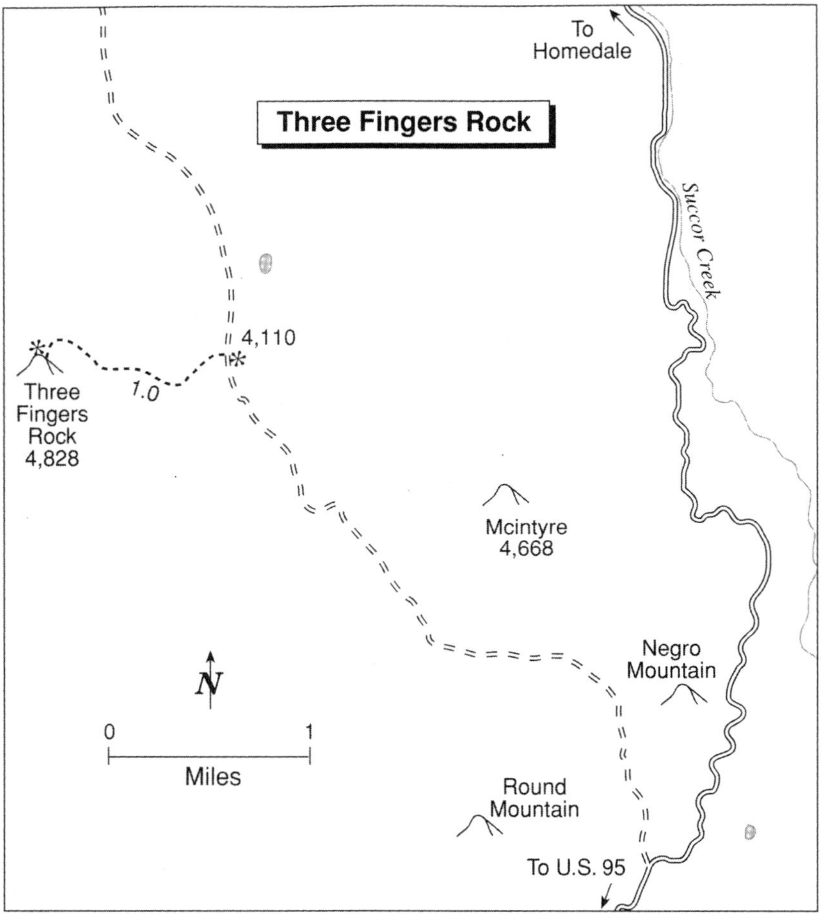


Just beyond the turnoff to Three Fingers Rock from the Succor Creek Road (5 miles north of the turnoff to Leslie Gulch) the rock looms ahead. The rutted dirt road climbs up and down, passing another which turns left. On top of the second rise at 3.5 miles, a jeep trail leads up a ridge to the left (west). Park here if you haven't already done so and walk up this track towards the hidden rock. When you see the rock from the top of the ridge you have been climbing, head cross-country towards its slanting north side. You may find a faint path leading this direction. Still on the north side of the rock, angle cross-country through grassy ravines up to the east one of the two notches. Climb to the little carpet of turf within the notch and then scramble 30 feet to the top of the east section of the main rock, which is 1 mile from the road. The more difficult 40-foot cliff of the middle section of the rock is suitable only for trained mountaineers with ropes. After climbing the rock, walk along below its south side .2 mile for a close view of its three sections.

# 82.

## Upper Leslie Gulch and Juniper Gulch

**Round trip:** 2 to 4 miles for Upper Leslie Gulch; 1.4 miles for Juniper Gulch

**Elevation gain:** 240 to 640 feet for Upper Leslie Gulch; 480 feet for Juniper Gulch

**Highest point:** 4,400 feet in Upper Leslie Gulch; 3,880 feet in Juniper Gulch

**Map:** Rooster Comb (Oregon), Bannock Ridge (Oregon)

**Difficulty:** easy; time: 1 hour plus for Upper Leslie Gulch (partly cross-country); 1 1/2 hours for Juniper Gulch

**Access:** Drive south on U.S. Highway 95 from the junction of Idaho Highway 55 and U.S. Highway 95 for 19.2 miles. Turn right (west) at McBride Creek and drive 8.7 miles to the site of Rockville where there is a junction with the Succor Creek Road. Turn right here towards Succor Creek State Park. At the Leslie Gulch turnoff at 10.4 miles, turn left (west) and drive over a summit at 17.1 miles and down to Upper Leslie Gulch at 19.6 miles and Juniper Gulch at 20.8 miles.

In Juniper Gulch and Upper Leslie Gulch miniature caves pit gold and orange cliffs above wildflowers, sagebrush and junipers. Rock towers blaze red, gold and orange here, and nearby at Owyhee Reservoir. These hikes up side canyons from Leslie Gulch give an intimate view of some of the colorful rock formations.

The Leslie Gulch area has been designated by the Bureau of Land Management as an Area of Critical Environmental Concern (ACEC) to protect its scenery, volcanic ash soils, five special status plant species, and animal life, especially the reintroduced California bighorn sheep. Much of the land in and around Leslie Gulch is within wilderness study areas. The only camping allowed is at the developed Slocum Creek campground near the shore of Owyhee Reservoir; therefore backpacking is not allowed. The towers have been formed by erosion and weathering of the Leslie Gulch ash flow tuffs, which resulted from the eruption of Mahogany Mountain 15 million years ago.

The road down Leslie Gulch leads to 50-mile-long Owyhee Reservoir. Construction on the dam that created the reservoir began in 1928 and was completed in 1932, bringing widespread irrigation to Malheur County, beginning in 1935.

To hike Upper Leslie Gulch, park at the sign for it and go along an unmaintained path on the left side of the little creek. As you begin, a spectacular striped cream and orange flat-topped tower is above on your right. At about .1 mile, the path crosses the creek to the right side. As you go along the creek, the valley widens and flattens out and the path becomes a network of faint traces. At about .4 mile, the path ends at the creek. Stay to the right of the creek here, hiking among the sagebrush as you go south. As you go up the canyon the colors of the cliffs fade to cream and peach. At about .6 mile, a steep side canyon tumbles down from your left (east). At this confluence the main canyon curves slightly to the right (south). Continue south past a row of 200-foot cliffs to where the canyon splits at 1 mile.

Here on the right, a row of isolated orange towers marks a ridge leading toward the timbered Mahogany Mountains straight ahead in the distance. Much of the

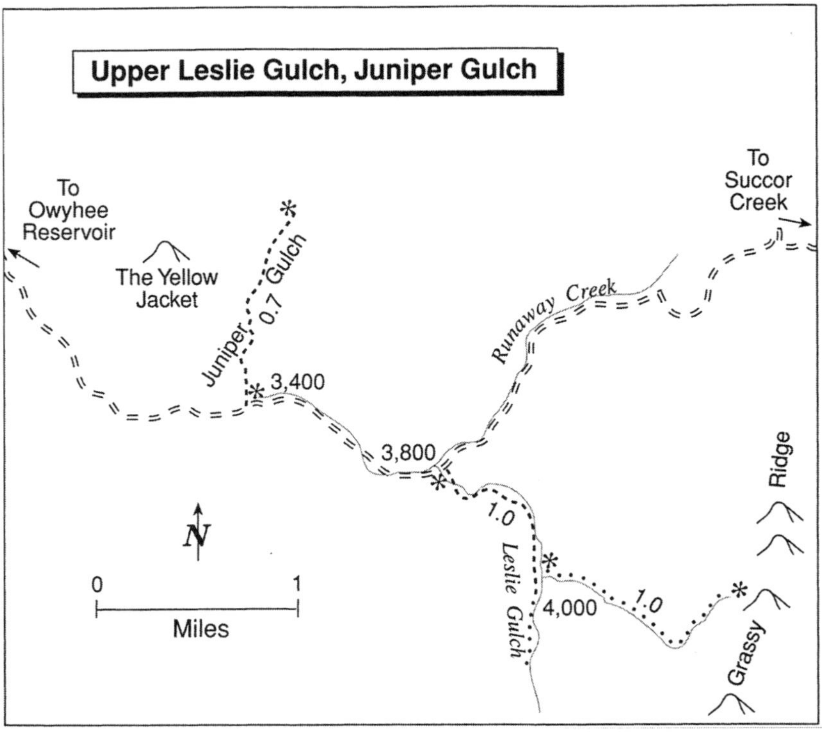


Mahogany Mountains is private land, and the canyon to the left is more spectacular. Therefore, if you want to continue farther, it is best to go east up the left canyon. In this canyon, cliffs continue along its west wall and include a 400-foot cliff at 1.5 miles. The canyon becomes steeper after that as it veers east and ends at about 2 miles just below a crest called Grassy Ridge.

Looking up Juniper Gulch from the parking area, a striped, cream-colored wall is topped with little towers pocketed with holes and leaning in such a way they appear to be dancing. To hike up Juniper Gulch from the parking area, ford the creek in Leslie Gulch and walk north up a path that soon becomes the canyon channel. Follow the channel up the gulch if the creek is dry. The path follows the gulch along its east side until its stream forks. At the fork, it heads between the streams onto a flat area and disappears under small cliffs at .7 mile.

# SALMON-CHALLIS NATIONAL FOREST
# MIDDLE FORK DISTRICT
# SEAFOAM AREA

## 83.

## Seafoam Lakes

**Round trip:** 6.8 miles
**Elevation gain:** 1,440 feet
**Highest point:** 8,200 feet
**Map:** Greyhound Mountain
**Difficulty:** moderate, but cross-country to third and fourth lakes; time: 6 hours
**Access:** Turn north off Idaho Highway 21 onto the Seafoam Road 18 miles northwest of Stanley. Drive 10 miles on gravel and 4 miles on dirt to the Seafoam Guard Station. Turn left (west) and go 2.7 miles on the primitive Seafoam Lakes Road. You used to be able to drive to the first and second lakes with four-wheel drive, but that part of the road is no longer maintained and its condition is deteriorating. The district ranger says it is DANGEROUS to try to drive it. Therefore, park at the ford of Seafoam Creek near the Fall Creek Trail sign and walk from there.

Mining began in the Seafoam area began when silver and gold were discovered there in 1886 by I.N. Daly and John Mullen. More than 20 mines were started on Seafoam, Float, Sulphur and Josephus Creeks. To serve them and the mines at Capehorn in the Stanley Basin, William Rideout built a supply station at the upper end of the basin in 1903. In 1905, the Greyhound Company constructed a rough toll road over Vanity Summit to the mines. At the foot of the grade over that summit, Mose Storher built a log store and hotel known as "Wagontown." The ruins of Wagontown are still visible along the road.

Misty green water forms four small lakes on Seafoam Creek below three dark gray peaks resembling three heads from the first lake and three pyramids from the fourth. At the first lake, a gray stripe across a buff-colored cliff on the middle peak gives that head a pleased smirk. The fourth lake sprawls amid grass and red mountain heath under a dark rock knoll beside the three peaks.

From the Fall Creek Trail sign on the Seafoam Lakes Road, ford Seafoam Creek and walk up the road. It switches back at 200 yards, passes a mine road at .2 mile, and makes two sharp bends at .5 mile. At 1 mile, the track passes two mine sheds as it zigzags up through rocks. At a fork at 1.5 miles, the left branch climbs boulders to a mine. Take the right (west) branch downhill to a ford at 2 miles where a track leads left 50 yards to the first lake.

To reach the second lake, continue on the road beyond the ford. At 200 yards, a side road dead-ends to the left (south) in the woods. When the main road splits 100 yards beyond this, take either branch, since these roads form a loop. At 2.5 miles, the road reaches the top of the loop, and turns back to the right (east) to complete it. At

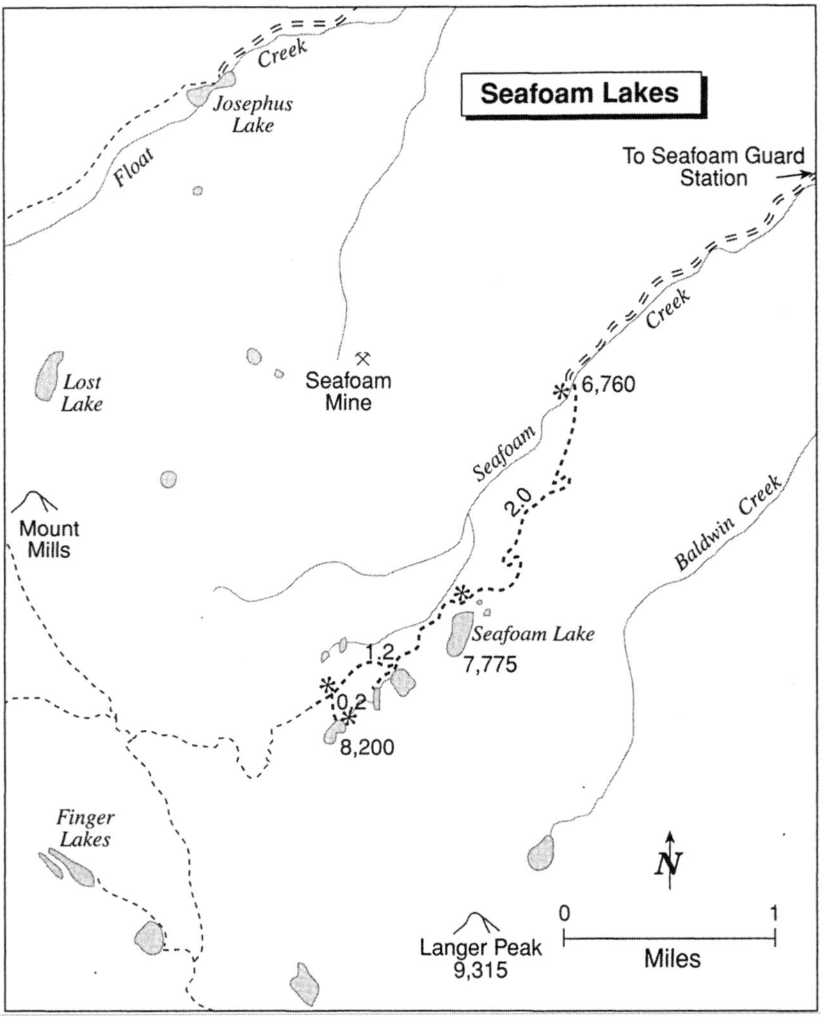


the top of the loop, the second lake is visible through the trees 100 yards cross-country to the south. To get to the third lake, climb cross-country up the creek between the lakes.

To find the fourth lake, go back down the right (north) branch of the loop for 100 yards to a blazed trail leading southwest. This is the Fall Creek Trail to the Middle Fork of the Salmon. Walk up this trail through firs and lodgepoles until opposite the first of the three dark gray peaks at 3.2 miles. Then cut south cross-country toward the middle one of the three peaks to reach the fourth lake at 3.4 miles.

# YANKEE FORK DISTRICT
# CAPE HORN AREA

## 84.

## Hindman Lake from Basin Butte

**Round trip:** 15 miles (from beginning of Hindman Lake jeep trail)
**Elevation gain:** 1,060 feet
**Elevation loss:** 1,300 feet (return climb)
**Highest point:** 8,760 feet
**Maps:** Basin Butte, Knapp Lakes
**Difficulty:** strenuous; time: 11 hours
**Access:** On Idaho Highway 21, 4.4 miles north of Stanley, turn right (east) on the rocky, rutted Basin Butte Road, which now requires four-wheel drive, and drive 11 miles to the Hindman Lake jeep trail, which is 1 mile below Basin Butte Lookout. You may be able to drive about 2 miles along the jeep trail with a four-wheel drive vehicle. However, the road has deteriorated so that it has more and bigger rocks, a narrower road bed, and side hilled sections. It is no longer recommended for four-wheel drive pickups or SUVs.

The basin of meadows west of the trail is called the Stanley Basin. It was discovered by fur trader Alexander Ross on September 18, 1824. After John Stanley discovered gold in the basin in 1864, 200 prospectors arrived. By 1869, Stanley had a store started by Arthur McGown to sell beef to the miners. Stanley continued to be a way station for miners as prospectors flocked to the Yankee Fork, Loon Creek and elsewhere. Beginning in 1873, several men discovered lodes or placers in the Stanley Basin in Kelly Gulch and Joes Gulch. Dredging occurred for about 25 years in the gulches, beginning in 1890.

Above Hindman Lake, Cabin Creek Peak unfurls a wrinkled wall of burnt orange and gray stripes. (This is the peak which is visible above wooded ridges to the north from Idaho Highway 75 just south of Stanley.) Northeast of Hindman Lake, the top of Red Mountain resembles a pile of crumbled bricks. Around the small green lake, red, yellow and pink Indian paintbrush dapples the grass, and springs bubble from beds of moss. From the top of Basin Butte, the chalky peaks of the White Clouds float in the distance. The northern end of the Sawtooths zigzags close by. Before the hike, be sure to drive or walk to the top of Basin Butte to enjoy the view.

The hike mileage given here begins at the start of the Hindman Lake jeep trail because it is DANGEROUS or impossible to drive some of the jeep trail in a four-wheel drive pickup or SUV as you used to be able to do. Because of the need for four-wheel drive from part way up the Basin Butte Road, the main use this track gets now is by ATVs. The route is too rocky to be enjoyable for most mountain bikers. Because of the heavy ATV use on weekends, it will be more pleasant for you to hike the trail during the week or in September. The hike is worth taking though to see Cabin Creek Peak up close.

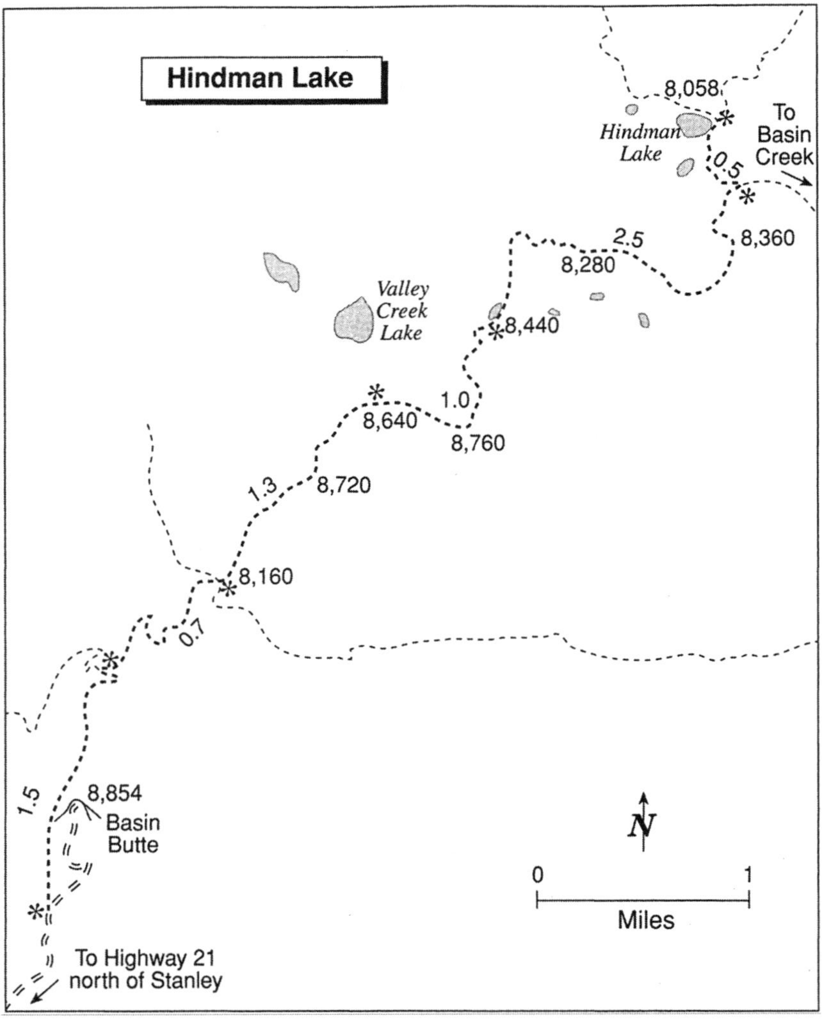


There is an alternate route the same length to Hindman Lake that avoids the ATV traffic, but it is not described in detail here. To find it drive east of Stanley on Idaho Highway 75 to Basin Creek and up Basin Creek for 4 miles to a trailhead just below Short Creek. This trail climbs 7.5 miles up Basin Creek with a 1,700-foot elevation gain to Hindman Lake. (There is no elevation loss to be reclimbed on the return on this route but the elevation gain is much greater than on the jeep trail.)

The Hindman Lake jeep trail begins by skirting the west side of Basin Butte and passes an old road from the lookout at 1.2 miles. At 1.5 miles, a trail turns off to the left down the East Fork of Valley Creek. On the main trail, the next mile drops 600 feet. At 2.2 miles, there is a junction from which trails lead down Prospect Creek to the west and Sunday Creek to the east.

The track next climbs northwest 500 feet over a wooded hill for 1 mile, and at 3.5 miles, parallels a saddle with a campsite on it. An unofficial trail leads north over the saddle and down 400 feet in .5 mile to Valley Creek Lake.

The track now climbs 120 feet in .5 mile, then skirts the end of a ridge and descends 320 feet to ponds at 4.5 miles. From the ponds it drops 200 feet and climbs 160 feet. Then it circles the end of another ridge, and drops 160 feet to a junction with the trail down Basin Creek at 7 miles where there is a view of Cabin Creek Peak and Red Mountain. From this junction, the track drops another 160 feet to the lake at 7.5 miles.

From the lake, the old jeep trail continues north toward Cabin Creek Peak and east below it to prospects. Also, a pack trail leads northwest 5 miles to Knapp Creek.

# SALMON-CHALLIS NATIONAL FOREST
# LOST RIVER DISTRICT
# TRAIL CREEK AREA

## 85.

## Summit Creek Trail

**Round trip:** 7.6 miles to saddle
**Elevation gain:** 1,560 feet
**Highest point:** 9,480 feet
**Maps:** Rock Roll Canyon, Phi Kappa Mountain
**Difficulty:** moderate; time: 6 hours
**Access:** From the junction of Sun Valley Road with Idaho Highway 75 in Ketchum, drive northeast on Trail Creek Road 9.4 miles on pavement and 2.9 miles on a dirt road with sharp rocks to Trail Creek Summit.

Trail Creek Road was first constructed in 1884, when H.C. Lewis built a toll road up Trail Creek from Ketchum to the Lost River, Bayhorse and Custer mines. This road allowed several mines, such as the Phi Kappa, Black Rock, and mines in Copper Basin, to be developed on the east side of the Pioneer Mountains.

This hike leads to a saddle across from the orange and light gray wall of the Devils Bedstead, which has so many sharp points giants would indeed find sleeping on it most uncomfortable. A grassy cirque indents the face of this mountain, and a ridge drops in stair steps from the summit to a notch. To the right of the notch, a sharp ridge runs down to a boulder-covered saddle. The trail to the saddle goes through meadows of paintbrush, cinquefoil, penstemon and bluebells and passes mossy springs. Above

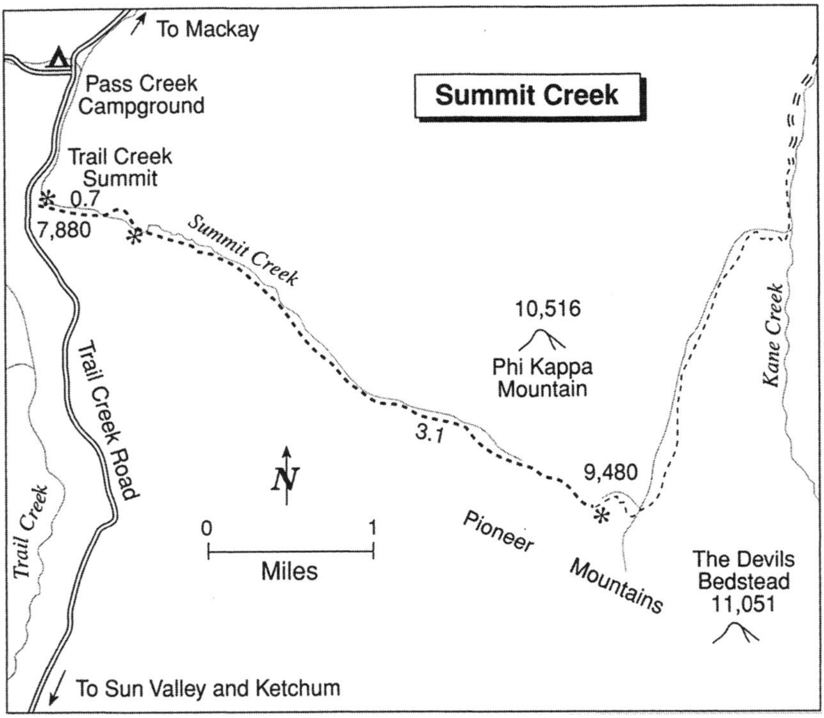


on the south, scalloped rose-colored cliffs edge the upper canyon across from the orange talus shoulder of Phi Kappa Mountain.

At Trail Creek Summit, park beside two snow markers where a jeep track leads 100 yards northeast to the creek. Walk down this track and ford the creek (in late summer cross on rocks). On the other side of the creek, the trail switchbacks back and forth up a hillside and then goes up the canyon across an open grass and lupine-covered hillside into woods. The trail passes a wet meadow at .5 miles and crosses the creek back to the south side at .7 mile.

The trail runs in the woods, then returns to the open at 1 mile. At 1.3 miles, it re-enters the forest at two avalanche areas and follows a .5 mile-long grassy hillside at 2 miles. At 2.5 miles, springs bubble from moss under big firs. The trail at 3 miles crosses a side stream and then climbs 200 yards along the left side of it.

A clearing is at 3.3 miles and a blaze on the far side marks where the trail drops to cross a stream. Across the stream, it climbs the left side of a bigger open area among little trees, winds through another open area and zigzags to the top of the saddle at 3.8 miles. The best view of the Devils Bedstead is from a grassy dell beyond the saddle. The trail descends 3 more miles to a half-mile trail leading down the west side of Kane Creek to the Kane Creek Road.

# 86.

## Kane Lake

**Round trip:** 8 miles
**Elevation gain:** 1,640 feet
**Highest point:** 9,240 feet
**Map:** Phi Kappa Mountain
**Difficulty:** strenuous; partly cross-country; time: 6½ hours
**Access:** Drive 19.2 miles northeast of Ketchum over the rocky Trail Creek Road to the primitive Kane Creek Road. Turn right (south) and drive along the creek, crossing it to the west side on a bridge. The Kane Creek Road fords a piece of the creek twice at 3.5 miles in a shallow place, with the second ford 100 yards beyond the first. These crossings are not shown on the topographic map and may require four-wheel drive. At 4.6 miles the road ends beside the creek at a closed to motor vehicles sign.

Across from 2,000-foot walls, turf carpets the north side of milky turquoise Kane Lake. Subalpine firs grow on the turf and in midsummer, buttercups, red mountain heath and dwarf paintbrush are in bloom. Above the south side of the lake rises a striped roof-shaped point of rock. Near it, a 300-foot waterfall splashes down a chimney in a black cliff. To the east, a second waterfall inscribes a unique dotted line. Three grayish-orange sections of the Devils Bedstead scribbled with stripes curve northwest of the lake.

From the south end of the informal parking area a recently-built trail goes along the right (west) side of the creek through forest, so you no longer have to ford the creek here. At .5 mile, is a rough plank bridge over the Right Fork of Kane Creek. Within a few yards, the trail joins one that has come 3 miles down the Right Fork from the Summit Creek Trail. At this junction, the trail crosses to the left (east) bank of Kane Creek on a footbridge. The jeep trail that used to come up the east side of the creek from the parking area has almost disappeared. From a campsite on the east bank beyond the footbridge, the trail to Kane Lake goes south up the canyon in woods, climbs the side of a small ridge, and returns to the creek bank at 1.7 miles for a few yards.

The official trail ends at 2.7 miles, but a trail which sometimes disappears continues through boulder fields. It crosses below a tongue of boulders, goes through a meadow by the creek, crosses a second tongue of boulders, and enters another meadow below more boulders. Then it climbs up granite ledges and through trees and disappears as it crosses the lower end of an immense slope of boulders. When the trail reappears, it climbs along the outlet of the lake between rock ledges and benches. Near the top, it splits, and either branch leads to the lake at 4 miles.

Kane Lake

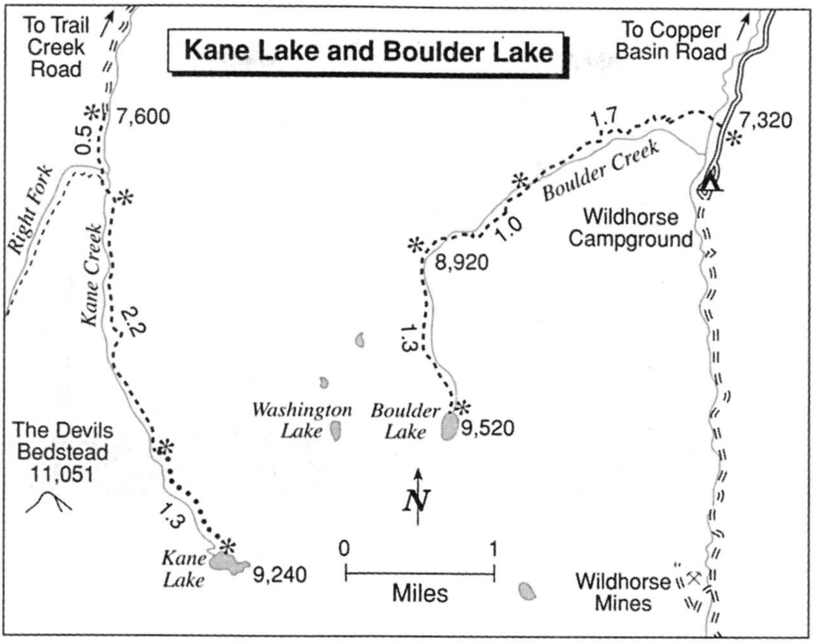


# 87.

## Boulder Lake

**Round trip:** 8 miles
**Elevation gain:** 2,200 feet
**Highest point:** 9,520 feet
**Maps:** Standhope Peak, Phi Kappa Mountain
**Difficulty:** strenuous; time: 7 hours
**Access:** Drive 22.5 miles northeast of Ketchum over the rocky Trail Creek Road to the turnoff for Copper Basin. Turn right (southeast) and drive 2.1 miles to the Wildhorse Creek Road. Turn right (south) and drive 4.6 miles to the Boulder Lake trailhead, which is just before the Wildhorse Campground on the right (west) side of the road.

Boulders and flower-studded grass surround the blue-green water of Boulder Lake. Pikas give insistent peeps while scampering among the rocks. A striped gray and orange wall flanks the east side of the lake and a knife-edged ridge of four jagged summits rises 1,800 feet at its head. To the west, a helmet-shaped summit near Washington Lake bulges behind an orange and white striped peak. A rose and light green ridge down the canyon ends in an elephant-shaped hill.

The trail first fords the creek and goes through willows into sagebrush and over to a forested hillside. It switchbacks up through the fir forest to the canyon of Boulder Creek and at .7 mile, runs along the edge of a 100-foot deep canyon.

An area of sagebrush, small firs and aspens is at 1.5 miles. At 1.7 miles, the trail crosses the creek to the east on logs and climbs beside a 20-foot chasm in the bedrock. Then it zigzags along the forest edge, and crosses the creek again to the west on rocks at 2.7 miles, 1,400 vertical feet from the trailhead.

As the trail levels out into an upper valley, unnamed peaks block the head of the canyon. Meadows sparkling with red paintbrush, white bistort and yellow buttercups are at 3.2 miles. Even though the trail may be confusing in the meadows, it is well blazed. At 3.7 miles, it continues up the west side of the creek to the lake at 4 miles, having climbed 800 feet in the last 1.3 miles.

# 88.

## Moose Lake

**Round trip:** 10 miles
**Elevation gain:** 2,255 feet
**Highest point:** 9,455 feet
**Map:** Standhope Peak
**Difficulty:** strenuous; time: 8 hours
**Access:** Drive 22.5 miles northeast of Ketchum over the rocky Trail Creek Road to the turnoff for Copper Basin. Turn right (southeast) and drive 2.1 miles to the Wildhorse Creek Road. Turn right (south) and go 3.5 miles to Fall Creek. Just beyond the bridge over the creek, turn left (east) and go .5 mile to the developed trailhead.

Jagged gray cliffs sweep to the apex of a mountain wall 2,300 feet above the head of Moose Lake. Below the wall, granite ridges create giant rounded steps. Three lower ridges disappear on the west into a massive mountain of gray rock. At Upper Moose Lake, a throne of rock tops a small peak, above gnarled trees and flowery meadows.

The old road shown on the map at Fall Creek as going 2 miles farther up the creek no longer exists. Instead, from the parking area walk north over Fall Creek on a bridge. In 200 yards, the trail turns right (east) through a gate in a pole fence and continues through sagebrush and past a display of blazing star. At 2 miles, it turns south and crosses the Left Fork of Fall Creek just before a junction with a trail up that creek. It is not a good plan to go up the trail on the right side of the creek to the falls and then ford the creek to the main trail, because it is so hard to ford the creek it isn't worth the .5 mile saved.

Beyond the junction with the trail up the Left Fork of Fall Creek, the main trail wanders through level meadows for 1 mile. At 3 miles, is a junction of the Fall Creek and Moose Lake trails. Turn right here on the Moose Lake Trail which fords Fall Creek and turns southwest up the canyon of the North Fork of Fall Creek. At 4 miles, it climbs in four large switchbacks not shown on the topographic map. The trail runs along the creek and crosses it at 4.5 miles amid a cloud of bluebells. It winds beside outcrops and a meadow to the lake at 5 miles. There are several campsites. To reach the higher lake, take a path along the east side of the lake to the inlet and walk up it.

# 89.

## Fall Creek Falls

**Round trip:** 2 miles
**Elevation gain:** 40 feet
**Highest Point:** 7,520 feet
**Map:** Standhope Peak
**Difficulty:** very easy, suitable for handicapped; time: 1 hour
**Access:** Drive 22.5 miles northeast of Ketchum over the rocky Trail Creek Road to the turnoff for Copper Basin. Turn right (southeast) and drive 2.1 miles to the Wildhorse Creek Road. Turn right (south) and go 3.5 miles to Fall Creek. Just beyond a bridge, turn left (east) and go .5 mile to the developed trailhead.

This trail leads from the Wildhorse Creek valley with its alp-like peaks up Fall Creek to a waterfall in the woods. The falls leap down mossy rock ledges in stair steps of spray, with a larger step on the fourth level formed by a six-foot-wide pool.

The 3-foot-wide gravel trail begins at the east edge of the parking lot and after 50 yards is running east in a Douglas fir forest 30 feet above the right side of Fall Creek. After about .2 mile, the trail comes out into a large flat of sagebrush and grass. At .8 mile, it goes into a grove of trees, curves right, then left and ends at a viewing platform in the woods at 1 mile.

# 90.

## Surprise Valley and Lakes

**Round trip:** 13 miles
**Elevation gain:** 2,940 feet
**This section:** 3.5 miles and 2,340 feet gain one-way
**Highest point:** 10,148 feet
**Map:** Standhope Peak
**Difficulty:** expert; time: 10 hours to 2 days
**Access:** Drive 22 .5 miles northeast of Ketchum over rocky Trail Creek Road to the turnoff for Copper Basin. Turn right (southeast) and drive 2.1 miles to the Wild-

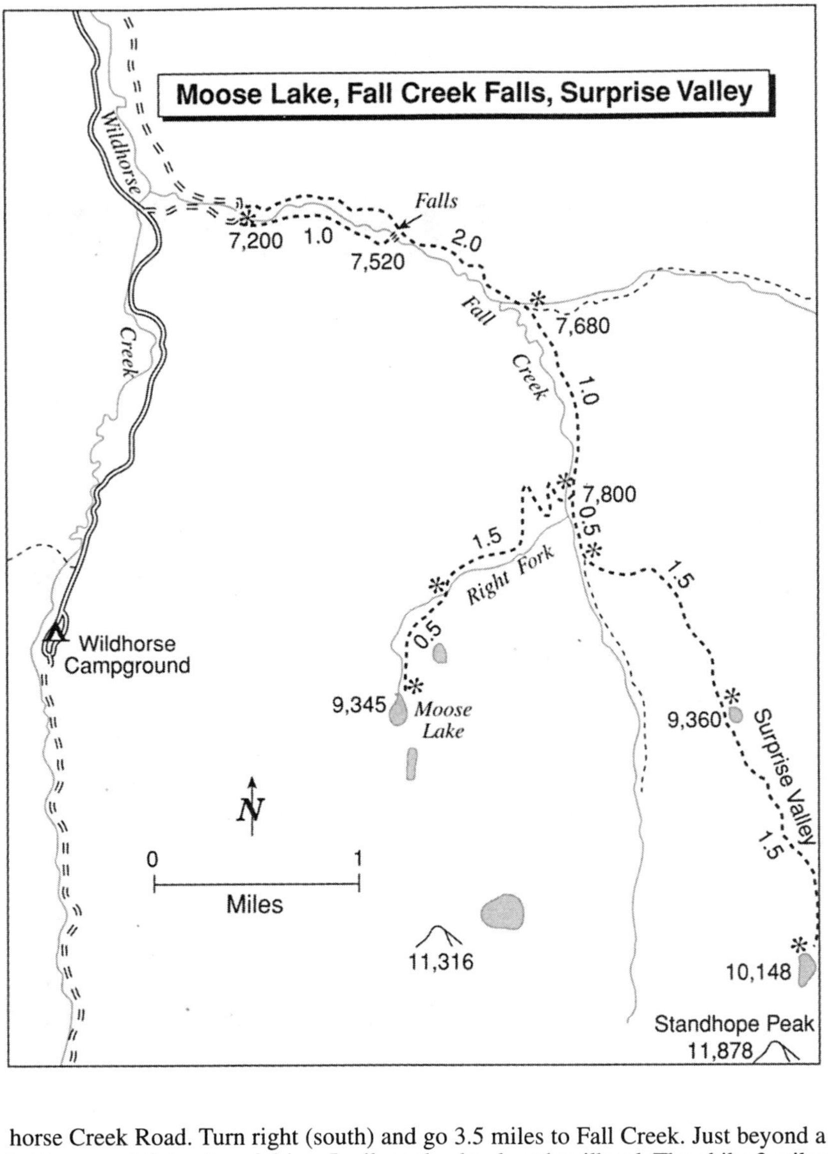


horse Creek Road. Turn right (south) and go 3.5 miles to Fall Creek. Just beyond a bridge, turn left (east) and drive .5 mile to the developed trailhead. Then hike 3 miles up Fall Creek to the Moose Lake junction, where this hike description begins.

At the lower end of Surprise Valley, a pale green lake dots a meadow under a double-pointed peak of slanting cliffs. To the west, the outlet has cut a gap in the canyon wall allowing it to fall into the canyon of Fall Creek. Through the gap, you can see jagged summits and dark cliffs on the other side of that canyon. From the lake, the meadows of Surprise Valley stretch .5 mile up the canyon past willows, scattered whitebark pines, hummocks of turf and a rainbow of wildflowers. Even in late August, there are paintbrush, cinquefoil, alpine sunflowers and gentians. On the west, talus rolls into the meadows from a ridge of fractured cliffs. At the head of the canyon a pale green lake sits below the wide triangle of Standhope Peak. Around this lake, a few whitebark pines, flattened by the wind to four feet tall, cling to barren benches.

From the junction with the Fall Creek Trail 3 miles from the Fall Creek trailhead, the route to the first lake is lightly used. There is little trail tread up the valley from this lake to the upper lake. From the Moose Lake junction, the Fall Creek Trail climbs 250 feet before reaching the Surprise Valley junction at .5 mile. The trail to the valley zigzags 720 feet up, ducks under a cliff, and crosses a small meadow near a spring at 1 mile. Beyond, you may need the blazes and cairns to follow it. At 1.3 miles, a long meadow provides a view of cream-colored towers on the canyon wall and the trail wanders through it to the first lake at 2 miles.

To reach the upper lake, walk cross-country between the talus and the stream on the west (right) side of the creek at the edge of the woods. Where a larger meadow begins at 2.3 miles, cross the creek to the left (east) side. Continue along the edge of the meadow, staying in hillside grass where possible. The creek branches at the upper end of the valley at 3.2 miles. The right (west) branch heads southwest up a slot in the cliffs to the lake. To reach it, circle left (east) into a small flat and cross the west branch of the stream. Then head southwest to the upper lake at 3.5 miles.

# COPPER BASIN AREA

## 91.

## Bellas Lakes

**Round trip:** 6.2 miles
**Elevation gain:** 1,660 feet
**Highest point:** 9,500 feet
**Map:** Big Black Dome
**Difficulty:** moderate; time: 5 1/2 hours

**Access:** Drive 22.5 miles northeast of Ketchum over the rocky Trail Creek Road to the turnoff for Copper Basin. Turn right (southeast) and drive 13 miles. Turn right (south) on the dirt Copper Basin Loop Road. Go 6.2 miles to Bellas Canyon. Turn right (west) and drive .1 mile up a rocky jeep trail to a grove of aspens. The trail begins about .1 mile farther up the track, but the track is so rocky it could damage even four-wheel-drive vehicles.

Above the first Bellas Lake, black stripes form an eye and mouth on the highest peak of a row of jagged cream-colored cliffs. On each side of the upper end of the lake, two green meadows, each ribboned by an inlet, slope into the green water. From the higher lake, cream-colored talus behind a rock knoll leads to the whitish top of Pyramid Peak. Across Copper Basin, plants patch copper peaks with green.

From the end of the jeep track, the trail climbs along the stream through aspens and lodgepoles. At .8 mile, it crosses the creek on rocks to the left (south) bank. Then the trail runs through large, dry meadows full of white mountain death camas, pale green elk thistle, blue littleleaf penstemon and yellow cinquefoil. At 2.2 miles, it enters a grassy basin of tiny subalpine firs and crosses to the east bank of the creek below a waterfall. From the ford, the trail climbs northeast away from the creek through sagebrush. At 2.7 miles, is a flat meadow with a view of a white wall of peaks. The first lake is at 3 miles and the three higher lakes may be reached by cross-country hiking. Visiting all three of these lakes adds 1.5 miles to the hike.

# 92.

## Betty Lake

**Round trip:** 10 miles
**Elevation gain:** 2,560 feet
**Highest point:** 10,379 feet
**Maps:** Standhope Peak, Big Black Dome
**Difficulty:** strenuous; time: 9 hours or 2 days;
**Access:** Drive 22.5 miles northeast of Ketchum over the rocky Trail Creek Road and turn right (southeast) on the dirt Copper Basin Road. Drive 13 miles and turn right (south) on the dirt Copper Basin Loop Road. Drive 7.7 miles to Broad Canyon and turn right (west) on a road up the canyon to a campground.

Above the trail to Betty Lake, crevices filled with snow slant up to the top of a 1,000-foot granite wall. Cliffs on a cream-colored peak divide into splinters northeast of the turquoise above-timberline lake. To the north, a gray ridge of slabs and talus sweeps west to the rounded tip of Standhope Peak. A short climb to a gap in a ridge to the south gives a view of Goat Lake on a bench below a peak of snow-filled fissures.

From the west end of the campground loop in Broad Canyon, hike up an old road which soon turns into a trail in a meadow full of willows. At 1 mile, it crosses to the north side of the creek and joins a trail that has come up from the campground on the other side of the creek. This second trail from the campground has a pack bridge at the beginning, which is useful when the creek is high. To find this alternate route back at the campground, go a quarter of the way around the loop road, turn right (north) and walk down a road leading to a little creek at the near side of the meadow. Ford the little creek and angle northwest across the meadow to a footbridge over the

**Trail to Betty Lake**

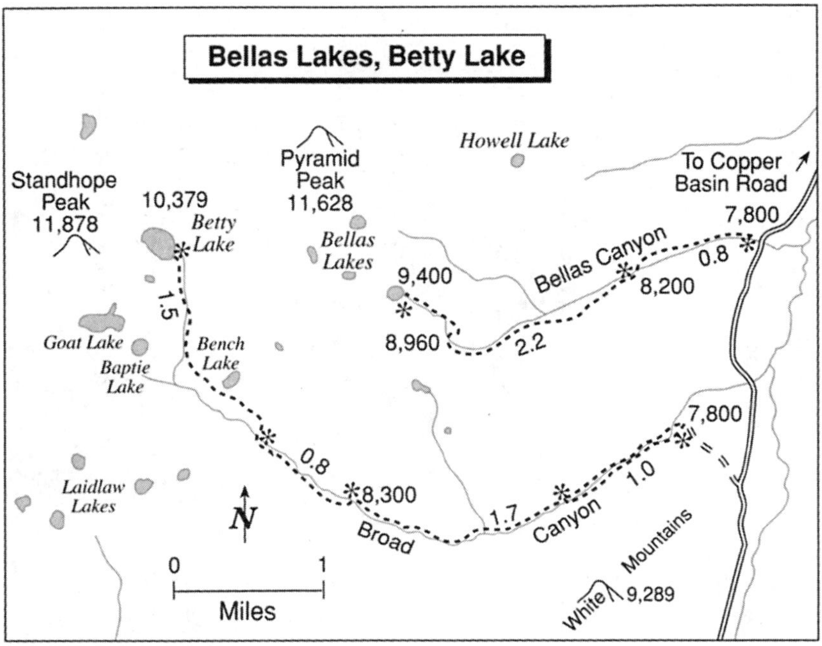


main creek.

After the two routes merge, the trail runs through a series of dry meadows, from which a pale pink and white ridge can be seen to the south. At the 2 mile point opposite a rose-gray rock knoll, the trail has climbed only 300 feet. A grassy area sloping to the creek is at 2.7 miles. The trail crosses back to the south side here.

Now the trail travels underneath a 1,000-foot row of cliffs. At the head of the canyon at 3 miles, rock benches form giant stair steps. It crosses back over Broad Creek to the north side at 3.5 miles. Early in the summer this crossing may be a problem. The route now has climbed 1,000 feet above the trailhead.

Next, the trail climbs an open hillside to a flat meadow at 3.7 miles containing a marsh (labeled "Bench Lake") at the upper end. The trail leads through whitebark pines and climbs 200 feet in 200 yards onto a bench. At 4.2 miles, the land flattens in another meadow where a stream meanders. A grassy basin with a campsite in the last stand of timber is at 4.5 miles. Beyond this point the trail is lightly used.

The route skirts the basin and climbs a grassy ridge studded with rocks. It stays east of the stream and does not cross as is shown on the map. From Betty Lake at 5 miles, cut southwest cross-country from the campsite in the timber to reach Baptie and Goat Lakes.

For a view of Goat Lake go southwest of Betty Lake and climb 400 feet in .5 mile up a draw to a barren gap. From here, it is possible to descend CAREFULLY to the lake.

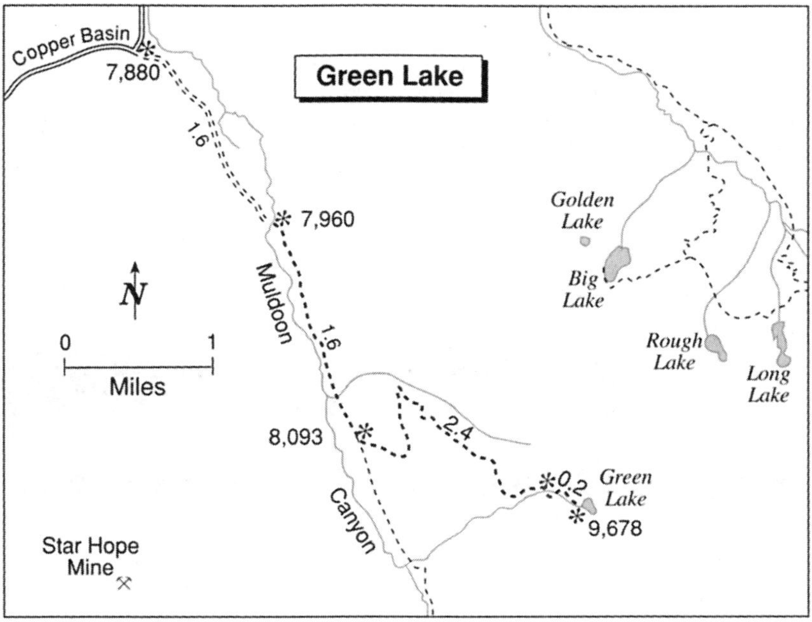


# 93.

## Green Lake

**Round trip:** 5.2 to 8.4 miles
**Elevation gain:** 1,600 feet
**Highest point:** 9,678 feet
**Maps:** Star Hope Mine, Smiley Mountain
**Difficulty:** moderate; time: 7 hours
**Access:** Drive 22.5 miles northeast of Ketchum over the rocky Trail Creek Road and turn right (southeast) on the Copper Basin Road. Drive 13 miles and turn right (south) on the dirt Copper Basin Loop Road and follow it for 10.5 miles. Turn right (southeast) and go 1.6 miles on the primitive Muldoon Canyon Road to a ford of Muldoon Creek. Four-wheel drive vehicles may be able to drive 1.6 miles farther to the Green Lake jeep trail, but not up it due to its sideways slant.

On the way to Green Lake you can see near the head of Muldoon Canyon, a black dome and remnants of mining. A 1,600-foot circle of charcoal gray peaks tinted rose and orange hems in the lake. Below the peaks, talus nibbles at the grass dusting the border of the milky, pale green lake. The only trees at Green Lake are a few white-bark pines, so the landscape of barren rock and milky green water resembles a setting from another planet.

After fording Muldoon Creek 1.6 miles up the canyon from the Copper Basin loop road, walk along the level road through sagebrush. At 1.6 miles, turn left (east) up an unsigned jeep track which climbs southeast through sagebrush, switchbacks up a sagebrush-covered ridge and then branches. Take either track since they soon rejoin. The jeep trail winds south across the sagebrush to Green Creek and ends at the ruins of an old cabin at 3.8 miles. Here, turn left and climb up to the trail, which you can see going across the talus. This trail reaches the lake 2.6 miles from the bottom of the jeep trail.

# 94.

## Iron Bog and Fishpole Lakes from Muldoon Canyon

**Round trip:** 17.2 miles
**Elevation gain:** 1,840 feet
**Elevation loss:** 560 feet (return climb)
**Highest point:** 9,600 feet
**Maps:** Star Hope Mine, Smiley Mountain
**Difficulty:** strenuous; time: 2 days
**Access:** Drive 22.5 miles northeast of Ketchum over the rocky Trail Creek Road and turn right (southeast) on the road to Copper Basin. Go 13 miles and turn right (south) on the dirt Copper Basin Loop Road and follow it for 10.5 miles. Turn right (southeast) and go 1.6 miles on the primitive Muldoon Canyon Road to a ford of Muldoon Creek. Those with four-wheel drive may be able to continue 2.6 miles farther to the end of the road, which is about 1 mile beyond the Green Lake jeep trail turnoff.

From above, Fishpole and Bobber Lakes resemble turquoise eyes in a grass and sagebrush basin below a ring of gray, orange and copper-colored crags. At the head of the basin, triangular peaks of dark gray slabs alternate with burnt-orange needles. Below these lakes sprawls milky blue-green Iron Bog Lake. A 800-foot face of dark gray cliffs splashed with yellow green lichen drops to its lake shore.

Mileage for this hike, which is partly along the Muldoon Canyon Road, starts at the ford of Muldoon Creek 1.6 miles from the Copper Basin Loop Road because only those with four-wheel drive vehicles should attempt to drive farther. The canyon is named for an defunct mining town, Muldoon, that is nearby on the west side of the Pioneer Range. Mining there began in 1882 and at one time the town had 1,500 people. There is little shade, so the hike will be more pleasant on a cool day.

From the ford, walk along the road up the canyon through the sagebrush. The Green Lake jeep trail turns off to the right at 1.6 miles. At 2.6 miles the road is closed to motor vehicles. At 3.1 miles, the trail crosses Muldoon Creek to the west and climbs above it. An old jeep trail turns off to the west to a mine at 3.3 miles, but the main trail returns to the edge of the creek. At 3.5 miles, it crosses a small deep side stream. Beaver ponds strung on the creek like beads soon appear. From here on the

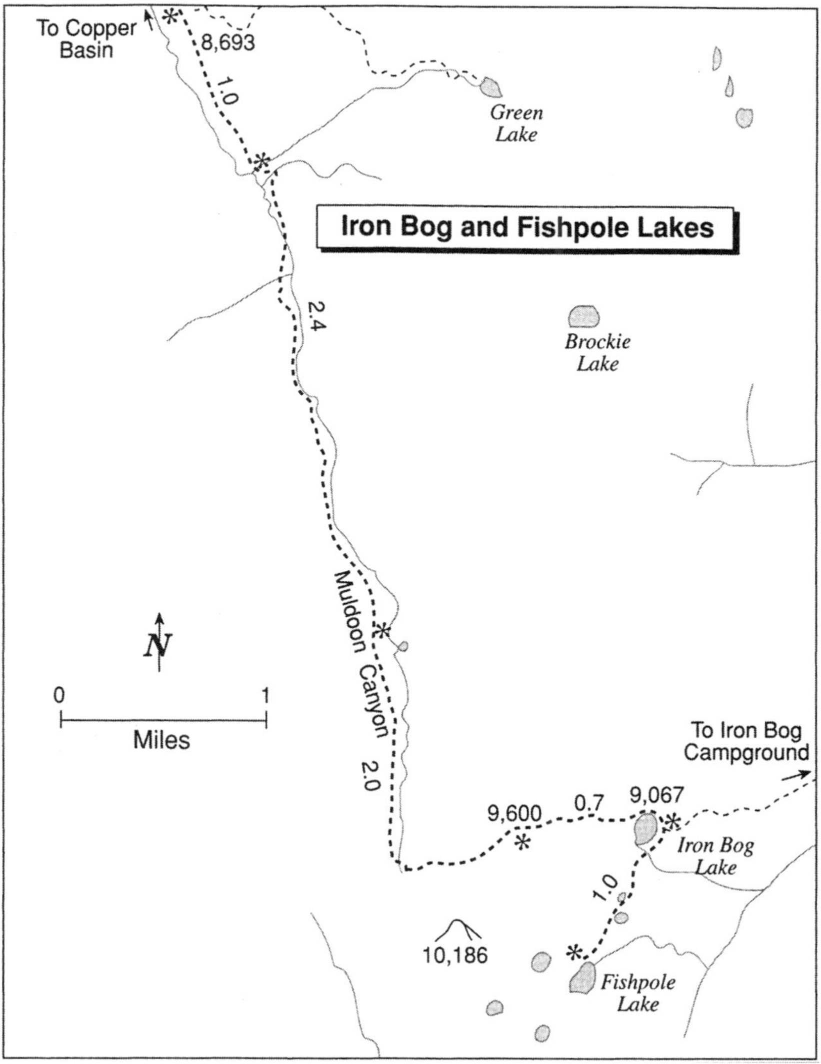


trail has been reconstructed to stay on the west side of the creek to the head of the canyon. This allows it to avoid boggy areas on the east side of the canyon just beyond the small sagebrush hill in the center of the canyon at 5.2 miles. Beginning at about 5.9 miles the trail climbs 400 feet in .5 mile. At the head of the canyon at 6.4 miles, it turns left (northeast) beside springs bubbling out of moss on a shelf just under the cliffs (A path leading west from the springs is not the trail.)

The trail contours a stony hillside to a pass at 7 miles on the east wall of the canyon. Beyond the pass, it sometimes disappears but reappears near Iron Bog Lake at 7.7 miles. Note that it's a 560-foot climb to return to the pass by the trail from the lake. To continue from Iron Bog Lake to Fishpole and Bobber Lakes, follow the trail around the north side of the lake and start down below it for about 100 yards to where a trail turns off to the right (southwest) Take this trail, which crosses the outlet of Iron Bog Lake, passes two tiny ponds, and climbs sagebrush hills to Fishpole Lake at 8.6 miles.

The adventurous can take a different route to Fishpole Lake. From the pass at 7 miles you can climb south to a grassy saddle and then CAREFULLY descend gullies and talus between cliffs, past another small lake sometimes called Bobber Lake to Fishpole Lake at 8 miles. The saddle also gives a fine view of the lakes without the effort of hiking to them.

It is only 4 and 6 miles to Iron Bog and Fishpole Lakes round trip from an 8-mile primitive road that goes up the Left Fork of Iron Bog Creek, but this road can be reached only from near Antelope Guard Station, and it requires four-wheel drive. To reach it, drive 23 miles from the Copper Basin Loop Road over Antelope Pass on a primitive road, or drive 12 miles north of Arco on U.S. 93 and then go 18 miles to the Iron Bog Campground. That route is described in *Trails of Eastern Idaho* by the author and Jerry Painter.

# 95.

## Round, Long, Rough, Big and Golden Lakes

**Round trip:** 12.5 miles (5.5 miles is a loop) plus 3.2 miles round trip on spur trails to see all five lakes

**Elevation gain:** 1,640 feet

**Elevation loss:** 960 feet (no return climb for loop hike)

**Highest point:** 9,680 feet

**Maps:** Copper Basin Knob, Smiley Mountain

**Difficulty:** strenuous; time: 10 hours or 2 days

**Access:** Drive 22.5 miles northeast of Ketchum over the rocky Trail Creek Road and turn right (southeast) on the road to Copper Basin. Go 13 miles and turn right (south) on the dirt Copper Basin Loop Road and follow it for 13.3 miles to the Lake Creek trailhead. It is 9.7 miles to the trailhead via the east side of the loop road. Then turn south .1 mile into a small campground and horse loading area. Note that the main trail and the side trails to all of the lakes are now open to ATVs.

The loop trail to these lakes gives views of white, black and orange peaks. The sharp white peaks behind Bellas Lakes across the basin contrast with the closer folded orange and white rocks of Copper Basin Knob. Still closer, tall peaks of crumbling black rock resembling pieces of licorice cake face hills of copper-colored talus. Round Lake sits beside a boulder field below copper and gray hills across from the wall of high black peaks. Above Long Lake, three of the black peaks overlook a glacier-sculptured ridge. Mountains of black rock blotted with snow overshadow Rough Lake. South of Big Lake rises a black rock monster with an ape-like head, triangular

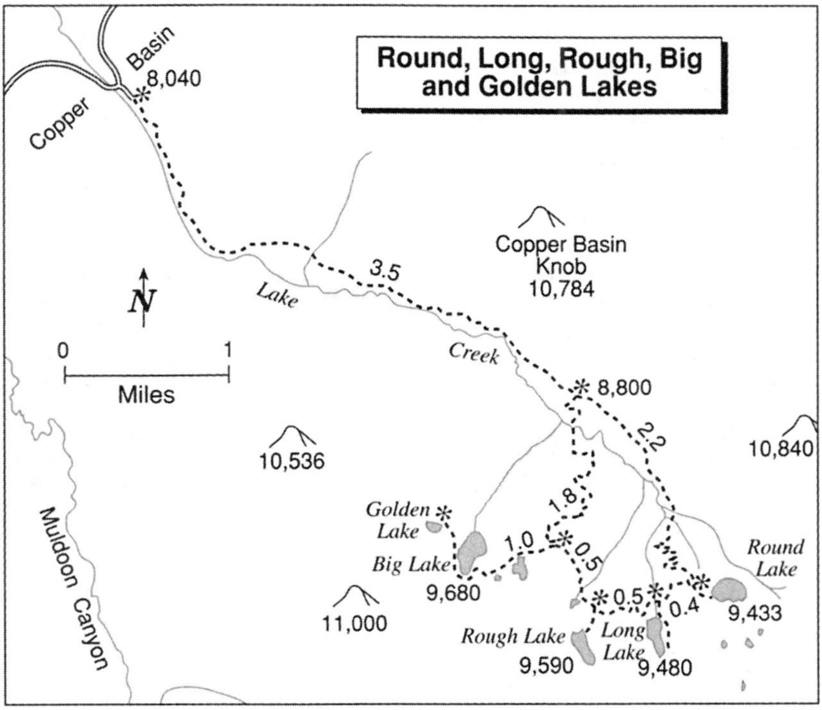


rump, and backbone of enormous vertebrae. Tiny tea-colored Golden Lake huddles under rock slabs.

As the trail begins at the far end of the campground it squeezes between two large boulders. Then it skirts a small meadow, follows the base of a ridge and climbs through trees and outcrops to a sagebrush bench that it follows it for .5 mile. At 1.3 miles, it crosses a stream and goes into forest. It skirts a large meadow at 2 miles and wanders under rose and white cliffs at 2.5 miles. Beyond log cabin ruins at 3 miles, it edges the east side of a meadow. The Big Lake and Round Lake trails meet to form a loop at the far end of the meadow at 3.5 miles. The loop is 5.5 miles long and that distance does not include the side trails to the lakes.

It is easier to go to Round Lake first, because the climb is less abrupt. The trail to Big Lake from the junction climbs 960 feet in 2.9 miles, but the climb to Round Lake is only 640 feet in 2.2 miles. The Round Lake Trail crosses a stream and then bends left toward the canyon wall. At 4.5 miles from the trailhead, it turns back towards the creek. It crosses a boulder field and two streams at 5.1 miles, and climbs a wooded ridge to the Round Lake turnoff at 5.7 miles. It is .1 mile east over a marsh and rocks to the lake.

To reach Long Lake, go .3 mile beyond the Round Lake turnoff along the main trail and turn off on a side trail to the left (south) at a junction just before the main trail crosses the outlet of Long Lake. Follow the side trail south along the east side of the lake to its end on a big peninsula at .3 mile. A big meadow along this spur trail contains horse-tie racks.

From its junction with the spur trail to Long Lake, the main trail crosses the outlet of Long Lake, then climbs west .3 mile over an 80-foot ridge, passing snow ponds and drops to a junction. Take the left (south) branch here and climb 200 yards to Rough Lake.

To reach Big Lake from the Rough Lake junction, continue northwest on the main trail. It crosses the outlet of Rough Lake, then ascends an open slope. Just beyond a rise, .3 mile from the Rough Lake junction is a junction with the west side of the loop trail that takes you back to the first junction on Lake Creek. To reach Big and Golden Lakes, keep straight ahead here. This side trail passes a pale green pond with a view of the backbone ridge at .3 mile and reaches Big Lake at .7 mile. To continue to Golden Lake, take a path around the lower (northern) end of Big Lake and cross its outlet. Then turn left (west) and climb over a low ridge to the lake about 1 mile from the junction with the loop trail.

To return from Big Lake to the beginning of the 5.5-mile loop, go 1 mile back to the junction of the spur trail to Big and Golden lakes with the main loop trail. From here, the loop trail drops down a grassy hillside, and switchbacks through woods down to the junction with the other side of the loop, 1.8 miles from the junction with the Big Lake Trail. It is another 3.5 miles down Lake Creek back to the trailhead. Round trips on the short side trails to Round, Long, Rough, Big and Golden Lakes add 3.2 miles to the hike.

# SAWTOOTH NATIONAL FOREST
# KETCHUM DISTRICT
# WARM SPRINGS AREA

## 96.

## Bald Mountain Trails

**Round trip:** 12 miles to the summit and back from the Warm Springs Lodge via the Warm Springs, Warm Springs Traverse, and Bald Mountain trails; 9.4 miles to the summit and back via the Bald Mountain Trail, which begins at River Run Lodge; in season you can ride down the Lookout and River Run lifts to the River Run Lodge free and halve the distance

**Elevation gain:** 3,400 feet

**Highest point:** 9,150 feet

**Maps:** Griffin Butte, Sun Valley

**Difficulty:** strenuous; time: 7 hours if you return on the ski lift

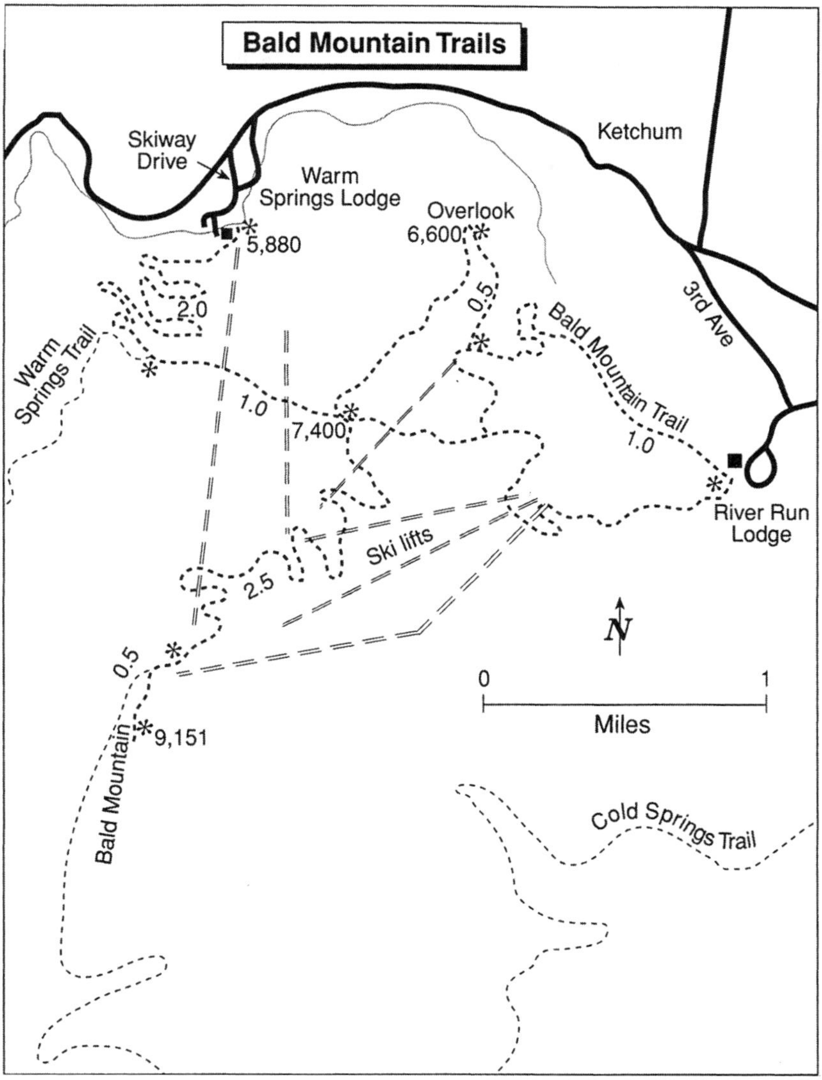


**Access:** There are two main trails up Bald Mountain from Ketchum and they join part way up the mountain. Either route is a beautiful, but long steep hike. To reach the Warm Springs Trail when going north on Idaho Highway 75 through Ketchum, turn left (northwest) on Warm Springs Avenue and drive to a stop sign at Skiway Drive. Turn left (south) and drive to the parking area for the Warm Springs lift. The trail begins in front of the day lodge. To reach the Bald Mountain Trail where it begins at the River Run Lodge, when going north on Idaho Highway 75 through Ketchum, turn left (west) on Sun Valley Road, then turn left (south) on Third Avenue and drive to the parking area. The trail begins in front of the lodge.

The nearby Wood River mines, which started in 1879, were successful because railroads and better processing made lead profitable for the first time in Idaho. When the U.S. government wouldn't grant a post office to a second Leadville, the town's original name was changed to Ketchum after the second settler, David Ketchum. The ski resort, Sun Valley, was begun by W. Averell Harriman of Union Pacific after he commissioned Count Felix Schaffgotsch to find the best place for a ski resort in the west. The lodge opened in 1936 and at first visitors mostly arrived by train. Sun Valley installed the first chairlift in the world (on Proctor Mountain) near the Trail Creek Cabin at Sun Valley.

The view from the top of Baldy is one of the best in Idaho. To the north, you can see the jagged outlines of the Sawtooths and White Clouds, to the east the curves and point of the Pioneers, to the south the vast expanse of the Snake River plain, and to the west the blue ridges of the Boise Mountains. Below, you can look down on the condominiums and trophy homes of Ketchum and Sun Valley.

On Bald Mountain there is a network of 28 miles of trails for hiking and mountain biking. The trails include the Warm Springs, Cold Springs, Broadway and Bald Mountain and assorted spur and connecting trails.

This description begins on the Warm Springs Trail and then cuts over to the Bald Mountain Trail part way up. The Warm Springs Trail starts by zigzagging back and forth several times across the open grassy slopes served by the Grayhawk and Challenger lifts, with the eastern switchbacks in forest. At 2 miles is a junction at the east edge of wide open slopes. To reach the summit most directly from here, turn left (southwest) here on the River Run — Warm Springs Traverse Trail. It zigzags up to meet the Bald Mountain trail at 3 miles.

Turn right here on the Bald Mountain trail. A couple of switchbacks above this junction is a drinking fountain built in memory of climber Louis Stur. The trail climbs in hairpin turns up the right sides of the Sunnyside and Lookout Express lifts to the Lookout Restaurant at 5.5 miles, where you can buy lunch when the lift is open. The view is splendid from the nearby slopes but if you want to say you have climbed Baldy, hike .5 mile southwest along the Lookout Trail to the summit at 6 miles.

If you plan to take the ski lift down and have someone in your party who has never ridden ski lifts or has only ridden them uphill, be sure to warn them before the hike that riding down on a high speed quad may bother those who have any fear of heights. If you ride down only, the ride is free. For those wanting a shorter hike you can walk up the trail from the River Run side mostly through forest for 1.5 miles to a viewing platform. From it there is an excellent view of Ketchum and the mountains around it.

**Hyndman Peak from Pioneer Cabin**

# TRAIL CREEK AREA

## 97.

## Pioneer Cabin

**Round trip:** 7.4 miles
**Elevation gain:** 2,680 feet
**Highest point:** 9,460 feet
**Map:** Hyndman Peak
**Difficulty:** strenuous; time: 7 hours
**Access:** From the junction of Idaho Highway 75 and Sun Valley Road in Ketchum, drive 5.1 miles northeast of Ketchum on Trail Creek Road to Corral Creek. Turn right (east) and drive 3.7 miles on a primitive road to a developed trailhead.

From a field of blue lupine, this brown board and batten cabin with a tar paper roof overlooks an orange and gray panorama of the Pioneer Mountains. To the east, pleated Cobb Peak peers from behind fluted, sway-backed Hyndman Peak. Handwerk Peak rises on the northeast in an orange double-pointed knob. Between them, corrugated Duncan Ridge joins the head wall. As seen from the trail below the cabin,

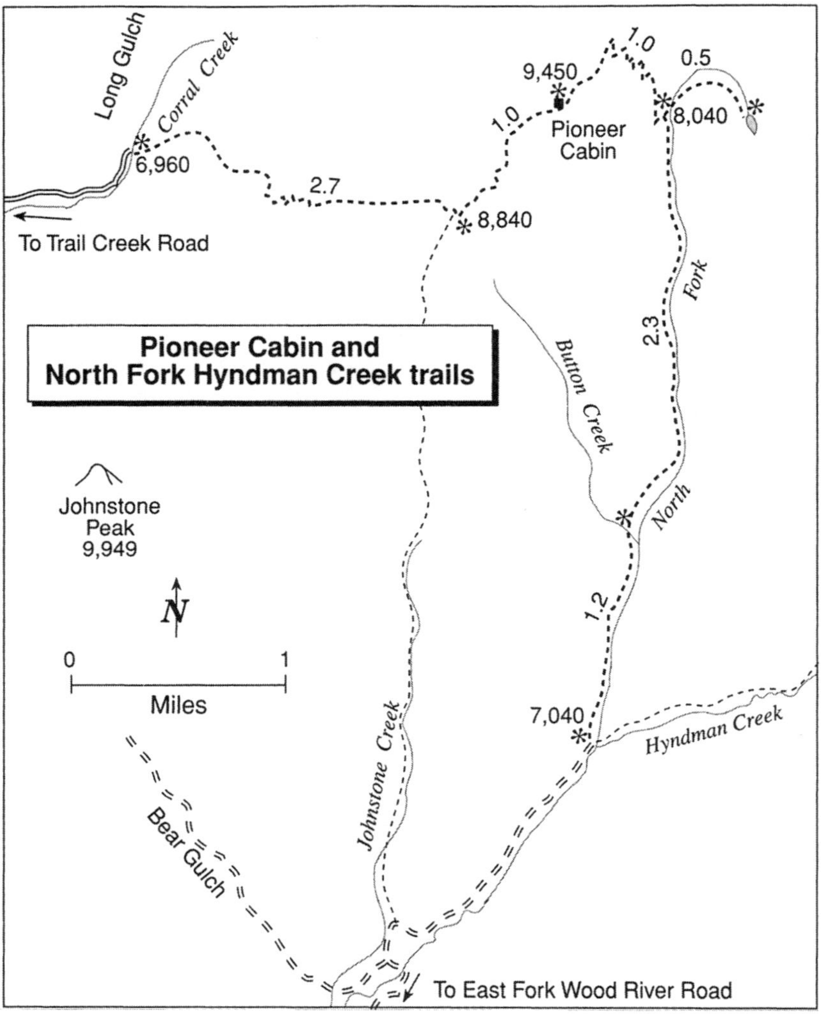


successive blue ridges lead toward the Smoky Mountains to the west..

From the trailhead on Corral Creek, the trail crosses the creek on a bridge and follows a branch of the creek in aspens and firs. A stream at .5 mile is the last water on the trail in late season. At .7 mile, the trail crosses another stream, goes into forest and climbs in seven 200-yard switchbacks.

At 2 miles, the trail follows a ridge in the open above grassy canyons. It flattens in a basin at 2.5 miles and reaches a junction at 2.7 miles with the Johnstone Creek Trail, 1,900 feet above the trailhead. The trail to the cabin turns south for 150 yards and then goes northeast along a ridge.

It climbs between small gray and orange hills, then edges the talus of a barren ridge. Finally it climbs the side of the ridge to a grassy saddle and crosses it to the cabin at 3.7 miles. The last 1.5 miles has no shade, so it is best to start the hike in early morning on a hot day. The cabin was built by the Union Pacific Railroad in 1937 as a ski hut.

From the cabin you can descend the Long Gulch Trail to the northwest back to the Pioneer Cabin trailhead for a great view of the Boulder Mountains on your return if you wish, making an 8.5 mile loop. It is also possible to descend the North Fork of Hyndman Creek or Johnstone Creek trails to the East Fork of the Wood River if you have arranged a car shuttle.

# WOOD RIVER AREA

## 98.

## North Fork Hyndman Creek: Pioneer Cabin and Hyndman Lake

**Round trip:** 8 miles (1 mile cross-country) for lake; 9 miles for cabin
**Elevation gain:** 1,640 feet to lake; 2,440 feet to cabin
**Highest point:** 8,640 feet at lake; 9,440 feet at cabin
**Map:** Hyndman Peak
**Difficulty:** strenuous to Pioneer Cabin, partly cross-country to lake; time: 7 hours for lake, 8 hours for cabin
**Access:** From Sun Valley Road in Ketchum drive 5.7 miles south on Idaho Highway 75, turn east on the paved East Fork of Wood River Road and drive 7.1 miles. Turn north on the gravel and dirt Hyndman Creek Road and drive 4.7 miles to a parking area.

On the way to the trailhead the road passes the site of the Triumph Mine. It was discovered in 1889, and became the most productive of the Wood River mines, producing silver, lead, and zinc. Its greatest production didn't occur until 1957, the year before the mill serving it was sold to a Cuban company to be taken to Cuba and reassembled.

A huge meadow woven with wildflowers cushions tiny pale green Hyndman Lake. Orange and white boulders of quartz choke the outlet of the lake. To the north of the lake the pale orange backbone of Handwerk Peak turns gray as it drops off like a lovers' leap. To the left of that peak, a jagged gray cliff wall, netted with white, merges with burnt orange and cream triangles. Below the lake, Orange and gray cliffs squeeze the upper end of the canyon of the North Fork of Hyndman Creek before opening into a vast dry meadow. The trail has many switchbacks from this meadow to Pioneer Cabin.

Park at the parking area, just before the North Fork of Hyndman Creek where the road is closed to motor vehicles and two trails turn off, one up Hyndman Creek and one up its north fork. From the upper end of the parking area, walk north up a jeep track across the grass. From the end of this track, the trail angles up the steep hillside of the canyon wall through sagebrush, Douglas fir and aspen and then levels out, but is slid away in places. At 1 mile, it drops to a grassy bench above the creek and goes along it. Ahead, a gray lava bluff overshadows the side canyon of three-foot-wide Button Creek, which you cross at 1.2 miles. Beyond a sagebrush flat at 1.7 miles, the canyon narrows and the trail enters mixed aspens and firs. At about 2.5 miles, is another grassy flat with cliffs ahead on the left that resemble giant rock steps. The trail climbs more steeply here, first up an open gravelly slope and then across a rocky one. At 3 miles, you are right below big cliffs and just above the creek. The trail winds through patches of white quartzite stained red and gold and then goes through subalpine fir, staying well above the creek.

At 3.5 miles, the trail starts climbing above the creek through a Douglas fir forest and then switchbacks left. From the point of the switchback a path runs down into the canyon ahead. It is the access for the route to the lake. Continue up the main trail which immediately switchbacks to the right across open sagebrush slopes. It heads over to the ravine of a dry creek and continues switchbacking up beside it to Pioneer Cabin on top of the ridge at 4.5 miles.

There is no trail to the lake. To reach it, take the path downhill to the right (north) from the first of the many switchbacks onto grass and sagebrush slopes. Look across the creek at the opposite canyon wall where a small tongue of grass pokes up into this forest at 4 miles. Cross the creek and climb this grassy tongue and a tiny ridge cross-country for 400 vertical feet to the lake at 4.5 miles. Or you can stay on the left side of the lake's outlet and climb over the open slopes which are a little steeper than those on the right. For variety on your return from Pioneer Cabin, you can walk down the Johnstone Creek Trail and then hike 1 mile on the Hyndman Creek Road to get back to your car.

# 99.

## Baker Lake

**Round trip:** 4 miles
**Elevation gain:** 870 feet
**Highest point:** 8,796 feet
**Map:** Baker Peak
**Difficulty:** easy; time: 4 hours

**Access:** Turn left (south) off Idaho Highway 75, at the Baker Creek Road, 15 miles north of Ketchum. Go 10.5 miles on an oiled road to a developed trailhead with a large parking area.

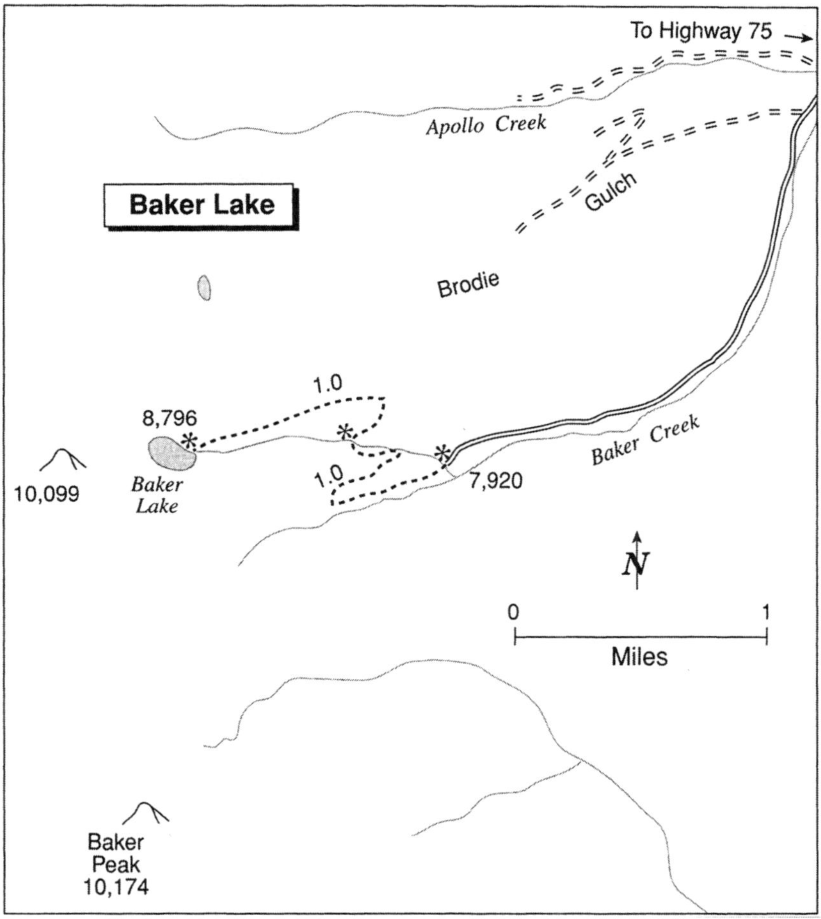


A 400-foot rose-colored cliff forms the face of a thumb-shaped peak above pink talus and the blue-green oval of Baker Lake. On the opposite side of the lake grow whitebark pines, shrubs and shooting stars. Terns sometimes swoop down to the water, duck under, and come up with fish in their beaks.

The trail has been completely rerouted since the last edition of this book. It is now twice as long but has a much easier grade. The trail begins by crossing a branch of Baker Creek on flat-topped boulders and heads west across sagebrush and lupine-covered slopes into a Douglas fir forest. At .5 mile, it switches back to the right. Then at .7 mile, it begins to wind through the woods on the left (south) side of the lake's outlet. Right after the outlet goes through a little gorge, the trail curves back into its canyon and crosses the creek at 1 mile. At the crossing it switches back to the right (northeast) and climbs an open hillside. At 1.2 miles, it switches back to the left (west) and after .3 mile passes through clumps of trees. At 1.6 miles, is a sign for a trail to Apollo Creek going off to the right (north). This trail is well-worn as far as an unnamed lake at the head of Brodie Gulch, but is a primitive trail from there to Apollo Creek and down it to the Baker Creek Road.

Beyond the junction, the Baker Lake trail enters woods again. At 1.8 miles, it wiggles back and forth across a little draw with a view of the thumblike peak above. Next it goes through stands of firs and lodgepoles and across hillsides embroidered with flowers to the lake at 1 mile. Along the trail, the rounded top of Baker Peak is visible to the southwest. Start early, as there is no shade most of the way. The few campsites have been overused, so this hike is best as a day hike. The trail continues along the east side of the lake into high alpine basins.

# 100.

## Norton Lakes

**Round trip:** 4.4 miles
**Elevation gain:** 1,510 feet
**Highest point:** 9,107 feet
**Map:** Baker Peak
**Difficulty:** moderate; time: 5 hours
**Access:** Turn left (south) off Idaho Highway 75 at Baker Creek, 15 miles north of Ketchum and drive 7.2 miles on an oiled road. Turn right (northwest) and drive 1.3 miles on a dirt road to the Norton Lakes trailhead. Park at the end of the road beside the creek.

From above, lower Norton Lake resembles a great glowing emerald. A gravel beach is on one side of the lake and white talus rising to a small peak on the other. In early summer, a garden of bluebells, pink mimulus and forget-me-nots lines the stream joining the two lakes. Talus and grass circling the highest lake blend with the rich colors of Norton Peak. East of the lake, rock needles stand on a brown, buff and rose-striped wall. Along the lower trail, yellow senecio, blue littleleaf penstemon and red paintbrush color the meadows.

From the end of the Norton Creek Road, the trail ascends the forested west side of the creek. It crosses a side creek at .5 mile and then continues up a hillside of flowers. Below talus and cliffs at 1.5 miles, pikas often cry "peep, peep."

Soon the trail crosses the outlet and makes a switchback to reach the lake at 2 miles. The trail runs along the north side of the lake to the inlet. Then it climbs .2 mile to the upper lake. From the upper lake, a more difficult trail leads 2 miles over Norton Saddle to Miner Lake in a 480-foot climb.

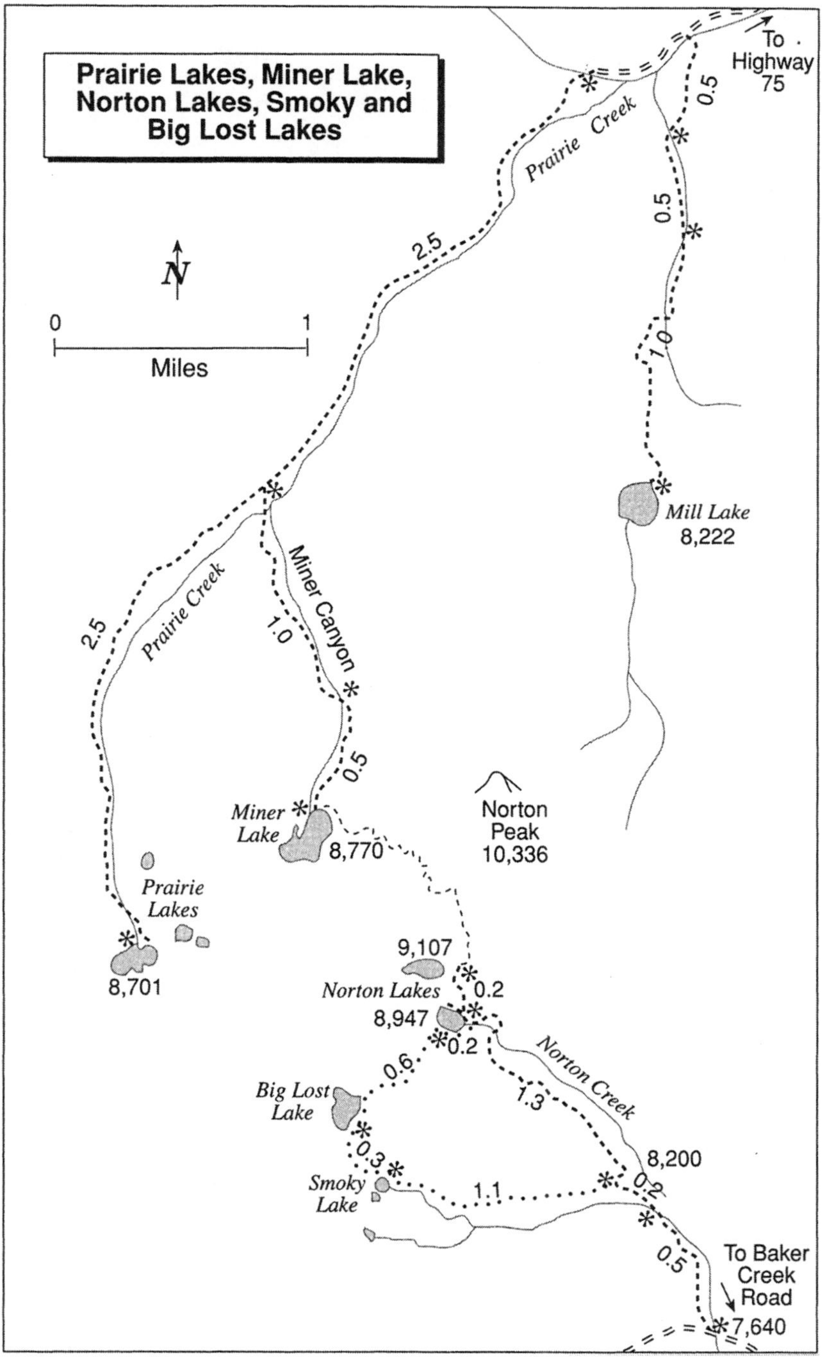
Prairie Lakes, Miner Lake, Norton Lakes, Smoky and Big Lost Lakes
N
0
1
Miles
To Highway 75
Prairie Creek
Miner Canyon
Mill Lake
8,222
Miner Lake
8,770
Norton Peak
10,336
Prairie Lakes
8,701
9,107
Norton Lakes
8,947
Norton Creek
Big Lost Lake
Smoky Lake
8,200
To Baker Creek Road
7,640
2.5
0.5
1.0
0.2
0.6
1.3
0.3
1.1

**Big Lost Lake**

# 101.

## Smoky and Big Lost Lakes

**Round trip:** 4.9 miles including 3.5 mile loop
**Elevation gain:** 1,640 feet
**Highest point:** 9,280 feet
**Map:** Baker Peak
**Difficulty:** cross-country; time: 6 hours;
**Access:** Turn left (south) off Idaho Highway 75 at Baker Creek, 15 miles north of Ketchum and drive 7.2 miles on an oiled road. Turn right (northwest) and drive 1.3 miles on a dirt road to the Norton Lakes trailhead. Park at the end of the road beside the creek.

Smoky Lake and the pond behind it are set in a basin below a dark gray mountain of glacier-carved slabs and cliffs. At the upper end, red mountain heather creates a garden among boulders. Over a divide from there, a ridge of crumbled rock, scored with avalanche paths, faces the long, blue strip of Big Lost Lake. These lakes are easily reached from Lower Norton Lake or the trail to it. Because the lakes are managed as a trailless area, be especially careful to leave no trace of your passage: no litter, no fires. Spreading out your party and walking off trail will help prevent erosion in the steeper places.

Hike up the Norton Lakes Trail until an unofficial trail turns off to the left (west) 400 yards after the Norton Lakes Trail crosses a side creek at .5 mile. The turnoff is at .7 mile at the right (east) edge of an open area after the main trail has climbed about 80 feet above the creek. To find the turnoff watch for a trail branching off the Norton Lakes Trail on a grassy slope. For a few yards beyond the turn you can see this trail running below and parallel to the main trail. Follow it along the north canyon wall of the side creek as it crosses slopes of grass and wildflowers and goes through patches of forest. The occasional downed log requires detouring above or below it, since this trail is not a maintained one. At about .9 mile, the creek's canyon narrows to a ravine and the trail is steep with uncertain footing. At 1.1 miles from the Norton Lakes Trail, you reach Smoky Lake. A campsite amid rock outcrops and pink mountain heather is at the northeast corner of the lake.

Circle the right (east) shore of the lake and then head northwest over a 9,200-foot saddle between Smoky and Big Lost lakes. The trail disappears as it climbs to the saddle and at a couple of places you have to scramble over rocks. From here on it continues to appear and disappear. Descend to the south shore of Big Lost Lake at 1.4 miles, then go along its east shore to a pond at the lake's northeast corner. Go between the lake and the pond and then head east and zigzag up to a 9,280-foot saddle that looks down on Lower Norton Lake. From here on the trail heads down, between the open talus and scree on the west and the forest on the east, to the lake shore at 2 miles. Until midsummer, this section will be under snow and you will have to detour over talus on the left or descend steep dirt through the forest on the right. Go around the south side of the lake to return to the main trail at 2.2 miles. Then descend it back to the Norton Lakes trailhead. From the lower lake it is 1.3 miles back to the point where you turned off the main trail to Smoky Lake and .7 mile from there back to the trailhead.

# TRAILS MANAGED BY THE SAWTOOTH NATIONAL RECREATION AREA IN THE KETCHUM DISTRICT

## 102.

## Mill Lake

**Round trip:** 4 miles
**Elevation gain:** 1,060 feet
**Highest point:** 8,222 feet
**Map:** Galena
**Difficulty:** moderate; time: 4 hours
**Access:** Drive 19 miles north of Ketchum on Idaho Highway 75. Turn left (west) onto the gravel Prairie Creek Road and drive 2.2 miles to a sign for Mill Lake.

Driftwood and dark gray talus surround the aqua-green water of Mill Lake below the crumbled cliffs and pointed cap of Norton Peak. From the peak, square crags run along the west side of the lake, forming a wall above the lake. An outcrop high above the opposite side of the lake resembles a lovers' leap. There is no real inlet, so the water line lowers as the summer passes.

At a sign for Mill Lake, turn left off the main road and park near the creek. The trail begins by fording Prairie Creek into forest. This will be difficult in early summer because of high water. At first it is an old jeep track that is open to motorcycles but not to motor vehicles. At .5 mile, the track crosses Mill Creek to the right (west) side, shrinks to a pack trail and begins to climb. At 1 mile, it returns to the east side of the creek and enters a valley of wildflowers. After about 200 yards it climbs into forest to the left, then curves right, climbing steeply. At 1.3 miles, it recrosses the creek and then goes along to the right of a big open area. The next part of the trail is the hardest because it has no shade and climbs about 300 feet over ball-bearing gravel, with rock-hard dirt underneath it. Be very careful here on your way back. Just before the lake, the trail tops a little rise and descends to the woods along the east shore at 2 miles.

# 103.

## Miner Lake

**Round trip:** 8 miles
**Elevation gain:** 1,570 feet
**Highest point:** 8,770 feet
**Map:** Galena
**Difficulty:** moderate; time: 6 1/2 hours
**Access:** Drive 19 miles north of Ketchum on Idaho Highway 75. Turn left (west) onto the gravel Prairie Creek Road and go 2.6 miles to the trailhead. The trail starts at the left (south) side of the parking area. (Another trail, the West Fork of Prairie Creek Trail angles off from the west side of the parking area.)

Galena (now just a lodge and cross-country ski center farther up Idaho Highway 75 from the turnoff for this hike) was the first town in the area, beginning in 1879. Before then no one had settled in the upper Wood River area because of Indian problems even though Warren Callahan discovered the lead ore, galena, there in 1864.

Bleached driftwood and feathery horsetails surround the jade green water of Miner Lake. Under the water, logs create brown stripes. Talus and plants above the south side lead to the pointed top of Norton Peak. Above the east side, loose rocks on the shore congeal into crags above.

The trail begins at the Prairie Creek Road trailhead at 2.6 miles. It fords the West Fork of Prairie Creek and turns south. The trail climbs for 1 mile along the west (right) side of Prairie Creek, which has banks of emerald green moss and yellow mimulus. At a big meadow at 1.2 miles, hikers can look back at the striped Boulder Mountains. A second meadow is at 1.7 miles and another is at 2 miles.

The trail to Miner Lake splits off to the southeast at 2.5 miles. This trail is closed to motorcycles and is not recommended for mountain bikes, although the Prairie Creek trail is open to motorcycles. It fords Prairie Creek and enters the woods. In the next 1.5 miles, the trail climbs 1,100 feet. At 3.5 miles, it crosses the outlet of the lake to the east side, where paintbrush reddens a meadow. The way continues through forest and meadows below a talus ridge to the lake at 4 miles.

# 104.

## Prairie Lakes

**Round trip:** 10 miles
**Elevation gain:** 1,500 feet

**This section one-way:** 2.5 miles with 1,020 feet gain
**Highest point:** 8,701 feet
**Map:** Galena
**Difficulty:** moderate; time: 7 1/2 hours
**Access:** Drive 19 miles north of Ketchum on Idaho Highway 75. Turn left (west) onto the gravel Prairie Creek Road and go 2.6 miles to the trailhead.

Logs thatched with bright green grass edge the apple green water of the largest Prairie Lake. Rust-brown patches of lake bottom show through the pale green water. Twisted stripes of chocolate brown etch the face of a peak south of the lake. Below the lake, furrowed and cracked buff-colored peaks line Prairie Creek Canyon.

The hike description and mileage begins at the Miner Lake Junction, 2.5 miles up the Miner-Prairie Lakes trail. From this junction, continue straight ahead up the canyon. Cliffs on the west canyon wall hang over the trail at 1.2 miles. At 2.2 miles, in a marshy meadow, it crosses Prairie Creek and reaches the lake at 2.5 miles. There is a large campsite on the south shore. Two miniature lakes hide 200 yards off the trail over a rise to the east. A third tiny lake is .5 mile to the northwest. Beyond the largest Prairie Lake, the trail continues over a pass and down the West Fork of Prairie Creek to the Norton Lakes trailhead. Above Prairie Lakes this trail is closed to motorized travel.

# TRAILS MANAGED BY THE SAWTOOTH NATIONAL RECREATION AREA IN THE FAIRFIELD DISTRICT VIENNA AREA

## 105.

## Smiley Creek Trail

**Round trip:** 6 miles
**Elevation gain:** 1,440 feet
**Highest point:** 9,040 feet
**Map:** Frenchman Creek
**Difficulty:** moderate; time: 5 1/2 hours
**Access:** Turn south off Idaho Highway 75 onto the dirt Smiley Creek Road 1.5 miles south of Smiley Creek Lodge and drive 6.2 miles to the sign for Vienna on the

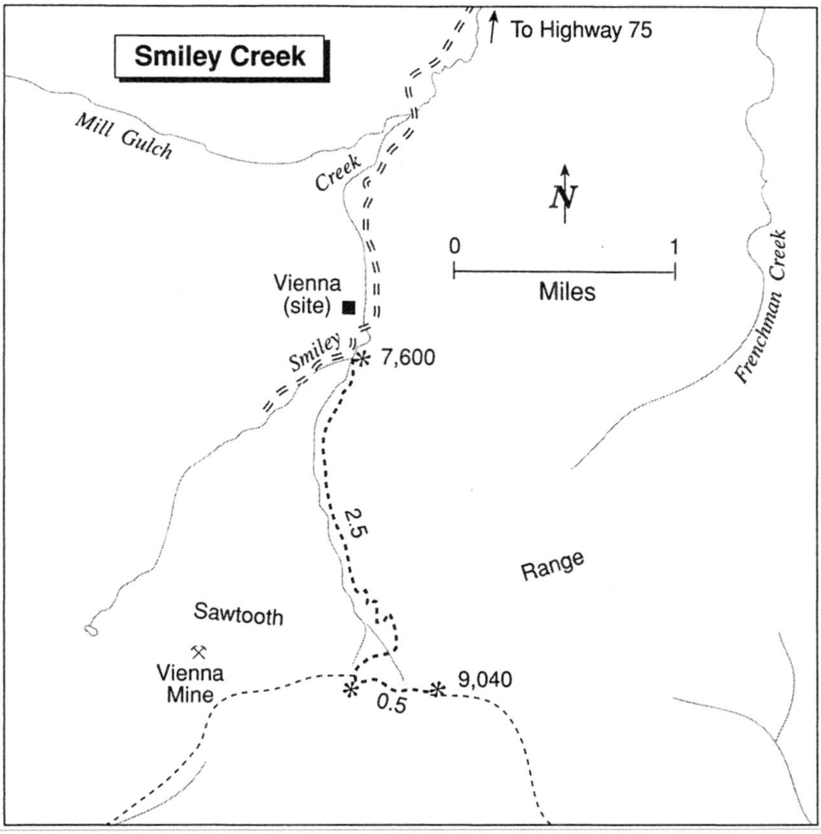


right side of the road. Across the main road from the sign and ruins is a parking area. The trail begins at the east end of the parking area next to the creek. Do not continue any farther up the main road because it enters the posted private property of some of the mines that served Vienna.

Vienna started in 1878, when Levi Smiley and T.B. Mulkey discovered and staked claims on a quartz vein at the head of Smiley Creek. Three settlements and several other mines started as a result: Vienna on Smiley Creek, Sawtooth City on Beaver Creek, and Eureka in Alturas Lake Creek Canyon. In 1880, the owners of the Pilgrim Mine at Sawtooth City built a toll road over Galena Summit to the mines.

The Vienna Mine was the largest in Smiley Creek Canyon, but there were others such as the Silver King. By 1882, there were 50 buildings in Vienna, including 14 saloons and a sawmill. A 20-stamp mill duplicated the General Custer Mill at Custer. In 1892, a fire in the Silver King Mine led to the end of mining at Vienna and 20,000 cords of wood for mine timbers were left cut and stacked in the canyon. The timbers are still there.

Only the ruins of one cabin marks the site of Vienna. North of there, red and orange outcrops sprout from an orange peak. A granite ridge holds jointed pillars on the divide between Smiley Creek and the West Fork of Big Smoky Creek. This divide provides access via a trail south down the West Fork of Big Smoky Creek and up Helen Creek to Snowslide and Paradise Lakes, about 7 miles from the trailhead. From the divide, the Emma Creek Trail goes southwest 5.5 miles to a road up the South Fork of the Boise.

Begin hiking where the trail fords the creek. On the other side, it passes a 100-yard long pile of mine timbers at .2 mile. Then it climbs through lodgepole pines, past smaller timber piles and the ruins of cabins. The second mile has many more switchbacks and stays on the east side of the creek longer than shown on the topographic map.

At 1.5 miles, the trail zigzags up a grassy hillside, crosses Smiley Creek at 2.2 miles and passes through a meadow below small cliffs. A junction with Emma Creek and the West Fork of Big Smoky Creek trails is at 2.5 miles. Follow the West Fork Trail east up a forested slope to the divide at 3 miles.

# TRAILS MANAGED BY THE SAWTOOTH NATIONAL FOREST IN THE FAIRFIELD DISTRICT SOUTH FORK BOISE RIVER AREA

## 106.

## Ross Fork Basin and Lakes

**Round trip to Ross Fork Basin:** 13 to 14 miles
**Round trip to Ross Fork Lakes:** 24.4 to 26.6 miles
**Elevation gain:** 2,400 to 3,040 feet
**Elevation loss:** 640 feet (return climb) on the longer route
**Highest point:** 8,600 feet
**Maps:** Ross Peak, Marshall Peak, Atlanta East, Newman Peak
**Difficulty:** strenuous, except that fording the river on the horse trail requires expert ability; time: 3 days;

**Access:** From Fairfield, take the road north through town that goes toward the Soldier Mountain Ski Area. At 1.1 miles, turn right at a sign for the ski area, then left at 2.2 miles at a sign for the Methodist Camp. Keep to the paved road when a dirt road to Wells Summit goes off to the right. At 9.9 miles, keep right when the road to the

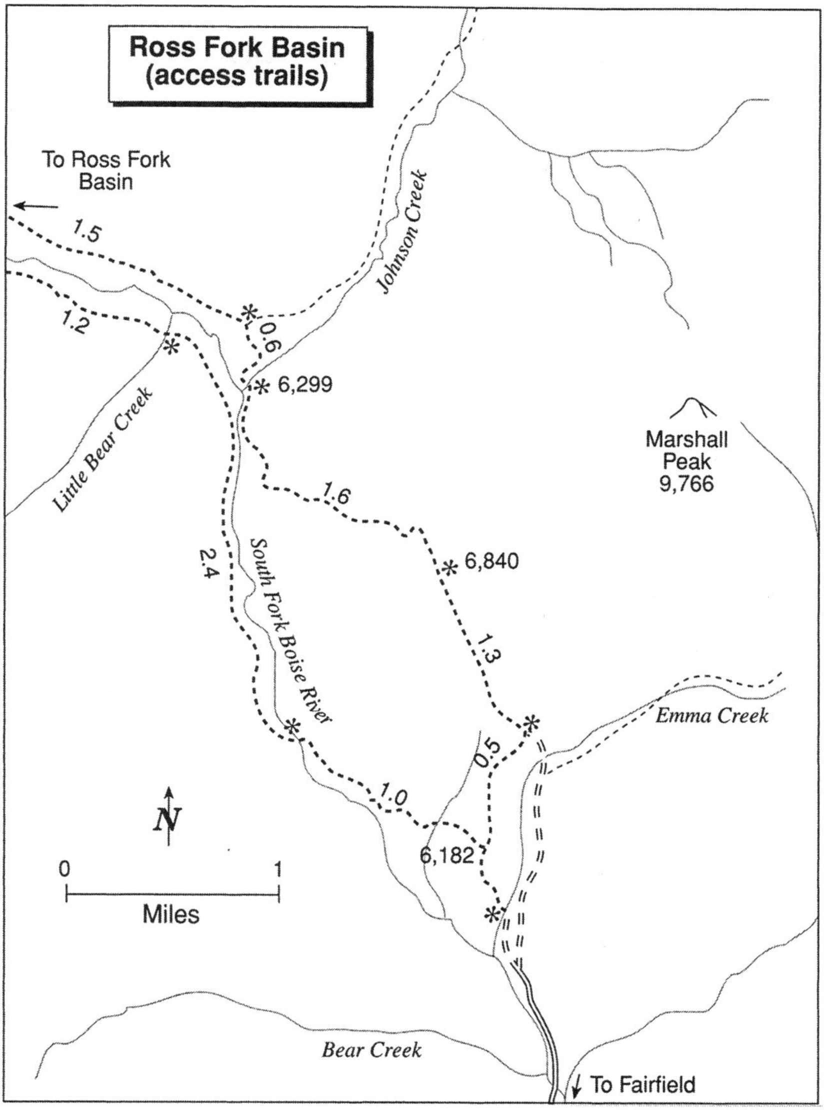


ski area turns left. Here the road becomes gravel. Drive over Couch Summit at 14.3 miles, and avoiding a side road to Ketchum, descend to a junction on the north side of the river at 24.4 miles. Or you can reach that junction by a 25-mile drive east from Featherville on a road that tends to have a washboard surface. Turn right here and at a junction with a side road to Canyon campground go straight ahead. Follow the dirt road north over Fleck Summit at 27 miles and down into an area sprinkled with vacation cabins. The road then passes a turnoff for the Methodist Camp at 32.5 miles and a junction with a road to the left to the Bear Creek transfer camp at 33.6 miles. At

33.9 miles, the road crosses the South Fork of the Boise River on a bridge to a parking area and toilet. Beyond here the road is primitive and very rocky. Drive or walk 1 mile farther to a ford of Emma Creek, which is at the bottom of a ravine, and requires four-wheel-drive to cross.

Ross Fork Basin, a level wooded and sagebrush area along the Ross Fork of the South Fork of the Boise, provides access to several lakes. Above the basin, pointed outcrops like granite Christmas trees stud sandy peaks along the canyon walls. The 100-yard wide river bed of white stones winds through the basin carrying the water of the Ross Fork.

Along the usual road to Ross Fork Basin is the town of Fairfield, located on the southernmost of Idaho's two camas prairies where the Bannocks and Shoshonis used to gather camas bulbs. A shortcut on the Oregon Trail, known as "Tim Goodale's Cutoff," crossed the Prairie. The first known settler, William Spencer, who ran a blacksmith shop for a year, shot and killed himself in 1880. Charley Babington built the first residence, a 1 1/2 story log house which still stands.

Jimmy Peck established the first town, Soldier, two miles north of Fairfield in 1880, naming it for the soldiers from Fort Boise who once camped there. The first post office, at Corral, was established in 1881. By 1910, there were 1,800 settlers. When the railroad arrived in 1911, Soldier was moved south to the tracks and rechristened "Fairfield."

On the way to Ross Fork Lakes from the basin, the trail passes through dry meadows scattered with rocks and wildflowers. Part way up the canyon, a peak in a side canyon resembling a big tooth overlooks Ross Fork Lake No. 1. Two points on top of 300-foot dark cliffs make the peak above the upper Ross Fork Lakes resemble the ears of a black cat. Below these cliffs, the highest Ross Fork Lake No. 5 sprawls in a bog and the blue water of Ross Lake No. 4 laps turf and whitened logs.

At Emma Creek, those with two-wheel drive trucks can take the right fork of the road to the north. This road makes a loop (see map) that can be used to reach the intersection of the Ross Fork jeep trail with the horse trail without fording Emma Creek. The hike mileage begins at this intersection. If you have four-wheel drive and decide to drive through the ford of Emma Creek, this intersection is .5 mile from the ford.

From this intersection, you can take a jeep trail and then a pack trail to the river to access the horse trail. When the trail reaches the river, it fords it to the left (west) side. Because this ford is thigh deep even in late summer IT IS SAFE ONLY FOR EXPERTS. Early in the summer everyone should take the jeep trail from the first junction. From that junction, you can drive a four-wheel-drive vehicle to the end of the loop and then follow the Ross Fork jeep trail north over a summit and down to a ford of Johnson Creek at 3.4 miles. This ford prevents all but the most gung ho from driving clear to Ross Fork Basin. The horse trail is .7 mile shorter and avoids a 640-foot climb over the summit.

From the beginning of the horse trail, the old road crosses a branch of the river at .5 mile, becomes a pack trail below a talus slope at .7 mile and reaches the river at 1 mile. Before fording, look downstream to find the trail on the other side.

At about 2 miles, the river splits into Johnson Creek and the Ross Fork, and the trail goes along the Ross Fork on the south side. It goes through sagebrush flats and forest and crosses Little Bear Creek on rocks at 3.4 miles.

The trail passes through a forested swamp before reaching Perkons Creek at 4.6 miles, where a faint trail up Perkons Creek to Perkons Lakes begins. At 5.4 miles, the horse trail ends at the Bass Creek Trail in a sagebrush flat. Take this trail north across the Ross Fork on rocks and turn left (west) onto the jeep trail at 5.7 miles. Follow this

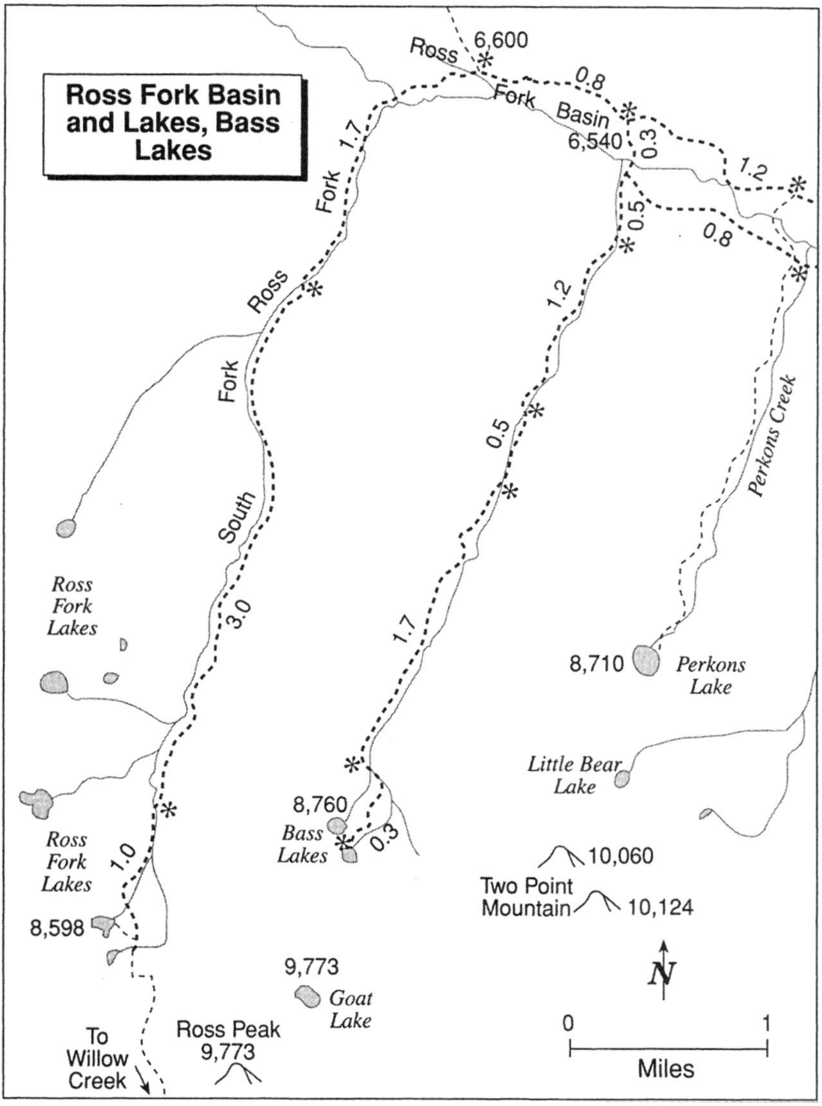


track to grassy Ross Fork Basin at 6.5 miles. A campsite is just beyond where the Ross Fork splits into its North and South Forks near the ruins of an old cabin.

To reach Ross Fork Basin by the jeep trail, go north from the end of the loop .7 mile from the intersection with the horse trail. From here, take a road north uphill through sagebrush. At a summit at 1.7 miles (640 feet above Emma Creek), it enters forest, switches back twice, crosses a creek in aspens and drops downhill. At 3.4 miles, the jeep trail fords Johnson Creek. To prevent damaging your pickup or SUV park here even if it has four-wheel drive. Walk along the track beyond the ford through trees to a signed junction with a trail up Johnson Creek at 4 miles.

The track continues along the bottom of a sagebrush hillside. At 5.5 miles, a post and a track toward the river mark the turnoff for Perkons Lake. Beyond here, the Ross Fork Trail fords a rocky creek and winds through mud. At 6 miles, it touches the riverbank and reaches the Bass Creek turnoff at 6.7 miles. Continue up the track to the basin at 7.5 miles.

To reach the Ross Fork Lakes, walk upriver from the basin on the old road. Distances on the lakes trail are measured from the ruins of an old cabin in the basin. Just beyond where a blazed pack trail leads north up the North Fork, cross the North Fork over yards of river stones. On the other side, the blazed jeep road leads through a lodgepole forest and passes some old cabins at .5 mile. The road becomes a pack trail .7 mile from the basin. At 1.7 miles, it crosses the South Fork of the Ross Fork on rocks in an open area where you can look up the canyon of the first Ross Fork Lake. Beyond this ford, a trail leads 2 miles up this side canyon to it. The main trail returns to forest, comes onto an open hillside at 2.5 miles, then enters wildflower meadows sprinkled with trees. Beyond a campsite and an open area of false hellebore at 4.7 miles, the trail crosses back to the west side of the creek.

After the crossing, the trail climbs along the creek and its west branch for 600 feet through forest with a view of the Sawtooths to the northeast. At 5.2 miles, it switchbacks west and then south back to the creek. To reach Lakes No. 4 and No. 5, before the ford, turn right (northwest) on a trail up an open hillside to Ross Fork Lake No. 4 at 5.7 miles. To reach Ross Fork Lake No. 5, walk up the creek cross-country from back where the trail fords it. Both these lakes are 5.7 miles from the old cabin at the forks — 12.2 miles and 13.3 miles from the trailhead. Once across the ford, the main trail climbs over a 9,200-foot pass west of Ross Peak and down Willow Creek to a trailhead near Featherville.

# 107.

## Bass Lakes

**Round trip:** 22.2 to 24.2 miles
**Elevation gain:** 2,580 to 3,220 feet
**Elevation loss:** 640 feet (return climb) on the longer route
**This section:** 4.7 miles with 2,220 feet gain
**Highest point:** 8,760 feet
**Maps:** Marshall Peak, Newman Peak, Ross Peak
**Difficulty:** strenuous; expert ability needed for a ford of the Ross Fork on the horse trail; time: 3 days

**Access:** Follow the directions under Ross Fork Basin and Lakes to reach the intersection of the Ross Fork horse and jeep trails. Then drive and hike a total of 7.5 miles up the Ross Fork on a jeep trail or hike 6.5 miles up the horse trail to Ross Fork Basin where this hike description begins.

The milky turquoise water of the higher Bass Lake laps against ledges matted with tiny trees. Behind the lake, a wall of dark gray and cream-colored cliffs hangs above a cirque containing the lake. Its grassy shores are decorated in early summer with penstemon, elephant's head, cinquefoil, alpine sunflower, aster and paintbrush. Cream-colored peaks of the Sawtooths float in the distance. At the lower, deeper lake, silvered logs, a grassy peninsula and a rock bench slide into green water.

From the jeep trail on the north side of the Ross Fork 6.7 miles from the trailhead, take the side track down to a ford of the Ross Fork. On the south side of the river the trail goes south across a sagebrush flat and climbs through trees and meadows along the northwest side of Bass Creek. Rock gnomes on the canyon wall overlook the trail at .5 mile. At .8 mile, it crosses the creek to the west side on rocks, crosses back at 2 miles, and at 2.5 miles returns to the west side.

Soon it disappears in the grass, where a path angles left to a campsite beside the creek. The trail on to the lakes goes along the grassy hillside about 150 yards above the campsite. Beyond are meadows and scattered bits of forest.

At 3.5 miles, the trail is opposite a peak on the end of the east canyon wall. It crosses a tiny stream in a meadow and continues up the right (west) of this meadow into the forest again. The trail then angles east across the head of the canyon.

It returns to the east side of the creek at 4.2 miles, leads up the bed of the left branch of the creek and switches back to the right (west). From here, you can see the mountains around Alice Lake in the distance. The trail crosses the branch of the creek at 4.4 miles and reaches the lake and a campsite at 4.7 miles. To reach the lower lake, walk northwest 200 yards.

**Sign in the Hells Canyon country**

# APPENDICES

## NOTES ON TRAILS NOT COVERED IN GUIDE

(Road numbers in this section refer to Forest Service roads.)

## HELLS CANYON NATIONAL RECREATION AREA AND WILDERNESS

**LITTLE GRANITE CREEK:** The access is from the Seven Devils Trail. The trail begins at a junction with it just above Hibbs Cow Camp and drops down Little Granite Creek and Granite Creek to the Snake River. It is 6 miles long and has a 6,160-foot elevation loss. The trail is steep and rocky, but is marked and maintained. Rattlesnakes and poison ivy are found in the lower section. The trail is only open from July to October due to snow. It offers backpackers the opportunity to descend from the Seven Devils to the Snake River. **Maps:** He Devil, Squirrel Prairie.

**STORMY POINT:** Formerly descended Sheep Creek to the Snake River from a rough dirt road that goes to Low Saddle from Lucile, Idaho. The trail has been washed out.

**RAPID RIVER:** The access is from the Rapid River Fish Hatchery. The trail begins at the West Fork Rapid River Trail at 4 miles and continues to the forest boundary and up the river to Smith Mountain near the Black Lake Road. It is 3.4 miles to the boundary with a 400-foot elevation gain. The trail is recommended only for spring and fall due to its low elevation. **Maps:** Heavens Gate, Pollock Mountain, Railroad Saddle.

**RANKIN MILL:** The access is from the Black Lake Road, Windy Saddle, or the Rapid River. The trail along the old road is now an ATV trail. It begins at the Black Lake Road and connects with the West Fork of Rapid River Trail. It is 12 miles to Rankin Mill with a 2,100-foot elevation gain and 2,900-foot elevation loss. Only ruins are left of the mill. It provides access by pack trail to Ruth Lake and by cross-country travel to Crystal Lake. Note that ATVs are not allowed beyond Paradise Creek. **Maps:** Purgatory Saddle, He Devil.

## PAYETTE NATIONAL FOREST (WEISER DISTRICT)

**EAST BROWNLEE:** The access is from near the summit of Idaho Highway 71, between Cambridge and Brownlee Reservoir, by the road that goes east from there past Brownlee Campground. It begins 1.5 miles northeast of the campground and continues over Cuddy Mountain to the abandoned Buck Park Guard Station. It is 6 miles long; with a 3,815-foot elevation gain. It provides a view of the entire Brownlee Reservoir drainage and goes through flat alpine meadows in the vicinity of Buck Park. **Map:** Cuddy Mountain.

## PAYETTE NATIONAL FOREST (NEW MEADOWS DISTRICT)

**BIG HAZARD LAKE:** The access is from the Hazard Lake—Elk Meadows Road 27 miles from Idaho 55. It begins at the road and goes to Big Hazard Lake. It is .5 mile long and has a 50- foot elevation loss. The trail leads through a burned forest to the 1 mile-long lake with a view south to Bruin Mountain. **Map:** Hazard Lake.

**JOHN AND MARY LAKES:** The access is from the Elk Lake Road through private land and therefore is not recommended. It is best to reach these lakes from the trail past Twin Lakes. This makes John Lake 7.5 miles from the Clayburn trailhead, with an 880-foot elevation gain and 1,680-foot elevation loss. **Maps:** Pollock, Patrick Butte.

**KENNETH LAKE:** The access is from the Elk Meadows Road. It begins at the Elk Meadows Road and climbs to Kenneth Lake. It is .2 mile long with a 160-foot elevation gain. It leads to a small lake in burned forest. **Map:** Black Tip.

## PAYETTE NATIONAL FOREST (MCCALL DISTRICT)

**PADDY FLAT-LAKE FORK:** The access is from the Paddy Flat Road or the Lick Creek Road. It begins on the Paddy Flat Road and goes to the Lick Creek Road. It is 9 miles long with a 2,180-foot elevation gain and 2,520-foot loss. It gives access to Boulder and Rapid Lakes when the Boulder Reservoir Road is too muddy to drive. It passes Anderson Lake. **Map:** Fitsum Summit.

**GOLDEN LAKE:** The access is from the Lick Creek Road; there is no trail. The cross-country route is 2 miles long with a 2,200-foot elevation gain. **Map:** Fitsum Summit.

**VICTOR CREEK:** The access is from the Warren Wagon Road. The trail begins at the Warren Wagon Road and continues to the Loon Lake Horse Trail. It is 12.5 miles long with a 2,000-foot elevation gain and 2,200 foot elevation loss. It gives access to Trail and Deep Lakes via cross-country travel. Much of the area along the trail is recovering from fire. **Maps:** Victor Peak, Loon Lake.

**CRESTLINE:** The access is from the Warren Wagon Road. The trail begins at the Pearl Creek Road and continues to a trailhead at the end of a road turning east off McCall's Lakeshore Drive. It passes through a lot of burned forest near Pearl, Heart, Brush, Squaw, Buck and Blackwell Lakes. It is 14 miles long with an 1,180 foot elevation gain and 2,240-foot elevation loss. **Maps:** Granite Lake, Box Lake, Fitsum Summit, McCall.

**BROWNS POND:** The access is from the Lick Creek Road. It is a jeep road that begins at the Lick Creek Road and goes to Browns Pond. It is .5 mile long with a 200-foot elevation loss. The pond is a 1 mile-long reservoir in woods with granite islands and a view of the lower Lake Fork Canyon. It is an easy stroll that is best for early summer. **Map:** McCall.

**PONDEROSA STATE PARK:** The access is from Lakeshore Drive. Those entering the park must pay a day use fee or have a season pass for Idaho state parks. The trails give views of Payette Lake and of marsh habitat. In winter, trails are groomed for cross-country skiing. You can obtain summer and winter maps of the trails at the Visitors Center. **Map:** McCall.

## BOISE NATIONAL FOREST (CASCADE DISTRICT)

**NEEDLES:** Access: Warm Lake Road. Begins at Gold Fork Meadow and continues to East Fork Kennally Creek. 14 miles long, 1,775 feet gain, 3,200 feet loss. Poor condition, no water. View of dramatic rocks of the Needles Peaks. **Maps:** Gold Fork Rock, Blackmare.

**TAMARACK:** New trails for hiking and mountain biking constructed by Tamarack Resort on the West Mountains above Cascade Lake. Consult www.tamarackidaho.com for information and to download trail map.

## PAYETTE NATIONAL FOREST (MCCALL DISTRICT)

**COUGAR LAKES:** The access is from the Kennally Creek Campground. The trail begins at the North Fork of Kennally Creek Trail and continues to the Cougar Creek Trail. It is 2.5 miles to the lake from the North Fork of Kennally Creek with a 1,600-foot elevation gain. **Map:** Blackmare.

**RIORDAN LAKE:** The access is from the Landmark-Yellow Pine Road. The

Stone cellar at Caribou Creek in Hells Canyon

**Payette Lakes from the Fall Creek Trail**

trail is 4 miles long with a 1,600-foot elevation gain. It leads to a. .7-mile-long lake in hills covered with partly burned forest. **Maps:** Yellow Pine, Chilcoot Peak.

**CATON AND RAINBOW LAKES:** The access is from the Landmark-Yellow Pine Road. It is 5 miles to Rainbow Lake with a 2,340-foot elevation gain and 9 miles to Caton Lake with a 2,140-foot elevation gain and 1,130 -foot elevation loss (return climb). **Maps:** Caton Lake, Log Mountain.

## BOISE NATIONAL FOREST (EMMETT DISTRICT)

**TRIPOD PEAK:** The access is from the north side of Sagehen Reservoir. The trail begins at the end of the primitive, 4-mile-long Joes Creek Road (622) and continues to the top of the peak. It is only 2.4 miles long but has a 2,000-foot elevation gain so it will seem longer. It gives a good view of Sagehen and Crane Creek Reservoirs and the surrounding mountains. **Map:** Tripod Peak.

**SAGEHEN NATURE TRAIL:** The access is from road 614 on the northeast side of Sagehen Reservoir. It is .5 mile long and mostly level. **Map:** Sagehen Reservoir.

**BOILING SPRINGS:** The access is from the Boiling Springs Road (698H). The trail begins at the Boiling Springs Guard Station and leads along the Middle Fork of the Payette River to the East Mountain Road (099) north of Clear Creek Summit. It is15.4 miles long with a 1,900-foot elevation gain. It passes undeveloped hot springs, but fords the Middle Fork of the Payette 17 times. These crossings are VERY DANGEROUS OR IMPASSABLE until August 1 and are still one to three feet deep in late summer. If you don't mind getting wet repeatedly, it provides a loop trip with the Bull Creek Trail. **Maps:** Boiling Springs, Bull Creek Hot Springs.

**East Twentymile Lake north of McCall**

**LONG FORK OF SILVER CREEK TRAIL:** The access is from Crouch on road 698 past Silver Creek Plunge and then on road 671. It offers rugged landscape and excellent views of the Sawtooths in the distance. It climbs the Long Fork of Silver Creek to a divide and descends east down Bitter Creek to the Deadwood Reservoir Road near its junction with the Landmark-Stanley Road. It is about a 2,700-foot gain and an equal loss. **Maps:** Boiling Springs, Wild Buck Peak.

**GABES PEAK:** The access is from the Gabes Peak Campground in Rammage Meadows on the Second Fork of Squaw Creek Road (609) north of Sagehen Reservoir. The trail leads up a ridge and over the side of Gabes Peak (7,665 feet) and down into Wilson Meadows .5 mile west of the Snowbank Mountain Road, passing within .2 mile of the lake called Gabes Bathtub. It provides a link via the West Mountain Trail with a network of trails, including the 5.3-mile Greenfield Flats Trail and the 2.9-mile Poison Creek Trail on the north and the 3.7-mile Antelope Creek Trail and the 4.1-mile Renwyck Trail on the south. From the trailhead it is 5 miles to the top of Gabes Peak and then .7 mile down into Wilson Meadows to a junction with the West Mountain Trail, with a 2,390-foot elevation gain and a 150-foot elevation loss. **Map:** Tripod Peak.

## BOISE NATIONAL FOREST (MOUNTAIN HOME DISTRICT)

**STACK ROCK:** Stack Rock is on PRIVATE PROPERTY and there is no way to reach the rock without going through other private land. The landowners have posted their property against trespassing. The major landowners hope that eventually through negotiations with the State of Idaho or other agencies a way will be found to allow access.

**HORSE HEAVEN:** The access is from the North Fork of the Boise River Road (Forest Service Road 327). It begins at the Trail Creek Road 2 miles from the North Fork of the Boise, climbs Horse Heaven Creek on an old logging road for 1.5 miles, then switchbacks up Horse Heaven Creek to a saddle on the north side of Swanholm Peak. It drops to meet the Lodgepole Creek Trail and continues to Johnson Creek Campground on the North Fork of the Boise River near Graham. There is a beautiful view of the Sawtooths from the saddle. It gives a fine exhibit of four plant communities: ponderosa pine, Douglas fir, subalpine fir and lodgepole pine. It is 8 miles long with a 2,240-foot elevation gain and 1,840-foot elevation loss. **Maps:** Swanholm Peak, Bear River.

**SWANHOLM PEAK AND WARRIOR LAKES:** The access is from the North Fork of the Boise River Road via the Trail Creek Road. It begins at the primitive Horse Heaven Creek Road, climbs 2.5 miles to Swanholm Peak as a jeep trail, and continues past Warrior Lakes as a pack trail. It is 2 additional miles to the lakes and the first part of this is steep. It climbs 2,500 feet to the peak and drops 620 feet to the lakes. The trail is in poor condition. **Map:** Swanholm Peak.

**BLACK WARRIOR:** The access is from the Middle Fork of the Boise River Road 10 miles west of Atlanta. It begins at that road, climbs Black Warrior Creek, and connects with the Neinmeyer Creek Trail. It is 11 miles long with a 2,700-foot elevation gain and is in poor condition. There are many creek crossings and views of old mines. It provides a loop with the Little Queens River Trail via Neinmeyer Creek. **Maps:** Phifer Creek, Atlanta West.

## BOISE NATIONAL FOREST (IDAHO CITY DISTRICT)

**CORBUS CREEK:** The access is from the James Creek Road 6 miles above where it turns off the Middle Fork of the Boise River Road, 1.7 miles west of Atlanta. It is 9 miles long with much up and down. It connects with the trails up Grouse and Decker Creeks on the Sawtooth National Forest. From it, you can reach Corbus Lake by taking the trail .5 mile from the James Creek trailhead to an 8,200-foot pass and then going .5 mile south cross-country.

**CROOKED RIVER:** The access is from Idaho Highway 21 near the Edna Creek Campground and 1 mile of Forest Road 384, which goes toward Atlanta. The trail descends the Crooked River to the North Fork of the Boise River Road. It is 12 miles long with a 300 foot elevation gain and a 1,000-foot elevation loss. There are views of the rugged canyon, deep pools and the rushing river. A ford of the river at 1 mile will be difficult in early summer. Three other fords are now bridged. The lower 9 miles burned in 1994. The upper end makes a good day hike, especially as part of a 5.5 mile loop with the Whoop-em-up, Lamar Creek and Beaver Creek trails. **Maps:** Big Owl Creek, Barber Flat.

**HOT CREEK:** To reach this trail drive to the junction of the North Fork Boise River Road (307) with the Middle Fork of the Boise River Road. Then cross the Middle Fork and drive up the Phifer Creek Road (156) for 2 miles to the Hot Creek Road (241). From June 15-Sept.15 you can drive 4.5 miles farther to where a jeep road climbs up to the right to access the beginning of the trail. The trail begins other side of Hot Creek from the end of the road. Go up this trail 3.5 miles and turn off onto the trail that goes 2.7 miles to Lake Creek. Once on Lake Creek, you can take a fisherman's path from the east side of Lake Creek and go 1 mile to Lake Creek Lake. From the Hot Creek trailhead you can also follow a trail up Hot Creek that isn't maintained to a pass between Hot and Elk Creeks. From the pass you can climb Steel Mountain.

**IDAHO CITY AREA TRAIL SYSTEM:** There is a 56-mile network of groomed cross-country ski trails, and summer hiking and mountain biking trails north of Idaho City. Yurts along the trails can be rented all year by advance reservation. See the *Year Around Yurt and Trail Guide* available from the Idaho Department of Parks and Recreation for more information. The trail system begins at three different trailheads: Banner Ridge, Gold Fork and Whoop-em-up. (Yurts are domed, circular canvas tents with plywood floors and wood stoves.)

## BOISE NATIONAL FOREST (LOWMAN DISTRICT)

**LOST LAKES:** The access is by way of the Clear Creek, Bear Valley and East Side roads. To reach the trailhead, from Lowman, drive up the Clear Creek Road (582) towards Bear Valley for 16.7 miles. Turn right (east) on the East Side Road (502) for about 10 miles. Turn right (south) on a jeep trail for .2 mile to find a pack trail that goes left. It's easy to drive past the trail if you don't watch closely. It is 1 mile to the first lake with a 280-foot elevation gain. Other lakes can be reached cross-country with a compass or GPS unit from the first. The lakes are small ones in wooded country. **Map:** Cache Creek.

**JACKSON PEAK:** The access is from Idaho Highway 21 east of Lowman and Forest Road 531. On this road, go across the South Fork of the Payette, then curve right and go .2 mile more to the trailhead. It is 3.5 miles long with a 3,500-foot elevation gain to the summit, which has an excellent view of the Sawtooths. The trail avoids having to drive any of the rocky Graham Road to gain access to the summit.

**TEN MILE RIDGE:** 12 miles east of Lowman on Idaho Highway 21, turn right on Forest Road 531. Go across the South Fork of the Payette, then veer left. At 1 mile, go left to the trailhead. It is 11.7 miles long with a 4,200-foot elevation gain. It provides access to the Sawtooth Wilderness via Picket Mountain and Big Meadows. **Maps:** Jackson Peak, Tyee Mountain, Edaho Mountain

**WAPITI CREEK:** 20.5 miles east of Lowman on Idaho Highway 21, turn east on the Grandjean Road. Go 4.7 miles to the Wapiti Summer Home Area. Turn right onto that road, then sharp right on Road 525 in .1 mile. After .2 mile, turn left on Road 525A and go .6 mile to the trailhead. The trail goes from the Wapiti Summer Home Area to the Ten Mile Ridge Area. It is 7 miles long, with a 2,640-foot elevation gain. **Maps:** Grandjean, Edaho Mountain

**KIRKHAM RIDGE ATV TRAIL:** This trail begins on Idaho 21 just beyond Kirkham Hot Springs. It is 8 miles of new ATV trails that connect with the Upper Kirkham Ridge-Warm Springs trail system, which is not open to ATVs, and should not be confused with this trail.

## BOISE NATIONAL FOREST (MOUNTAIN HOME DISTRICT)

**ROARING RIVER:** The access is from Trinity Lakes. It begins at the Trinity Lakes Guard Station just off Forest Road 129 near Big Trinity Lake and continues to the Roaring River Road (265), passing a junction with the William H. Pogue Trail at about 6 miles, thus providing a through trip from the Middle Fork of the Boise River Road to the Trinity Lakes. It is 8 miles long with a 2,740-foot elevation loss. **Map:**

Little Trinity Lake.

## IDAHO STATE HISTORICAL SOCIETY (Boise)

**OLD PRISON QUARRY TRAIL:** The access is from the Old Penitentiary State Park in Boise. The trail is 1.5 miles long with a 200 foot elevation gain. The trail makes a loop to the old prison quarry west of Tablerock. **Map:** Boise South.

## BUREAU OF LAND MANAGEMENT (Lower Snake River District)

**RIDGE TO RIVERS TRAIL SYSTEM:** This system is a unique partnership among government agencies, private landowners, organizations and individuals to manage the roads and trails that travel 75,000 acres of land in the foothills just north of Boise. This area stretches from the Boise River to the Boise Ridge above the town. Many of the trails cross private property by agreement with the landowners and the agreements are limited to the trail corridors, so please stay on the trails. Going off trail on these private lands is trespassing.

**FLORIDA MOUNTAIN:** The access is from Silver City. This old road, much used by ATVs, begins at the campground just south of the city. It climbs Florida Mountain, passing old mines, and returns down Long Gulch. It is 6 miles long with a 1,600-foot elevation gain. It provides a fine view of Silver City. The top of the mountain has seen recent large-scale mining, so is not as attractive a destination as War Eagle Mountain. Because of high summer temperatures it is best for late June and October. **Maps:** Silver City, DeLamar.

**SOUTH MOUNTAIN:** The access is from Jordan Valley, Oregon. The road up South Mountain provides hiking opportunities on several jeep roads. There are early mining sites and in mid-June, especially fine wildflowers. Use the BLM maps to find the current roads. **Maps:** Williams Creek, Cliffs.

**OREGON TRAIL NEAR CANYON CREEK:** The access is from the Canyon Creek Road north of Mountain Home. Experienced hikers can follow the Oregon Trail several miles east and west of Canyon Creek. An interpretive map is available from the BLM. **Map:** Mountain Home North.

**THREE ISLAND CROSSING STATE PARK:** The access is from West Madison Street 1 mile south of Glens Ferry. There are interpretive trails and in summer, covered wagon rides. The park is located at the Oregon Trail crossing from the south to north sides of the river. **Map:** Glenns Ferry.

## CHALLIS NATIONAL FOREST (MIDDLE FORK DISTRICT)

**MIDDLE FORK OF SALMON RIVER:** This trail is described in full in the second edition of *Trails of the Frank Church-River of No Return Wilderness* by the author because it is in that wilderness.

**HELLDIVER, SOLDIER, AND CUTTHROAT LAKES; LANGER, ISLAND AND RUFFNECK LAKES; HORSESHOE LAKE FROM KNAPP CREEK; KNAPP LAKES; and CRIMSON LAKE:** These hike descriptions have been removed from the hike descriptions in this book because these trails are partly

**Swan Falls trail in the Birds of Prey National Conservation Area**

in the Frank Church Wilderness. They now appear in the second edition of *Trails of the Frank Church-River of No Return Wilderness* by the author.

## CHALLIS NATIONAL FOREST (YANKEE FORK DISTRICT)

**LIGHTNING CREEK TRAIL:** There are two ways to access the Lightning Creek Trail. One is from the Bonanza Guard Station and the West Fork of Yankee Fork trail and the other is from a jeep trail off the Loon Creek Summit Road at the first switchback after that road leaves Jordan Creek and begins climbing. The non-motorized trail begins at a new bridge over Lightning Creek 4 miles up the West Fork of Yankee Fork Trail and continues up Lightning Creek to the jeep trail that leads off the Loon Creek Summit Road. The Lightning Creek Trail is about 10.3 miles long and passes Lightning Lake at 8.6 miles. There is a 2,920-foot elevation gain from the bridge to the top of the divide above the lake. From the trail there is a view of colorful peaks.

By driving in on the jeep trail from the Loon Creek Summit Road for .5 mile, you can walk the next 2 miles of the road to the Lightning Creek Trail and then follow that trail 1.7 miles over a divide next to Mt. Jordan and down to Lightning Lake. If you do that, the elevation gain is 1,920 feet and the elevation loss (return climb) is

680 feet. (It is possible to drive a four-wheel drive vehicle to the end of the jeep trail, reducing the round trip to 3.4 miles, and the elevation gain to 500 feet, but that 2 miles of road is very rough.) **Maps:** Custer, Mt. Jordan.

**SULLIVAN LAKE:** This description has been removed from this book because the original access from Idaho 75, 2.5 miles east of the Yankee Fork Ranger Station, is blocked by posted private property. In addition, that trail up Sullivan Creek is a game trail and thus not maintained. It is probably best to reach Sullivan Lake by the Corral Creek Trail through the Sawtooth National Recreation Area from the north end of Jimmy Smith Lake. That trail is 6 miles long with a 1,540-foot gain. It mostly goes through sagebrush with no shade. There is also a little-known non-system trail to Sullivan Lake from Idaho 75, which starts on the opposite side of the road from the turnoff for the road that goes north up Squaw Creek to the Thompson Mine, but the author didn't find out about it in time to check it out. **Maps:** Clayton, Potaman Peak.

## CHALLIS NATIONAL FOREST (LOST RIVER DISTRICT)

**UPPER FALL CREEK:** The access is from the Wildhorse Creek Road. The lower part of the trail is covered in the descriptions for Moose Lake and Surprise Valley. The upper trail begins at the Surprise Valley junction and climbs part way up Fall Creek. It is about 2 miles long with a 600-foot elevation gain. It is little used, poorly defined, and goes through much fallen timber, but from it there is a magnificent view of the head wall of Fall Creek Canyon. Hikers can continue cross-country to the head of the canyon at about 4 miles. **Map:** Standhope Peak.

## SAWTOOTH NATIONAL FOREST (KETCHUM DISTRICT)

**BIG WOOD RIVER TRAIL (LAKE CREEK TRAIL):** The access is by footbridge from the Lake Creek trailhead 3 miles north of Ketchum on Idaho Highway 75. It climbs 700 feet in 5 miles and provides access to the 40-mile Adams Gulch and Fox Creek Trail system (see below). In winter, the Lake Creek Trail is groomed for cross-country skiing. **Maps:** Sun Valley, Griffin Butte.

**ADAMS GULCH TRAILS:** There are a series of loop and one-way trails in Adams Gulch. The access is from Idaho Highway 75, 1.5 miles north of Ketchum. To reach the trailhead from the highway, turn west on Adams Gulch Road, and go .7 mile. The trails include the 2.5-mile Sunnyside-Lane's trail, the 1.5-mile Shadyside Trail, the 5.5-mile Adams Gulch loop, the 6-mile Eve's Gulch — West Fork Warm Springs trail, and a new trail called Sunnyside. **Map:** Griffin Butte.

**FOX CREEK TRAILS:** There are several loop trails in the Fox Creek drainage that are reached from the Lake Creek trailhead. They include the 5-mile Fox Creek loop, the 3-mile North Fork loop, the 1-mile Chocolate Gulch loop, and the 5-mile trail to Oregon Gulch. These trails are primarily used by residents and visitors for exercise on foot or mountain bike. **Maps:** Griffin Butte, Amber Lakes.

**HARRIMAN TRAIL:** The access is from Idaho Highway 75 at North Fork or from Galena Lodge. It begins at the North Fork Campground 10 miles north of Ketchum and goes along near the highway and the Wood River for 18.8 miles with a basic elevation gain of 100 feet. Because the trail isn't on the topographic map, the ups and downs that add to the elevation gain haven't been figured. The trail provides a safer alternative to riding on the highway for bicyclists and in winter it is groomed for cross-country skiing. It is named for Averell Harriman, founder of Sun Valley.

**Shirts Lake above Cascade Reservoir**

**Maps:** Amber Lakes, Easley Hot Springs, Galena.

**HIGH RIDGE:** The access is from the Lake Creek or Park Creek Road. It begins at the Lake Creek Road, climbs to a saddle and around the end of a ridge before dropping to the Park Creek Road. A through trip requires car shuttle. It is 7 miles long with a 2,000-foot elevation gain. The trail provides challenging hiking at high elevations with excellent views of the Pioneer and Boulder Mountains. It is snow-free only after mid-July. **Map:** Rock Roll Canyon.

**HYNDMAN CREEK:** The access is from the East Fork of the Wood River Road. It begins at the Hyndman Creek Road and will connect, when completed, with the trail up the North Fork of Hyndman Creek to Pioneer Cabin. It is 2 miles to the saddle with the best view of the peaks with an 1,800-foot elevation gain. It gives you a spectacular view of Hyndman and Cobb peaks. **Map:** Hyndman Peak.

**JOHNSTONE PASS AND BOX CANYON LAKES:** This description has been removed from this edition. A landslide has obliterated the trail near the top of the pass. Since the trail wasn't a maintained one, the Forest Service has, understandably, decided not to clear the landslide. Because of the danger in crossing the landslide, the author no longer recommends this route. The lakes can still be reached from the east by 12 or so miles of trail from the Starhope Campground in Copper Basin. **Map:** Grays Peak.

**TRAIL CREEK TRAILS:** From Idaho Highway 75 in Ketchum, turn east on Sun Valley Road and go 3 miles to Trail Creek Cabin or a little farther to the Boundary Campground. Trails include the 3.5-mile Corral Creek Trail, the 1.7-mile Aspen loop trail, the 1.5-mile Trail Creek Trail, and the 5- mile one-way Proctor Mountain Trail. This last climbs to the top of Proctor Mountain, which has an excellent view of Sun Valley and Bald Mountain and holds remnants of the world's first chairlift. **Map:** Sun Valley.

**Jordan's House in Hells Canyon**

# SAWTOOTH NATIONAL FOREST (FAIRFIELD DISTRICT)

**BIG SMOKY:** The access is from Couch Summit near Fairfield or from the South Fork of the Boise River Road from Featherville. The trail begins at Canyon Campground and continues to the road from Chemetkan Campground at the south end of the Sawtooth Valley. The section from Sawtooth Valley to the summit is described fully in the forth edition of *Trails of the Sawtooth and White Cloud Mountains* by the author. The trail is 21 miles long with a 2,920-foot elevation gain and an 800-foot elevation loss. The trail runs up Big Smoky Creek over the top of the Salmon River Divide, passing Skillern Hot springs at 3 miles, and the headwaters of the Salmon River at 18.5 miles. **Maps:** Sidney Butte, Paradise Peak, Baker Peak, Frenchman Creek, Galena.

**GOAT LAKE:** The access is from the upper South Fork of the Boise River Road. It begins at the Bear Creek Road and continues to the lake. It is 3 miles long with a 1,540-foot elevation gain. Two miles of it is jeep trail, and the Bear Creek Road requires four-wheel drive. **Maps:** Newman Peak, Ross Peak.

**PERKONS LAKE:** The access is from the upper South Fork of the Boise River Road via the horse trail on the south side of the Ross Fork. It begins at the Ross Fork Trail and climbs to Perkons Lake. It is 3 miles long with a 2,100-foot elevation gain. It is extremely steep for the last mile. **Map:** Marshall Peak.

**NORTH FORK ROSS FORK — JOHNSON CREEK LOOP**: The access is from the upper South Fork of Boise River Road via a trail or four-wheel drive road up the Ross Fork to Johnson Creek. It begins at the Ross Fork, goes up Johnson Creek, and comes down the North Fork of the Ross Fork. It is 15 miles long, including completing the loop on the Ross Fork Trail and has a 2,000-foot elevation gain and 1,800-foot elevation loss. It provides access to Johnson Lake by cross-country hiking and connects with the Alturas Creek Trail in the Sawtooth National Recreation Area via .7 mile of old trail from the upper end of Johnson Creek. **Map:** Marshall Peak.

**WEST FORK BIG SMOKY CREEK:** The access is from the Big Smoky Creek Trail. It begins at Big Smoky Creek and climbs its West Fork and goes over a saddle to a junction with the Emma Creek and Smiley Creek trails. It is 6.5 miles long with a 3,500-foot elevation gain. It provides access to Snowslide and Paradise lakes via a trail from Helen Creek. **Maps:** Baker Peak, Galena, Frenchman Creek, Paradise Peak.

# WALLOWA-WHITMAN NATIONAL FOREST (OREGON) BAKER DISTRICT

**ANTHONY LAKES:** There are three short hikes beginning at or near Anthony Lakes, Oregon. The access is by 21-mile road from North Powder, Oregon (18 miles north of Baker on Interstate 84). Van Patton Lake is 2 miles with a 1,000-foot elevation gain. Hoffer Lakes are .5 mile with a 280-foot elevation gain. Black Lake is 1.5 miles with a 200-foot elevation gain. The trails have views of small triangular peaks with cliffs. There are campgrounds at Anthony Lakes at the base of the ski area. No motor boats are allowed at Anthony Lakes. **Map:** Anthony Lake.

# SOURCES FOR MORE INFORMATION

When you telephone all but three of these offices, you need to use the Idaho Area Code, which is 208. Also, note that Web sites for the national forest and national recreation area offices are available at www.fs.fed.us.

**BOISE DEPARTMENT OF PARKS & RECREATION (for the Greenbelt)**
1104 Royal Boulevard, Boise, Idaho 83706 (384-4240) www.cityofboise.org

**BOISE NATIONAL FOREST (CASCADE DISTRICT)**
Highway 55, P.O. Box 696, Cascade, Idaho 83611 (382-7400)

**BOISE NATIONAL FOREST (EMMETT DISTRICT)**
1805 Highway 16 #5, Emmett, Idaho 83617 (365-7000)

**BOISE NATIONAL FOREST (IDAHO CITY DISTRICT)**
P. O. Box 129, (Highway 21, Milepost 38.5,) Idaho City ID 83631 (392-6681)

**BOISE NATIONAL FOREST (LOWMAN DISTRICT)**
7359 Highway 21, Lowman, Idaho 83637 (259-3361)

**BOISE NATIONAL FOREST (MOUNTAIN HOME DISTRICT)**
2180 American Legion Blvd., Mountain Home, Idaho 83647 (587-7961)

**BOISE NATIONAL FOREST (SUPERVISOR'S OFFICE)**
1249 S. Vinnell Way, Suite 200, Boise, Idaho 83709 (373-4100)

**BRUNEAU SAND DUNES STATE PARK**
HC85 Box 41, Mountain Home, ID 83647 (366-7919)
www.idahoparks.org

**BUREAU OF LAND MANAGEMENT (Lower Snake River District)**
3948 Development Avenue, Boise, Idaho 83705 (384-3300) www.id..blm.gov

**BUREAU OF LAND MANAGEMENT (SHOSHONE DISTRICT)**
P.O. Box 2B, Shoshone ID 83352,
www.id.blm.gov

**BUREAU OF LAND MANAGEMENT (VALE DISTRICT)**
100 Oregon Street E, P.O. Box 700, Vale, Oregon 97918 (541-473-3144)
www.or.blm.gov

**FRIENDS OF THE WEISER RIVER TRAIL**
2165 Seid Creek Road, Cambridge, Idaho 83610. 1-888-MY TRAIL.
www.weiserrivertrail.org

**HAGERMAN FOSSIL BEDS NATIONAL MONUMENT**
P.O. Box 750, Hagerman ID 83332 (837-4793)
www.nps.gov

**Baldy Lake in the Seven Devils**

**HELLS CANYON ADVENTURES**
P.O. Box 159, Oxbow OR 97840 (541-785-3353)
www.hellscanyonadventures.com

**HELLS CANYON NATIONAL RECREATION AREA (Headquarters)**
88401 Highway 82, Enterprise OR 97828 (541-426-4978)

**HELLS CANYON NATIONAL RECREATION AREA (SALMON RIVER DISTRICT)**
P.O. Box 832, Riggins, Idaho 83549 (628-3916)

**IDAHO OUTFITTERS AND GUIDES ASSOCIATION**
P.O. Box 95, Boise ID 83701 (1-800-49-IDAHO); www.ioga.org

**MALAD GORGE STATE PARK**
1074 E. 2350 South, Hagerman ID 83332 (837-4505) www.idahoparks.org

**MALHEUR COUNTY SHERIFF**
(541-473-5126) for road conditions on back roads in eastern Oregon

**OWYHEE COUNTY SHERIFF**
(337-4222) for road conditions on back roads in the Owyhees

**Cabin below Skein Lake near Cascade Reservoir**

**PAYETTE NATIONAL FOREST (COUNCIL DISTRICT)**
P.O. Box 567, (500 East Whitely Avenue) Council, Idaho 83612 (253-0100)

**PAYETTE NATIONAL FOREST (MCCALL DISTRICT)**
P.O. Box 1026, (102 W. Lake St.), McCall, Idaho 83638 (634-0400)

**PAYETTE NATIONAL FOREST (NEW MEADOWS DISTRICT)**
P.O. Box J, (700 Virginia Ave.), New Meadows, Idaho 83654 (347-0300)

**PAYETTE NATIONAL FOREST (KRASSEL DISTRICT)**
P.O. Box 1026 (500 N. Mission St.), McCall ID 83638 (634-0600)

**PAYETTE NATIONAL FOREST (SUPERVISOR'S OFFICE)**
P.O. Box 1026, (804 W. Lakeside Avenue), McCall, Idaho 83638 (634-0700)

**PAYETTE NATIONAL FOREST (WEISER DISTRICT)**
851 E. 9th, Weiser, Idaho 83672 (549-4200)

**RIDGE TO RIVERS TRAIL SYSTEM**
3948 Development Ave., Boise ID 83705 (384-3360); www.ridgetorivers.org

**SALMON-CHALLIS NATIONAL FOREST (LOST RIVER DISTRICT)**
P.O. Box 507, (716 W. Custer), Mackay ID 83251 (588-3400)

**SALMON-CHALLIS NATIONAL FOREST (MIDDLE FORK DISTRICT)**
P.O. Box 750, (Highway 93 North) Challis, Idaho 83226 (879-4101)

**SALMON-CHALLIS NATIONAL FOREST (YANKEE FORK DISTRICT)**
HC 67, Box 650, Clayton, Idaho 83277 (838-3300)

**SALMON-CHALLIS NATIONAL FOREST (SUPERVISOR'S OFFICE)**
50 Highway 93 South, Salmon ID 83467. (756-5100)

**SAWTOOTH NATIONAL FOREST (FAIRFIELD DISTRICT)**
P.O. Box 189, Fairfield, Idaho 83327 (764-3202)

**SAWTOOTH NATIONAL FOREST (KETCHUM DISTRICT)**
P.O. Box 2356, (206 Sun Valley Road) Ketchum, Idaho 83340 (622-5371)

**SAWTOOTH NATIONAL FOREST (SUPERVISOR'S OFFICE)**
2467 Kimberly Road East, Twin Falls, Idaho 83301 (737-3200)

**SAWTOOTH NATIONAL RECREATION AREA**
HC 64, Box 8291, Ketchum ID 83340 (727-5000)

**SNAKE RIVER BIRDS OF PREY AREA**
3948 Development Avenue, Boise ID 83705 (384-3300)
www.id.blm.gov.

# GUIDE TO HIKES

## Easy

**(Up to 7 miles round trip and up to 1,000 feet elevation gain)**
Baker Lake
Big Jacks Creek
Blue Lake
Boise Greenbelt (depending on length of section)
Box Canyon
Bruneau Sand Dunes
Duck Lake
Fall Creek Falls

Juniper Gulch — Leslie Gulch, Oregon

Goose Creek Falls
Grassy Twin and Coffee Cup Lakes
Halverson Lakes
Heavens Gate
Hulls Gulch
Indian Bathtub
Jordan Craters
Josephine Lake
Jump Creek
Little City of Rocks
Lizard Butte
Louie Lake
Mores Mountain
North Fork Kennally Creek
Oregon Trail at Bonneville Point
Reynolds Creek
Scribner Lake
Sheep Rock
Skein and Raft Lakes
Snake River Birds of Prey Area at Swan Falls
Snowslide Lake
Spanish Town
Squaw Creek
Twin Lakes (Granite Mountain)
Upper Hazard Lake
Upper Leslie Gulch and Juniper Gulch
Vulcan Hot Springs
Weiser River Trail (depending on length of section)

## MODERATE HIKES

**(7 to 10 miles with 1,000 to 2,000 feet gain)**
Avondale Basin
Bellas Lakes
Boulder and Rapid Lakes
Box Lake
Cottonwood Creek
Emerald Lake
Grassy Twin and Coffee Cup Lakes
Green Lake
Hard Butte, Twin, and Rainbow
Hum Lake
Jennie Lake
Lava Butte Lakes
Loon Lake
Mill Lake
Miner Lake
Norton Lakes
Oregon Trail South Alternate (Sinker Creek)
Prairie Lakes
Rainbow Basin

Seafoam Lakes #1 and #2
Six Lakes Basin
Smiley Creek
Summit Creek Trail
West Fork Rapid River Trail
William H. Pogue Trail (Sheep Creek)
Windy Saddle to Cannon Lake

## HIKES WITH CROSS-COUNTRY TRAVEL

Blackmare Lake
Blackwell and Crystal Lakes
Smoky and Big Lost Lakes
Gooding City of Rocks
Kane Lake (last mile)
Little Jacks Creek
Red Mountain Lakes
Satan Lake
Seafoam Lakes #3 and #4
Summit and Malony Lakes
Three Fingers Rock

## EXPERT ABILITY

**(Route finding problems or treacherous footing)**
Bass Lakes
Blackmare Lake
Gooding City of Rocks
Hyndman Lake
Jughandle Trail
Maki Lake from Snowslide Lake
Roberson Trail
Ross Fork horse trail
Shirts Lake
Surprise Valley and Lakes
War Eagle Mountain

## OPENING DATES FOR HIKES

**APRIL AND MAY**
Big Jacks Creek
Boise Greenbelt (all year)
Box Canyon
Bruneau Sand Dunes
Gooding City of Rocks
Hagerman Fossil Beds: Emigrant Trail
Halverson Lakes
Hells Canyon
Hulls Gulch
Indian Bathtub

**Rough Lake near Copper Basiin**

Jordan Craters
Jump Creek
Little City of Rocks
Lizard Butte
Oregon Trail (Bonneville Point)
Oregon Trail South Alternate (Sinker Creek)
Reynolds Creek
Roberson Trail
Sheep Creek
Snake River Birds of Prey Area at Swan Falls
Squaw Creek
Three Fingers Rock
Upper Leslie Gulch and Juniper Gulch
Weiser River Trail
West Fork Rapid River

**BY JULY 1**
Avondale Basin
Blue Lake
Loon Lake
Skein and Raft Lakes

**Surprise Valley in the Pioneer Mountains**

Spanish Town
Twin Lakes
Vulcan Hot Springs
War Eagle Mountain

**AFTER JULY 15**
Emerald Lake
Satan Lake
Six Lake Basin
Surprise Valley and Lakes

## OVERNIGHT OR LONGER REQUIRED

Bass Lakes
Hells Canyon
Link Trail
Ross Fork Lakes
Seven Devils (northern loop)
Upper Kirkham Ridge

## CROWDED

Baker Lake
Basin, Shelf, Gem and Sheep Lakes
Bellas Lakes
Blue Lake
Boise Greenbelt
Bruneau Sand Dunes
Goose Creek Falls
Hulls Gulch
Indian Bathtub
Jump Creek
Norton Lakes
Round, Long, Rough, etc. lakes
Shelf Lake
Vulcan Hot Springs

## SELDOM VISITED

Bass Lakes
Grouse Lakes
Little Jacks Creek
Roberson Trail
Satan Lake
Shirts Lake
Surprise Valley and Lakes
Three Fingers Rock

## ACCESS ROADS FOR TOUGH VEHICLES AND EXPERIENCED DRIVERS

Black Lake
Hindman Lake (its access road, the Basin Butte Road now requires four-wheel drive)
Josephine Lake
Kane Creek
Little Jacks Creek
Muldoon Canyon
Rice Peak and Long Lake
Roberson Trail
Three Fingers Rock
Windy Saddle (northern Seven Devils and Heavens Gate)

## NEW HIKES IN THIS EDITION

Bald Mountain Trails
Box Canyon
Falls Creek Falls
Gooding City of Rocks
Goose Creek Falls
Hagerman Fossil Beds: The Emigrant Trail

Halverson Lakes
Heavens Gate
Little City of Rocks
Malad Gorge: Devils Washbowl
Sheep Rock
Smoky and Big Lost Lakes
Weiser River Trail

## HIKES REMOVED FROM THIS EDITION

Crimson Lake — transferred to *Trails of the Frank Church-River of No Return Wilderness*
Helldiver and Soldier Lakes — transferred
Horseshoe Lake from Knapp Creek — transferred
Johnstone Pass and Box Canyon Lakes
Knapp Lakes — transferred
Langer, Island and Ruffneck Lakes — transferred
Stack Rock
Sullivan Lake — transferred

# BASIC EQUIPMENT

**CLOTHING:** avoid cotton and down because if they get wet they are useless. Faster-drying materials such as nylon and polyester are preferable except around a campfire, where wool and cotton are safer.

**Boots** (hiking; broken in)
**Clothes** (complete change)
***Hats** (two — sun and wool)
***Jacket** (warm — insulated)
**Mosquito headnet**
***Pants (long)** — nylon or polyester, not jeans
***Rain jacket or poncho and chaps**
***Shirt** (long-sleeved)
***Socks** (wool or synthetic)
**Sock liners** (nylon or polypropylene)
***Sunglasses**
**Wool sweater or fleece jacket**

**GENERAL:**
**Backpack** (comfortable)
***Compass**
***Flashlight or headlamp** with extra bulbs and batteries
***Map** (topographic)
**Rope** (20 feet of 1/8" nylon)
**Toilet paper** — and plastic bag in which to haul out the used paper

**Trowel** (plastic)

**COOKING:**

**Cooking pots** (aluminum or teflon lined )
***Firestarter**
***Food**, plus a little extra for emergency
**Gloves or pot gripper**
***Knife** (pocket)
***Matches** (waterproof with strike plate from their box or a butane lighter-strike anywhere kitchen matches are inadequate even if kept in a waterproof container)
**Pot scrubber**
**Soap** (biodegradable)
**Spoon and cup** (thick, unbreakable plastic, such as Lexan)
**Stove** (backpacking) — butane/propane is the easiest to operate
**Utensils**

**SLEEPING:**

**pad** (thermarest mattress or waffle imprinted closed cell foam)
**sleeping bag** (3-season down or synthetic) — cold blooded people may need a 4-season bag
**tent** (breathable fabric with waterproof fly)

**FIRST AID:**

**ace bandage**
**antibiotic ointment**
**bandaids**
**gauze and tape**
**lip salve**
**moleskin**
**mosquito repellant**
***prescription pain pills**
**prescriptions those in your party take regularly**
**sunburn cream**
**triangular bandage for use as a sling**

(* shows items essential for every hiker)

# SUGGESTED READING

Adams, Mildretta. *Historic Silver City*. Homedale, Idaho: Owyhee Chronicle, 1960.

Alt, David, and Hyndman, Donald. *Roadside Geology of Idaho*. Missoula, Montana: Mountain Press, 1989.

Bailey, Robert G. *Hell's Canyon*. Lewiston, Idaho: Lewiston Printing, 1984 (reprint of 1874 book).

Bird, Annie Laurie. *Boise, the Peace Valley*. Caldwell, Idaho: Caxton Printers,

**Rainbow Basin Trail near Anderson Ranch Reservoir**

1934.

Beal, Merrill and Wells, Merle. *History of Idaho*. New York: Lewis Historical Publishing Co., 1959.

Brosnan, Cornelius J. *History of the State of Idaho*. New York: Charles Scribners and Sons, 1918.

Callender, Signe, ed. *Early Days in Long Valley*. 1987.

Carrey, Johnny; Conley, Cort; and Barton, Ace. *Snake River of Hells Canyon*. Cambridge, Idaho: Backeddy Books, 1979.

Conley, Cort. *Idaho For the Curious*. Cambridge, Idaho: Backeddy Books, 1982.

Defenbach, Byron. *Idaho, the Land and Its People*. Chicago - New York: American Historical Society, Inc., 1933.

Derig, Betty. *Roadside History of Idaho*. Missoula, Montana: Mountain Press, 1996.

Elsensohn, Sister Alfreda. *Pioneer Days in Idaho County*. Caldwell, Idaho: Caxton Printers, 1951.

Gibbs, Rafe. *Beckoning the Bold*. Moscow, Idaho: The University of Idaho Press, 1976.

Gulick, Bill. *Snake River Country*. Caldwell, Idaho: Caxton Printers, 1971.

Hailey, John. *History of Idaho*. Boise, Idaho: Syms-York Co., 1910.

Hanley, Mike and Lucia, Ellis. *Owyhee Trails*. Caldwell, Idaho: Caxton Printers, 1950.

*Idaho, An Illustrated History*. Boise, Idaho: Idaho Historical Society, 1976.

McLeod, George. *History of Alturas and Blaine Counties, Idaho*. Hailey Idaho: The Hailey Times 1938.

Maley, Terry. *Exploring Idaho Geology*. Boise, Idaho: Mineral Land Publications

Miller, Donald. *Ghost Towns of Idaho*. Boulder, Colorado: Pruett Publishing, 1976.

*Mining Industry of Idaho*. Annual Reports. 1899-on.

Nettleton, Helen. *Sketches of Owyhee County*. Nampa, Idaho: Schwartz Printing, 1978.

O'Reilly, Betty. *The Magic of McCall: Footsteps Across a Century, 1890-1990*. McCall, Idaho: Better Books, 1989.

Oppenheimer, Doug and Poore, Jim. *Sun Valley, A Biography*. Boise, Idaho: Beatty, 1976.

Rollins, P.A. *The Discovery of the Oregon Trail*. New York: Charles Scribners and Sons, 1935.

Rowland, Frank. *Founding of McCall*. Caldwell, Idaho: Caxton Printers, 1960.

Ryan, John F. *A History of Camas Prairie*. Fairfield, Idaho: Camas County Historical Society, 1975.

*The Snake River Country*. New York: Time-Life Books, 1974.

Sparling, Wayne. *Southern Idaho Ghost Towns*. Caldwell, Idaho: Caxton Printers, 1976.

Strahorn, Carrie. *Fifteen Thousand Miles By Stage*. New York: G.P. Putnam & Sons, 1911.

Weis, Norman. *Ghost Towns of the Northwest*. Caldwell, Idaho: Caxton Printers, 1971.

Wells, Merle. *Gold Camps and Silver Cities: Nineteenth Century Mining in Central and Southern Idaho*. Boise, Idaho: Idaho Department of Lands (Bulletin #22, Idaho Bureau of Mines and Geology), 2nd ed. 1983.

Woods, Shelton ed. *Valley County Idaho, Pre-history to 1920*. Donnelly, Idaho: Action West Publishing, 2002.

Yarber, Esther. *Land of the Yankee Fork*. Denver, Colorado: Sage Books, 1963.

Yarber, Esther, and McGown, Edna. *Stanley-Sawtooth Country*. Salt Lake City: Publishers Press, 1976.

# ACKNOWLEDGMENTS

I would like to thank all those who helped me with this book, both the original 1982 book, the revised edition and this third edition. This guide couldn't have been written without the help and encouragement of my family: my husband, Wayne; and my children, Doug, Leslie, Neal, Hilary and Stuart. I would particularly like to thank my youngest son, Stuart, who was my companion on most of the hikes for the original edition of the book. I would also like to thank the friends, relatives, and organizations such as Mountain West who have helped with the hikes and transportation for all three editions. I would like to thank the many district rangers and forestry technicians who suggested trails and edited the hike descriptions for all three editions, and others who provided information on changes in the trails and trailheads over the years. I particularly want to thank the rangers and others who helped make sure the facts in the manuscript were correct for this third edition: Terry Bonner, Tim Breuer, Renee Catherin, Jim Ciardelli, Cathy Conover, Jay Dorr, Earl Dodds, Gary Elliott, Laurie Fink, Mike Foster, David Gordon, Tom Hass, Frank Jenks, John Kurtz, Laurie Matthews, Joe Miczulski, Clem Pope, Diane Pritchard, Dick Pugh, Larry Ridenour, Robert Romig, Jeff Schramm, Amy Stahl, Mike Stayton, Linda Strain, Paul Willard, Wes Whitworth, Mike Wissenbach, Jack Yarborough and Judi Zuckert.

I especially want to thank former Governor Cecil Andrus for writing the foreword and allowing me to use it again, Diana Hall for editing the manuscript, Beth Bolt for copyediting it, and Jerry Painter for doing the layout and maps for this third edition.

## Photo credits

Page 141, Wallace Cathcart; Page 254, Fritz Ward; Page 267, Wayne Ferrell. All other photos are by author.

Margaret Fuller is best known for writing four guidebooks to Idaho trails. The hiking guidebooks are four editions of *Trails of the Sawtooth and White Cloud Mountains*, two previous editions of *Trails of Western Idaho*, two editions of *Trails of the Frank Church-River of No Return Wilderness*, and two editions of *Trails of Eastern Idaho* (with Jerry Painter). She has also written three natural history books: *Forest Fires: An Introduction to Wildland Fire Behavior, Management, Firefighting, and Prevention; Mountains: A Natural History and Hiking Guide*; and *Wild Berries of the West* (with Betty Derig).

Three previous editions of *Trails of the Sawtooth and White Cloud Mountains*, published in 1979, was the first comprehensive guidebook to any Idaho trails. In 1982, the year *Trails of Western Idaho* was first published, Margaret received the Writer of the Year Award from the Idaho Writer's League. In 1989, the then three hiking guidebooks were endorsed by the Idaho Centennial Commission as official centennial publications. In 1991, Margaret received the Achievement Award from the Idaho Trails Council. In 1991, *Forest Fires* won first place for books in the Northwest Outdoor Writers annual contest. In 1996, she received the Women of Today and Tomorrow award for the outdoors from the Silver Sage Girl Scout Council. That year she was also awarded membership in the international Society of Woman Geographers. In 2002, the Outdoor Idaho program (Idaho Public Television, Channel 4) filmed a 5-minute spot on Margaret that is part of a program on older Idahoans who have contributed to the knowledge of Idaho's outdoors and are still active in it.

Margaret has taught backpacking and mountain ecology in workshops and community education courses and has given more than 240 slide shows about Idaho mountains to community, church and school groups.

Margaret was born and raised in Palo Alto, California, and received a B.A. in biology from Stanford University. She and her husband, Wayne, a retired district judge, live in Weiser, Idaho, and have five grown children and five grandchildren.